SAEED KOUROS

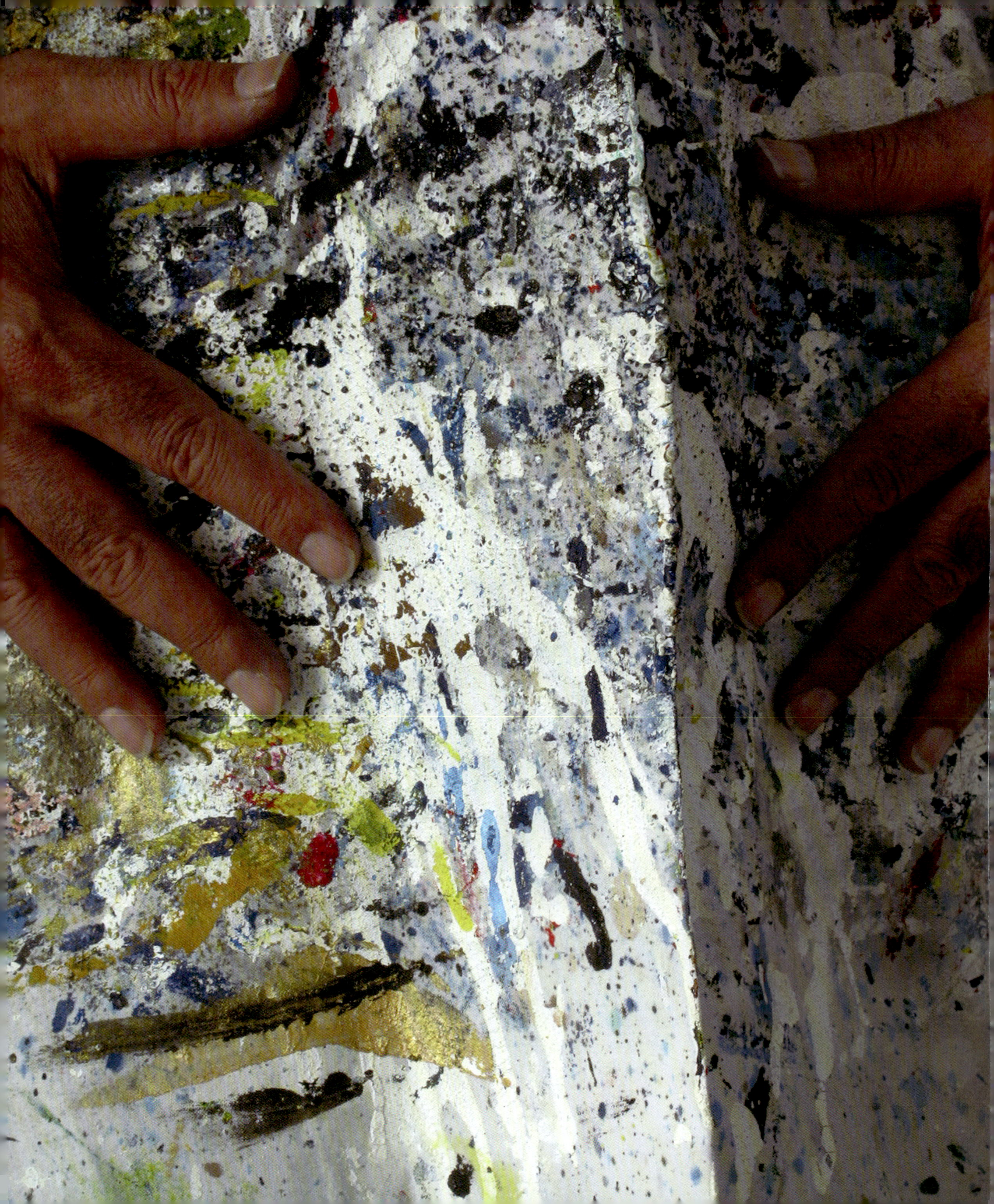

SAEED KOUROS

Picturing Life

Edited by
Hamid Keshmirshekan

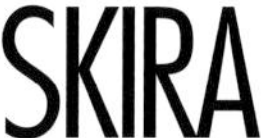

Contents

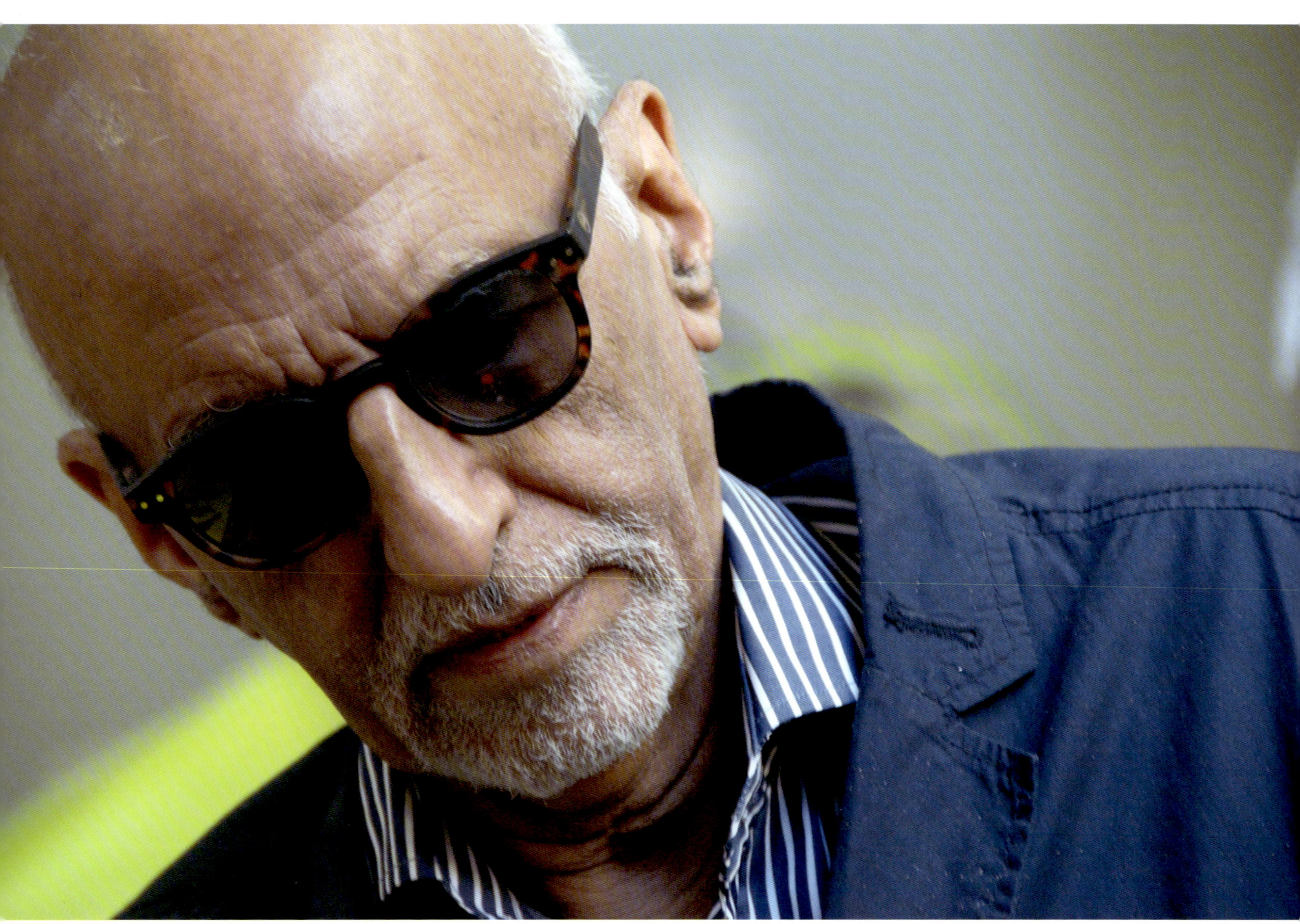

Picturing Life and Pain

Hamid Keshmirshekan

Saeed Kouros's (b. 1942) work embodies a range of approaches towards non-objective painting. Primarily abstract, his art depicts a variety of formal implications and technical strategies including the application of textural elements, spontaneous forms, textures and lines. His paintings portray a personal and unique experience and resist stylistic categorisation. However, the basic inclination in all of his works is an emphasis on dynamic and energetic gesture shaped through an intuitive and active approach. Many of them, if not all, have a close affinity with spontaneity and improvisation often associated with Abstract Expressionism and *Art Informel*.

An industrialist, export in Zand and Qajar and also *Qahveh-khaneh* (coffee-house) painting, art collector – a family practice –, as well as an amateur architect and a devoted entrepreneur, Kouros started his art practice in the early 2000s when he was in his sixties. Before that, however, he had a short but prolific period of art practice during his early twenties. Born in a family profoundly engaged in cultural initiatives, he became familiar with the arts through his parents, his mother in particular who was a qualified painter.[1] But it was in 1964 at the age of twenty-two while living in Montreal, Canada that Kouros started working on his early artworks seriously. Although it was short, about a year, it proved to be a very intensive and fruitful period. Being a self-taught artist, he started experimenting with materials such as sand and plaster on huge canvases and installations made up of hundreds of coloured, black and white geometrical forms of triangle and circle. While still in Montreal, he developed a friendship with artists, poets, gallerists and intellectuals and

1 She learnt painting from the distinguished Iranian realist painter and teacher Ali Mohammad Heydarian (1896-1990), one of Kamal al-Mulk's (the famous court artist in the late Qajar period) best-known disciples. She had a close affinity with several distinguished artists, poets and musicians and hosted frequent gatherings with the presence of several contemporary artists in their house.

succeeded to exhibit his works in a solo and a group shows. Undoubtedly this period remained the basis of Kourus's future artistic developments. However, this productive time had to be ended due to his emotional breakdown with his old mate in Montreal. That was a critical period in his life resulted in him leaving Canada together with his art with a lot of sadness. He returned to Iran in 1965 and became fully involved in his family business in industry, production and finance.[2]

In 2000 he was suddenly diagnosed with liver, stomach and pancreas failure. He had to go through a long and painful period of treatment and medication that took for years. He was then introduced to a Chinese lady in the US who offered him "alternative medication" to cure the severe inflammation caused by the disease. Curing process continued through a psychoanalyst in North London since after a long period of pain and medication, Kouros felt deeply depressed. The psychoanalyst had based her practice on shamanic healing. After diagnosing Kouros, she told him that he was genuinely an artist and so the remedy should be made through art practice to help him transfer the pains to his art. His early works in Greece were experimental drawings on paper with simple art materials – suggested by the psychoanalyst – such as pencil, colour pencil and ink. He personally believes it was an extremely useful therapy for both his physical and mental health. It was indeed another turning point in his life resulting in his serious art practice since then. Chiefly experimental and executed with a variety of materials spontaneously, these experiences were precisely different from his earlier works in the 1960s. The early examples were largely based on pure improvisation what remained markedly an important feature in the future periods. These chiefly small scale paintings demonstrate Kouros's eagerness to experiment with pigments and materials to develop his skill in using varieties of techniques. Later he developed a formal template from one canvas to several canvases while at the same time trying to experiment with different colour-schemes and textures. During this process each painting acts individually as a metamorphosis which is the outcome of changes from one canvas to the other.

Since those years of severe illness his biological time has changed and he basically works during nights rather than days. This has provided him with an opportunity to concentrate better while working spontaneously in silence. He has inevitably had to adapt himself to the constant physical pain and hence his artworks are inevitably attached to his very everyday life. As the art critic Behzad Hatam says, "Kouros communicates, complains, screams and calms himself through his art… He has been able to masterly combine colours and composition to allow his restless soul to create."[3]

Kouros's belief that the Universe and all physical conventions are ruled by an order led him in 2006-7 to become interested in geometrical

2 His father was an influential industrialist and pioneer of printed cotton and chintz factory in Iran, among others Chit-sazi-e Rey, an MP, senator and collector of Islamic art and objects.

3 Behzad Hatam, catalogue of Saeed Kouros Exhibition at the Gallery 10., Tehran, 2008: n.p.

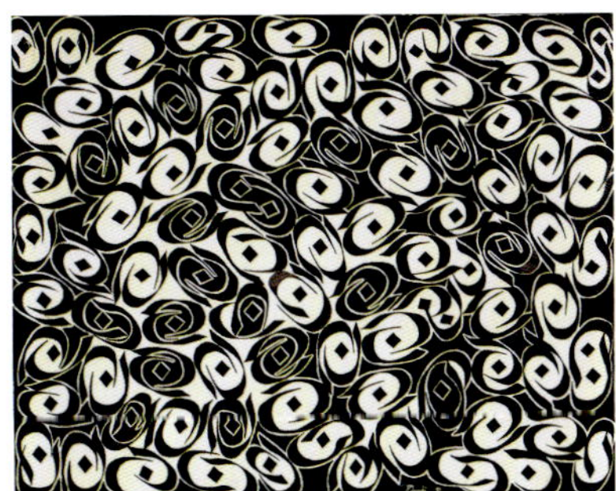

Fig. 1 Charles Hossein Zenderoudi, *Noon,* 1971, oil on canvas, 80 x 100cm

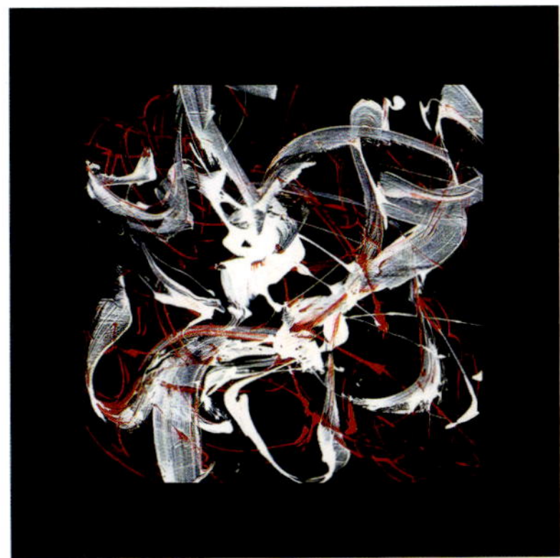

Fig. 2 Saeed Kouros, *Untitled,* 2007, acrylic on canvas, 70 x 70cm

foundations. In this period, all the elements and textures were situated on theses basis. From 2007 to 2009, however, Kouros gradually departed from those geometrical and calculated structures and filled his canvases with unreadable calligraphic-like textual elements with a diversity of shapes and compositions. This approach in nature was not truly novel and had many precedents in the history of modern Iranian art. The works of many artists in the 1960s onward both in Iran and several other countries in the Middle East and North Africa (MENA) regions epitomised this trend. Kouros must have been familiar with works of pioneer artists such as Charles Hossein Zenderoudi (b. 1937) and Mohammad Ehsai (b. 1939) whose works explicitly represent this genre. (Fig. 1) However, his paintings prove to be taking distance formalistically from those *lettrist* works of Zenderoudi and categorically readable works of Ehsai in terms of conveying literary, religious or specific cultural messages. (Fig. 2) They are rather, as the Italian art critic Luigi Menghelli defines them, signs of "calligraphic memory" which even do not try to connote any particular cultural code or signification. Menghelli rightly maintains that Kouros uses these means of calligraphic memory and pseudo-scripts by superimposing them on top of each other through sometimes complex and on occasion minimal compositions, leaving only a memory of the origin.[4] Kouros's work in this period represents an evident attempt to tracing the lines and forms to creating pure visual structure. The variety of shape, size and angle create a sense of depth in these compositions, making the squares, circles and rectangles appear to be moving in space. These speedy traces of calligraphic signs occasionally become reminiscent of the Chinese calligraphy or in his later works in 2016 are transferred to hieroglyph-like signs.[5] All these formal segments are seeking to create a space; a fragmented universe, but there is a sense of visual harmony too.

By examining Kouros's work; the observer would find a close affinity with the works of American Abstract Expressionists, in particular the way that those artists such as Jackson Pollock depicted inner feeling through the act of painting and directness of expression, best achieved through improvisation. Pollock's description of the process of painting clearly represents this fact, saying, "when I am *in* my painting, I'm not much aware of what I'm doing. It is only after a sort of 'get acquainted' period that I see what I have been about."[6] Breaking away from putative conventions in both technique and subject-matter, the artists affiliated to the Abstract Expressionism made works that stood as reflections of their individual psyches. Furthermore, these artists appreciated most spontaneity and improvisation, and they rendered the utmost importance to "process". Along the same line of Polack's early works, some of Kouros's works too feature pictographic elements transformed into personal code. Emotional energy and gestural surface which mark Abstract Expressionists and their understanding of painting itself as a struggle between self-expression and the chaos of the subconscious

4 Luigi Menghelli, "From Suprematism to Post-contemporary," a lecture given by him on the occasion of Saeed Kouros's exhibition in Milan, Italy in 2016.

5 See pages 53-56 and 187-190.

6 Jackson Pollock, "My Painting," *Possibilities* 1 (Winter 1947–48): 79

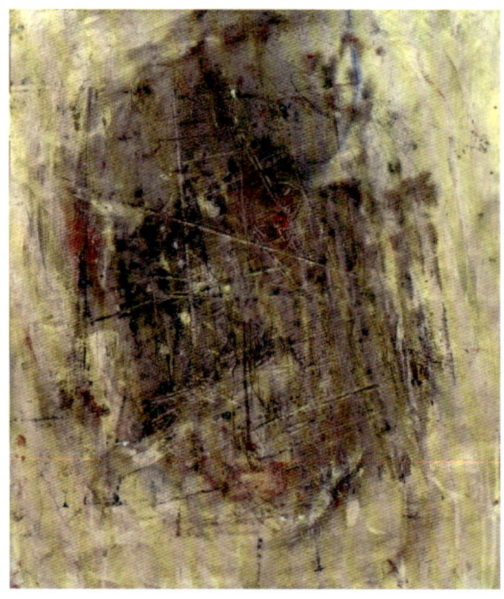

Fig. 3 Wols, *Composition IV*, 1947, oil on canvas, 65 x 54cm

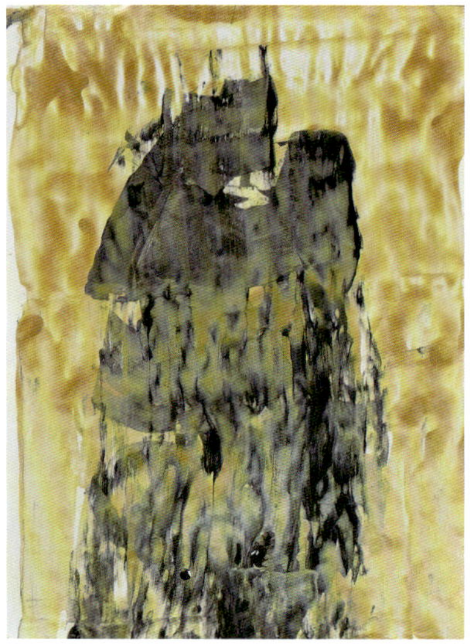

Fig. 5 Saeed Kouros, *Untitled*, 2016, mixed media on paper, 61 x 45.7cm

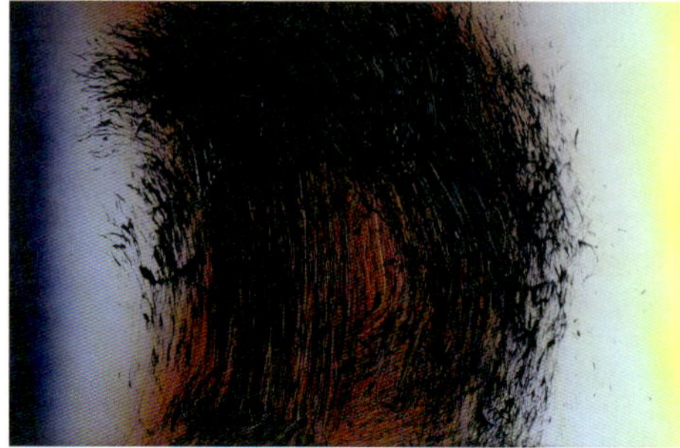

Fig. 4 Hans-Hartung, *T1982-E15-1982*, oil on canvas

can also be the case in his works. Similarly, Kouros's self-referential works address the inner world of the artist. The relationships within his compositional ingredients bring to mind the dance between light and dark – something he loves expressing, a self-described unification of pain and life.

Many art historians no longer assert that an abstract expressionist painting is unmediated,[7] it is rather said that the combination of chance and control became synonymous with Abstract Expressionism's evolution. In such process, the artist follows the picture and its unforeseen changes stimulate him to take unplanned actions. A new creative factor arises – the artist's spontaneity. But s/he then consciously controls when and how it should end. Kouros too instinctively chooses his pictorial theme and spontaneously follows the act of painting. He first allows chance into his artistic process and therefore it is improvisational in nature. However, the very amalgamation of the chance-based system and controlling the course of painting in fact happens in the Kouros's creation process.

As art historian Joan Marter identifies it, the Abstract Expressionists' "intention to release subjective response, hail the importance of chance, and continue the exploration of the subconscious" was shared with those associated with *Art Informel*.[8] Common features in these painting are spontaneous brushwork, drips and scribble-like marks. *Tachisme*, in particular, puts emphasis on gesturalism characterised by spontaneous brushwork, splotches of paint or calligraphic-like markings or scribblings. In many of Kouros's work, mainly those created during 2015-16, he tries to embrace anti-compositional forms and gestural techniques. Like what happens in the works of such artists as Wols and Hans Hartung, in Kouros's work too gestural painting allows him to embrace spontaneity and subvert the aesthetic standards. **(Figs. 3-5)** In his paintings the painterly material becomes an active participant in the process of creation. It is done by contributing unplanned new elements. Associated with Franz Kline's strong brush strokes, for example, a number of Kouros's paintings portray an energetic whirlpool of calligraphic lines which are extending from the centre depicting a kind of swirling nebula of colours. **(Figs. 6, 7)**

7 Valerie Hellstein, "The Cage-iness of Abstract Expressionism," *American Art*, 28: 1 (Spring 2014): 58.

8 Joan M. Marter, "Internationalism and Abstract Expressionism," in Joan M. Marter (ed), *Abstract Expressionism: The International Context* (New Brunswick, New Jersey: Rutgers University Press, 2007): 7.

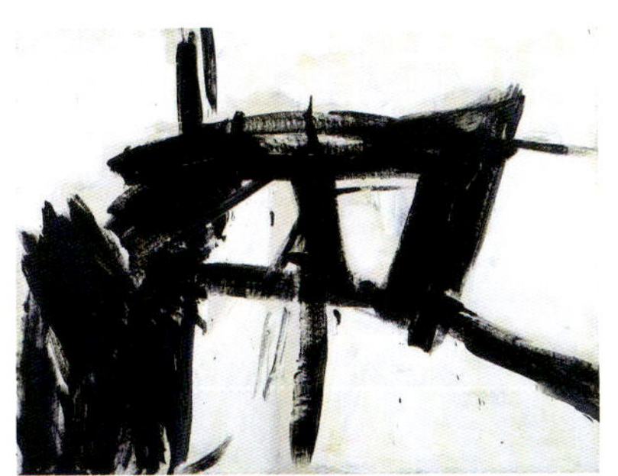

Fig. 6 Franz Kline, *Vawdavitch*, 1955, oil on canvas, 158 x 205cm

Kouros's paintings are formalistically powerful and indeed mature. But what is more important about them is that they reflect his personality, inner feeling and overall his life story. Although his artistic creativity flourished in a mature age, it was, in fact, a mark for a return to his true "self". It seems he had constantly been carrying this talent as a wishful treasure throughout years after the unexpected and regretful disconnection from artistic practice earlier at his young age!

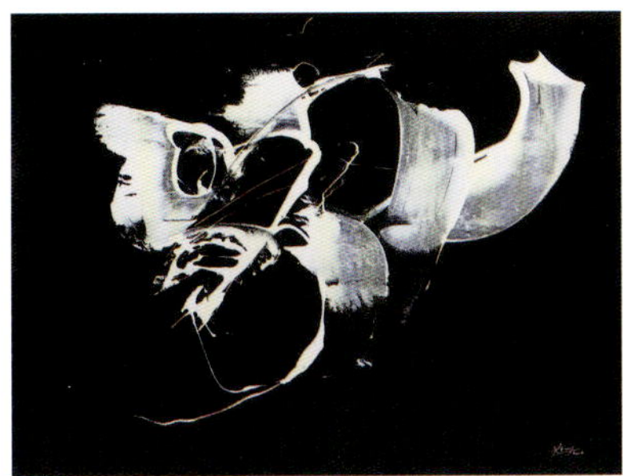

Fig. 7 Saeed Kouros, *Untitled*, 2009, acrylic on cardboard, 50 x 65cm

Beyond the Word ...[1]

Viana Conti

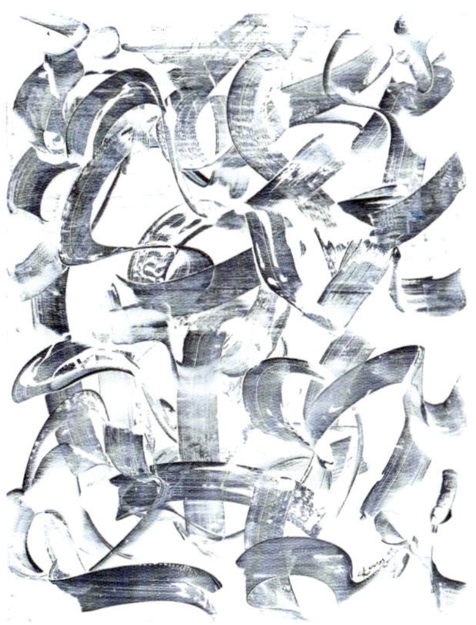

Fig. 1 Saeed Kouros, *Untitled*, 2008, mixed media on canvas, 100 x 80cm

1 Another version of this text already appeared in the Saeed Kouros's exhibition in Milan in 2016 http://www.tenstar-community.org/art/artists/

An exponent of abstract painting characterised by calligraphic memory and gestural appeal, Saeed Kouros raised in a family environment dedicated to collecting of Islamic Persian art, Safavid, Zand and Qajar eras in particular. The artist matured his personal sensitivity over time. His training during his young age in Switzerland and Canada next to his passion for collecting and entrepreneurship commitment was influential in this process. He is engaged in a type of painting – mostly acrylic on canvas – that combines the tradition of art of handwriting gestures with Western mood of painting. His intense experience in architecture and design stimulates his creativity when he paints and when he works on environmental creations. His emotional intensity is expressed through a profound writing mode, which emerges from his inner world; emotional experiences dating back to his childhood and the years of his education. His pictorial writing is not made up of recognisable letters of the alphabet, but gestural impulses that invent new alphabets, aiming to express the unconscious secret impulses and emotional moments of his life. The creative energy is running through it during the visual action. Influenced by the traditional culture of handwriting in the Middle East drawing light and elegant forms through the art of lettering and the decoration, Kouros's work, however, is freed from the burden of the literal meaning to speak, moving beyond the word, through the form, gesture, colour, the body and poetry.

In his daily practice, often at nights, painting becomes for Saeed Kouros the releasing action, a release of inner freedom practised with a kind of

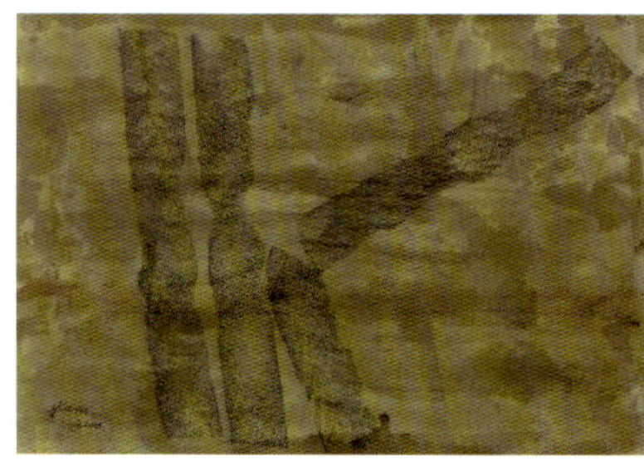

Fig. 2 Saeed Kouros, *Untitled*, 2015, charcoal, acrylic and graphite on paper, 50 x 70cm

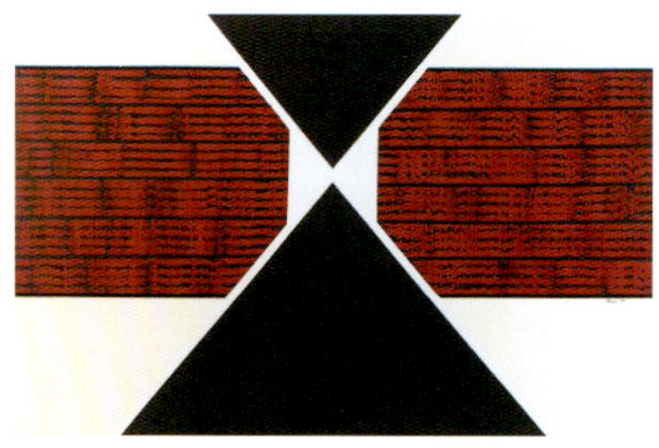

Fig. 3 Saeed Kouros, *Untitled*, 2007, acrylic on canvas, 120 x 200cm

meditation exercise in the silence of his studio which leads him to seek his most authentic secret identity. His mysterious inscriptions, from a dreamlike and surreal world, seem to be screwed by wind spirals. Particularly expressive are his charcoal drawings on paper or cardboard. His colour palette is based on whites, blacks, blues and golden ochres. His pictorial universe is divided into two main currents. On the one side, freed from the constraint of a sense of conventional and coded meanings, it takes shape from the current gestural, abstract and informal, built on empty, crossed by signs or instant writing gestures, emancipated from the readability. On another side it is shaped from geometric current, built on a Cartesian plane on a Euclidean metric such as the map of a living space, traversable, but still abstract, structured by a linear system which intersects with hatches and panels resulting from a "need" for mental order. The spirals and the curves express the dynamic calligraphic energy originated from the Soul of Kouros, while the squares and the lines are expressing the order and balance of his "Dimore Mentali".

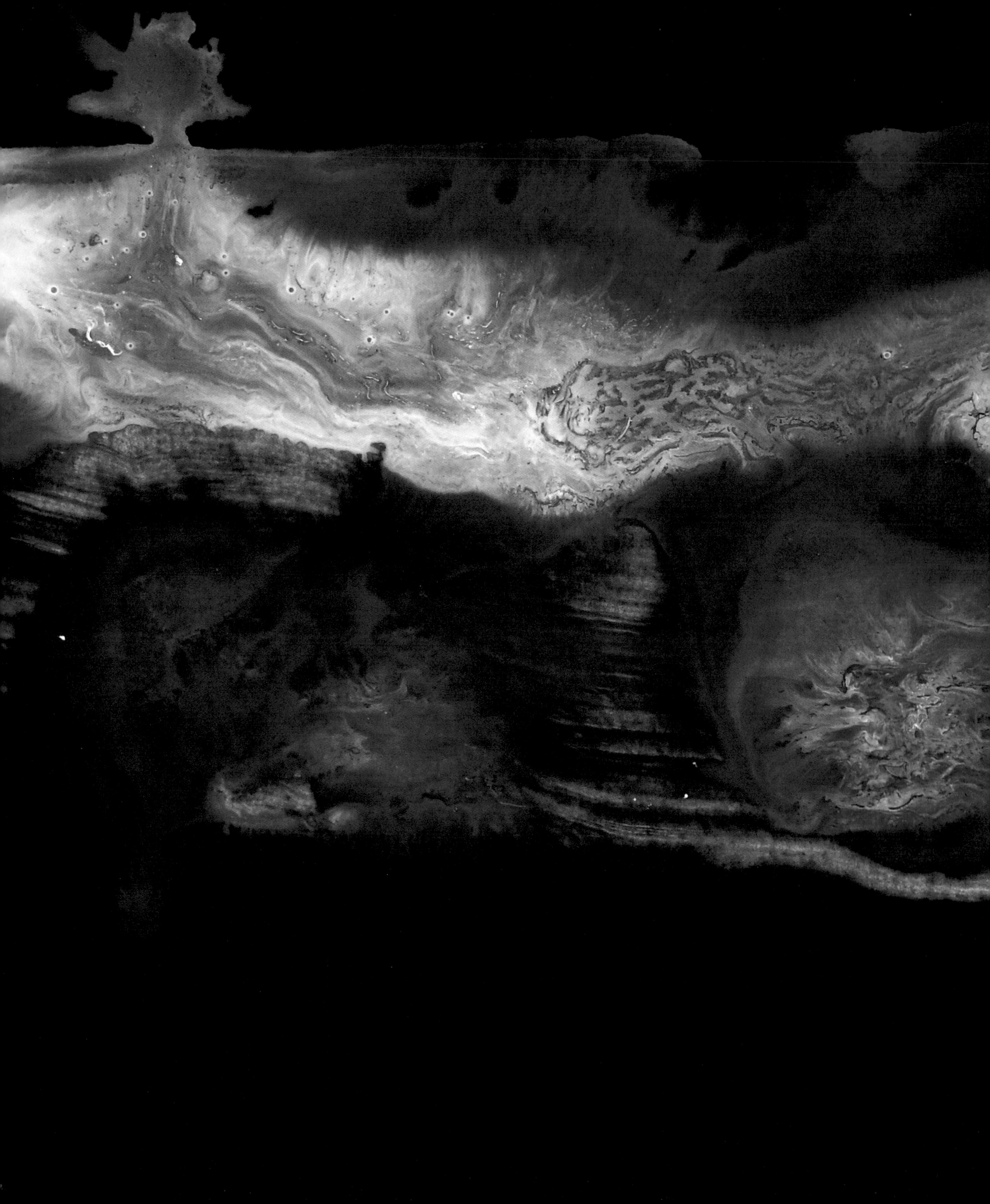

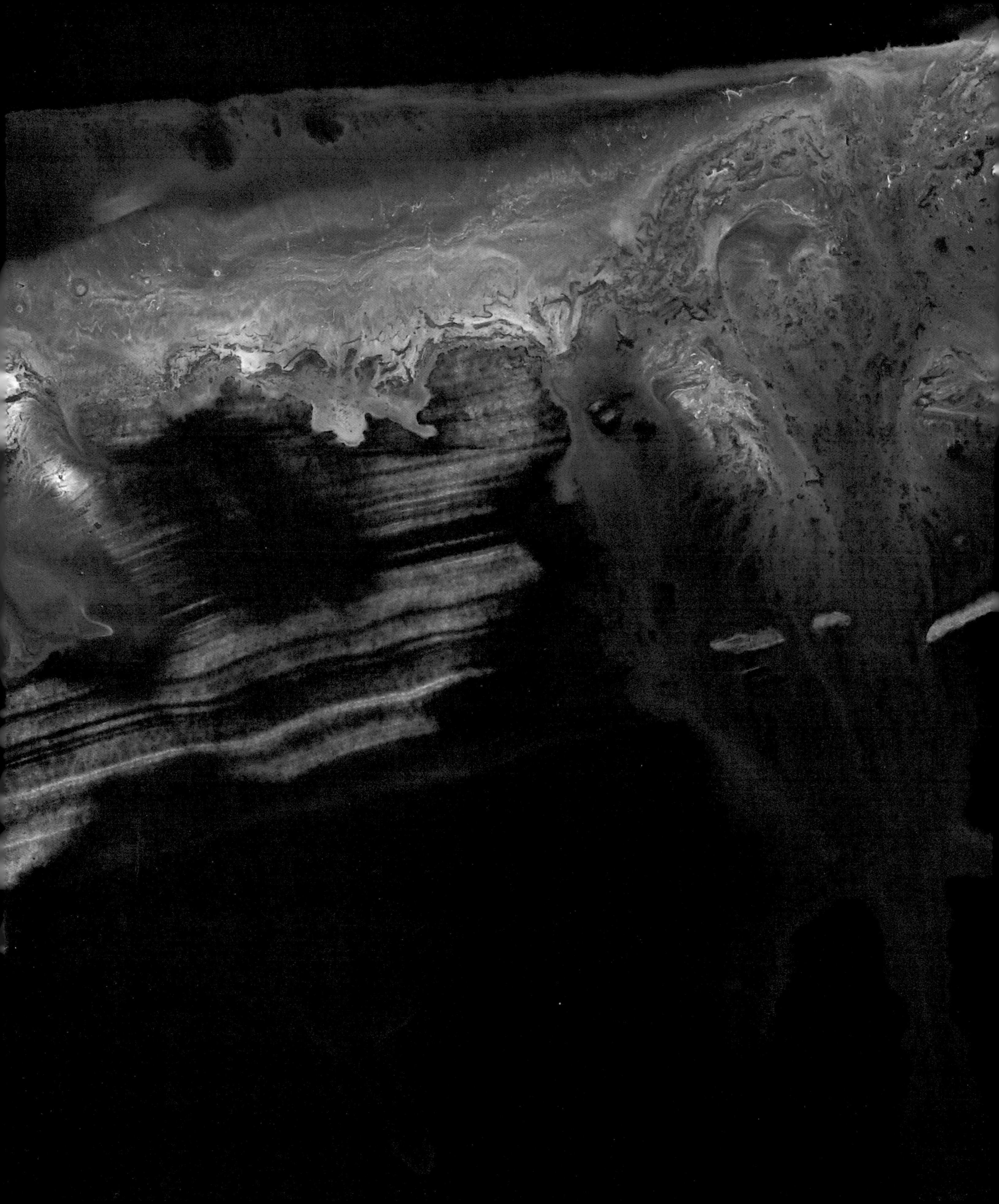

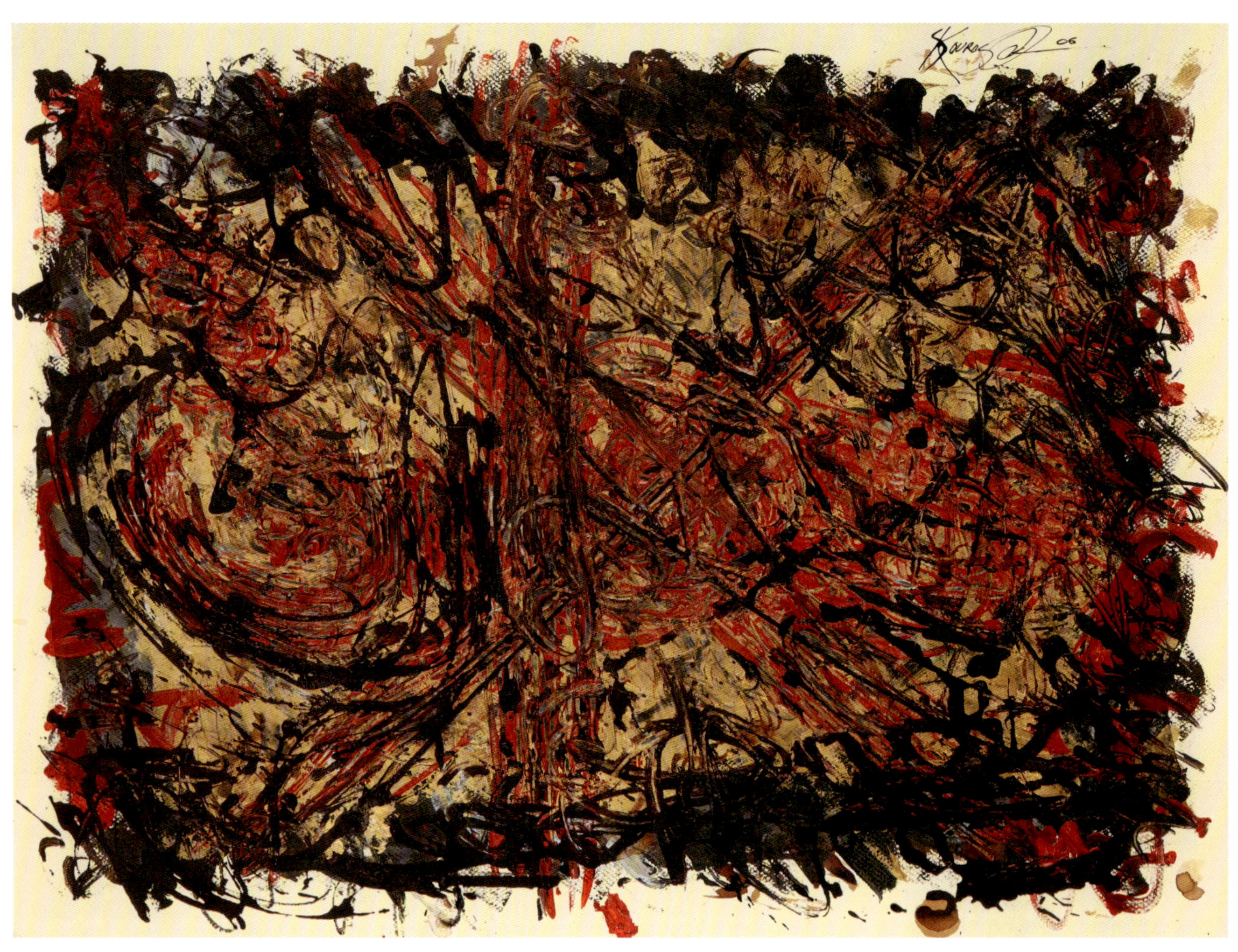

2006, ink and acrylic on paper,
50 x 65 cm

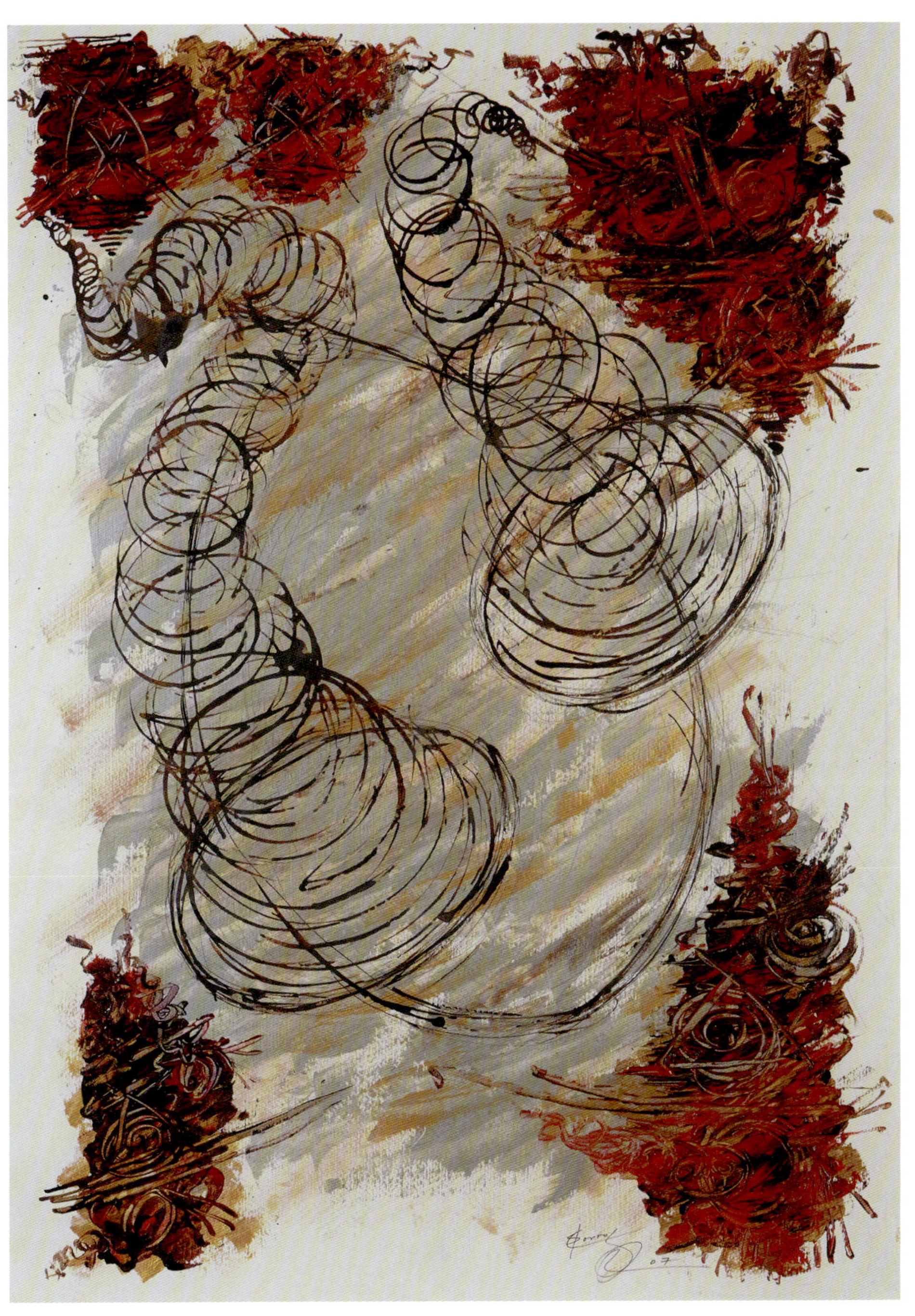

2007, acrylic on paper,
100 x 70 cm

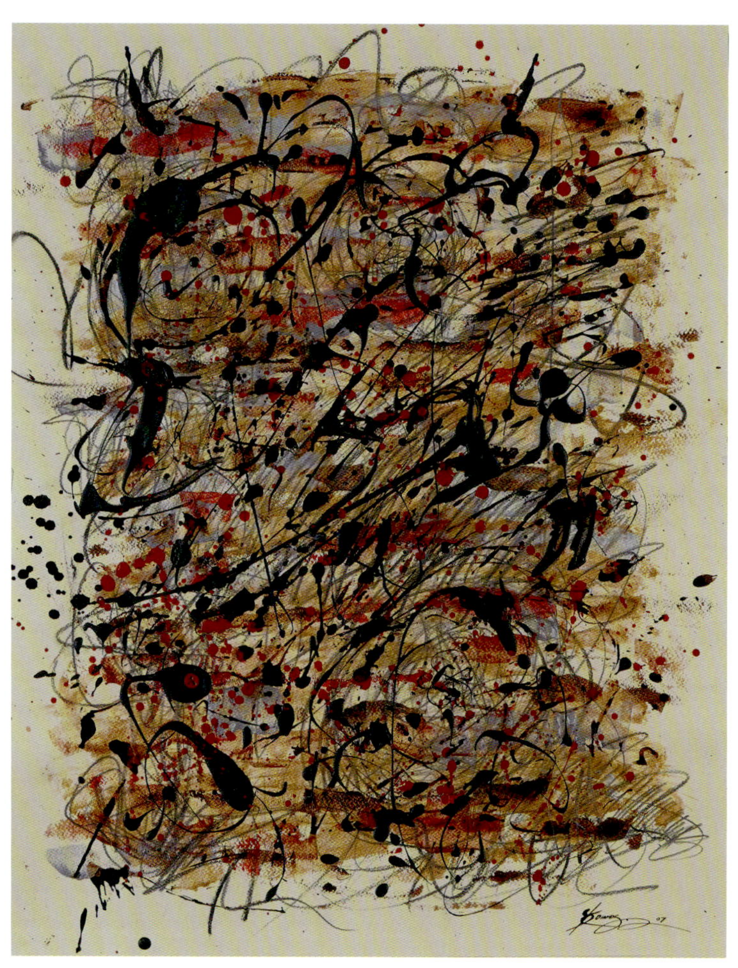

2007, mixed media on paper,
60 x 50 cm

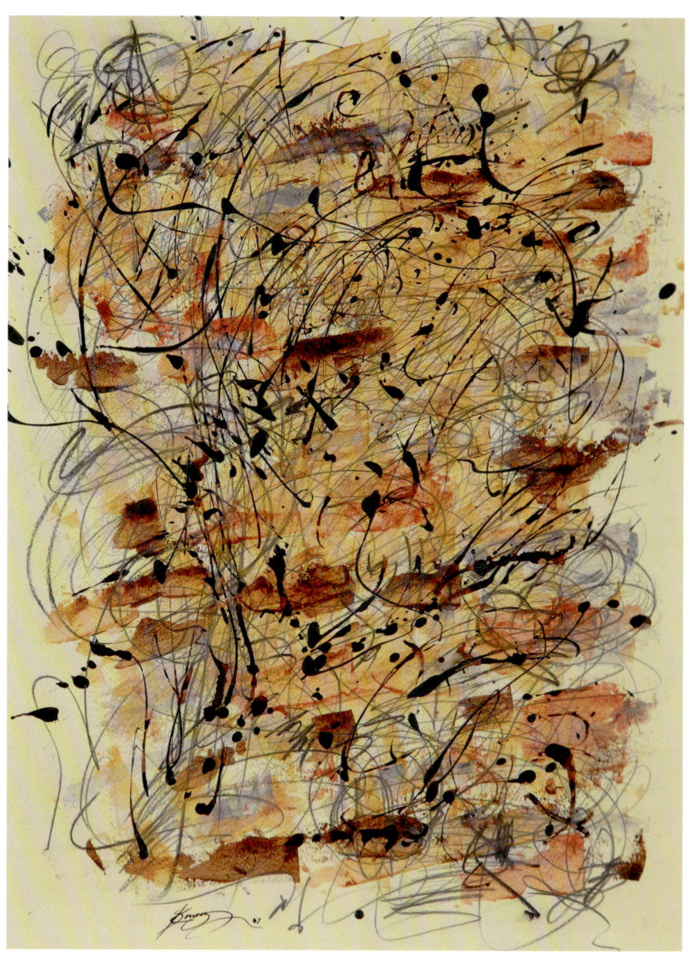

2007, mixed media on paper,
70 x 50 cm

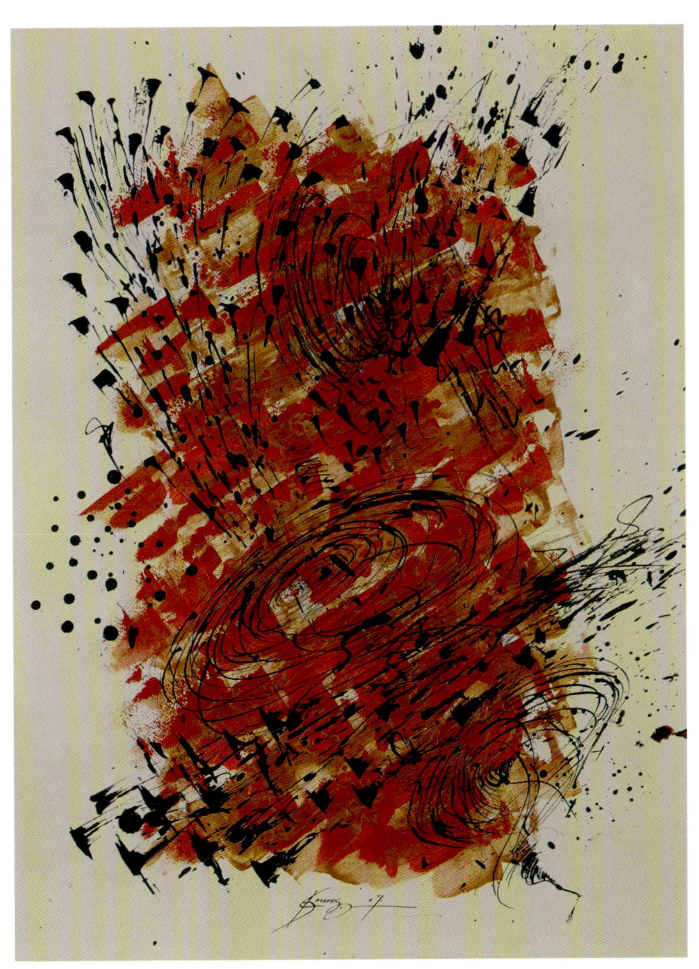

2007, mixed media on paper,
70 x 50 cm

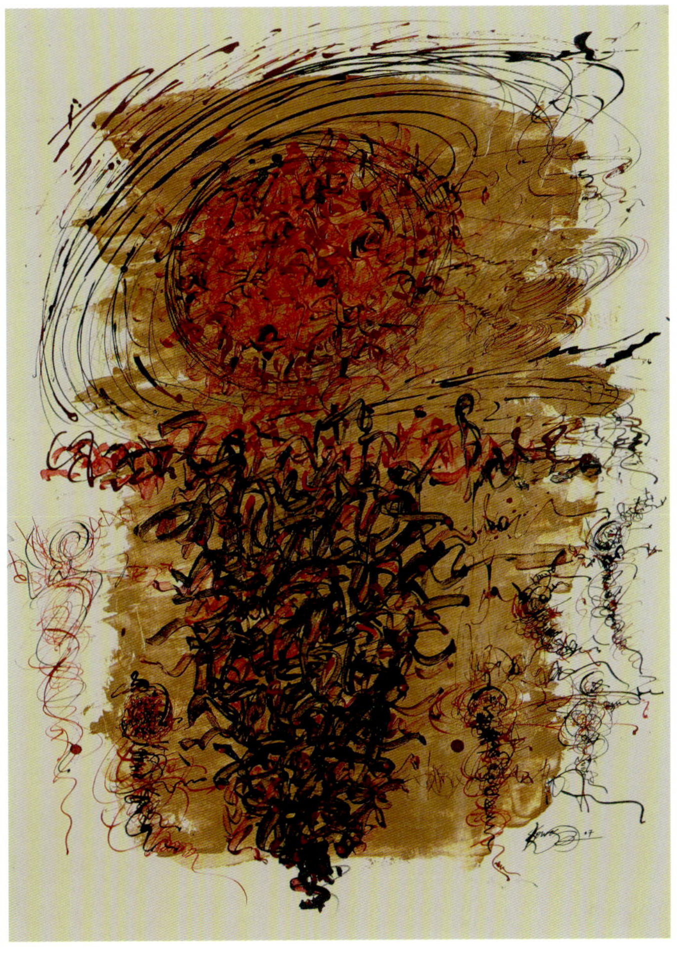

2007, mixed media on paper
70 x 50 cm

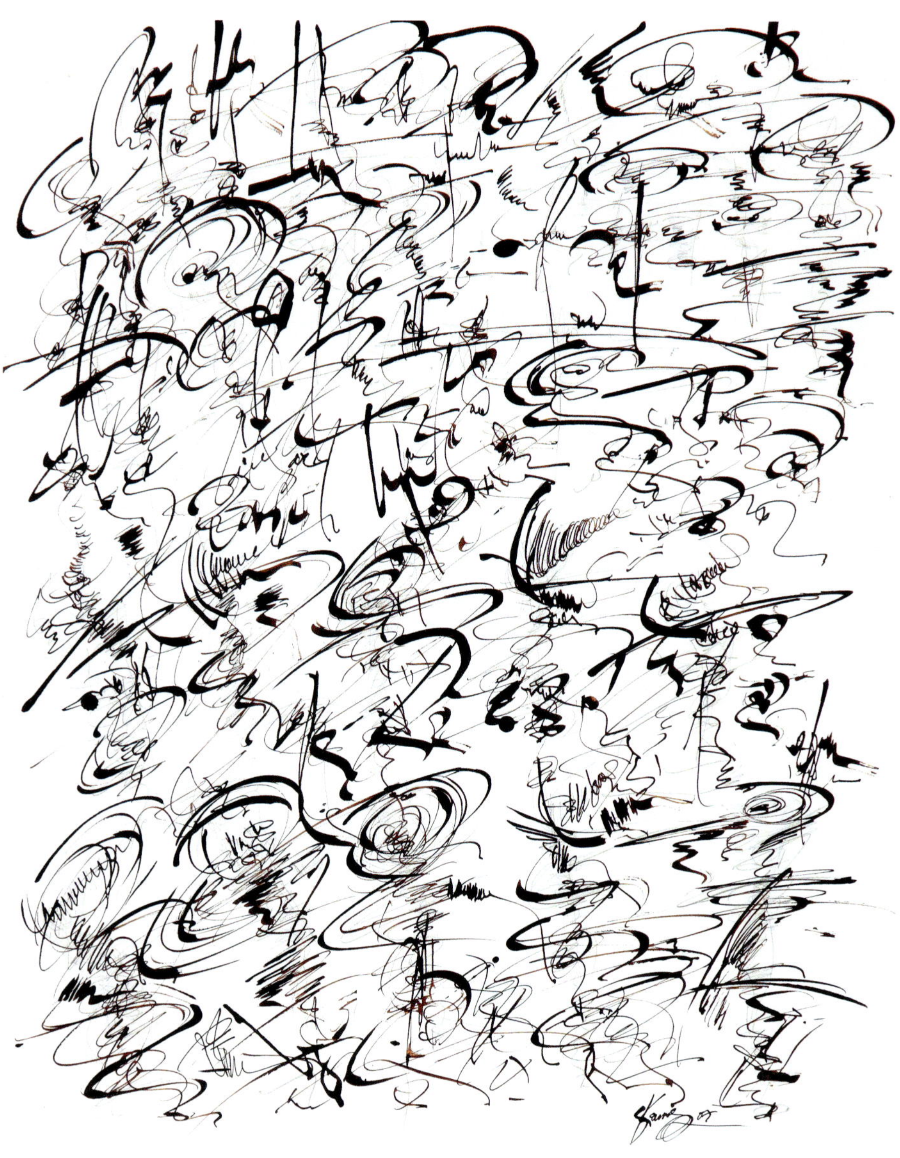

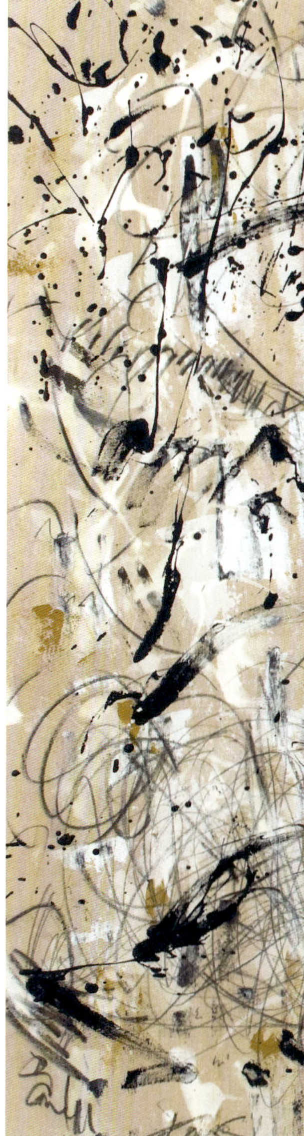

2007, ink on paper,
100 x 70 cm

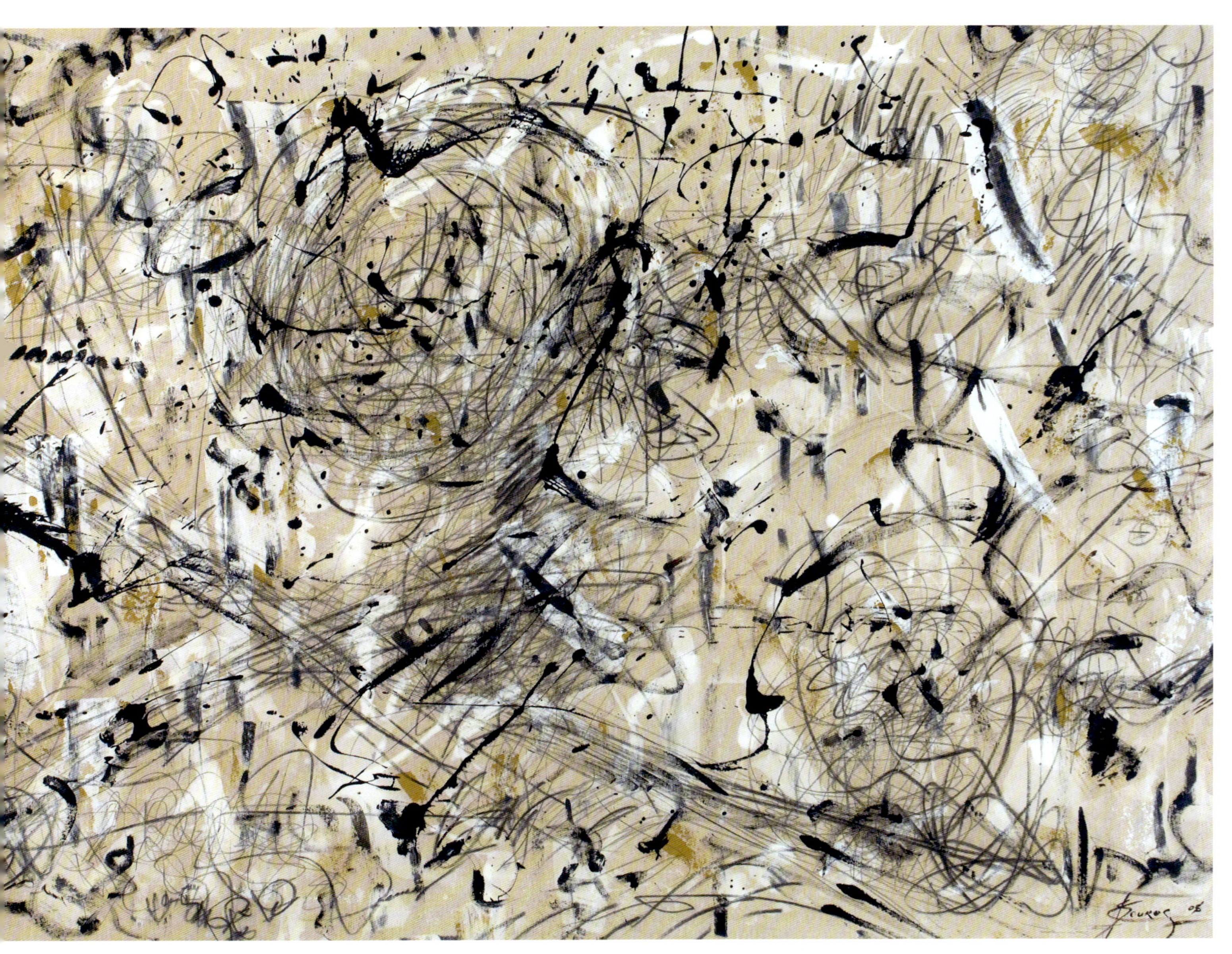

2008, mixed media on canvas,
120 x 200 cm

2007, acrylic on canvas,
120 x 120 cm

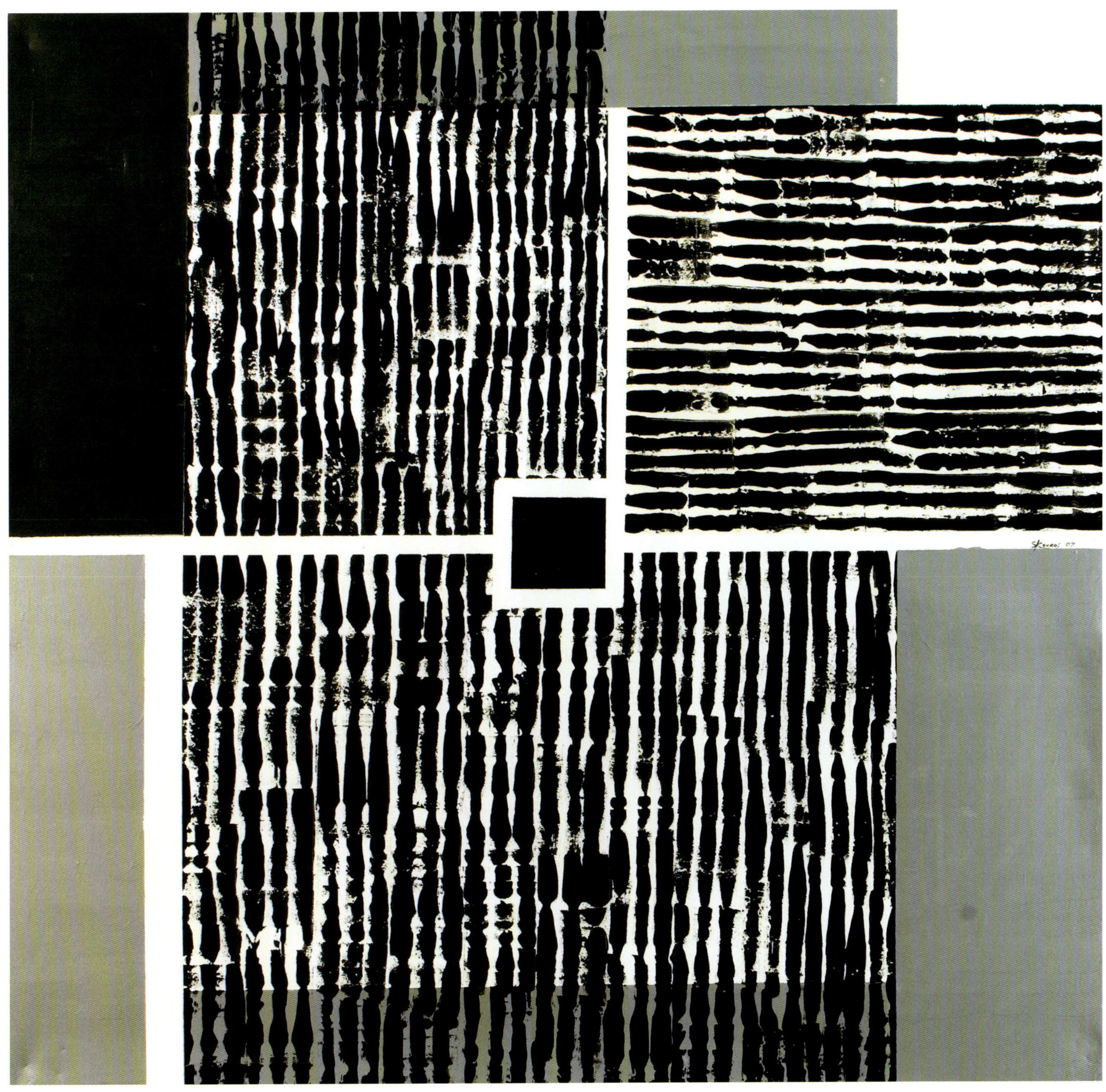

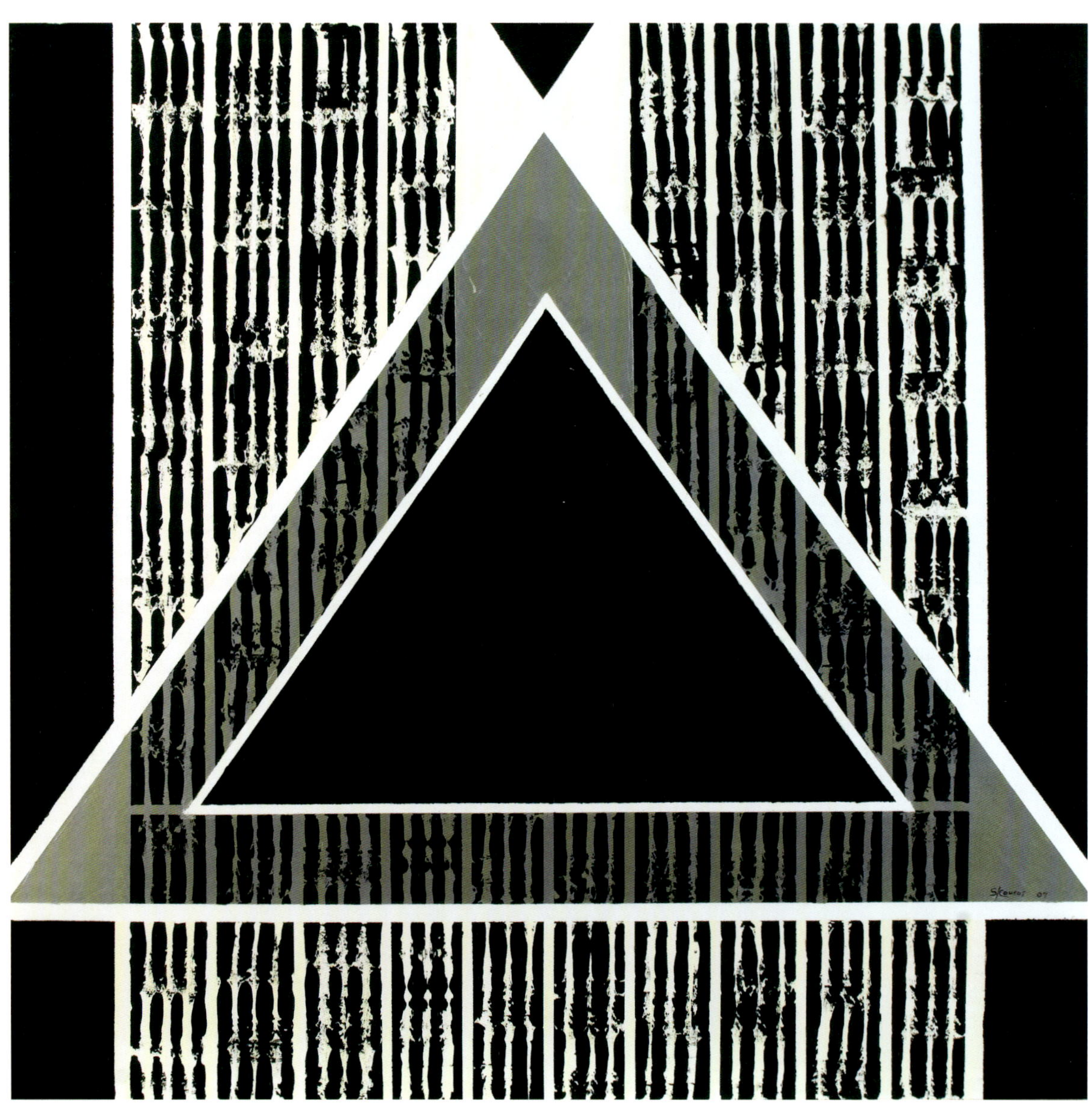

2007, acrylic on canvas,
120 x 120 cm

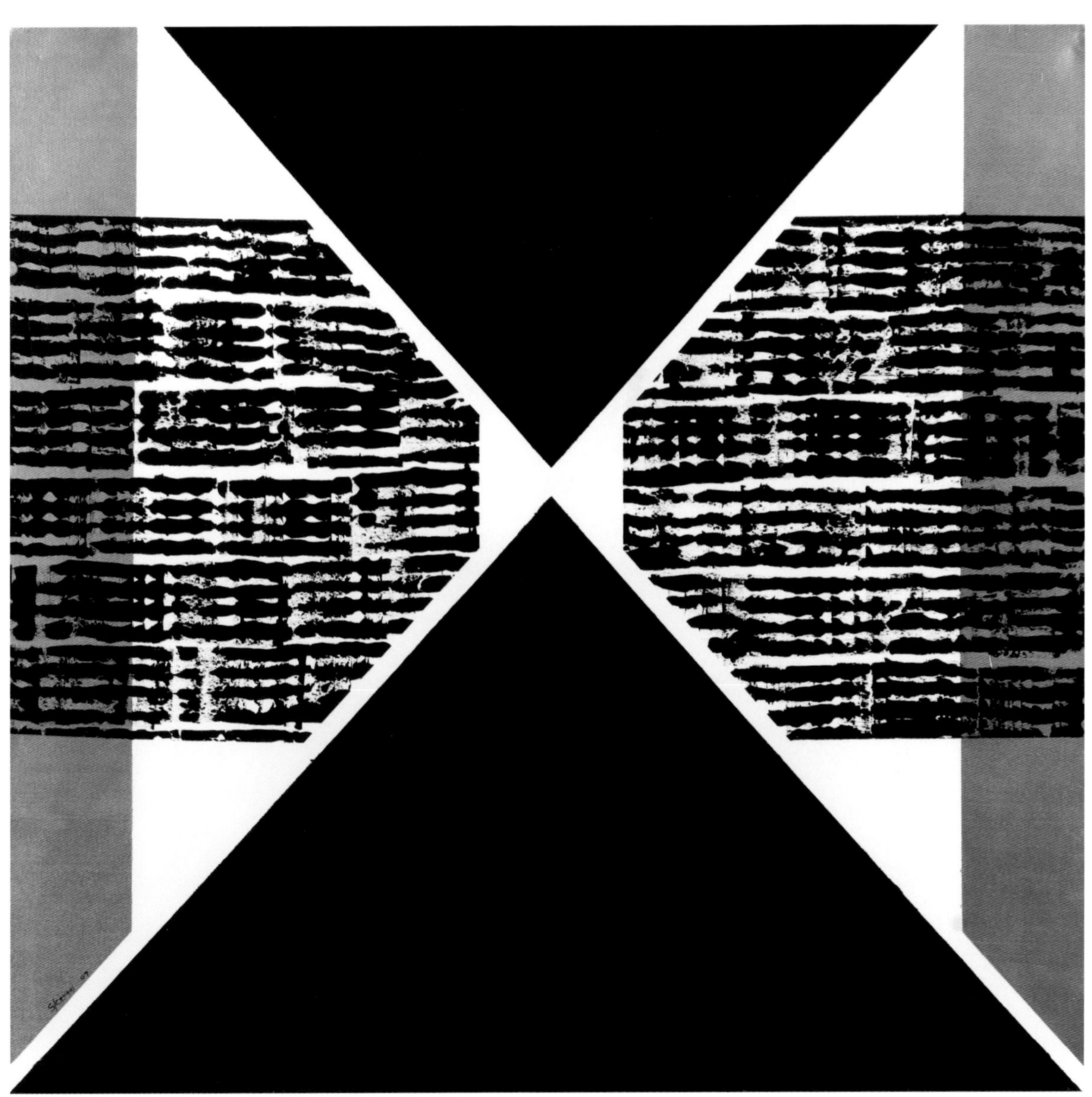

2007, acrylic on canvas,
120 x 120 cm

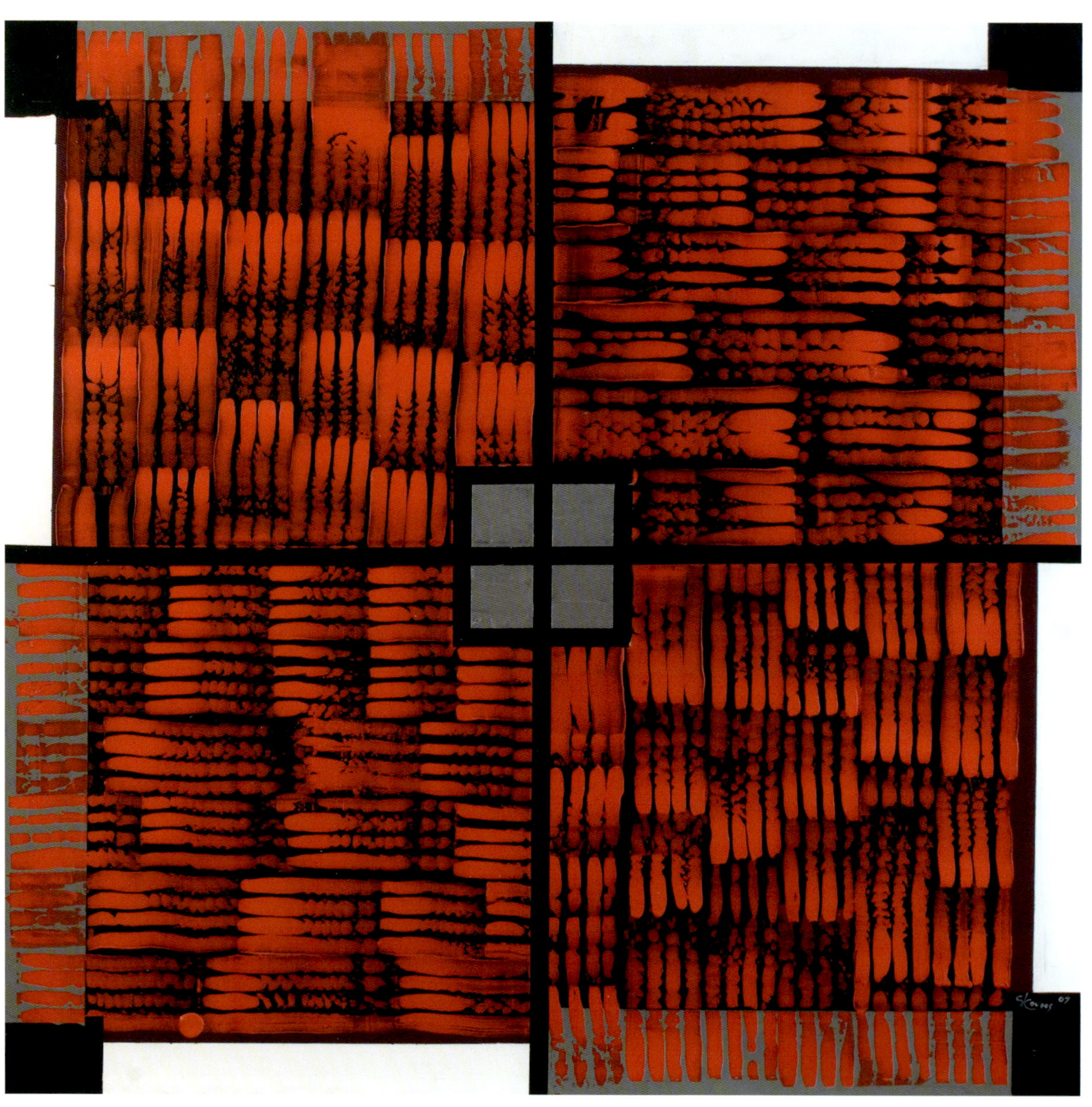

2007, acrylic on canvas,
120 x 120 cm

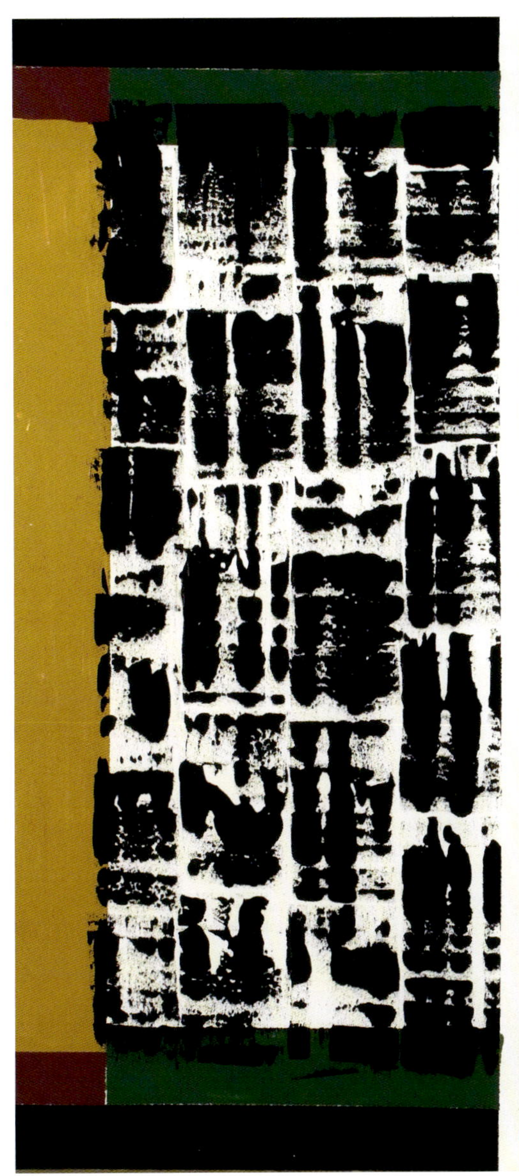

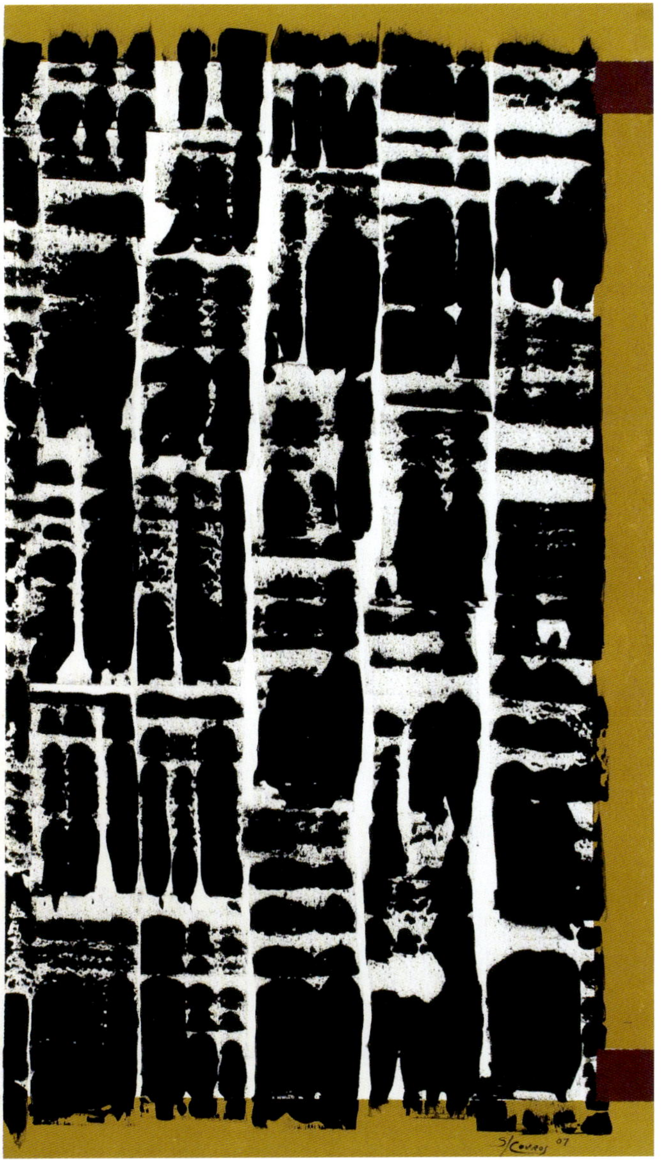

2007, acrylic on canvas,
120 x 120 cm

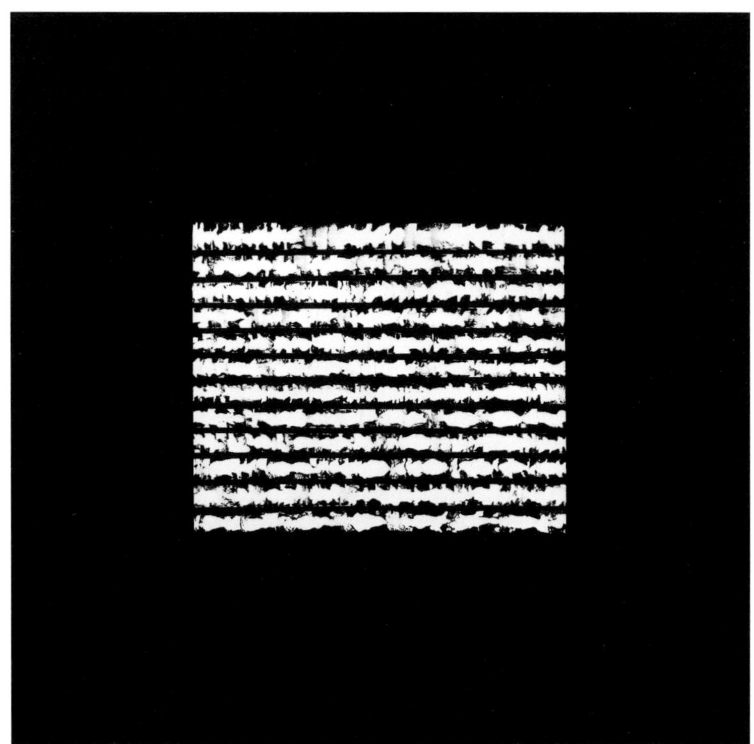

2007, acrylic on canvas,
120 x 120 cm

2007, acrylic on canvas,
120 x 120 cm

2007, acrylic on canvas,
120 x 120 cm

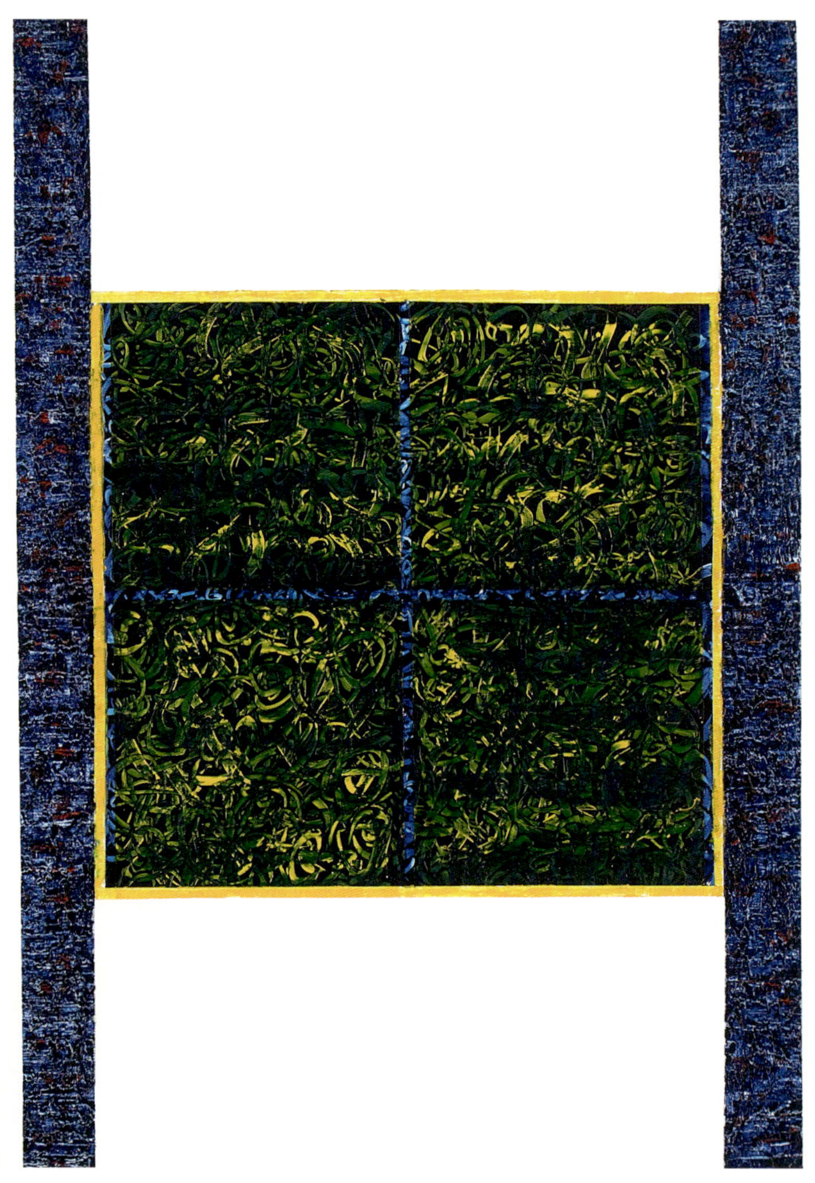

2007, mixed media on canvas,
120 x 120 cm

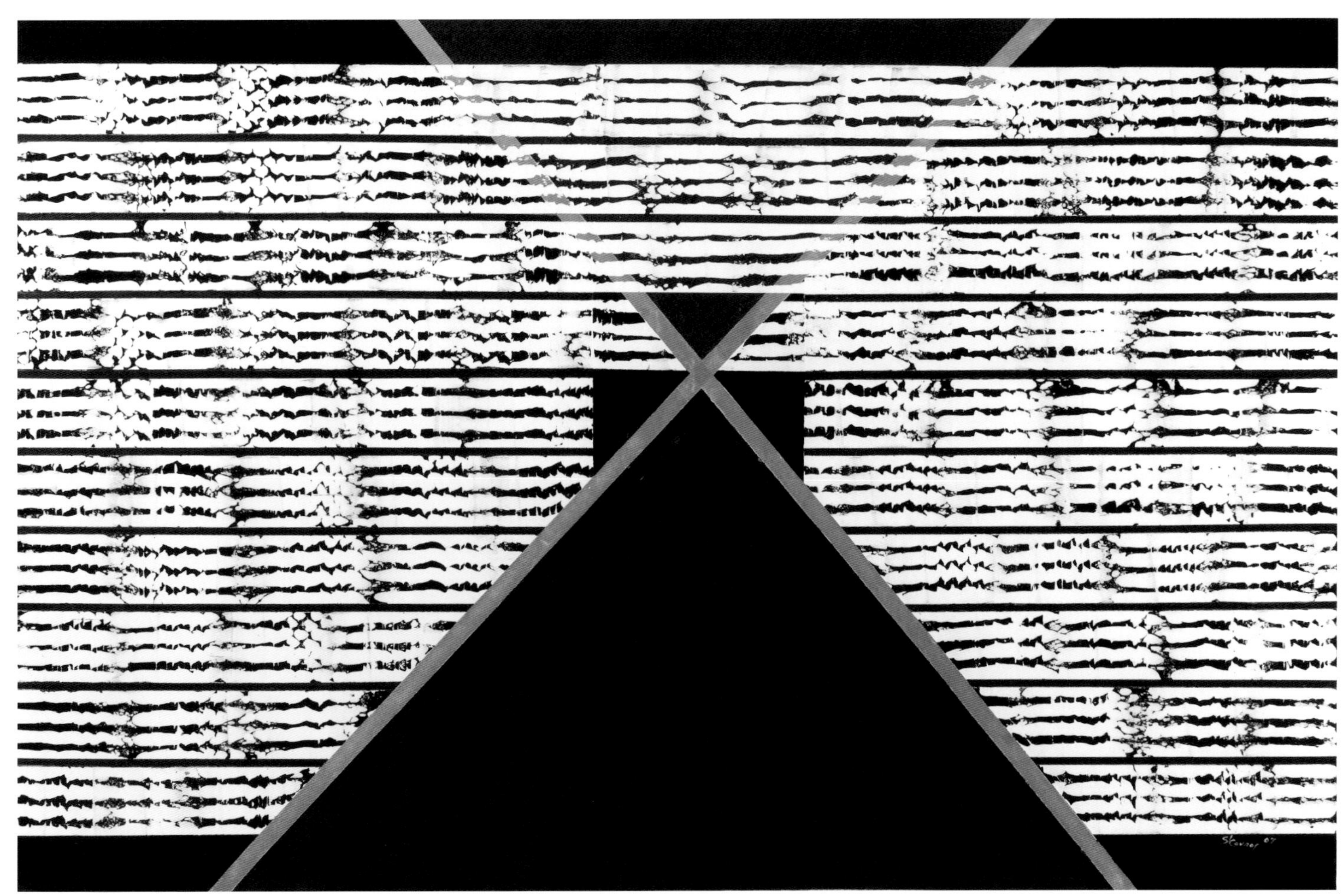

2007, acrylic on canvas,
120 x 200 cm

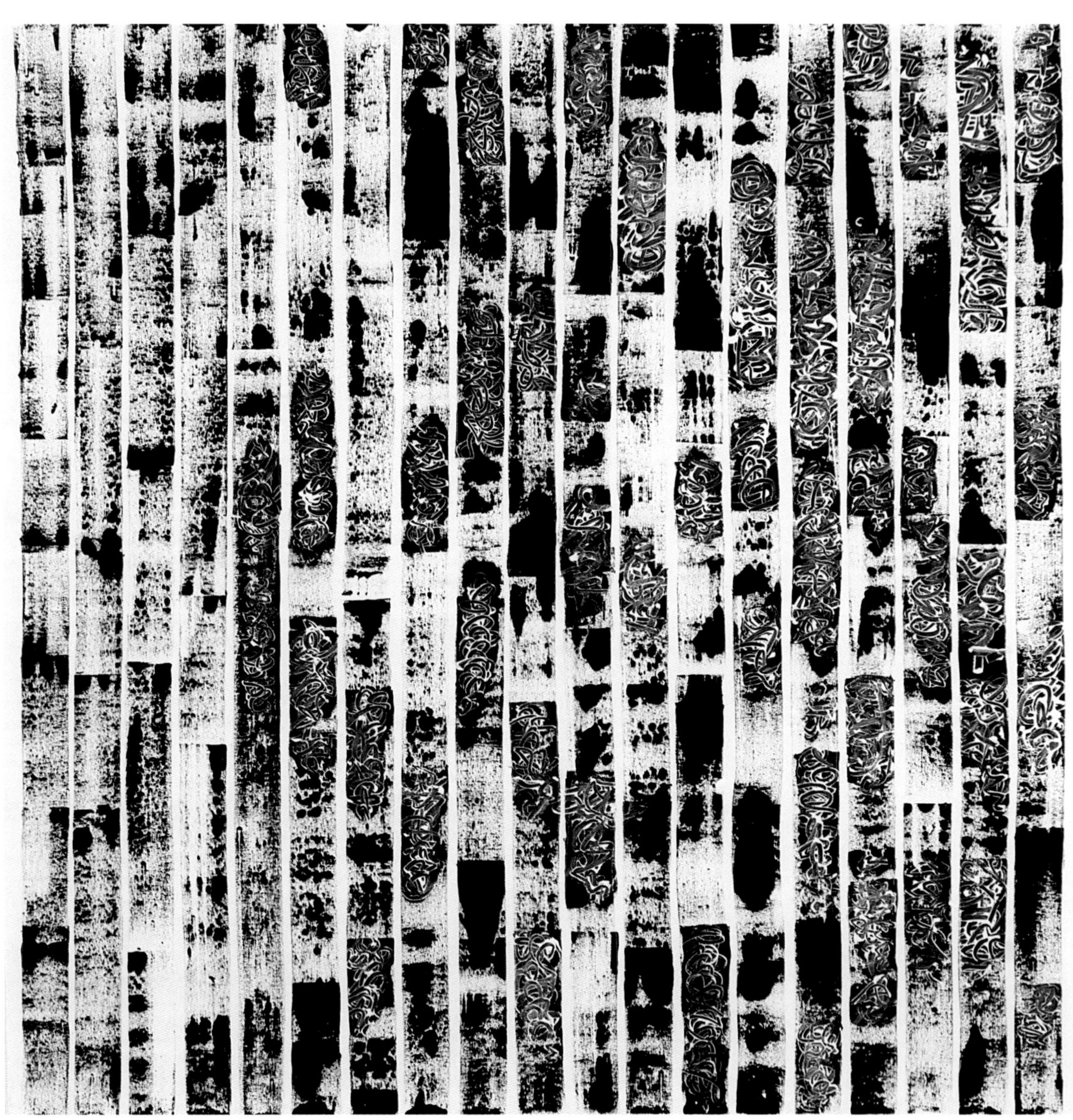

2007, mixed media on canvas,
120 x 120 cm

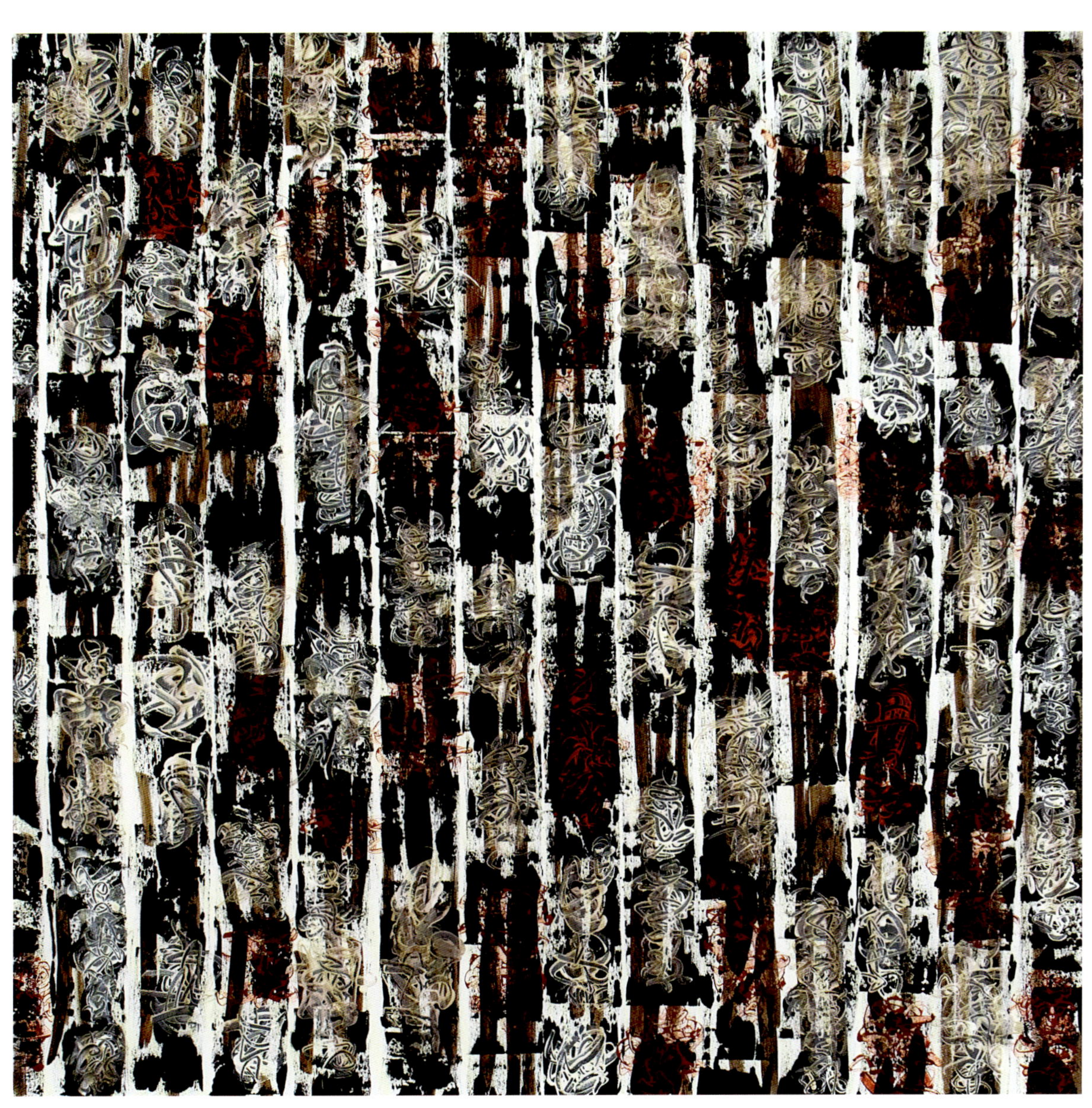

2007, mixed media on canvas,
120 x 120 cm

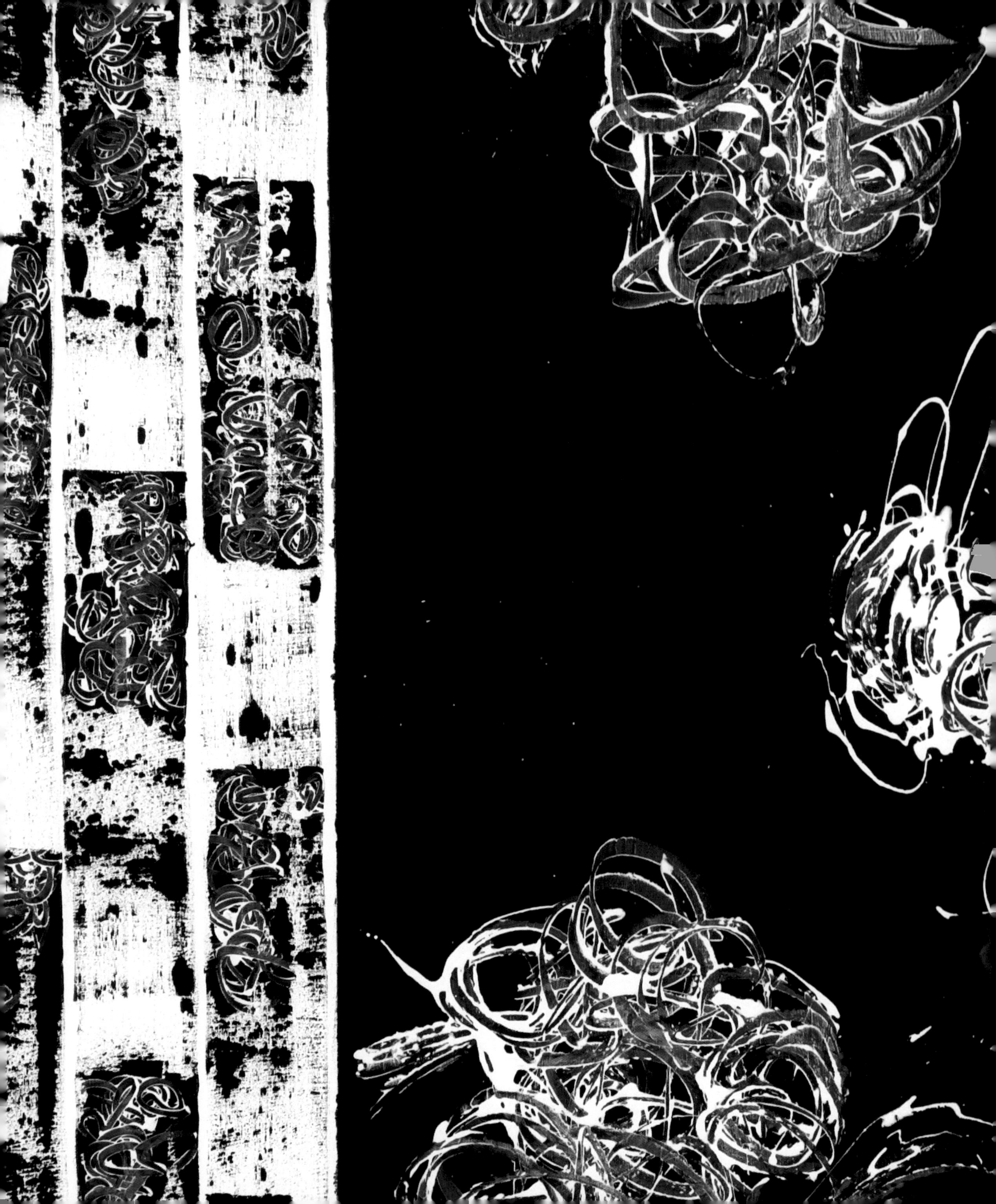

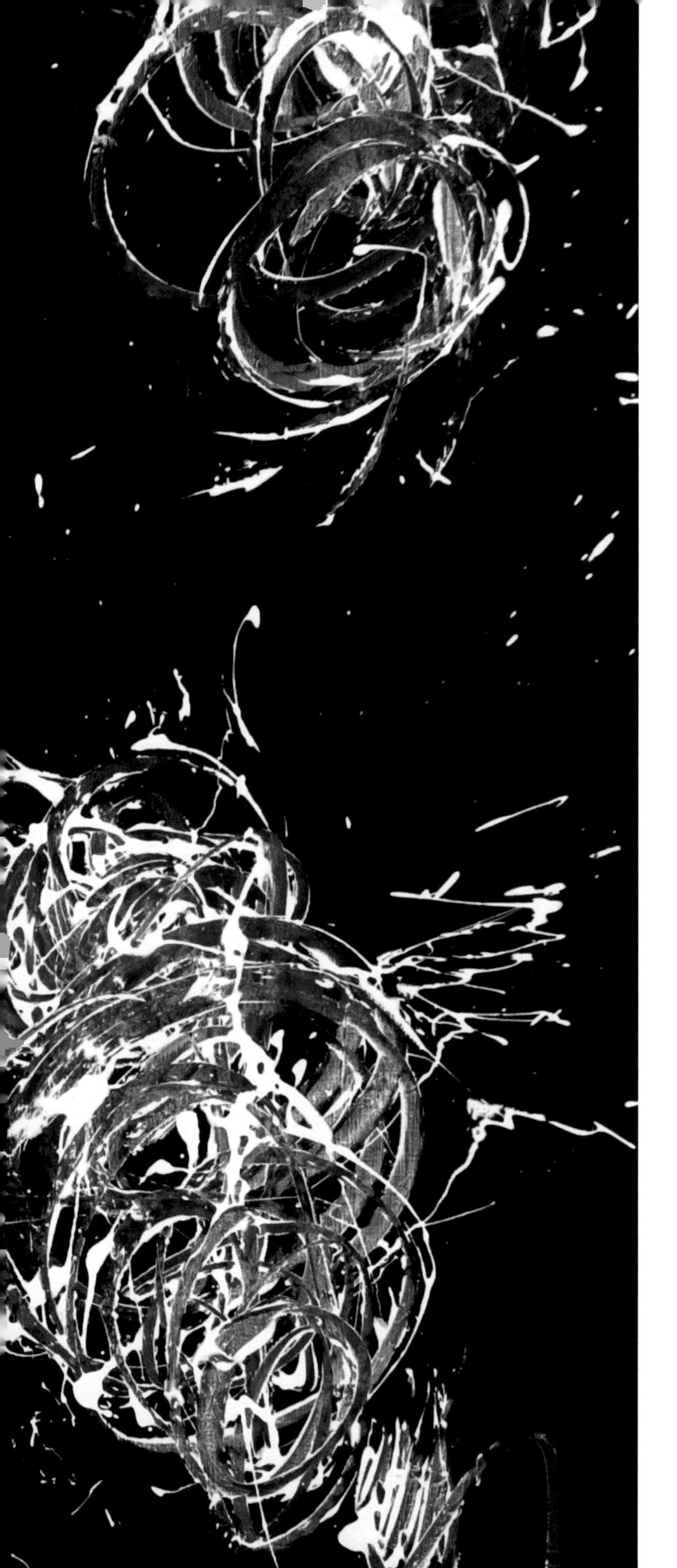

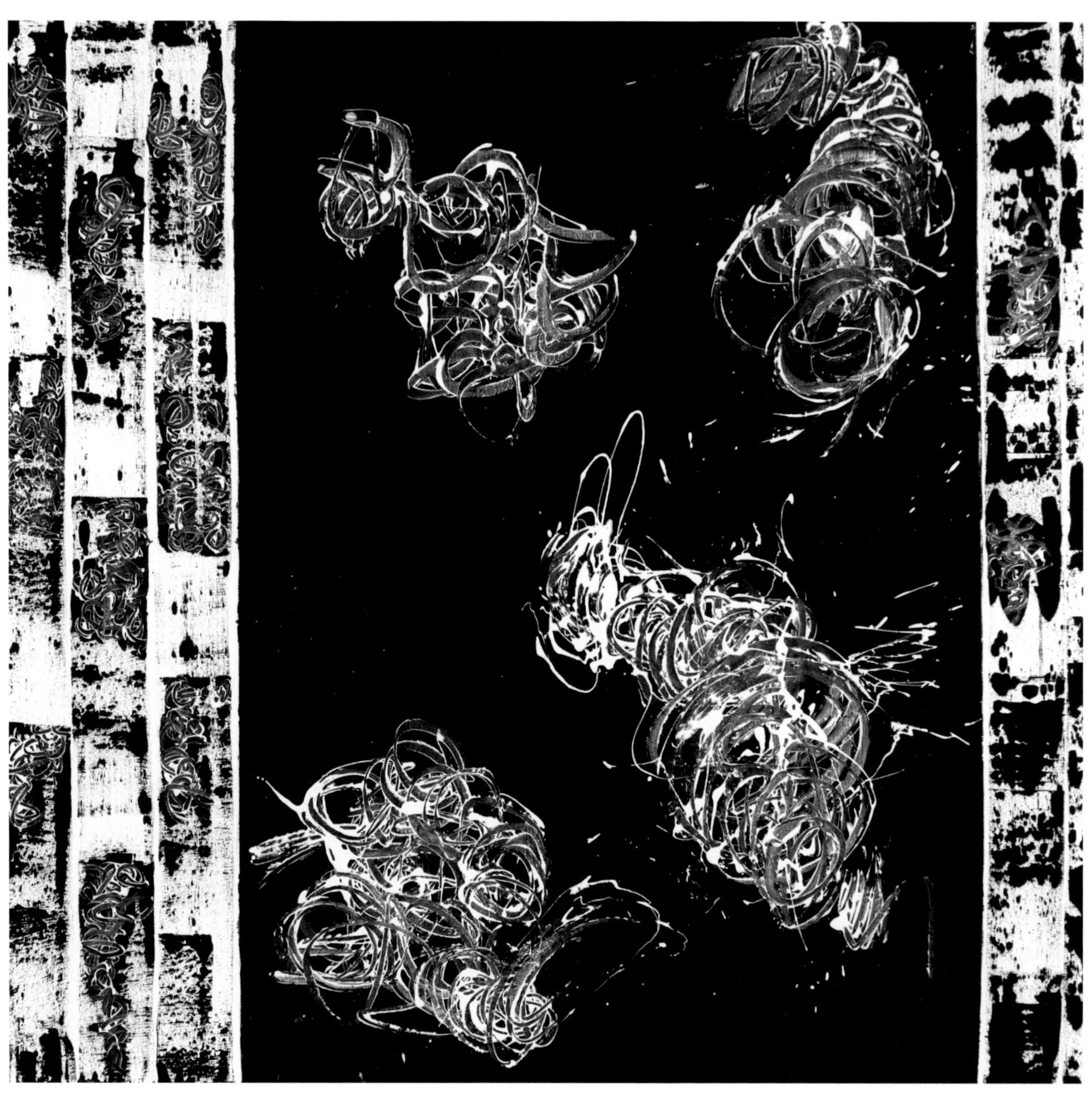

2007, mixed media on canvas,
120 x 120 cm

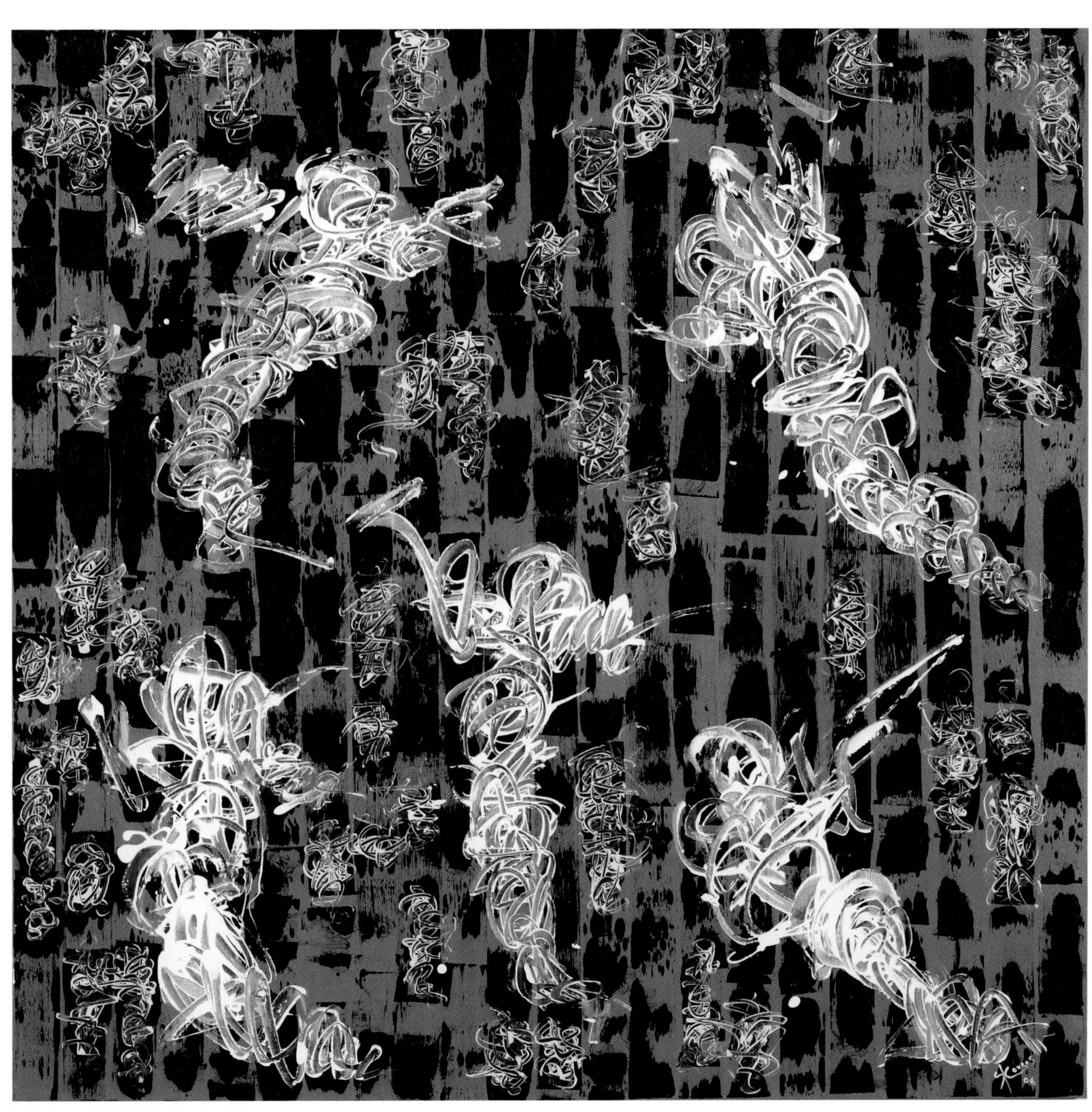

2008, mixed media on canvas,
120 x 120 cm

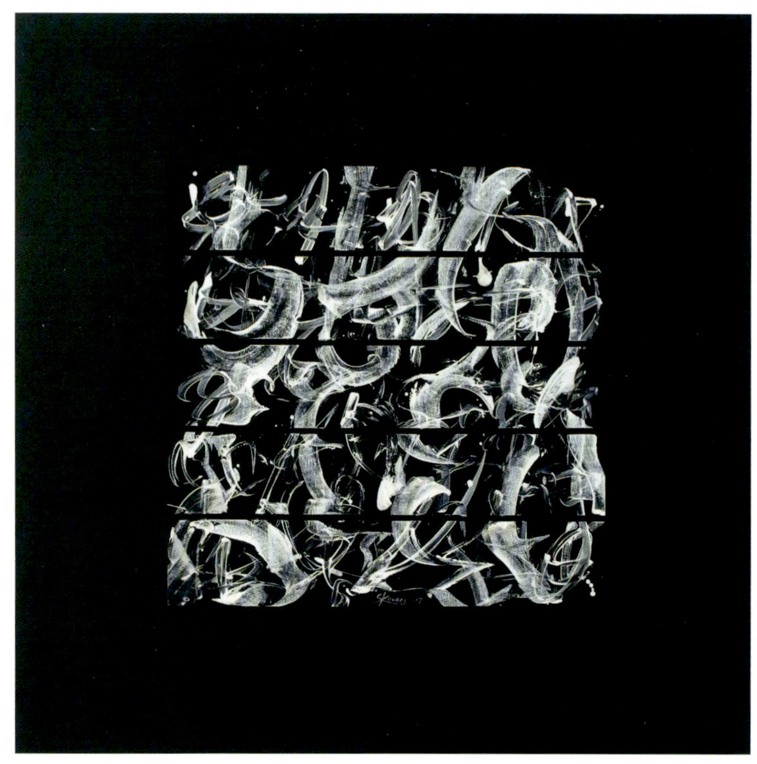

2007, mixed media on canvas,
120 x 120 cm

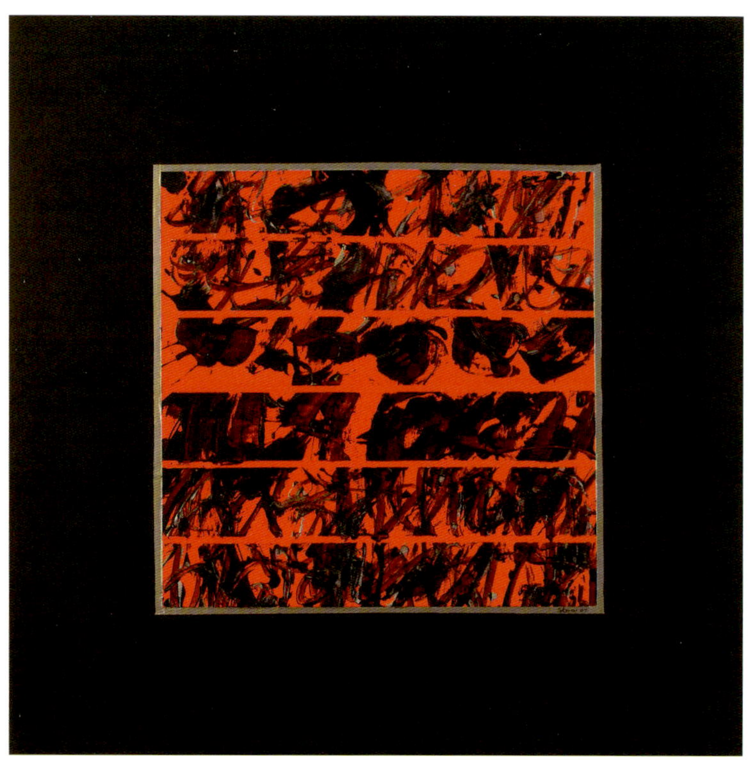

2007, acrylic on canvas,
120 x 120 cm

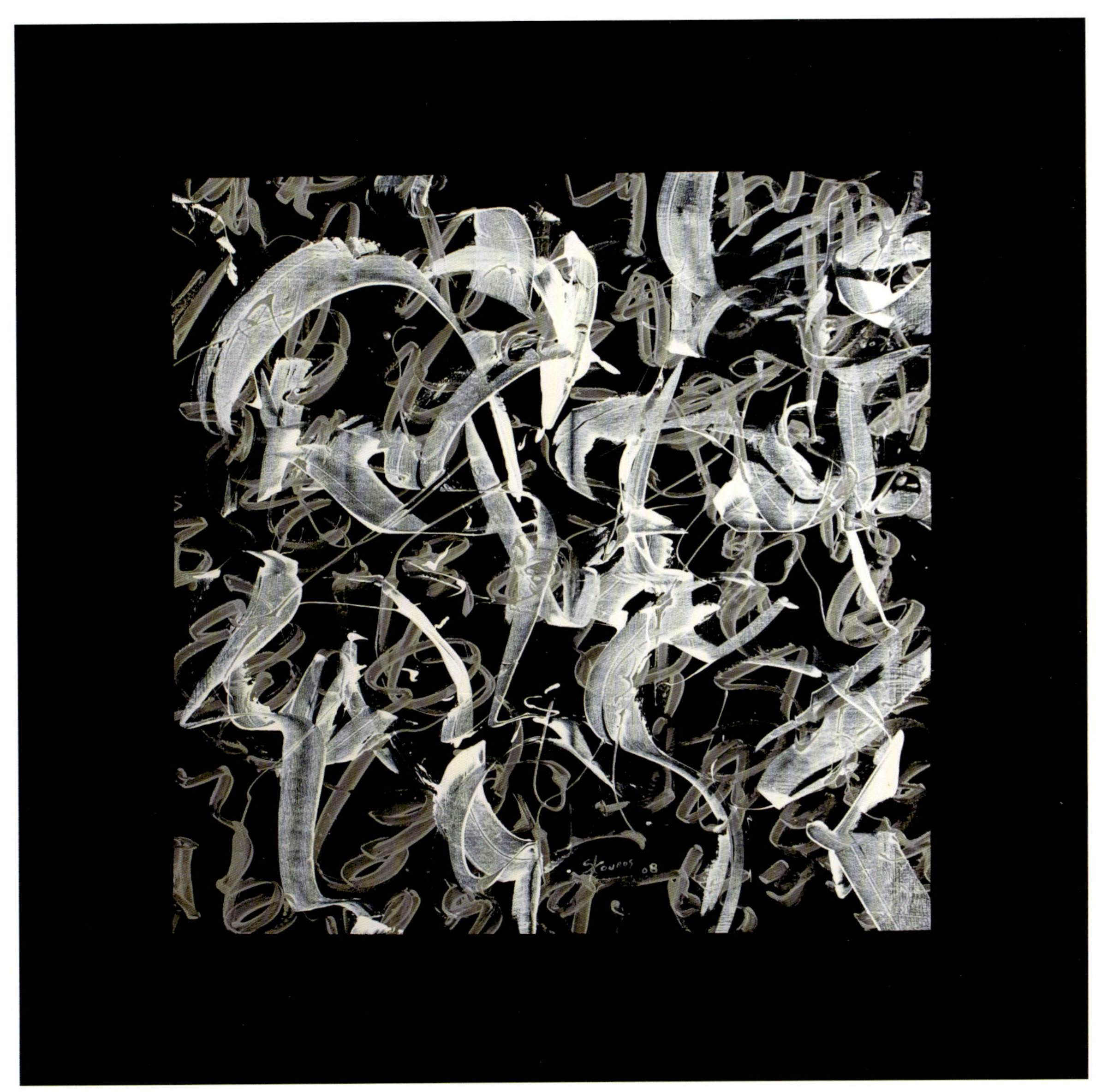

2007, mixed media on canvas,
120 x 120 cm

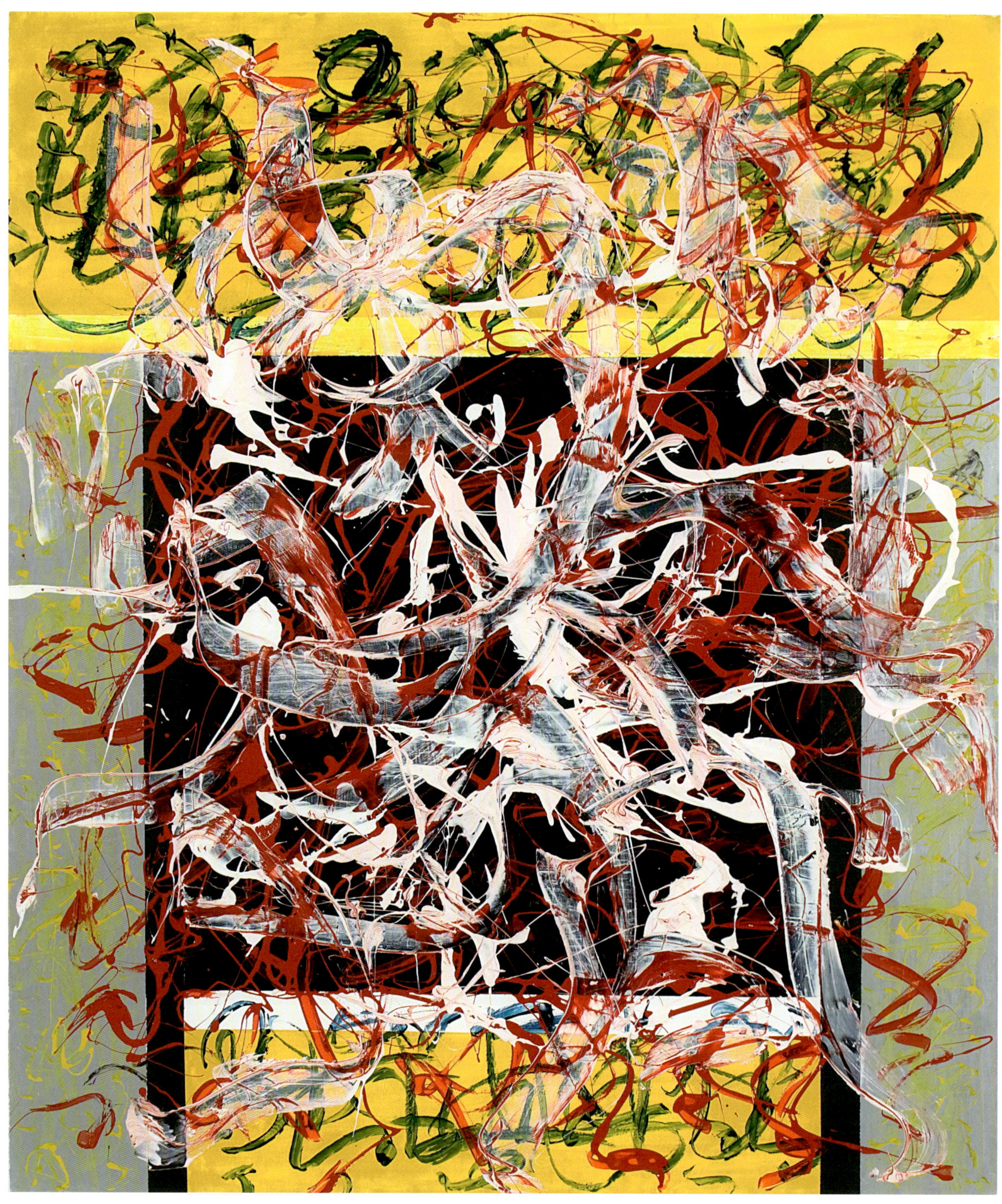

2007, mixed media on canvas,
120 x 100 cm

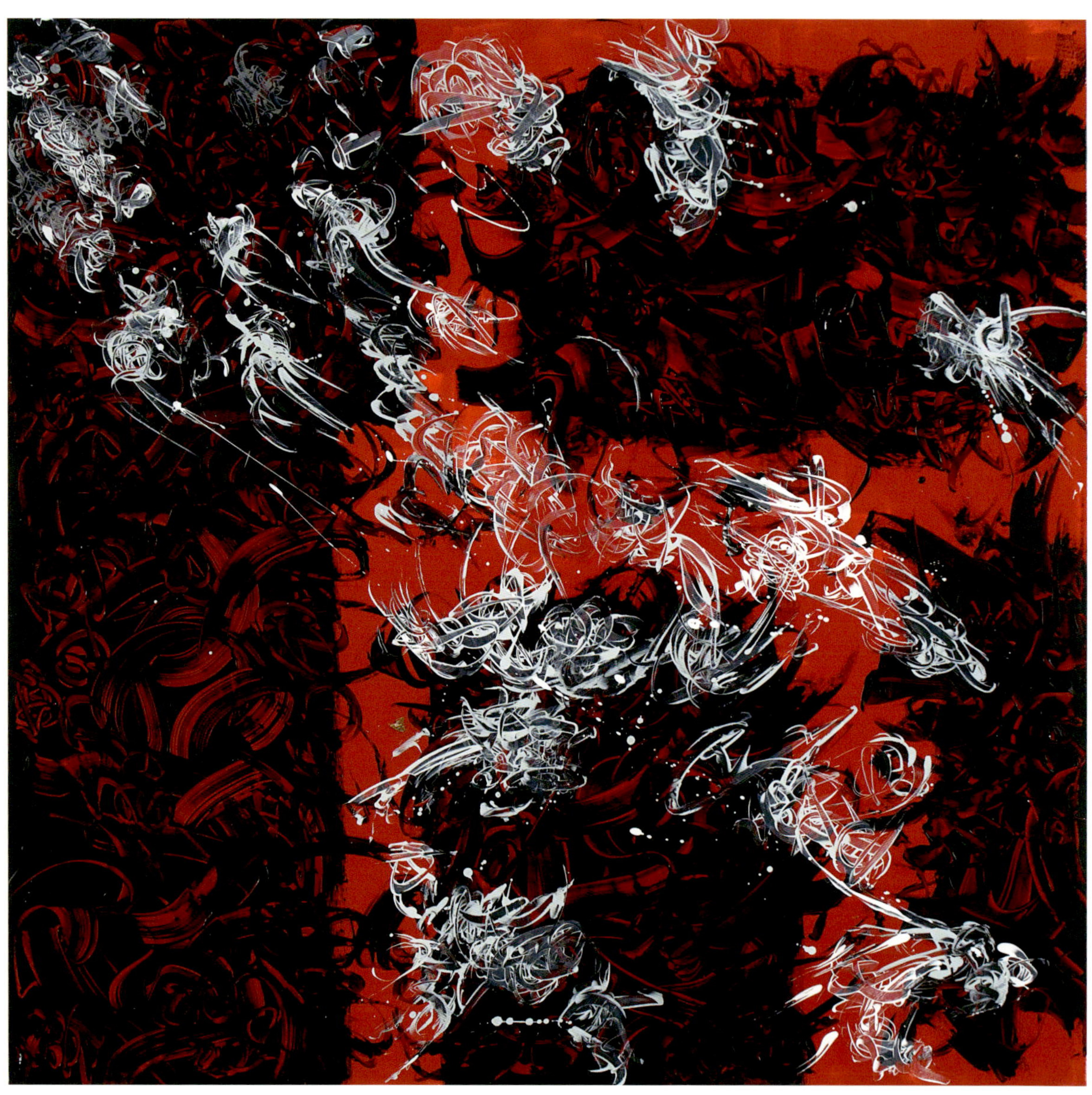

2007, mixed media on canvas,
120 x 120 cm

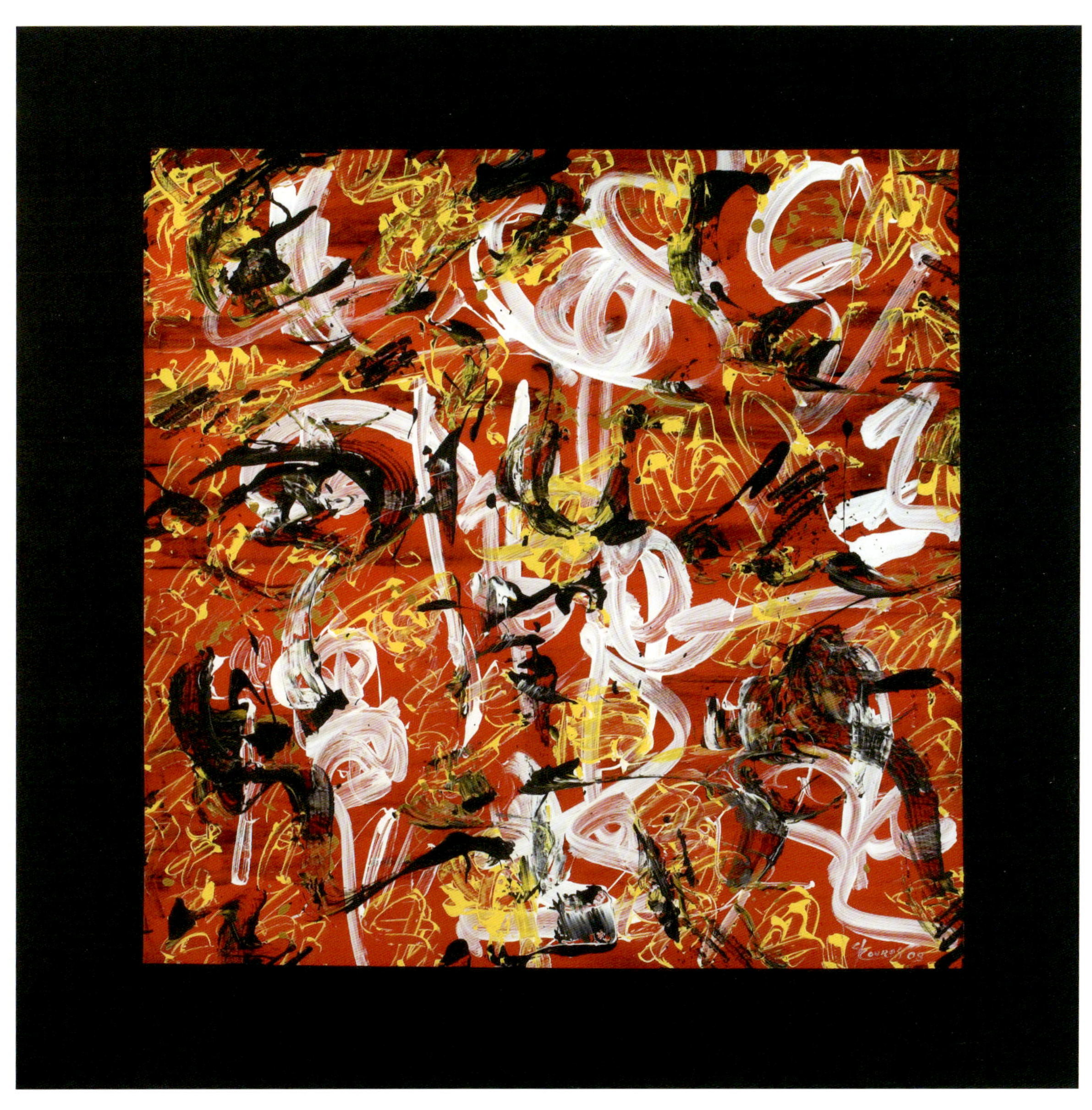

2007, mixed media on canvas,
120 x 120 cm

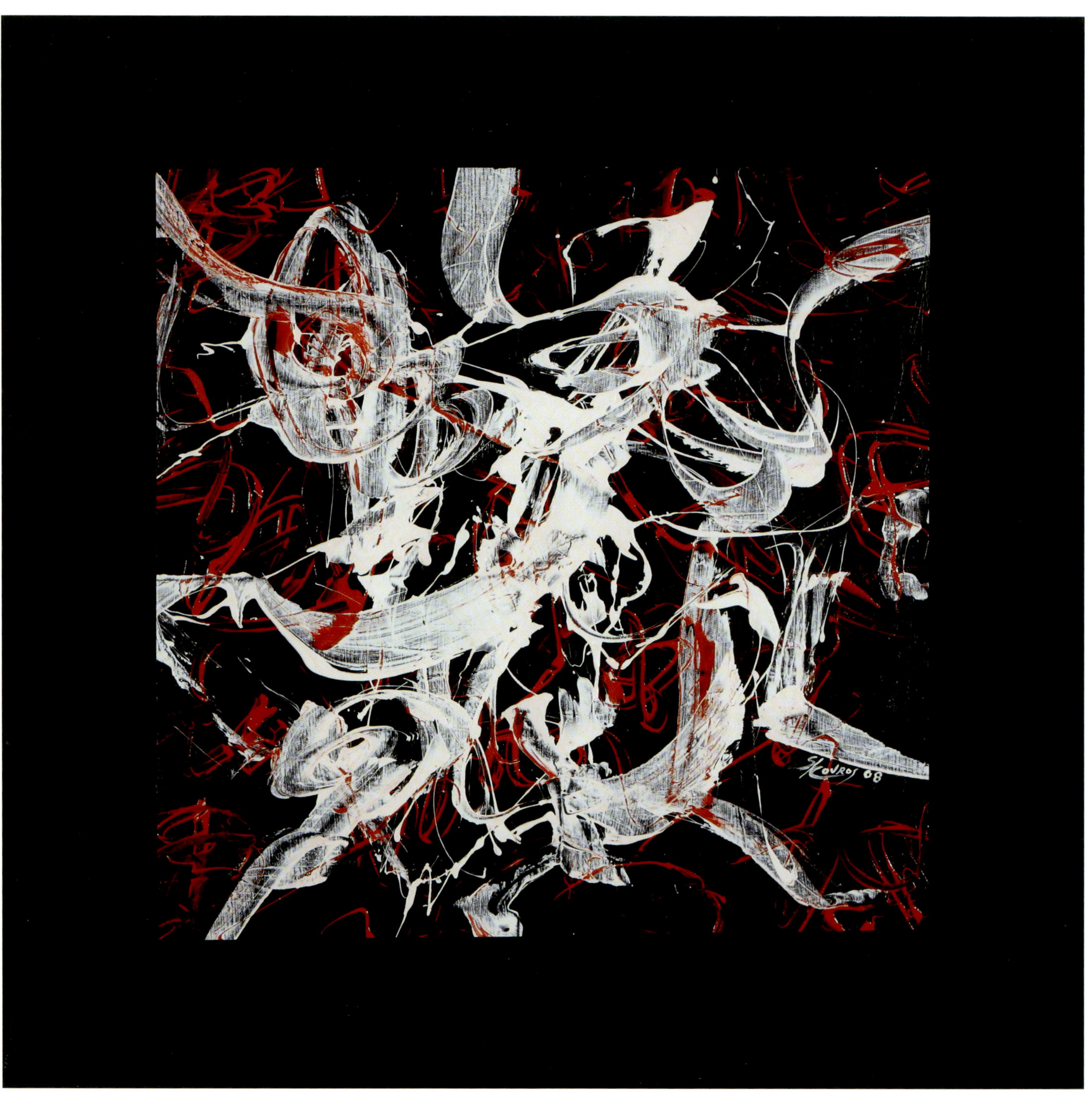
Skouros 08

2008, mixed media on canvas,
120 x 120 cm

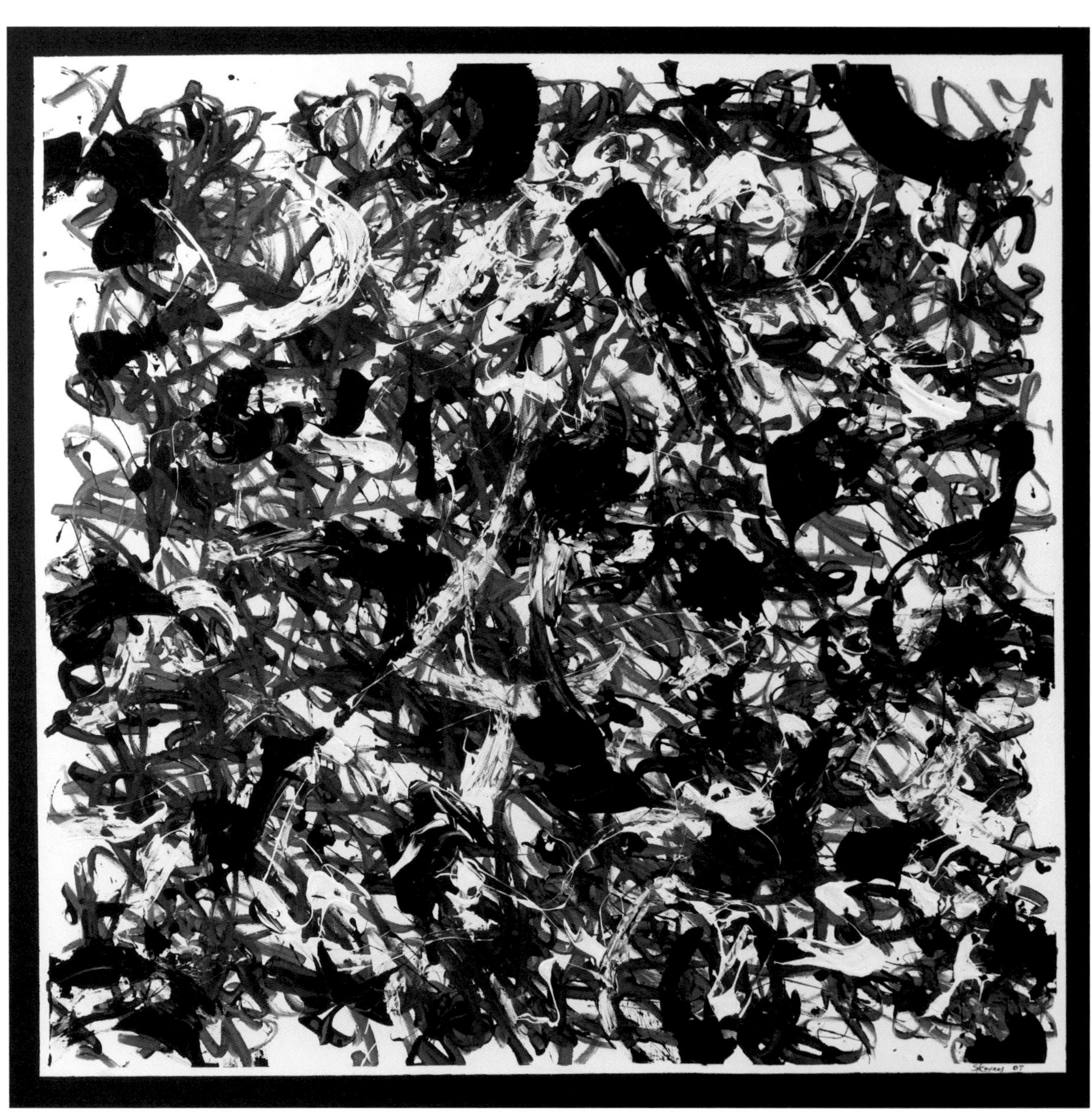

2007, mixed media on canvas,
120 x 120 cm

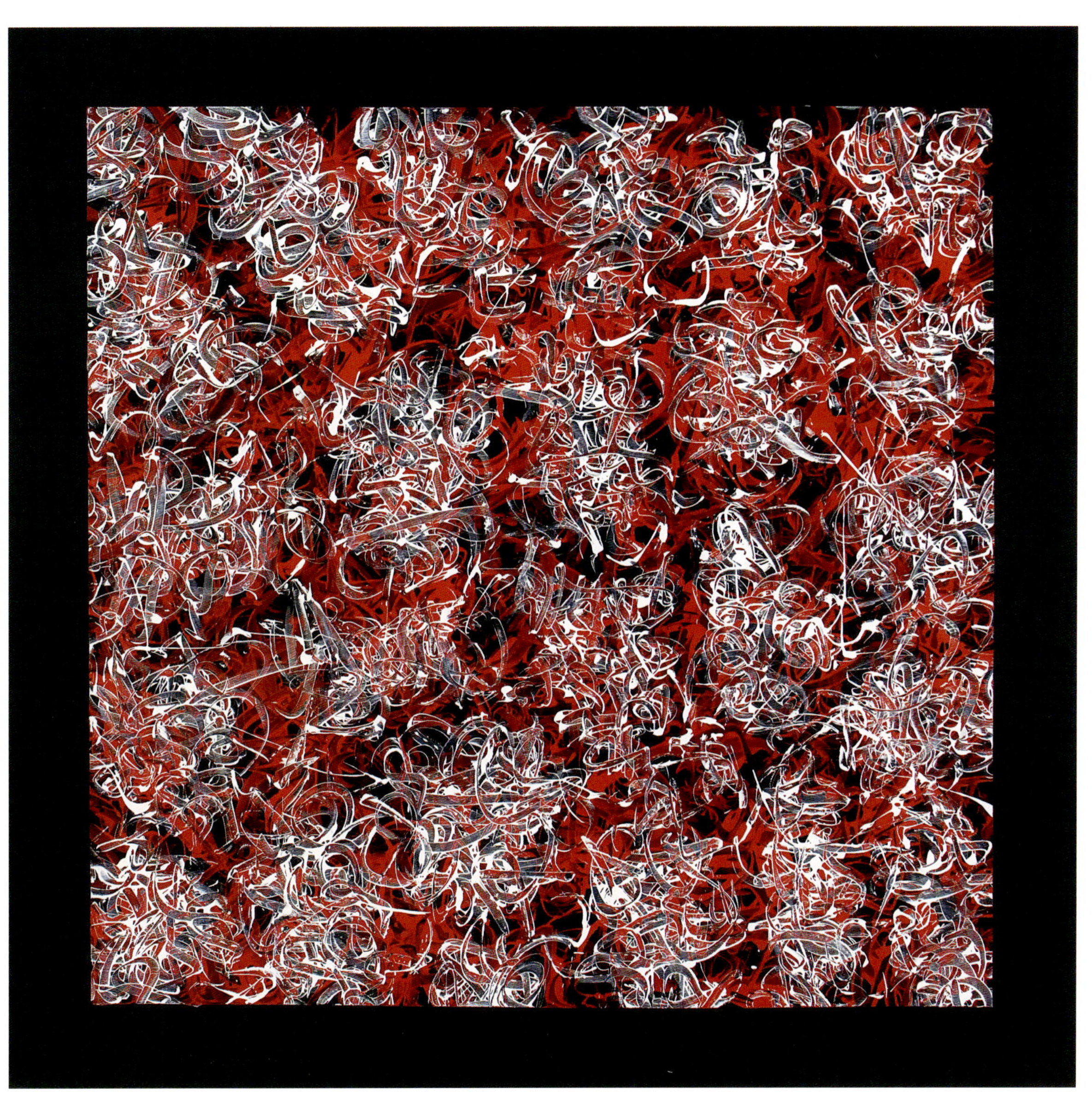

2007, mixed media on canvas,
120 x 120 cm

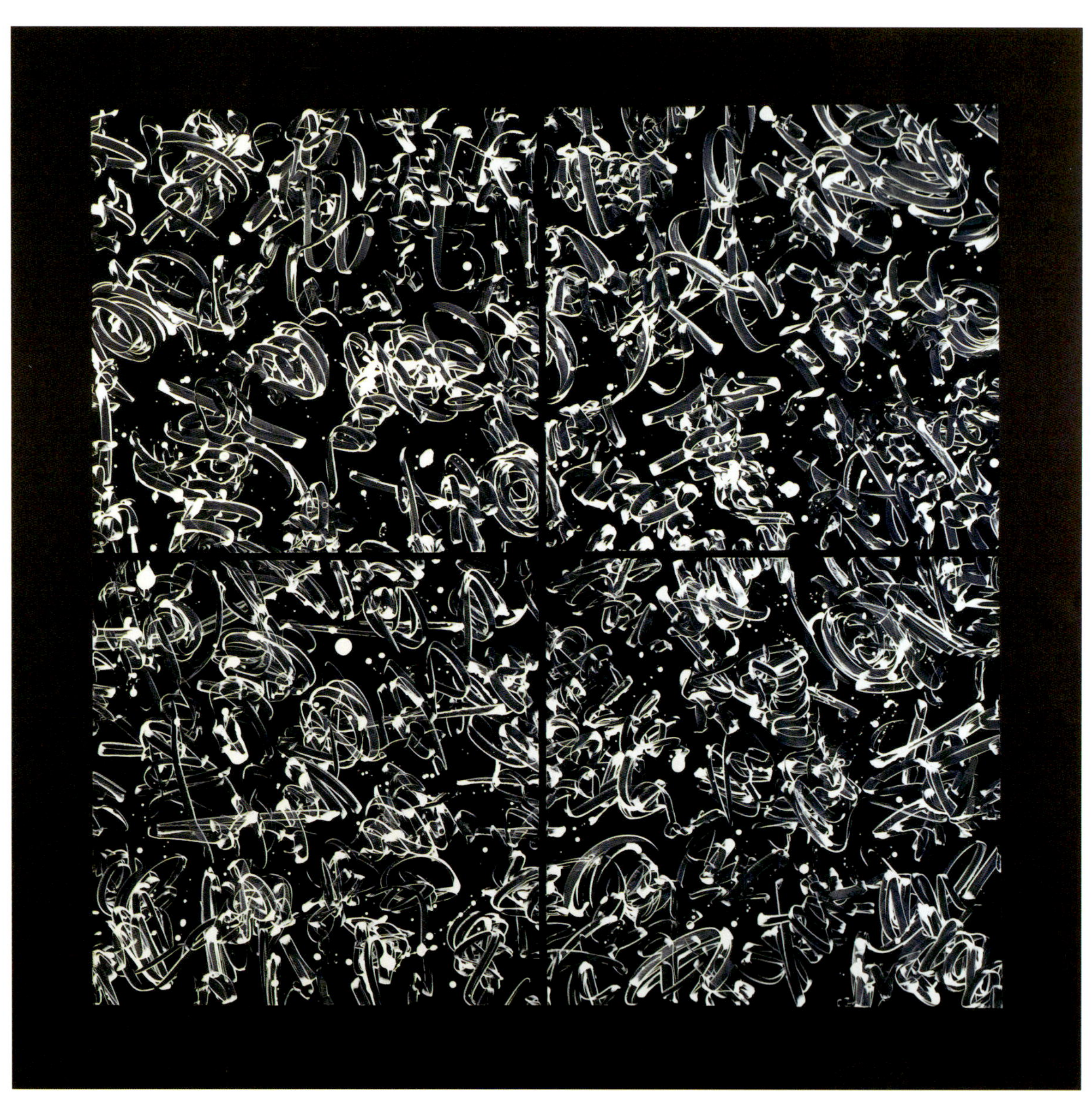

2008, mixed media on canvas,
120 x 120 cm

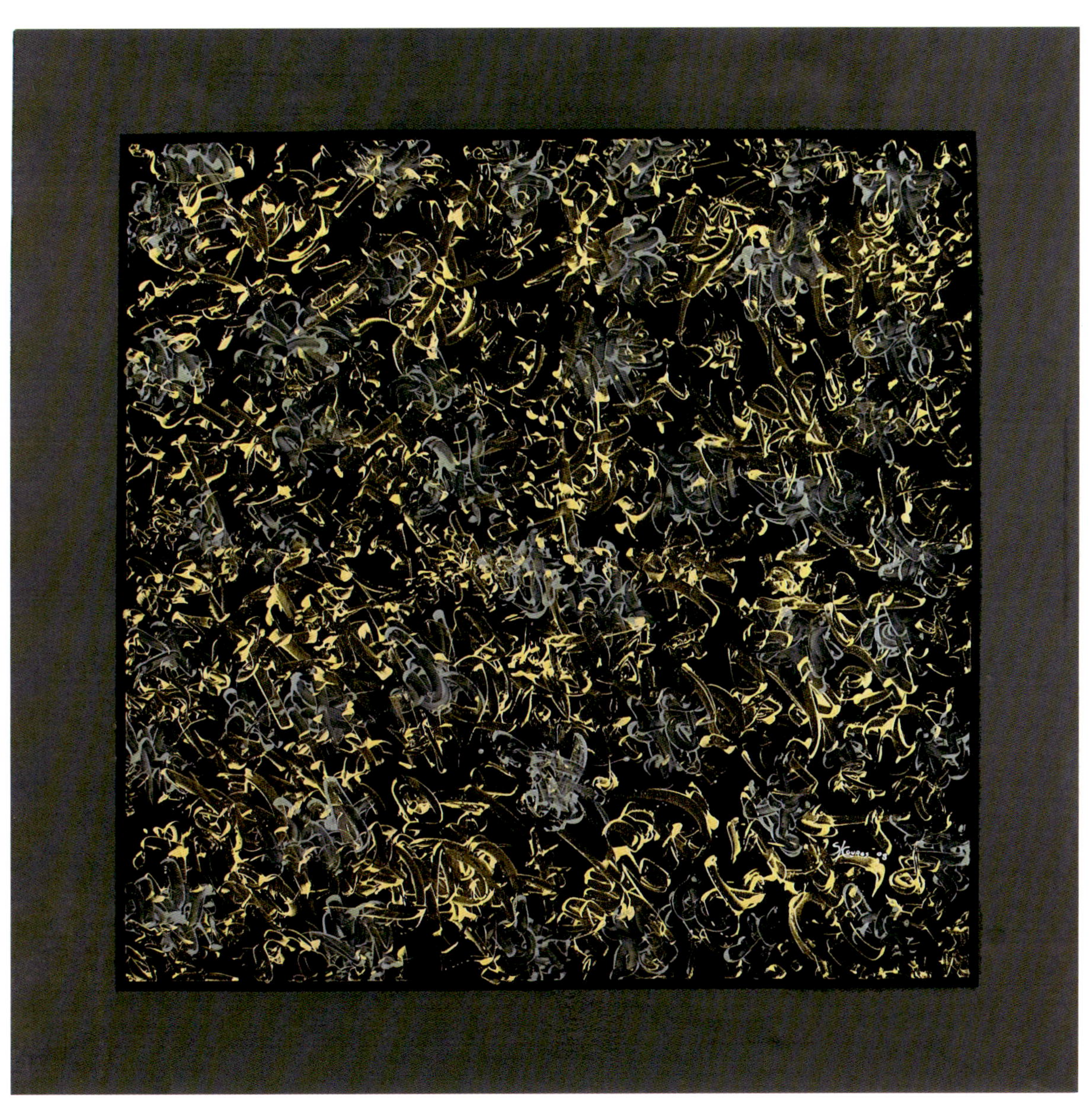

2008, mixed media on canvas,
120 x 120 cm

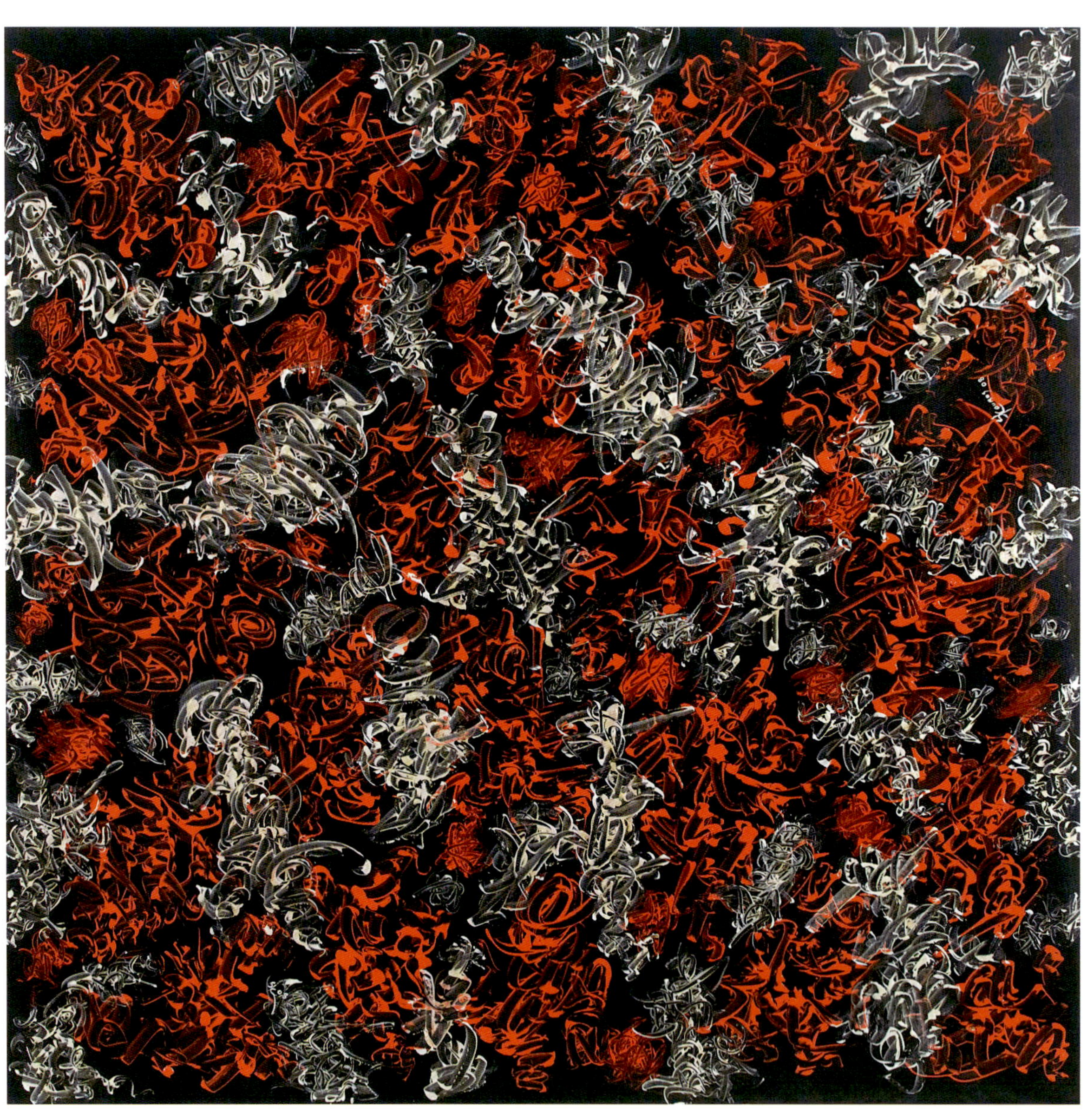

2007, mixed media on canvas,
120 x 120 cm

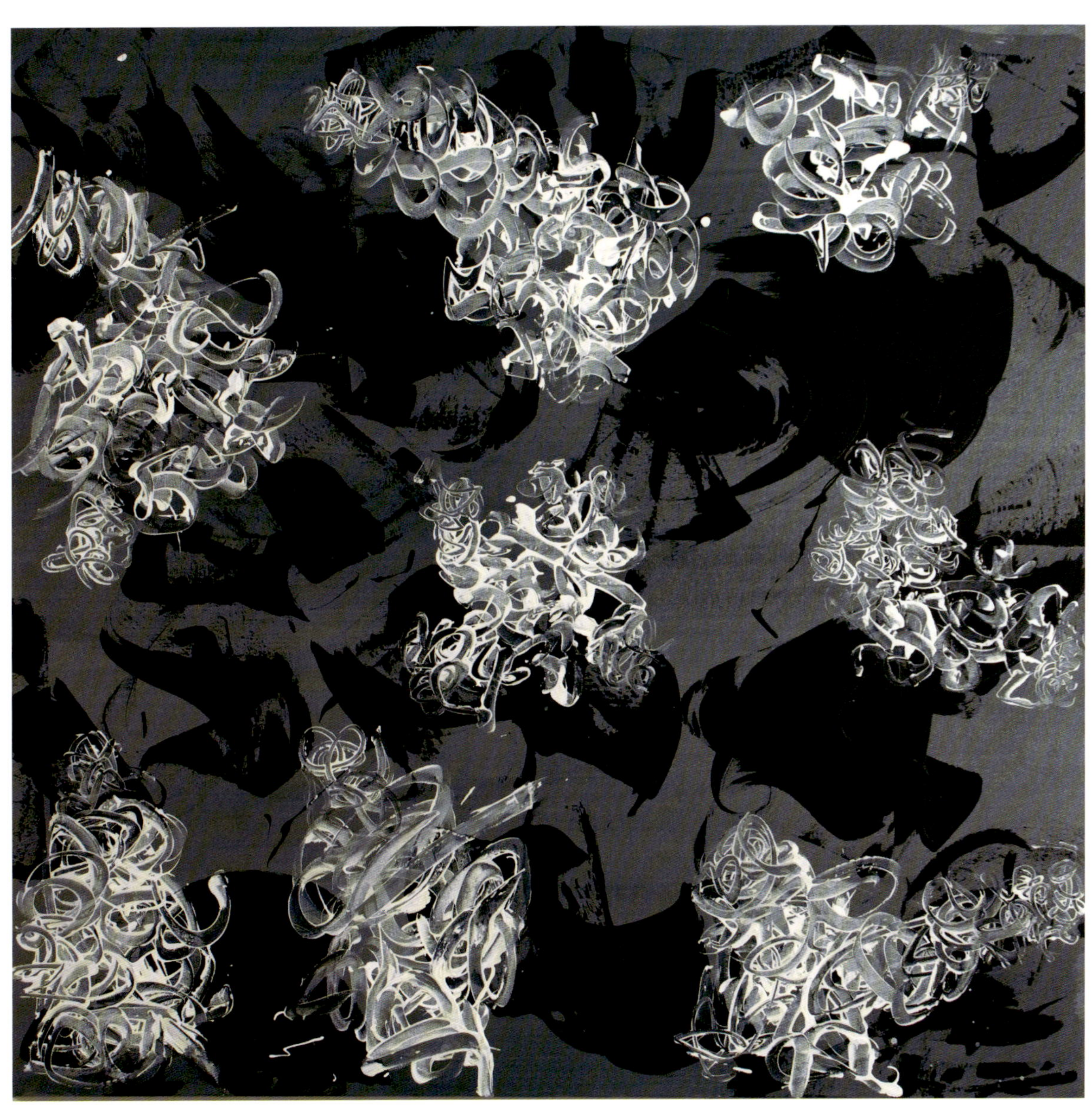

2007, mixed media on canvas,
120 x 120 cm

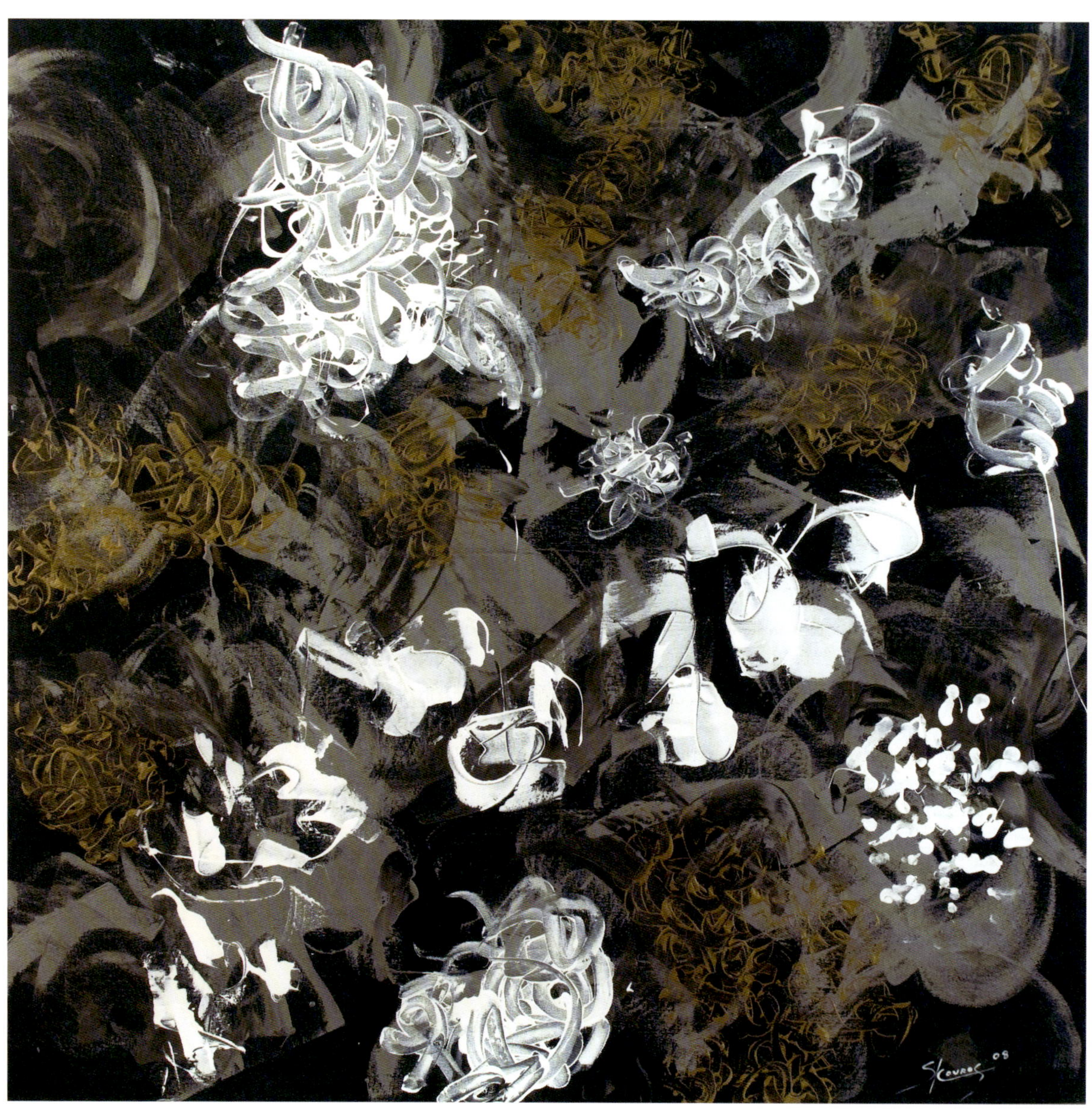

2007, mixed media on canvas,
120 x 120 cm

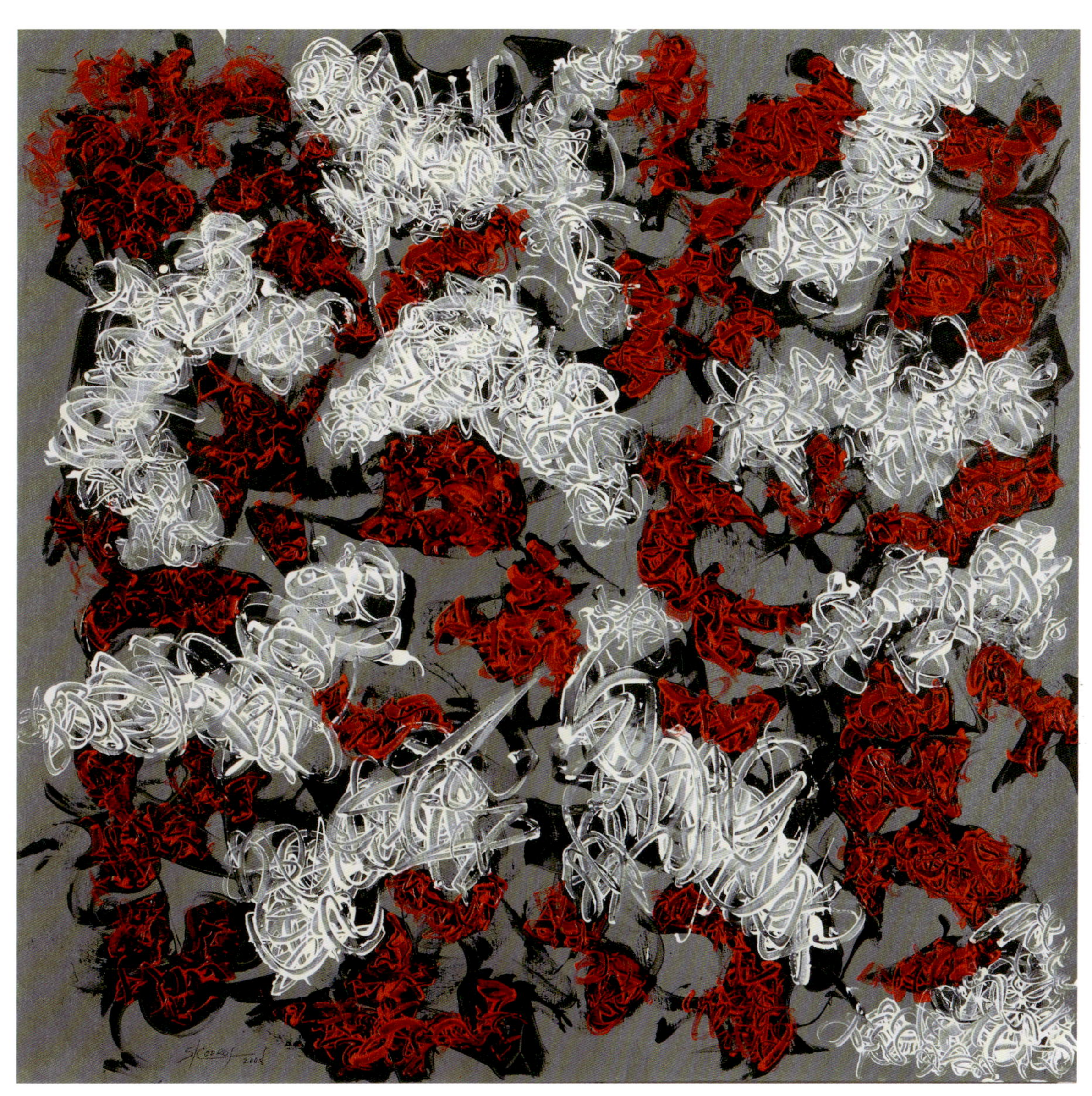

2008, mixed media on canvas,
120 x 120 cm

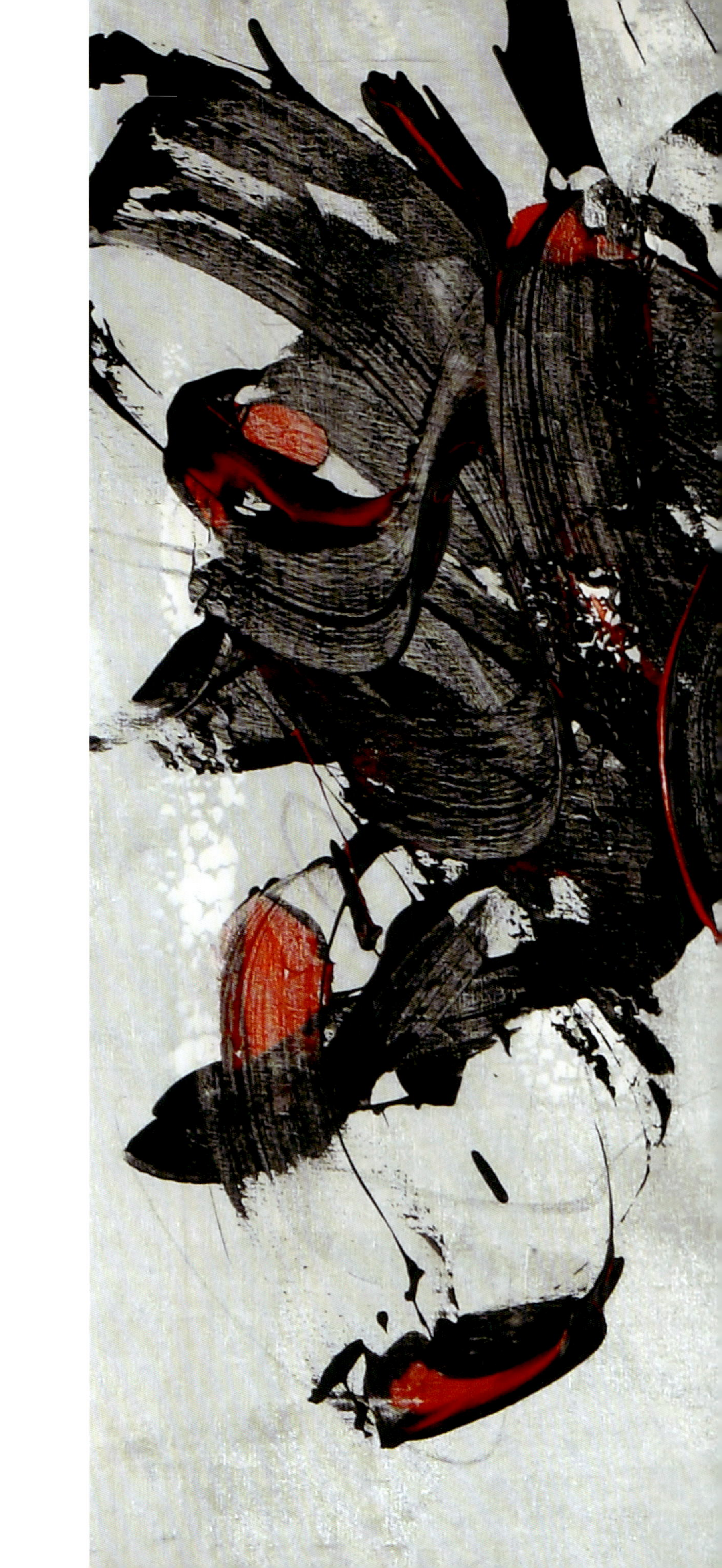

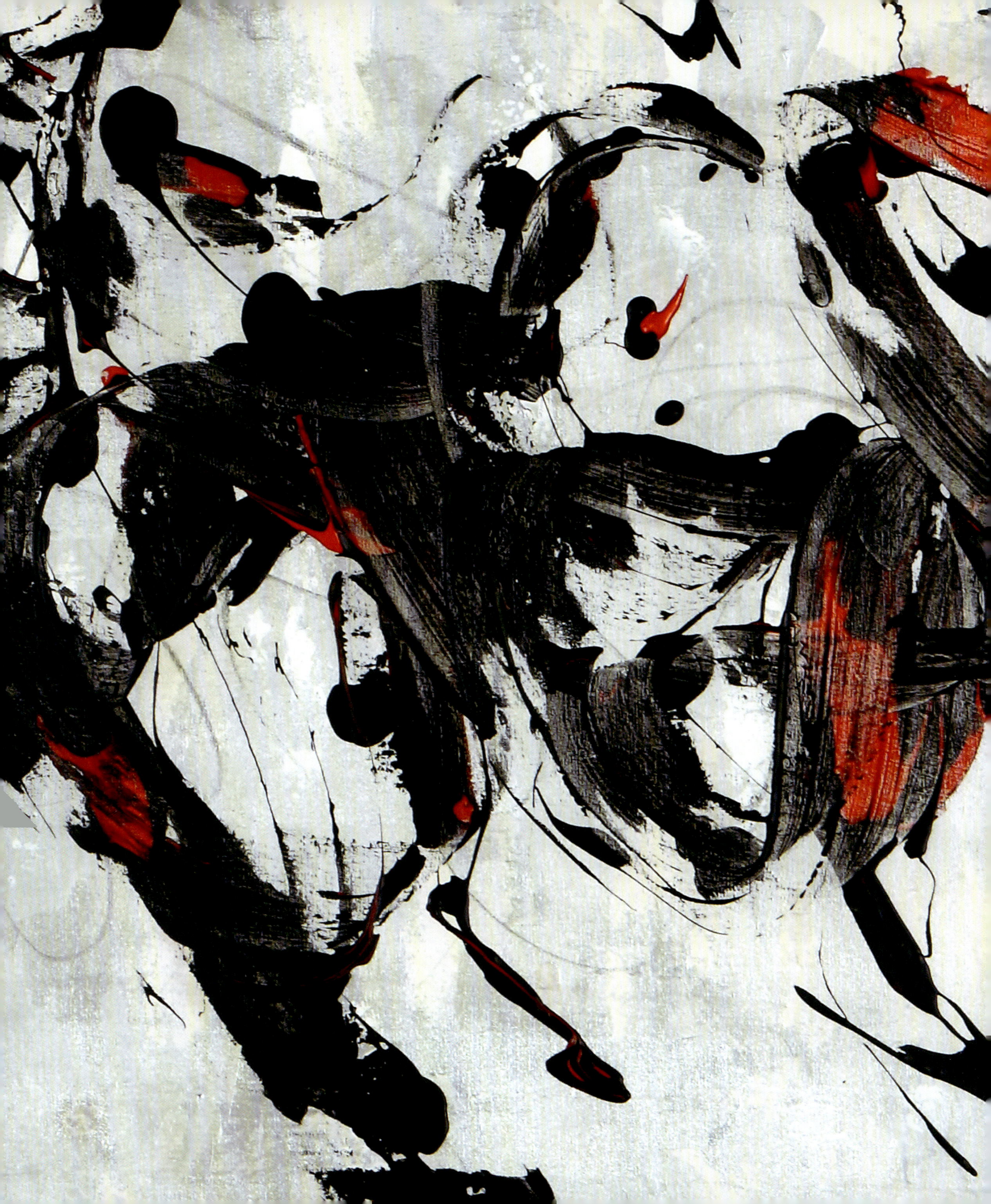

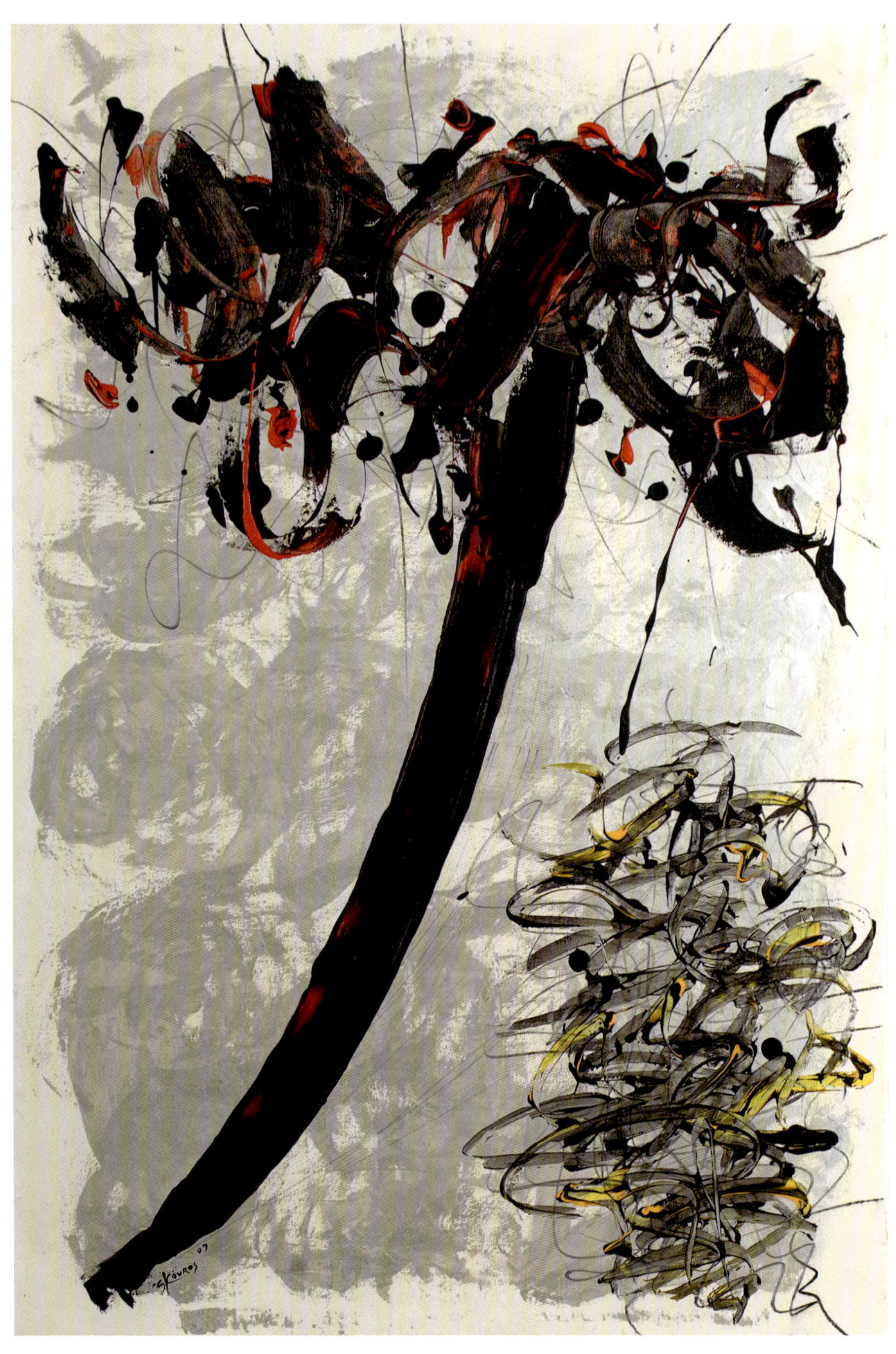

2007, acrylic on canvas,
140 x 80 cm

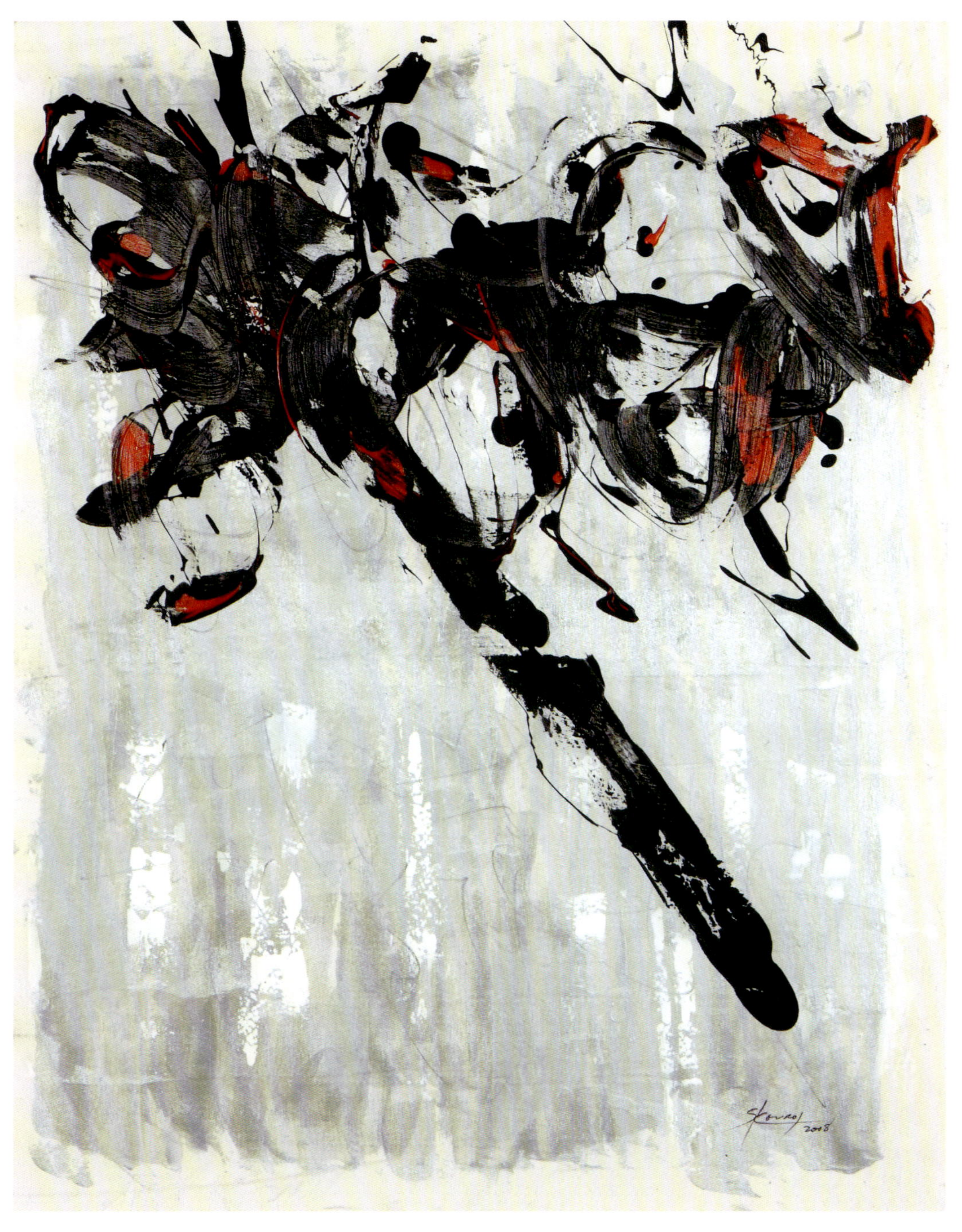

2008, acrylic on canvas,
140 x 100 cm

2007, acrylic on canvas,
140 x 80 cm

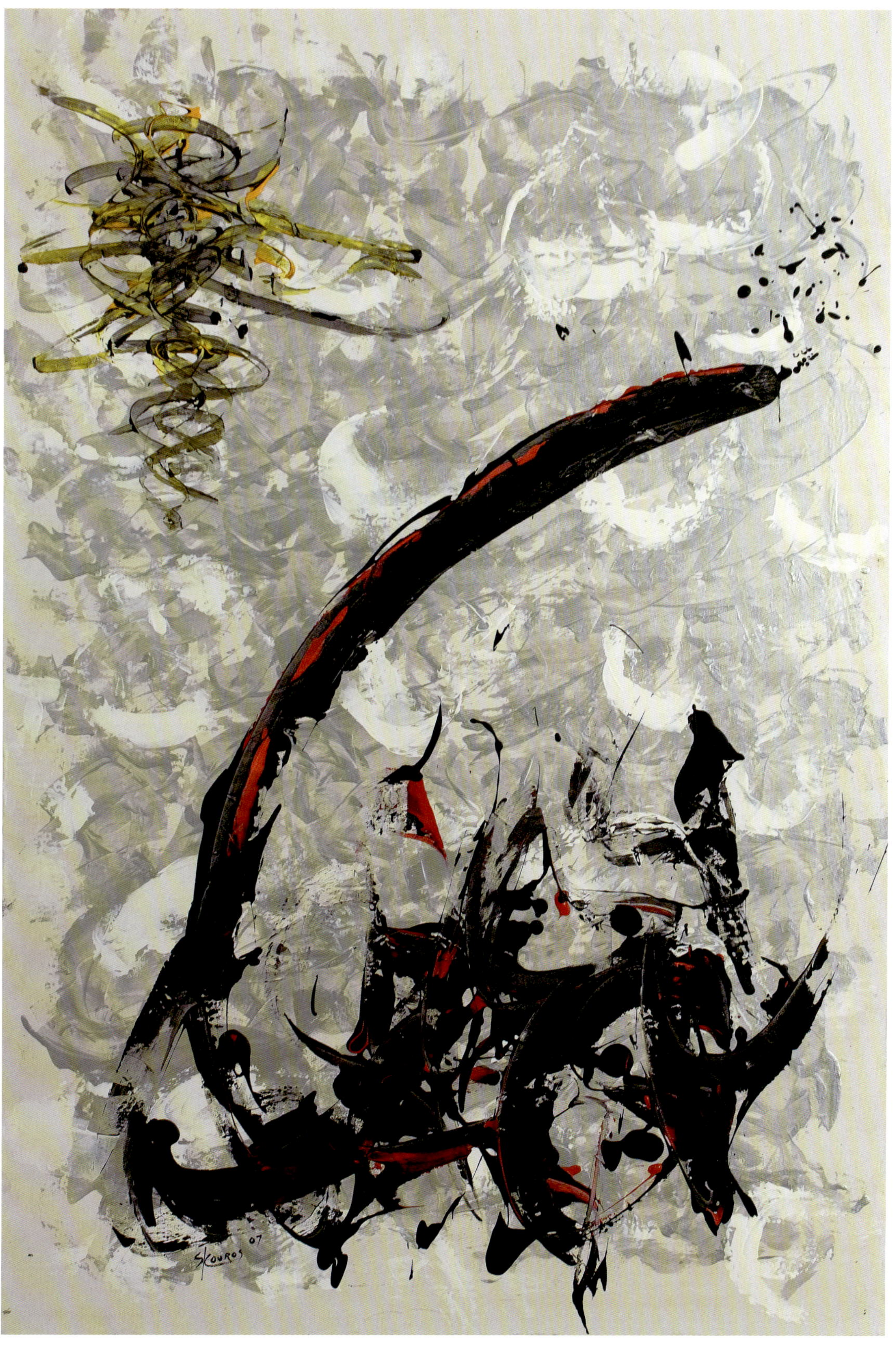
Skouros 07

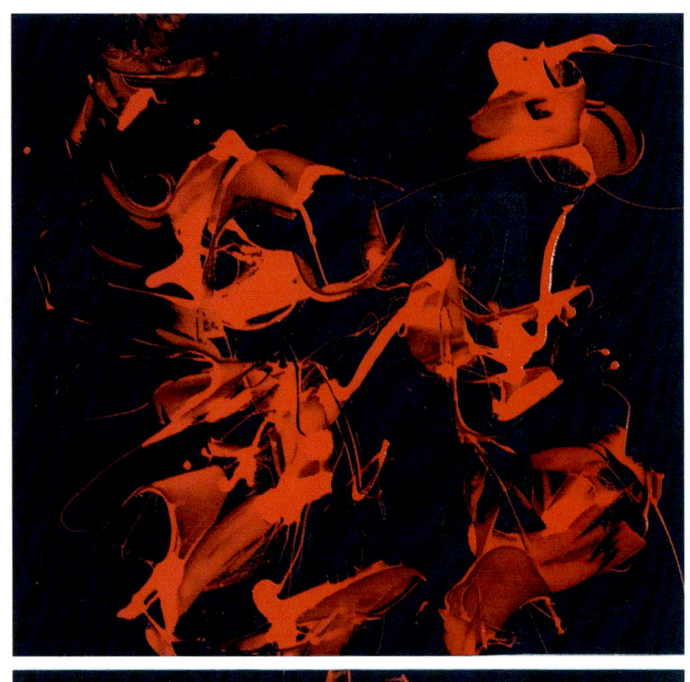

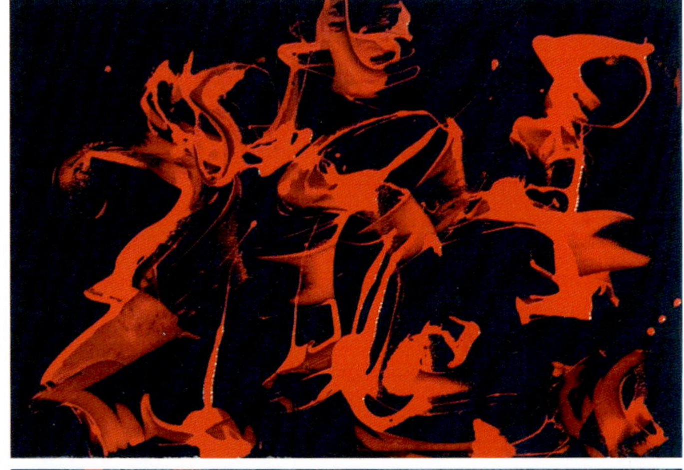

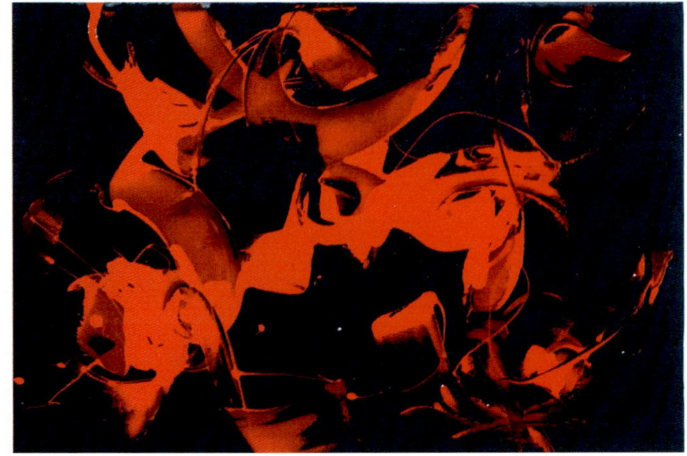

2007, acrylic on canvas, tryptich,
120 x 293 cm

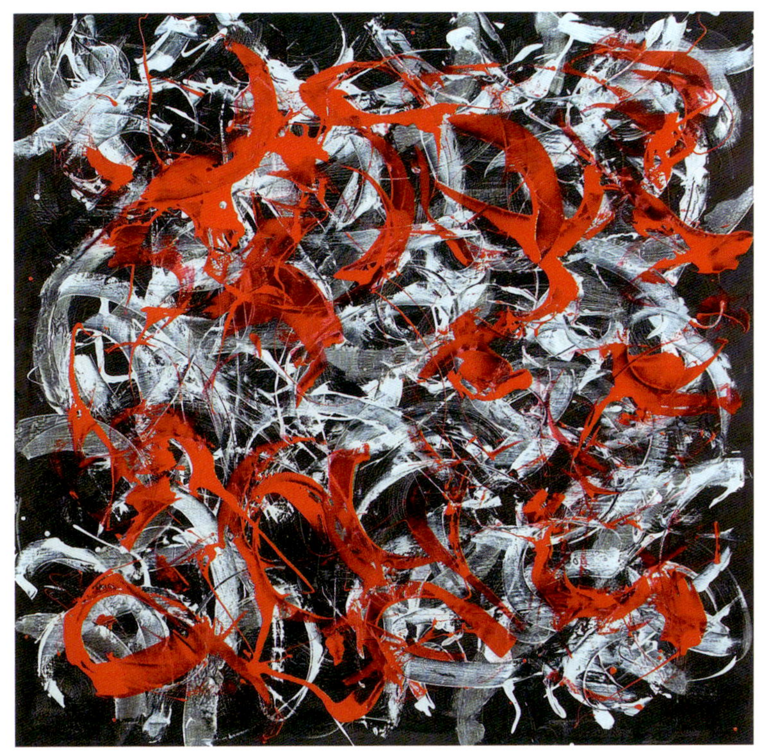

2007, mixed media on canvas,
120 x 120 cm

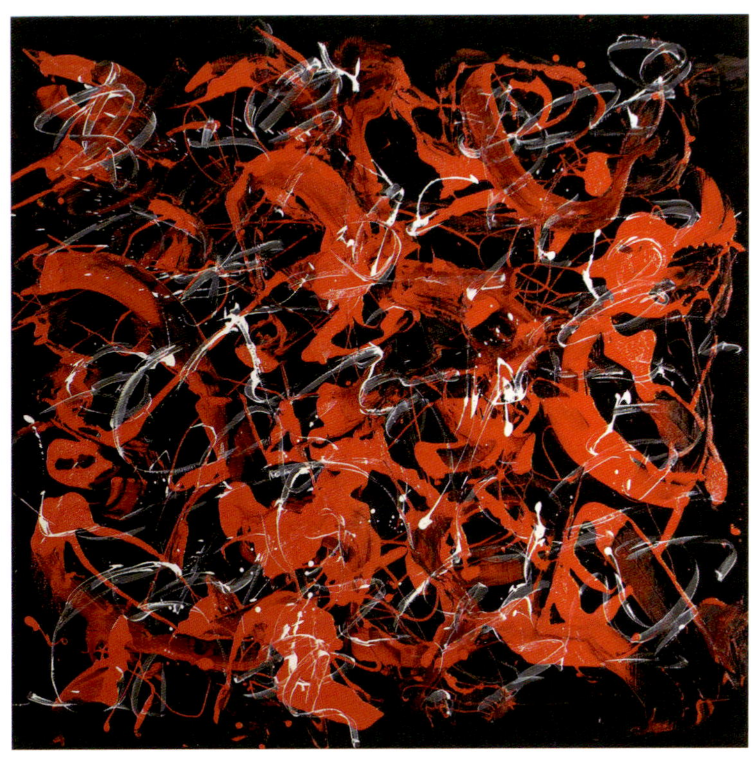

2007, mixed media on canvas,
120 x 120 cm

2007, mixed media on canvas,
120 x 120 cm

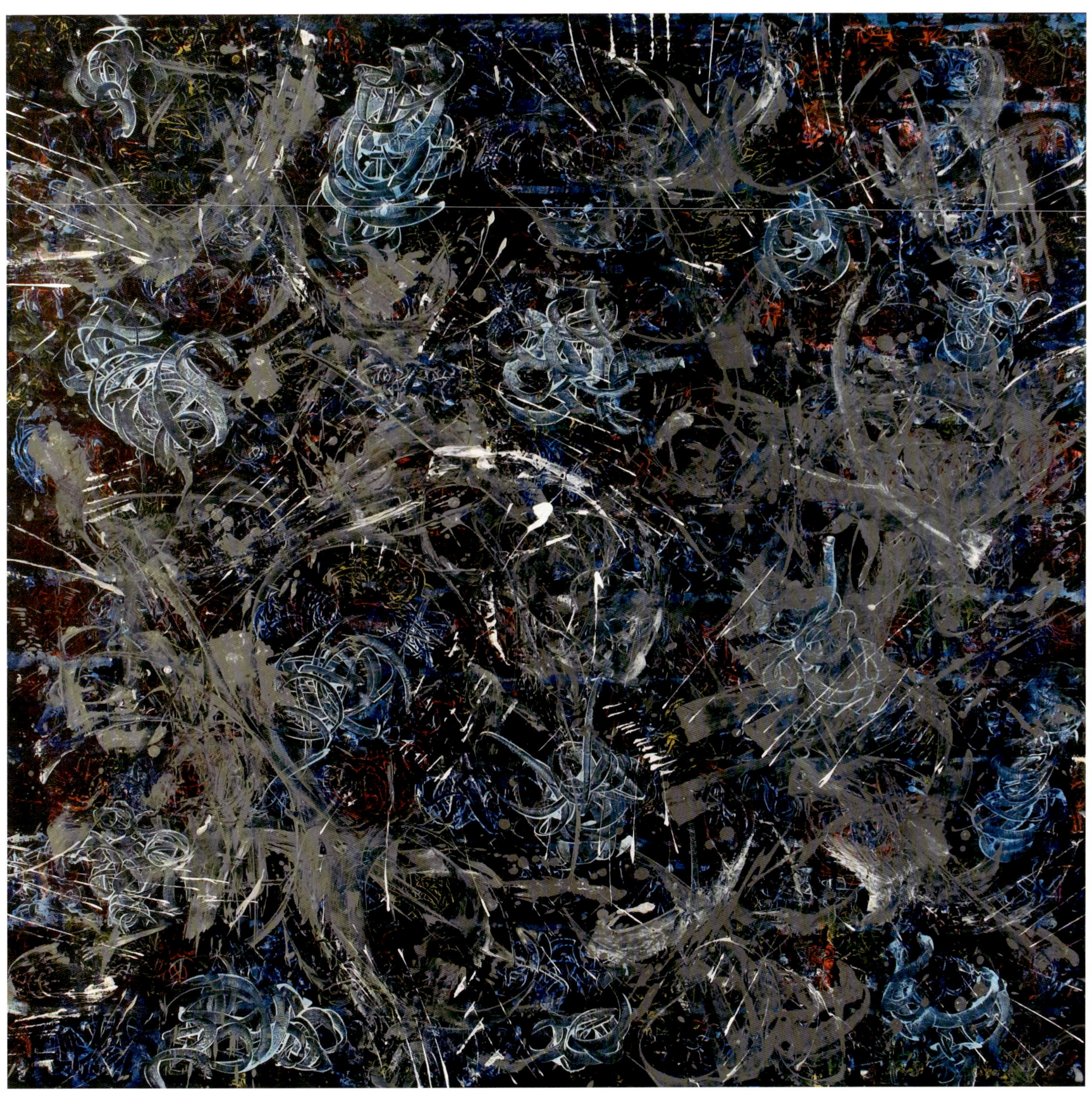

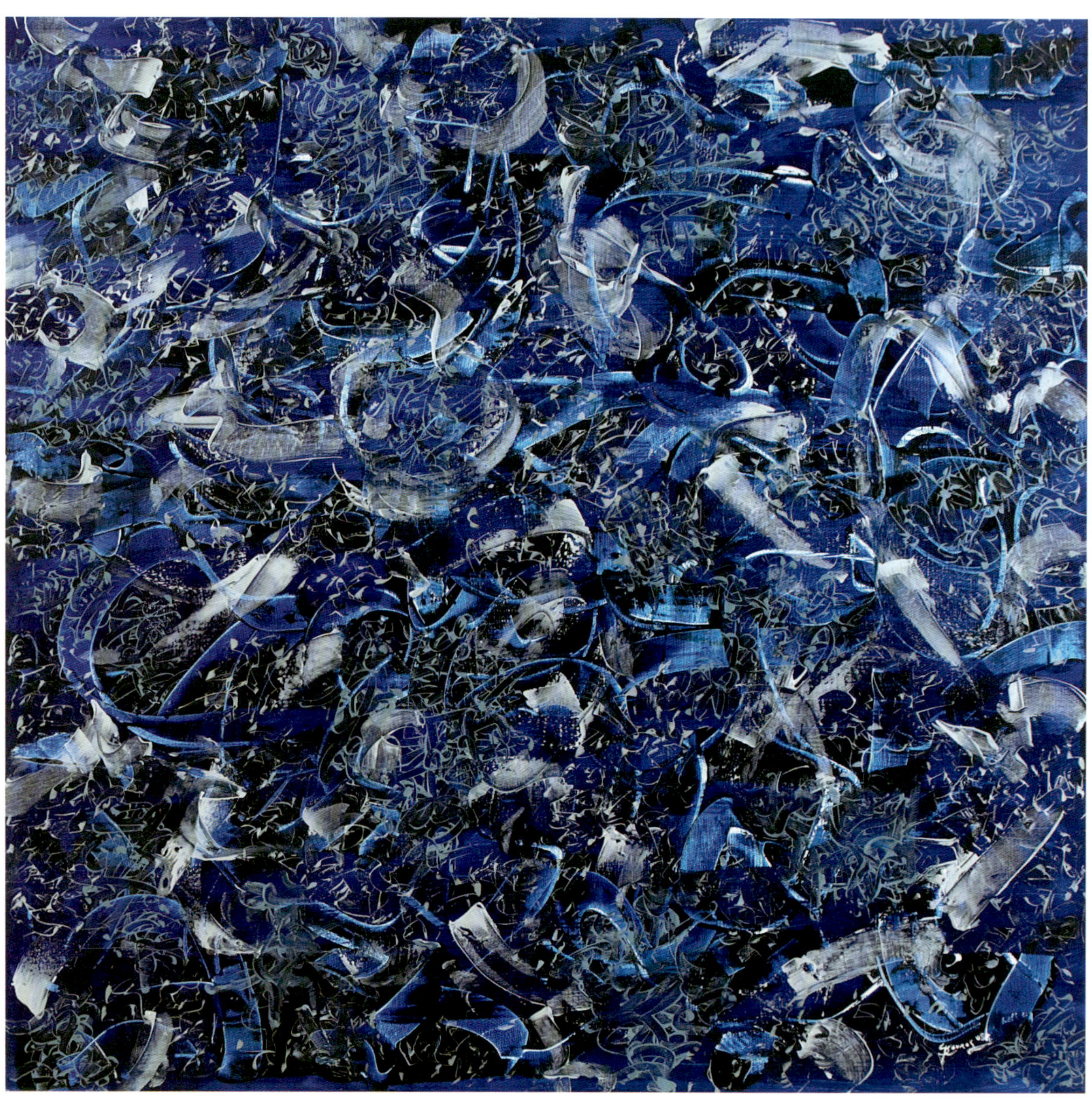

2007, mixed media on canvas,
120 x 120 cm

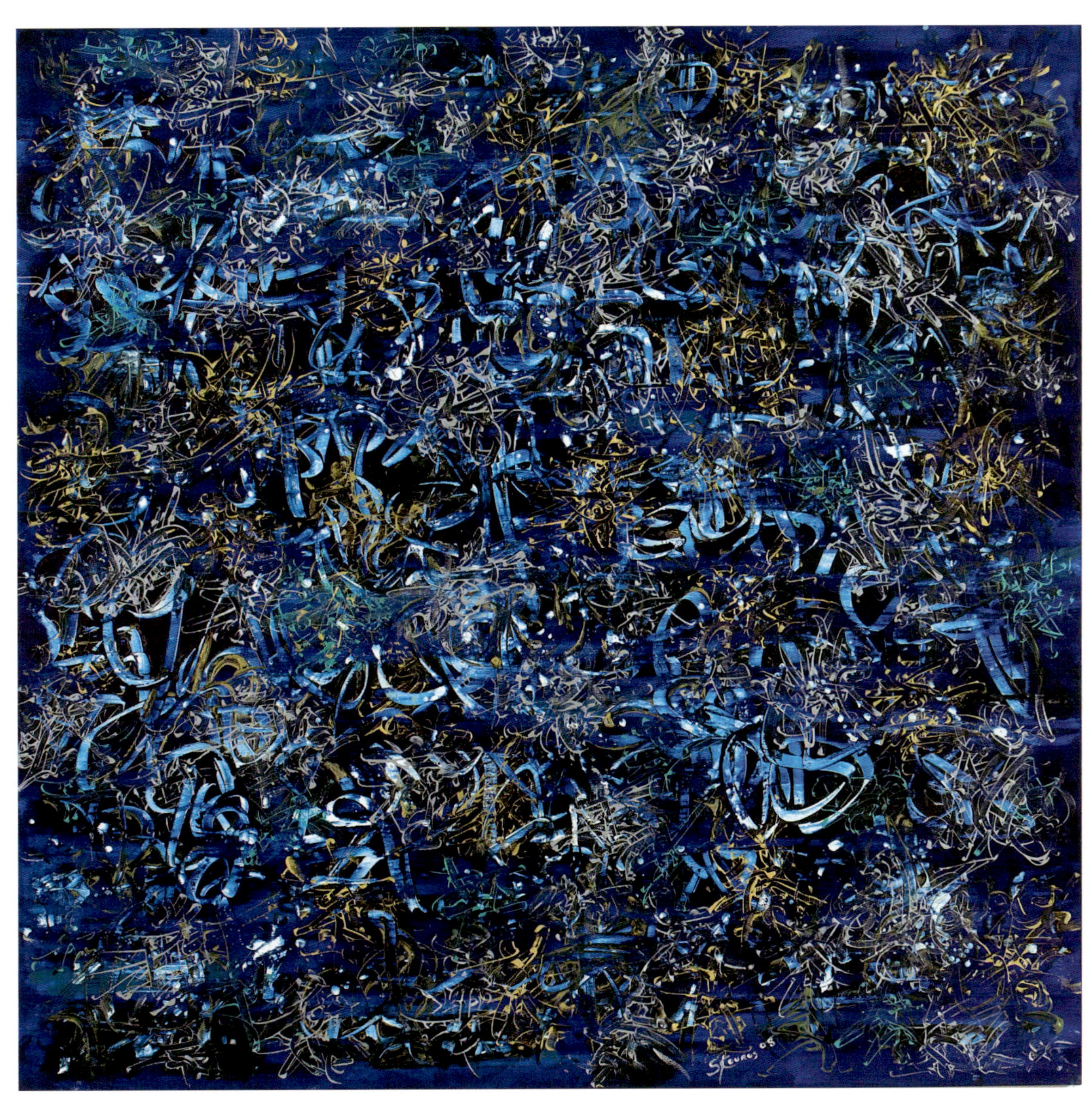

2007, mixed media on canvas,
120 x 120 cm

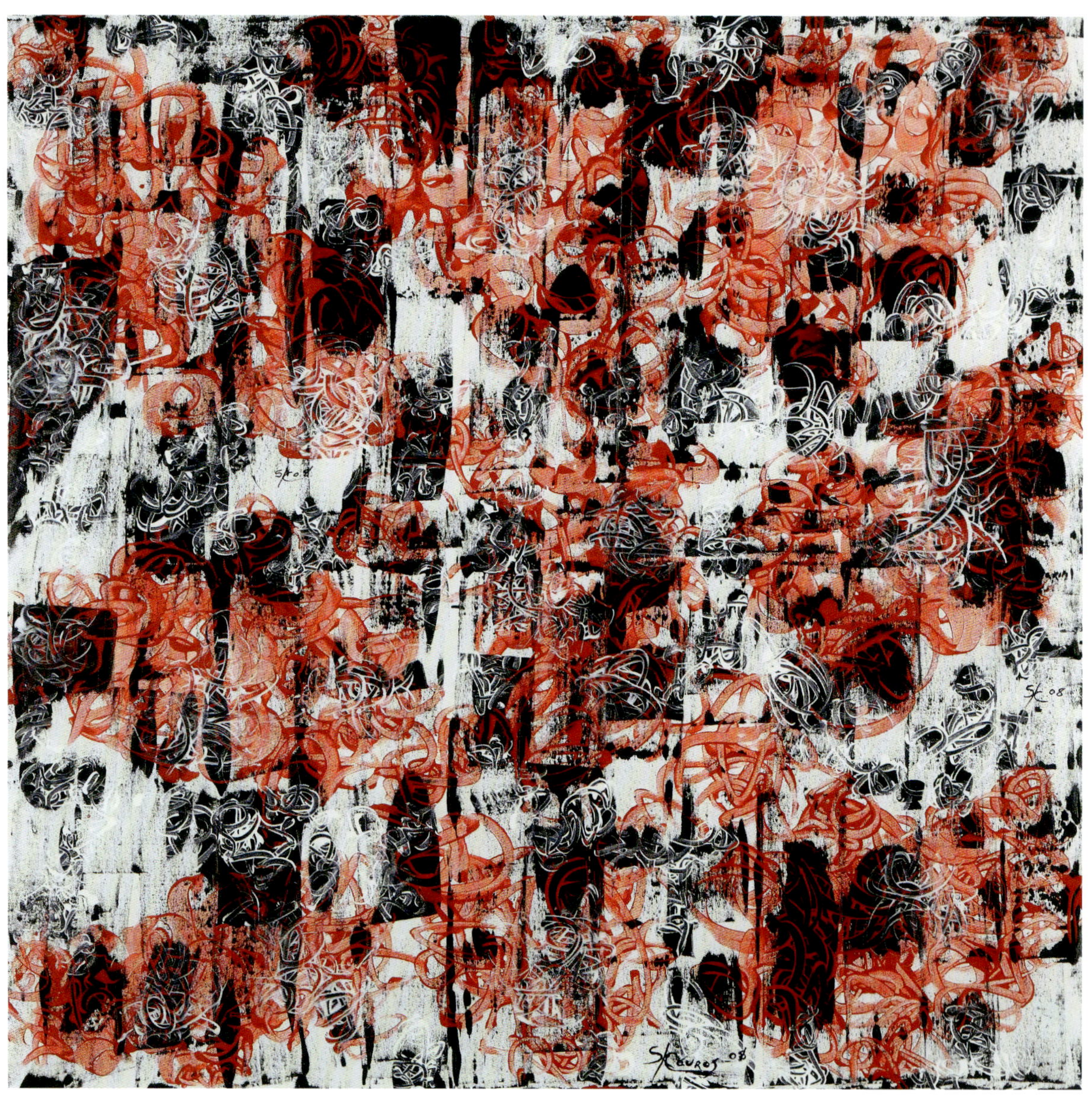

2008, acrylic on canvas,
70 x 70 cm

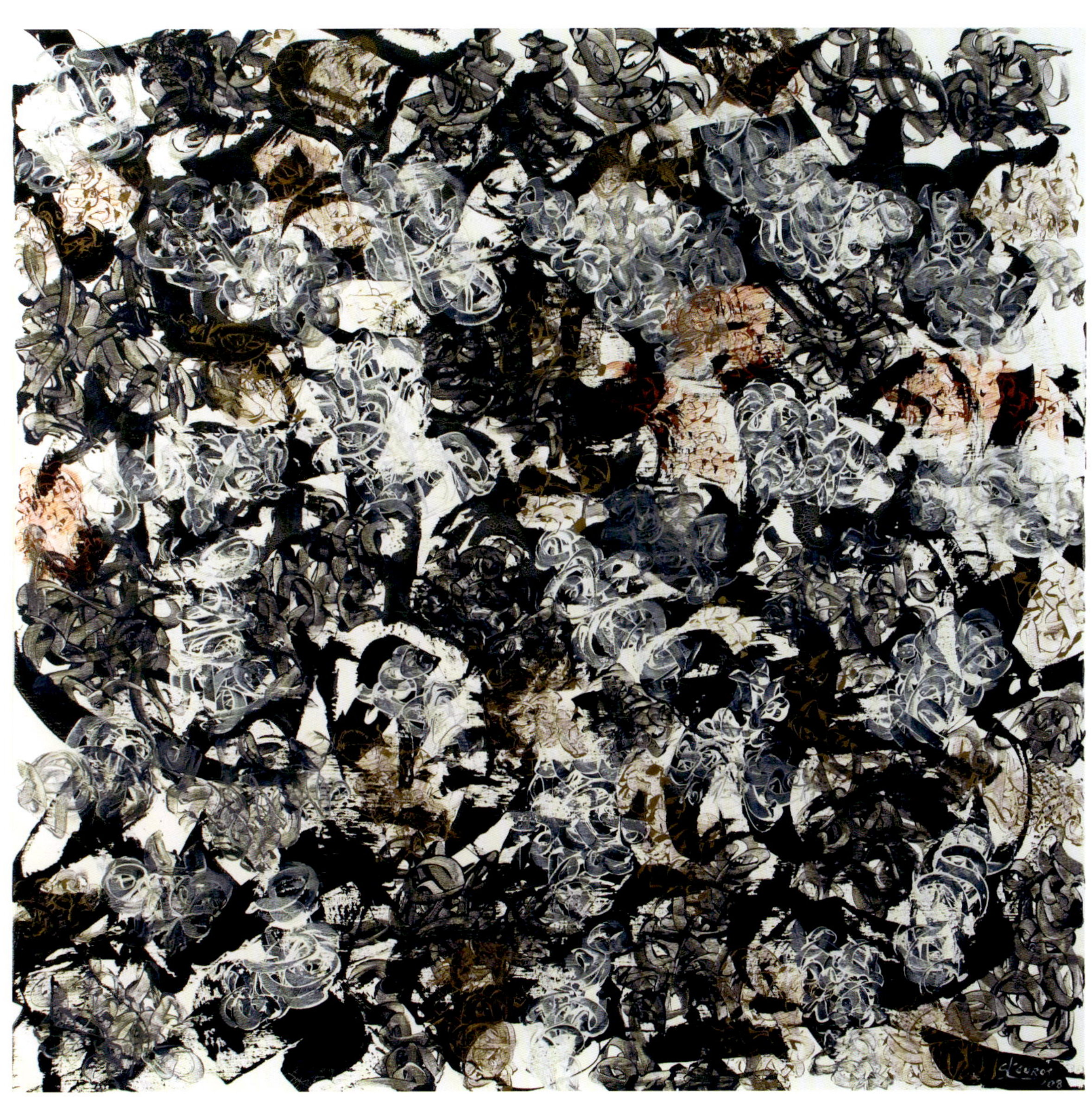

2008, mixed media on canvas,
120 x 120 cm

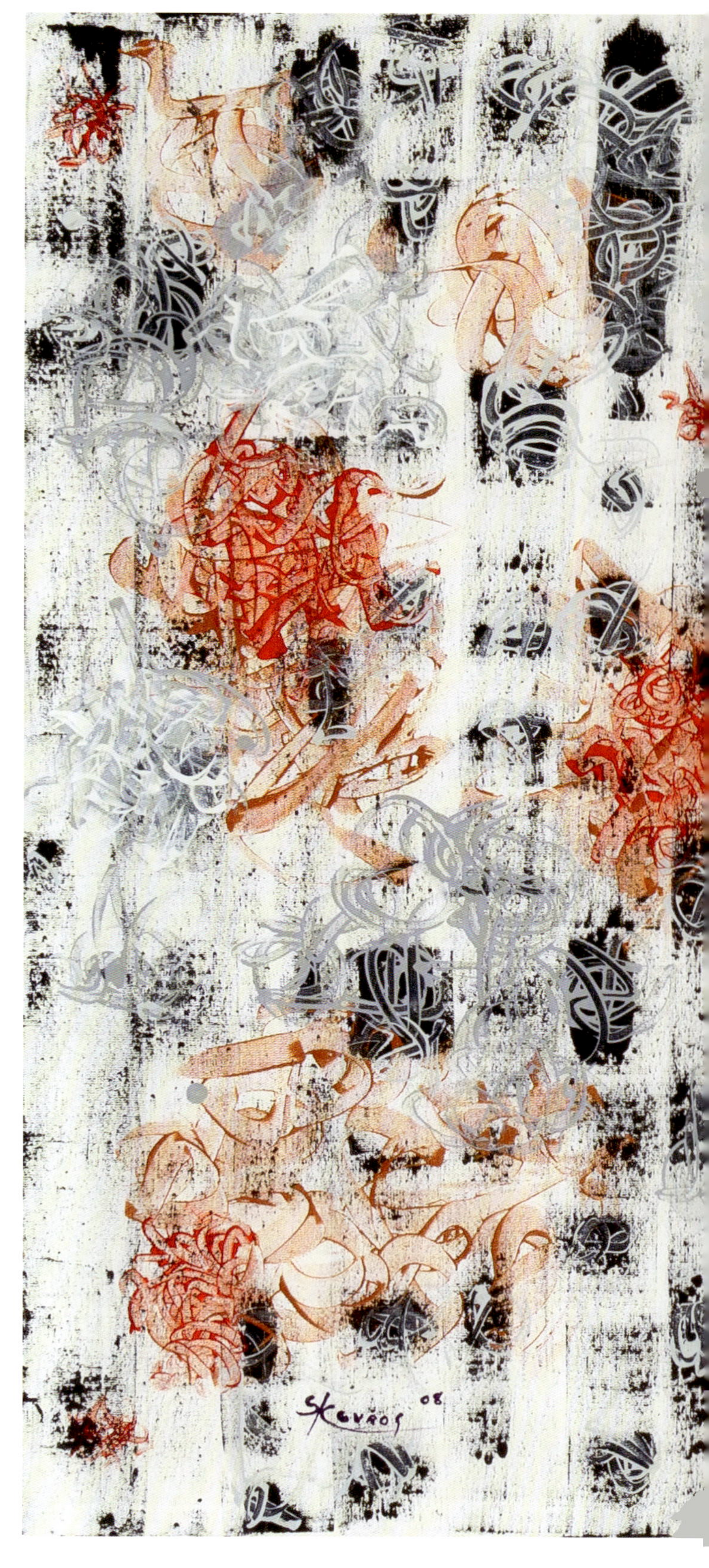

2008, acrylic on canvas,
70 x 100 cm

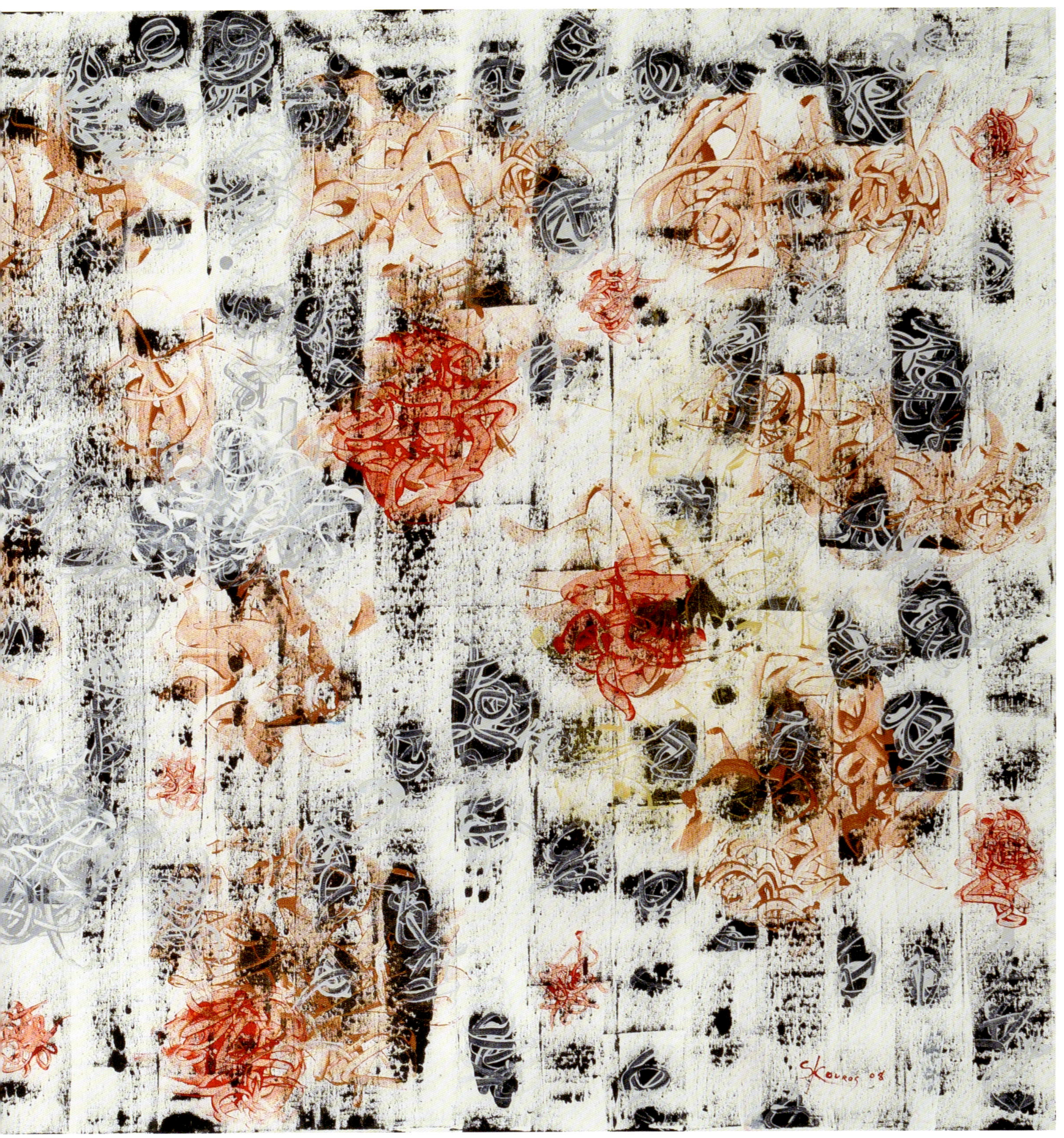
Skouros 08

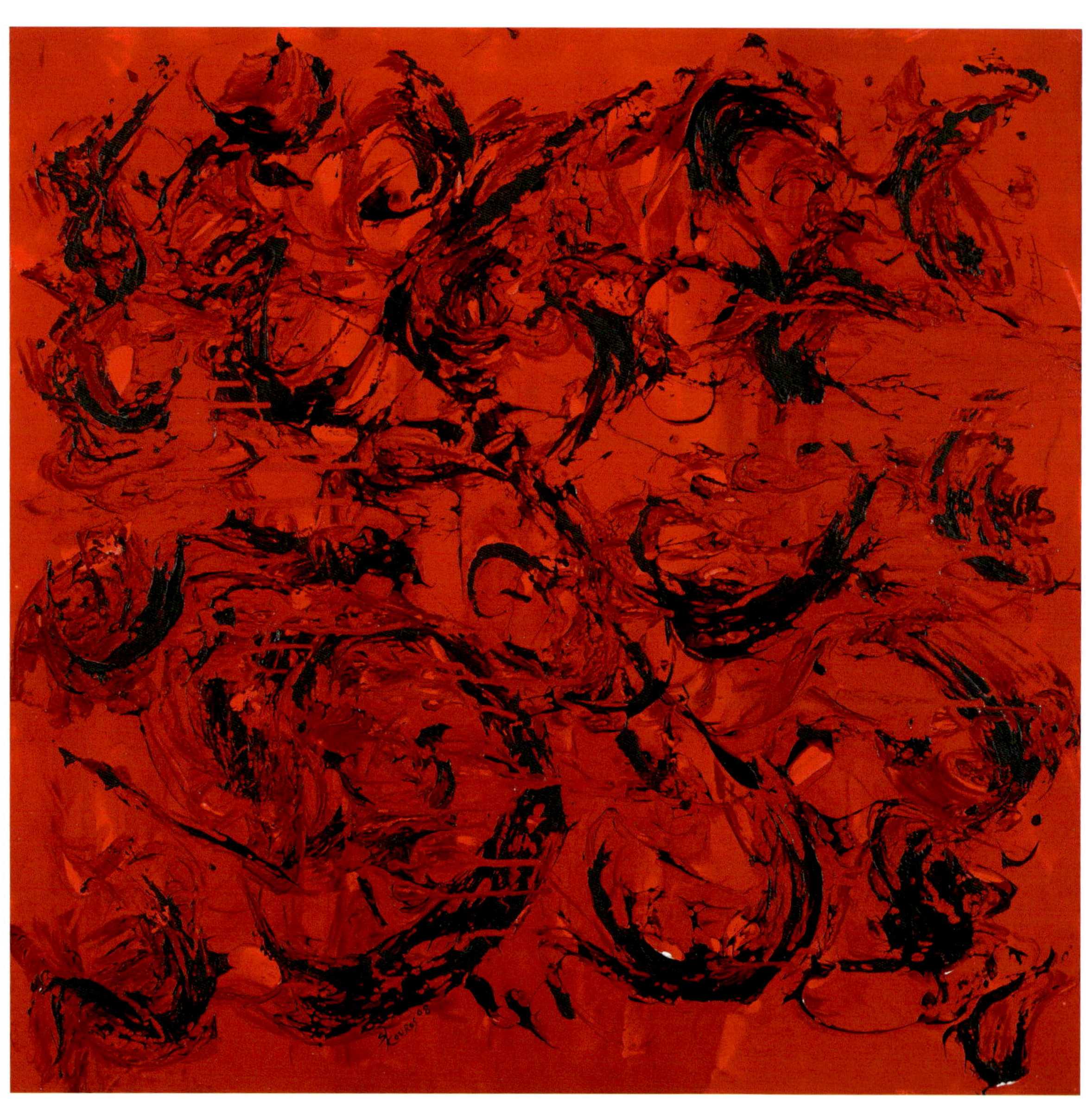

2008, mixed media on canvas,
100 x 100 cm

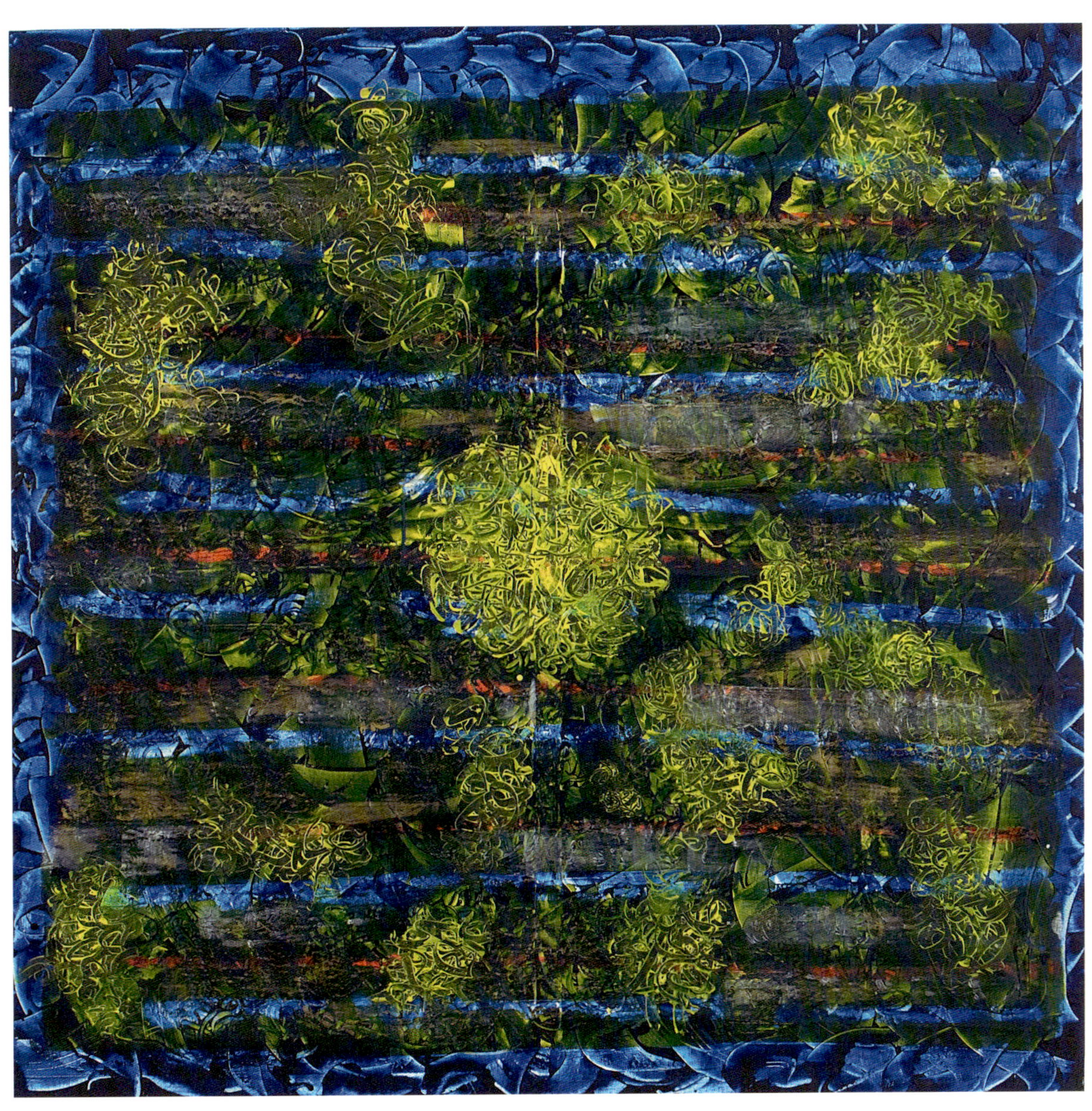

2007, mixed media on canvas,
120 x 120 cm

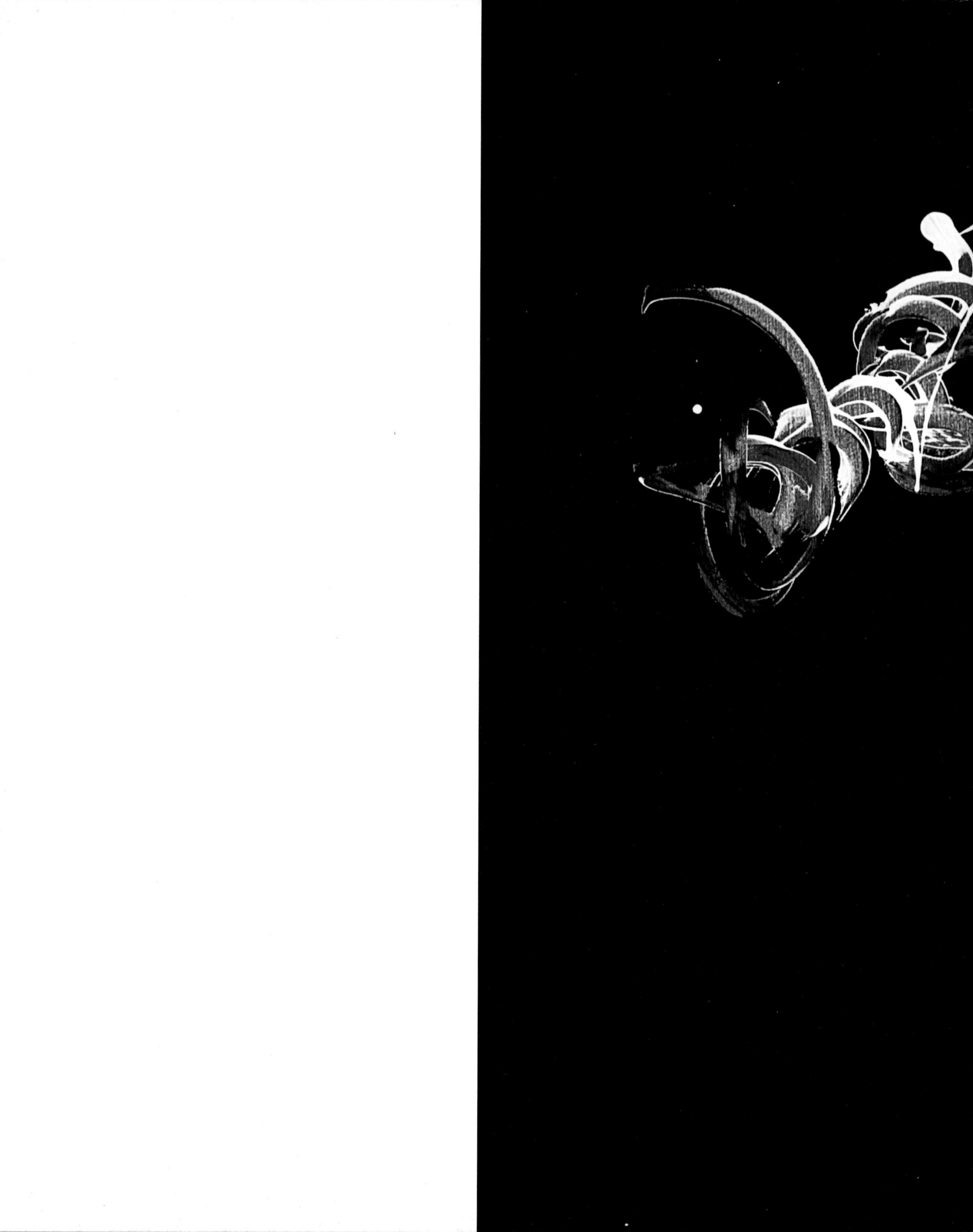

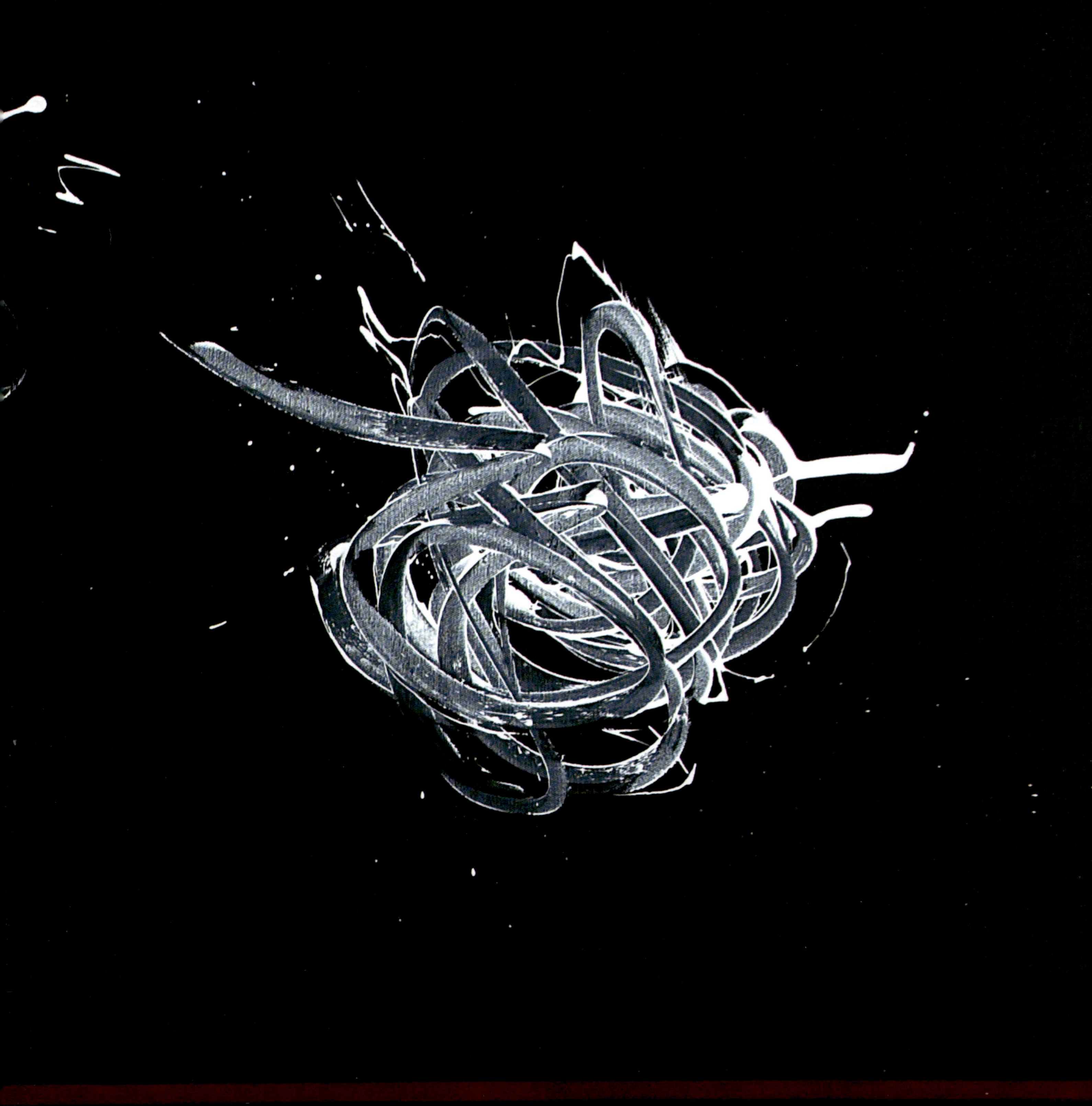

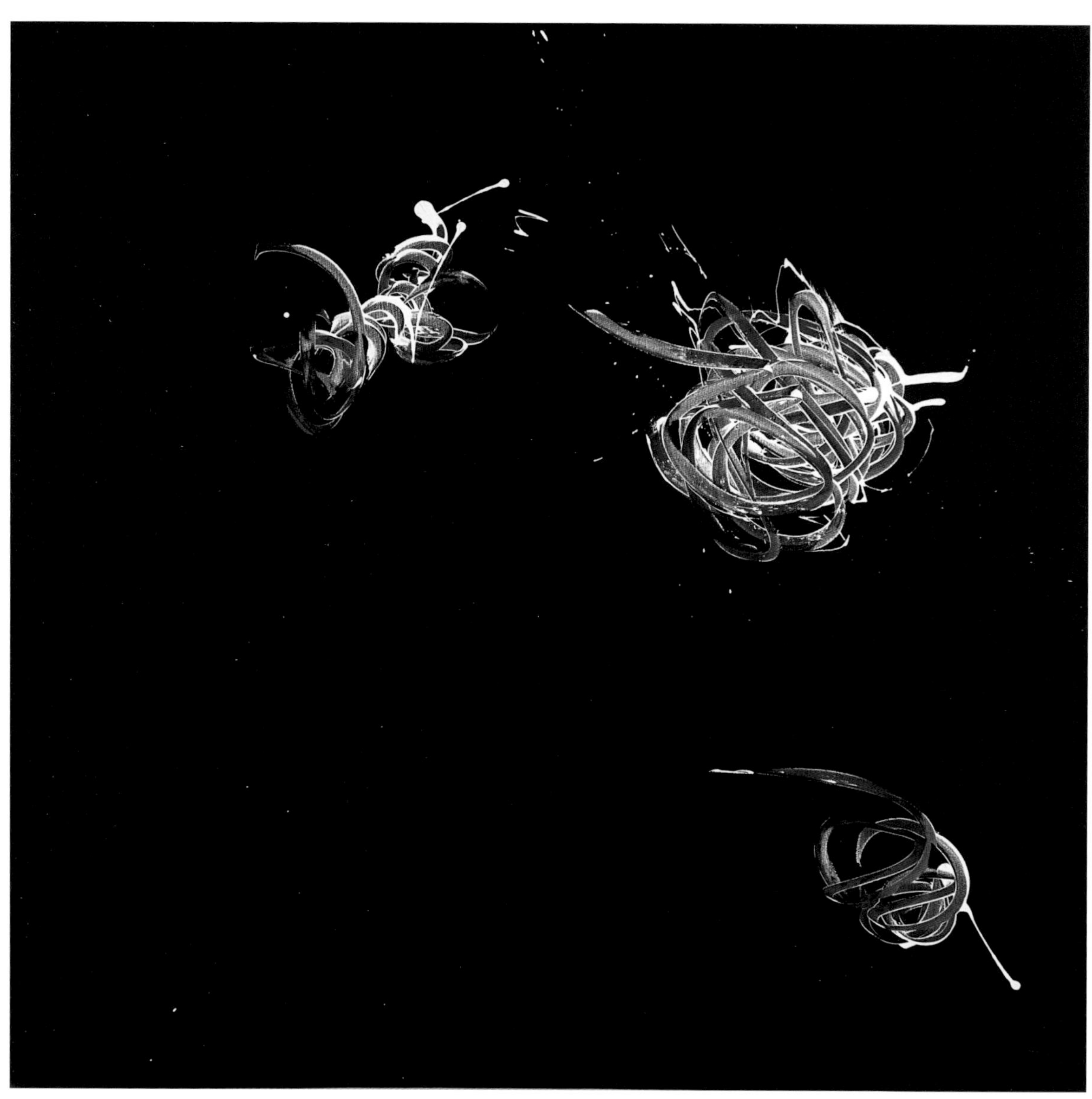

2007, mixed media on canvas,
120 x 120 cm

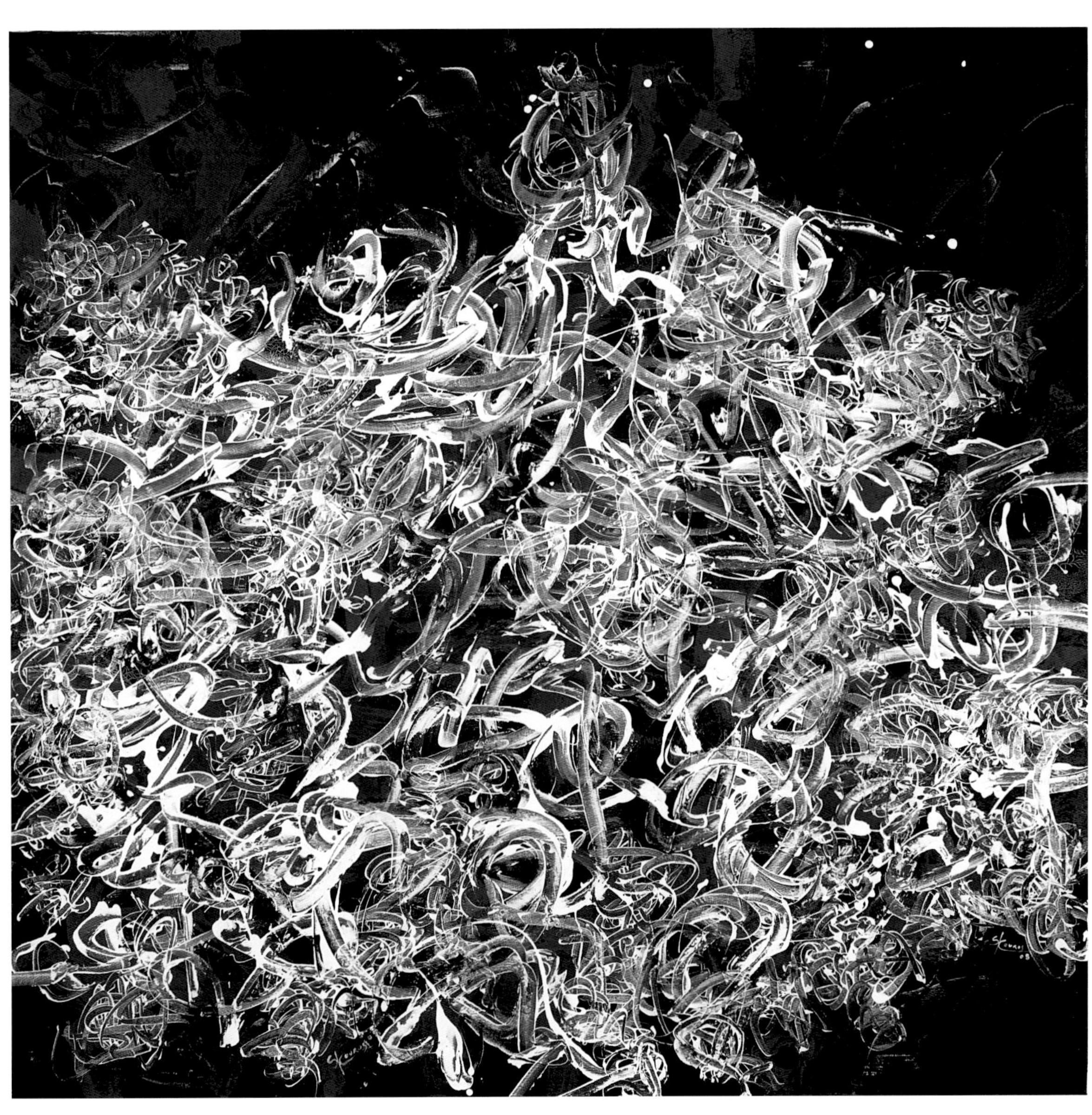

2007, mixed media on canvas,
120 x 120 cm

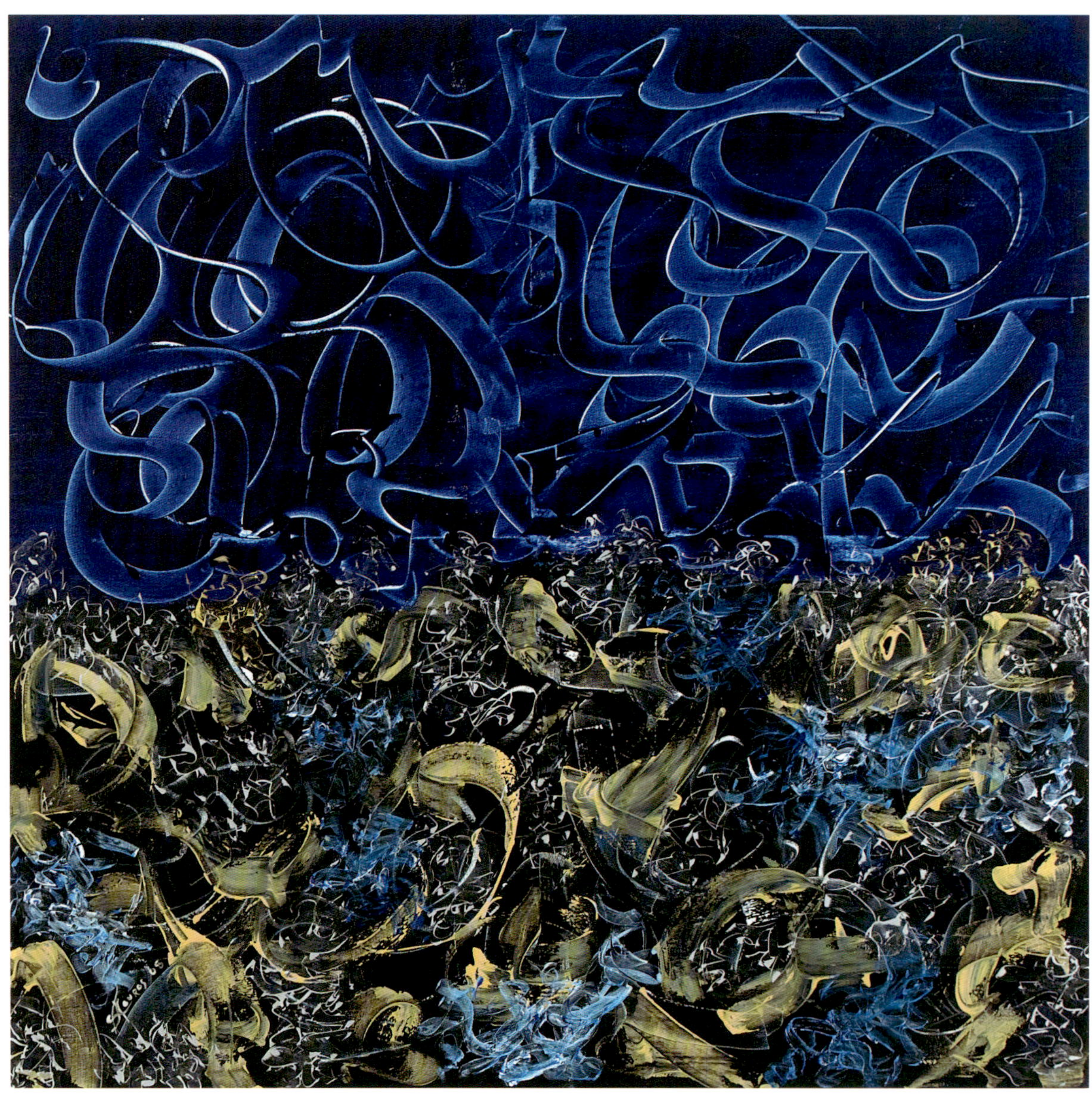

2007, mixed media on canvas,
120 x 120 cm

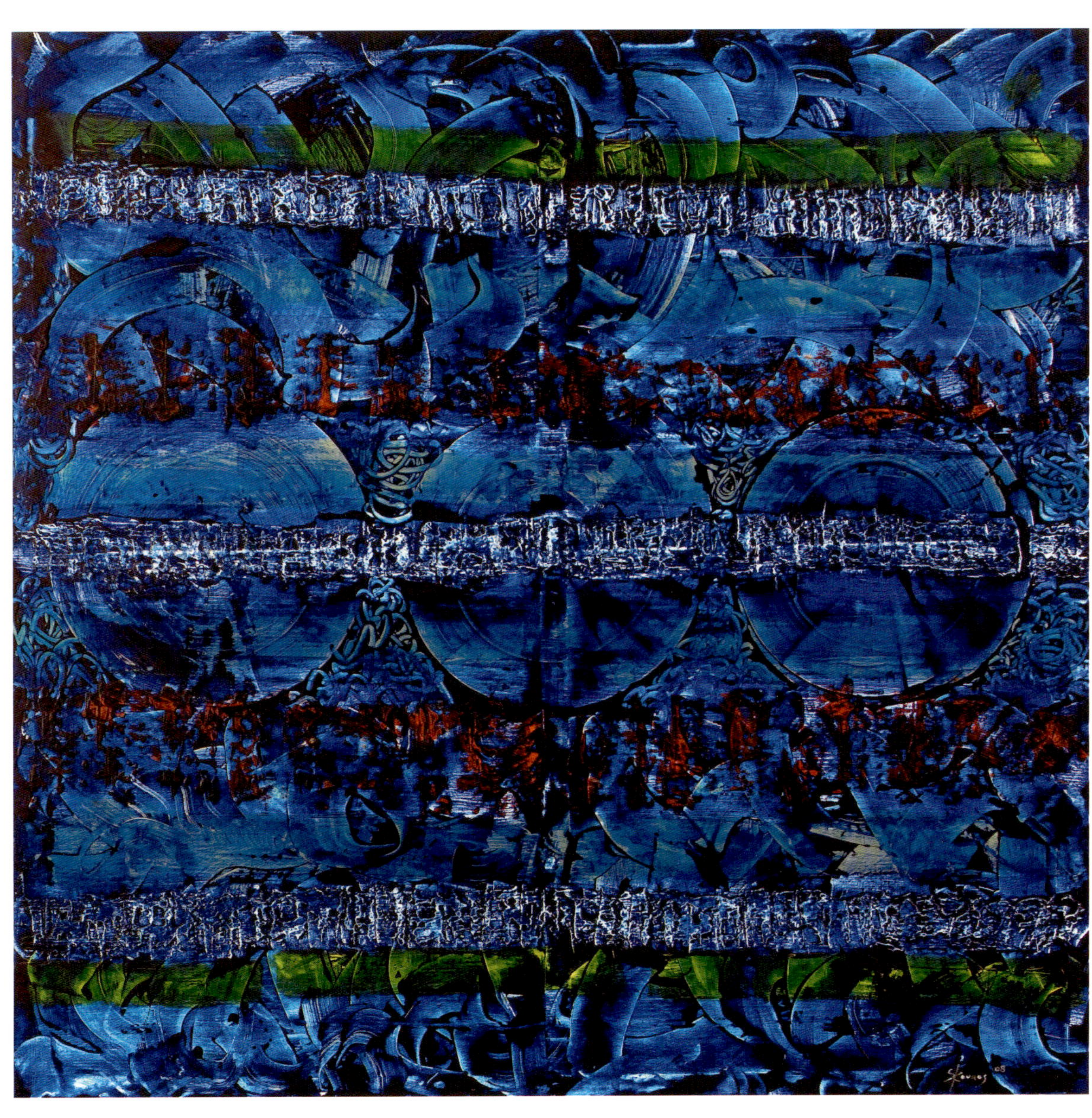

2008, mixed media on canvas,
120 x 120 cm

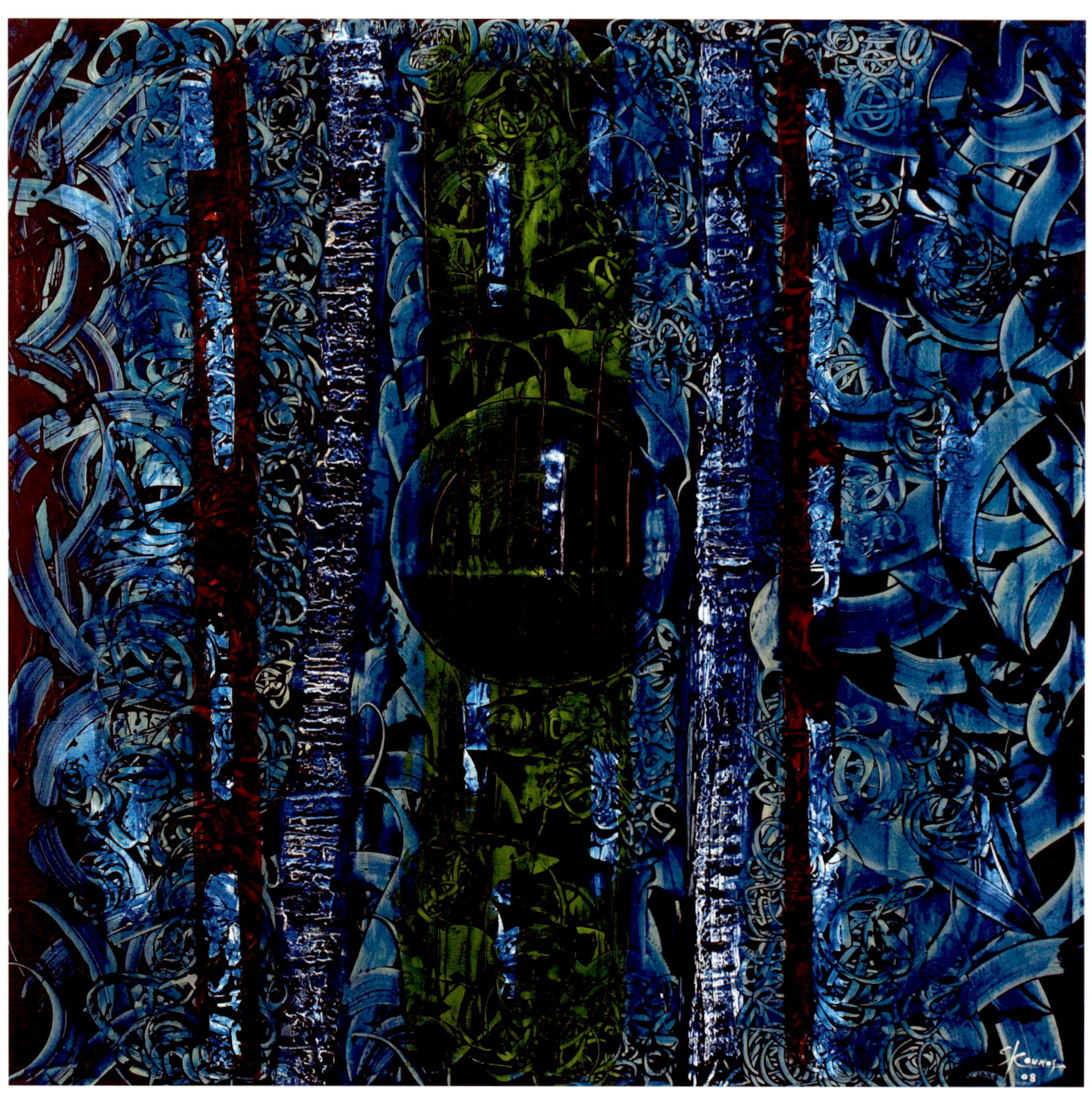

2008, mixed media on canvas,
120 x 120 cm

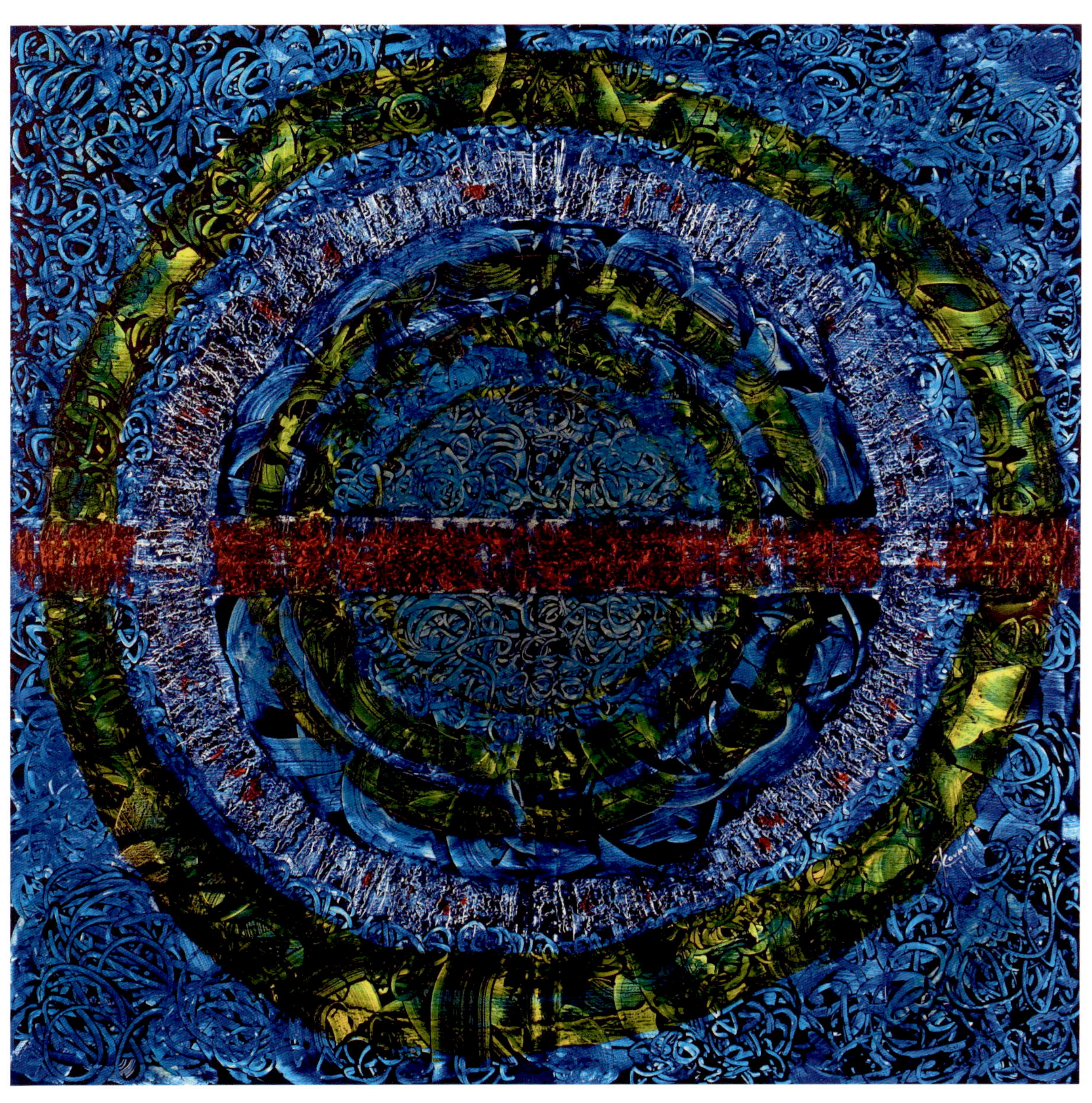

2008, mixed media on canvas,
120 x 120 cm

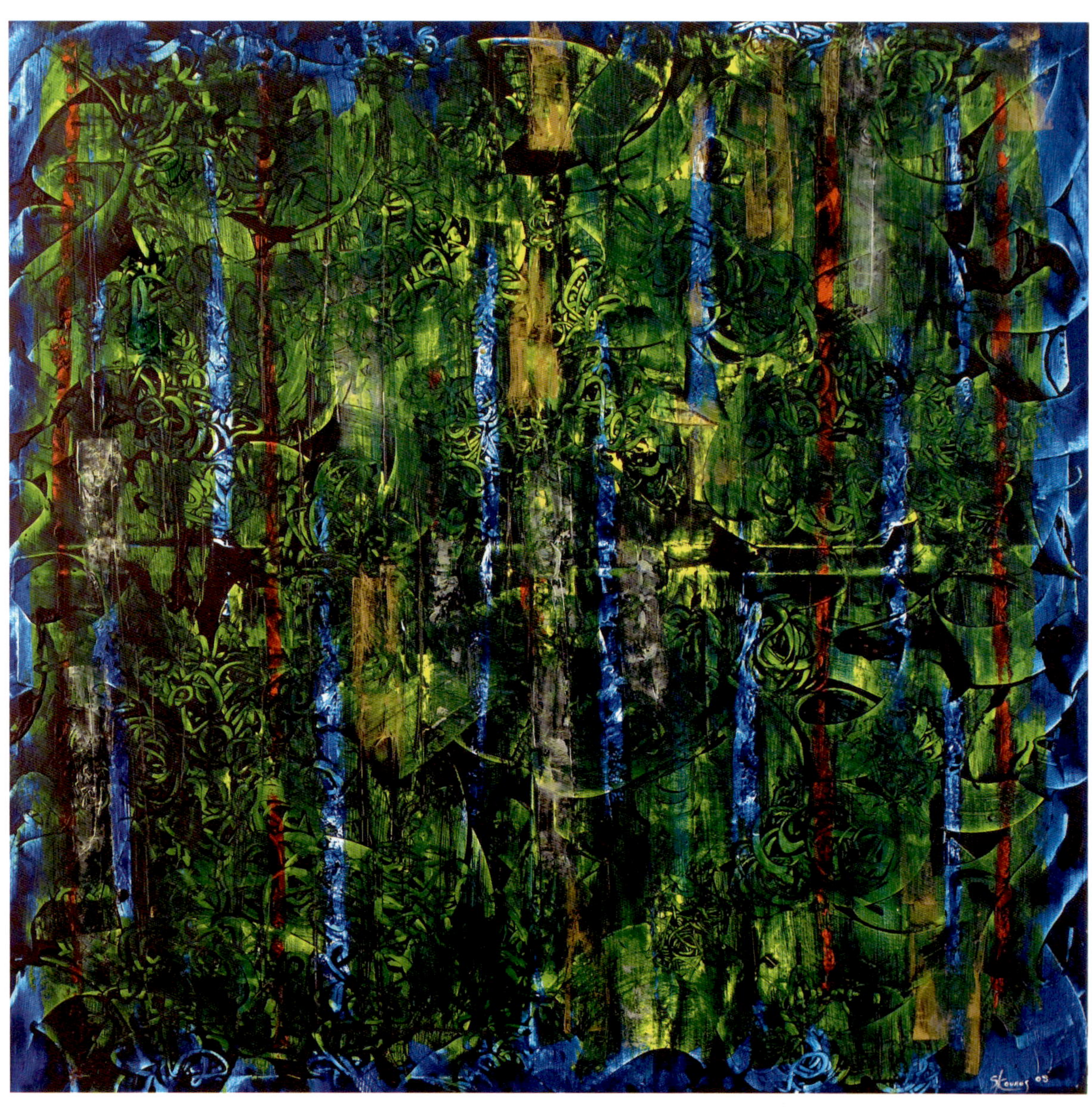

2008, mixed media on canvas,
120 x 120 cm

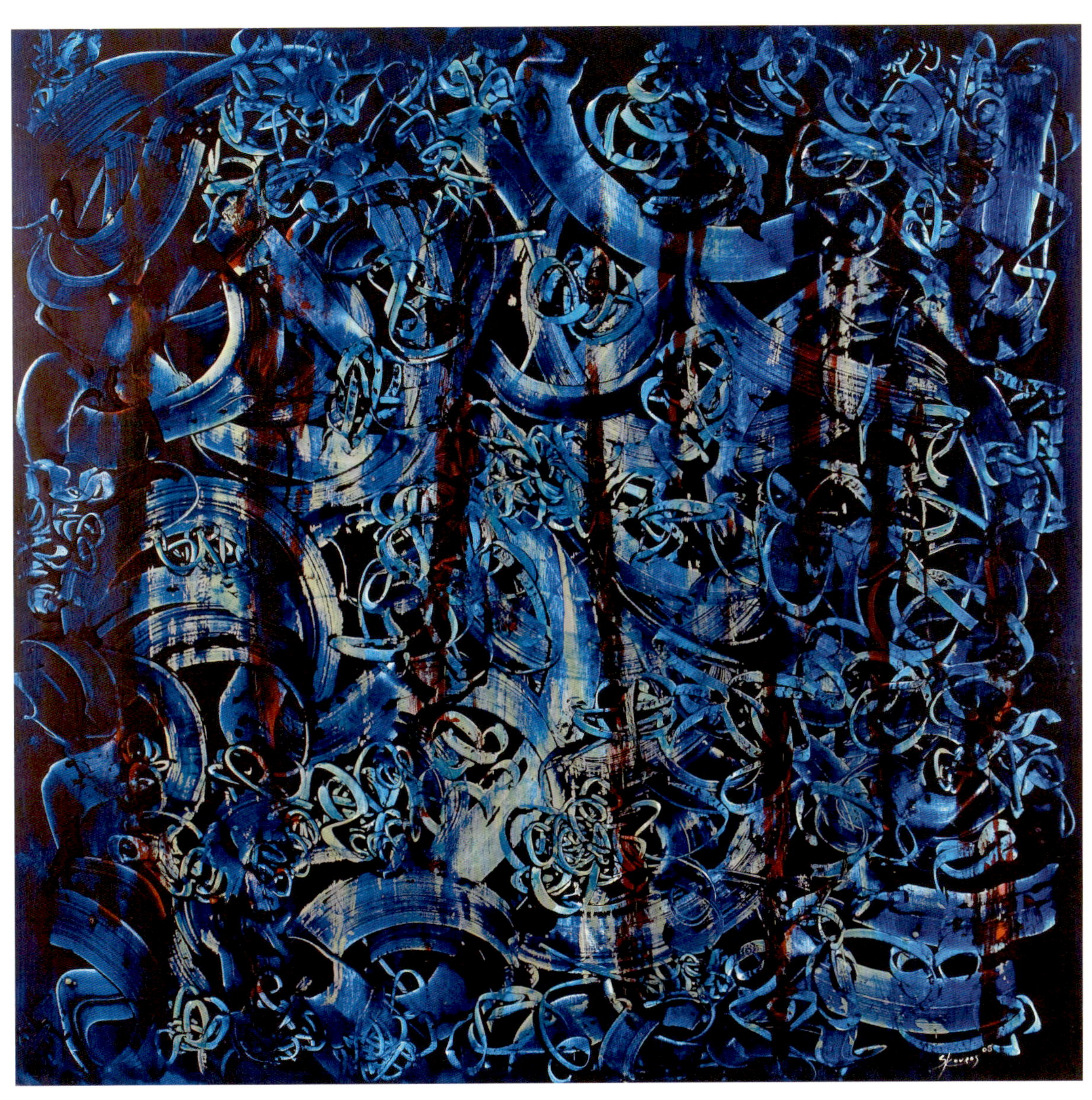

2008, mixed media on canvas,
120 x 120 cm

2008, mixed media on canvas,
120 x 120 cm

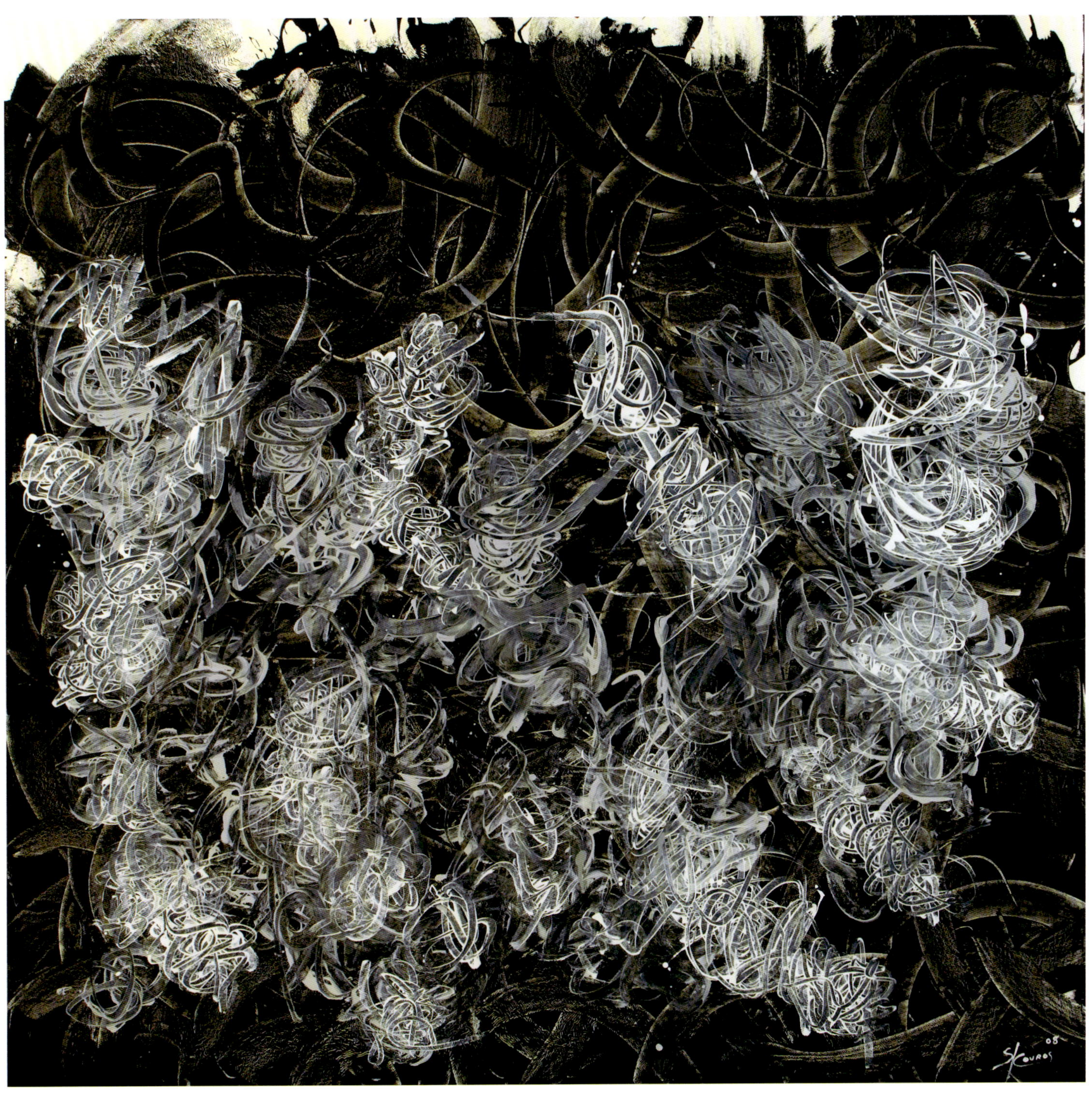

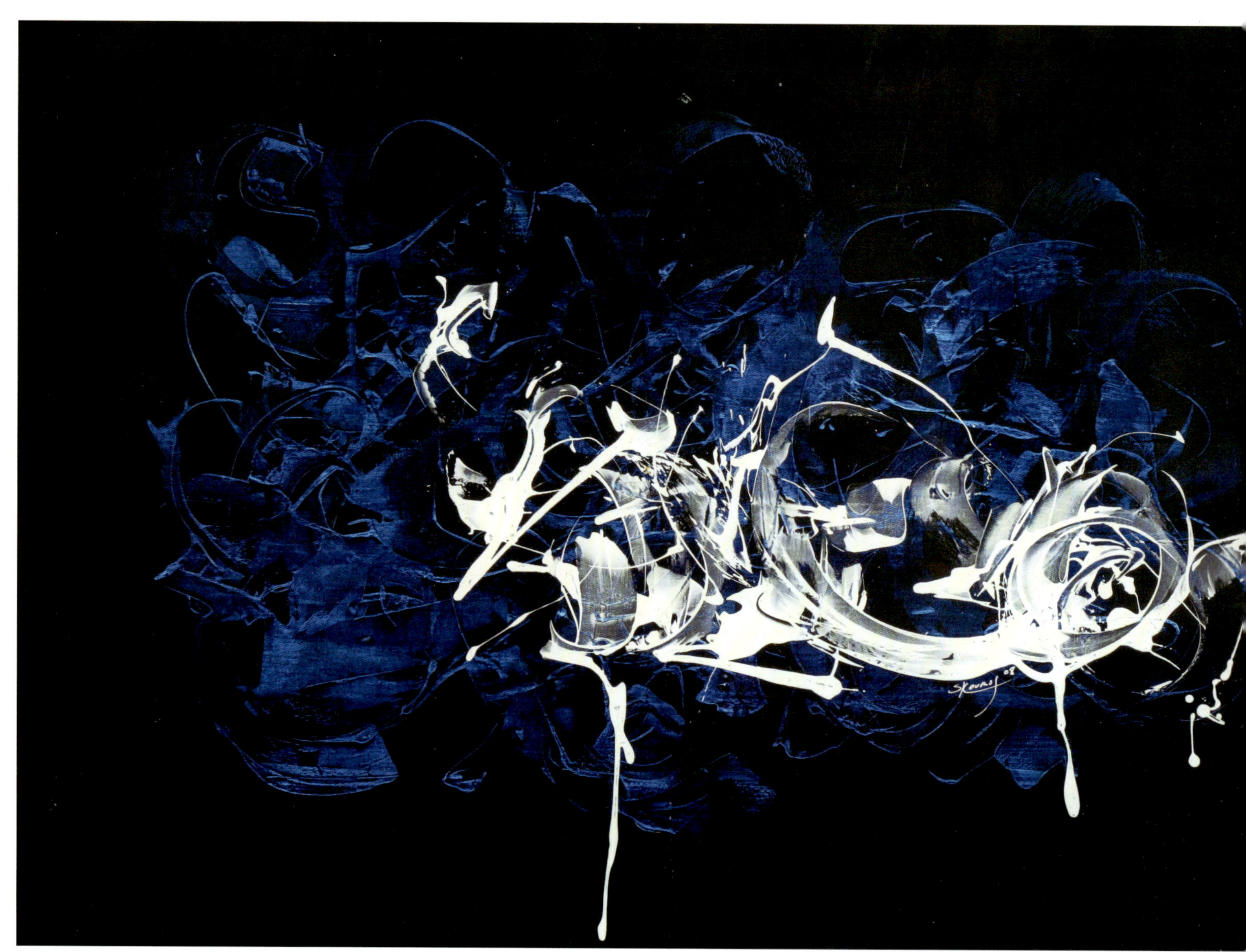

2008, mixed media on canvas,
80 x 120 cm

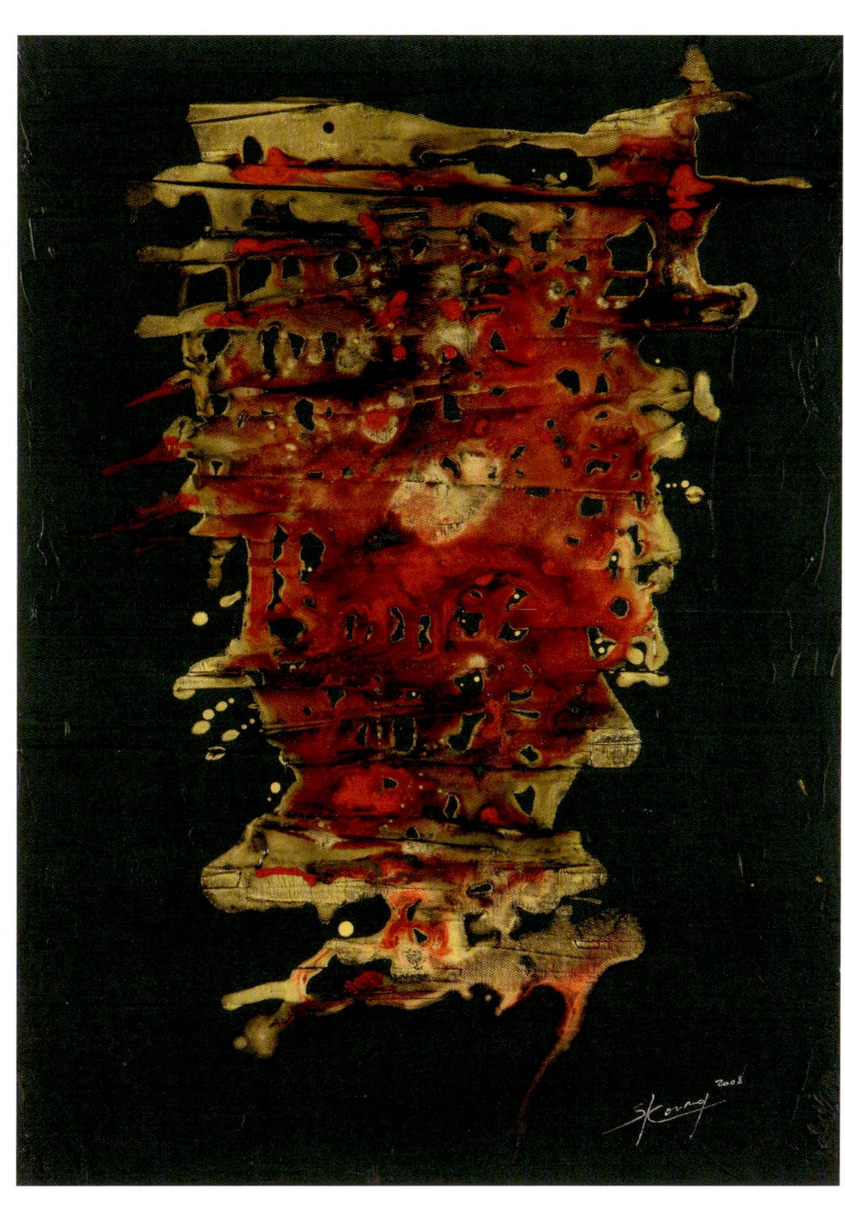

2008, acrylic on canvas,
70 x 50 cm

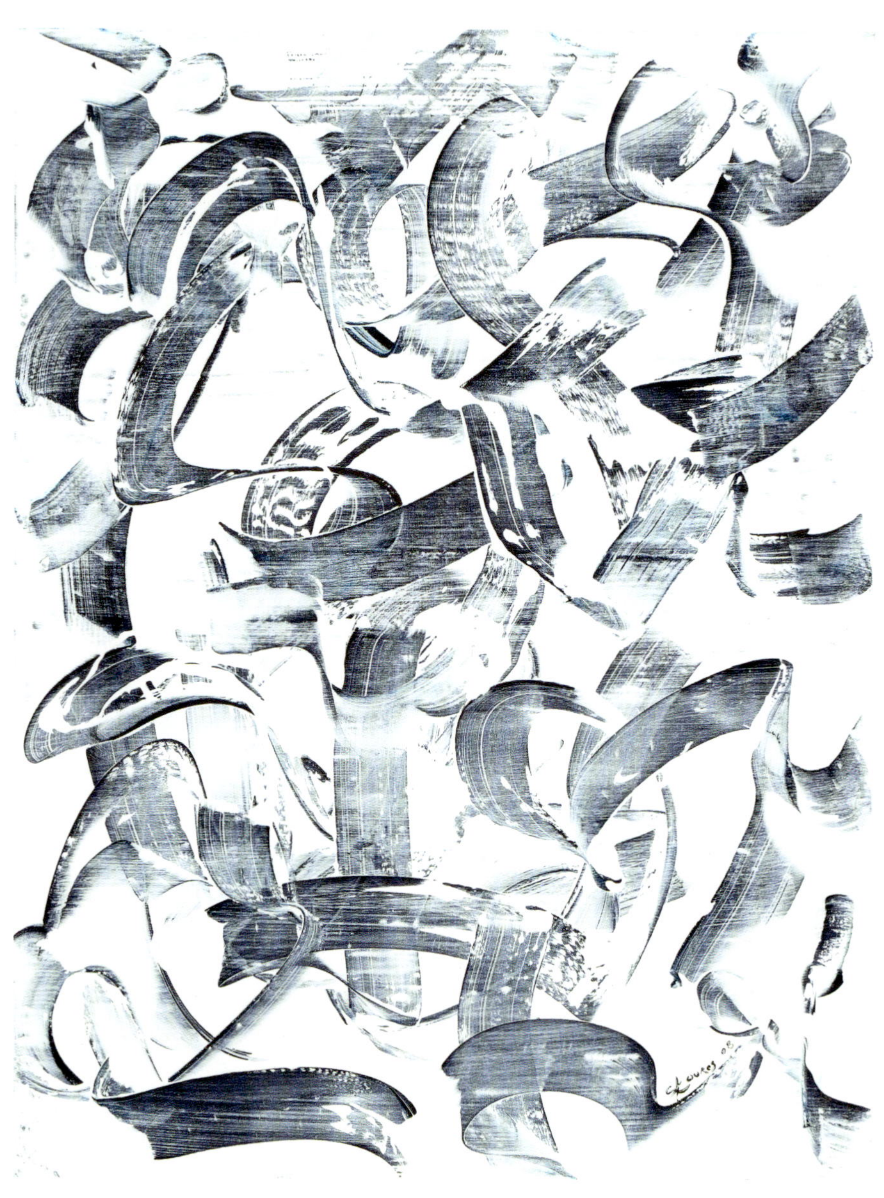

2008, mixed media on canvas
100 x 80 cm

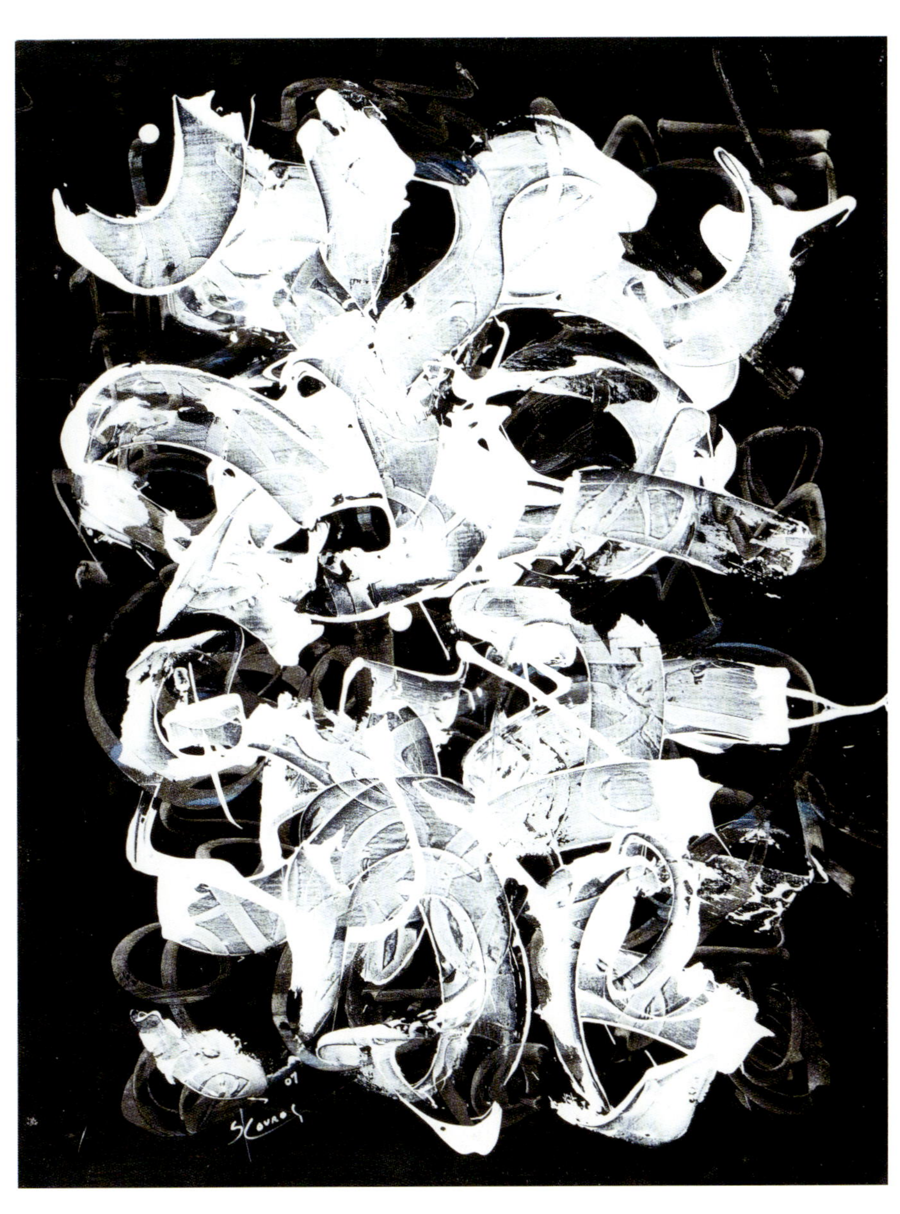

2007, acrylic on canvas,
80 x 60 cm

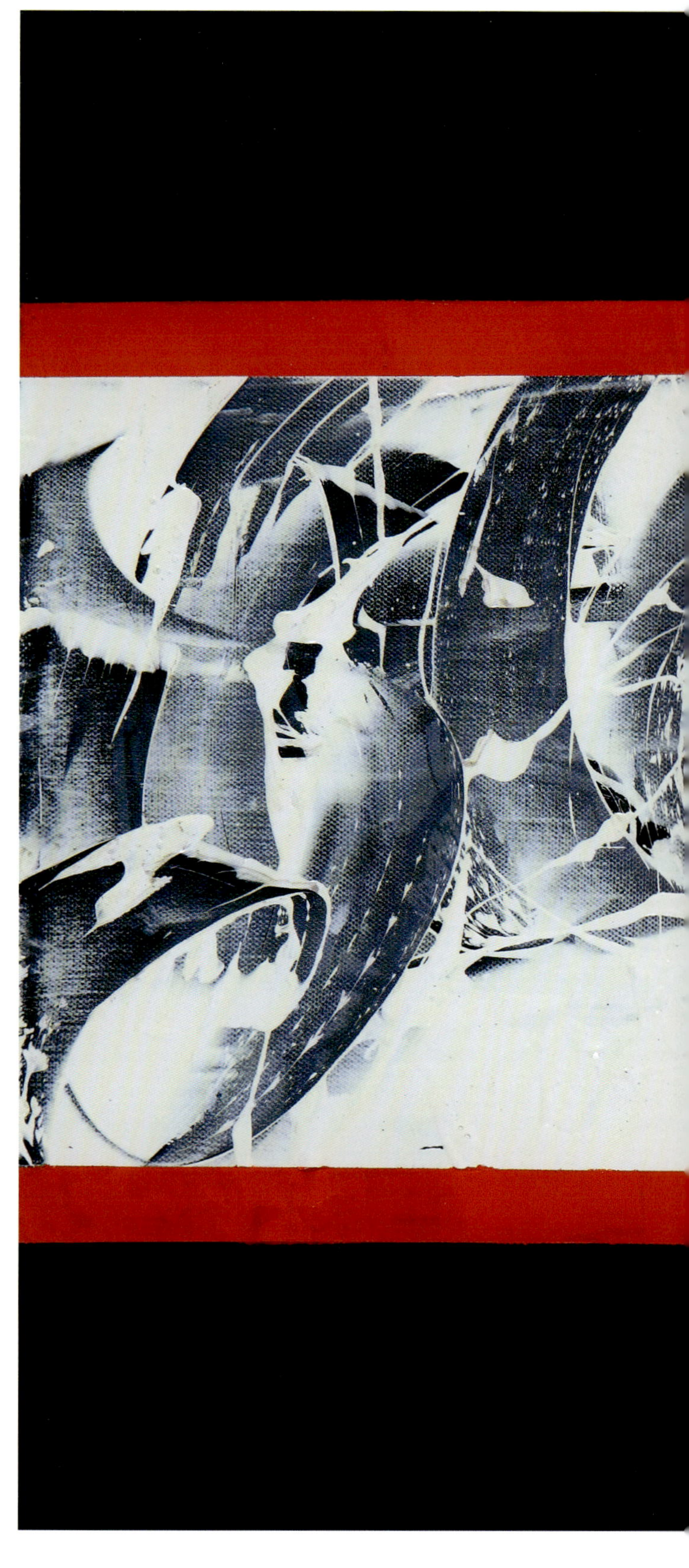

2009, acrylic on canvas,
50 x 70 cm

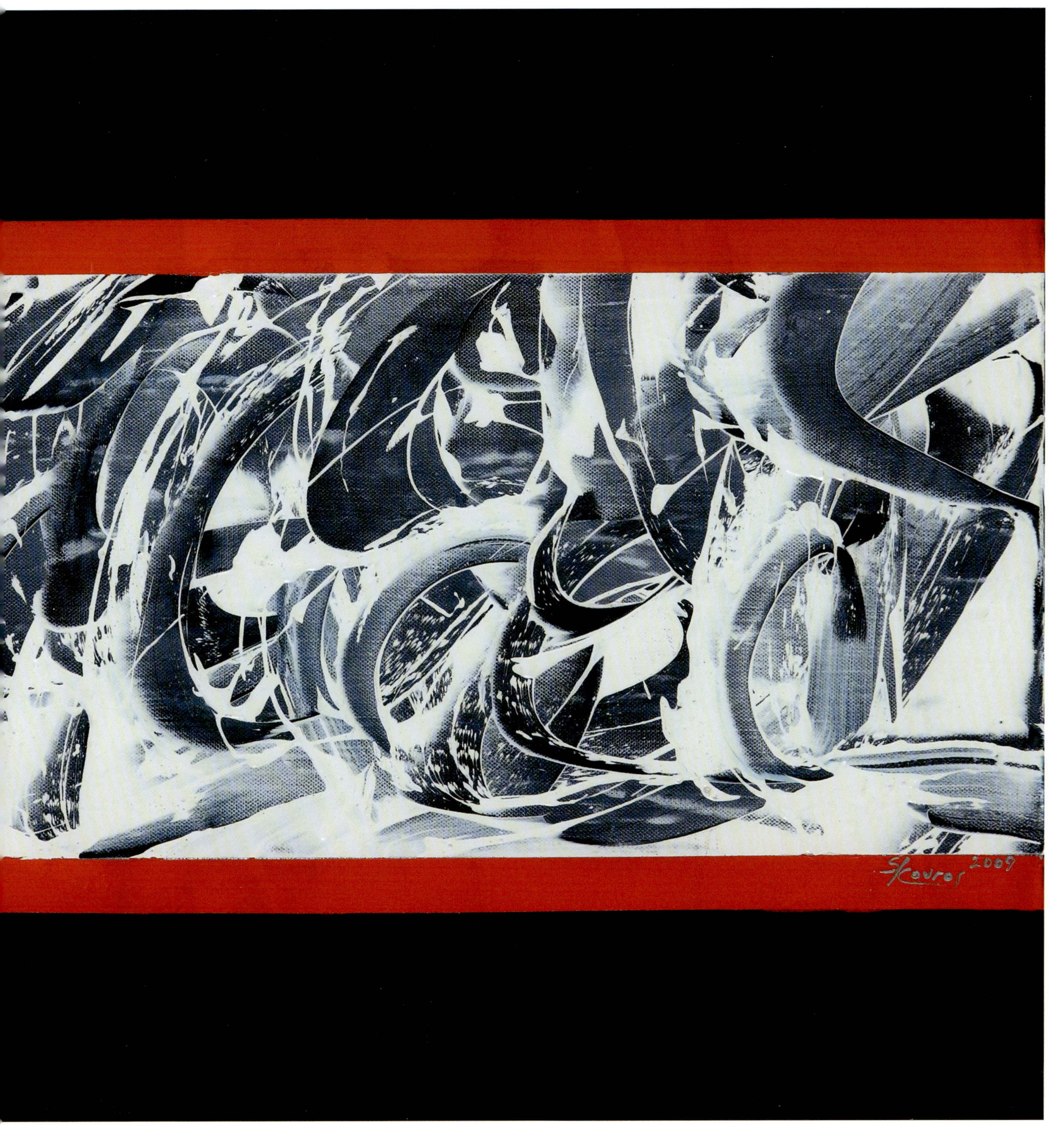
Skouros 2009

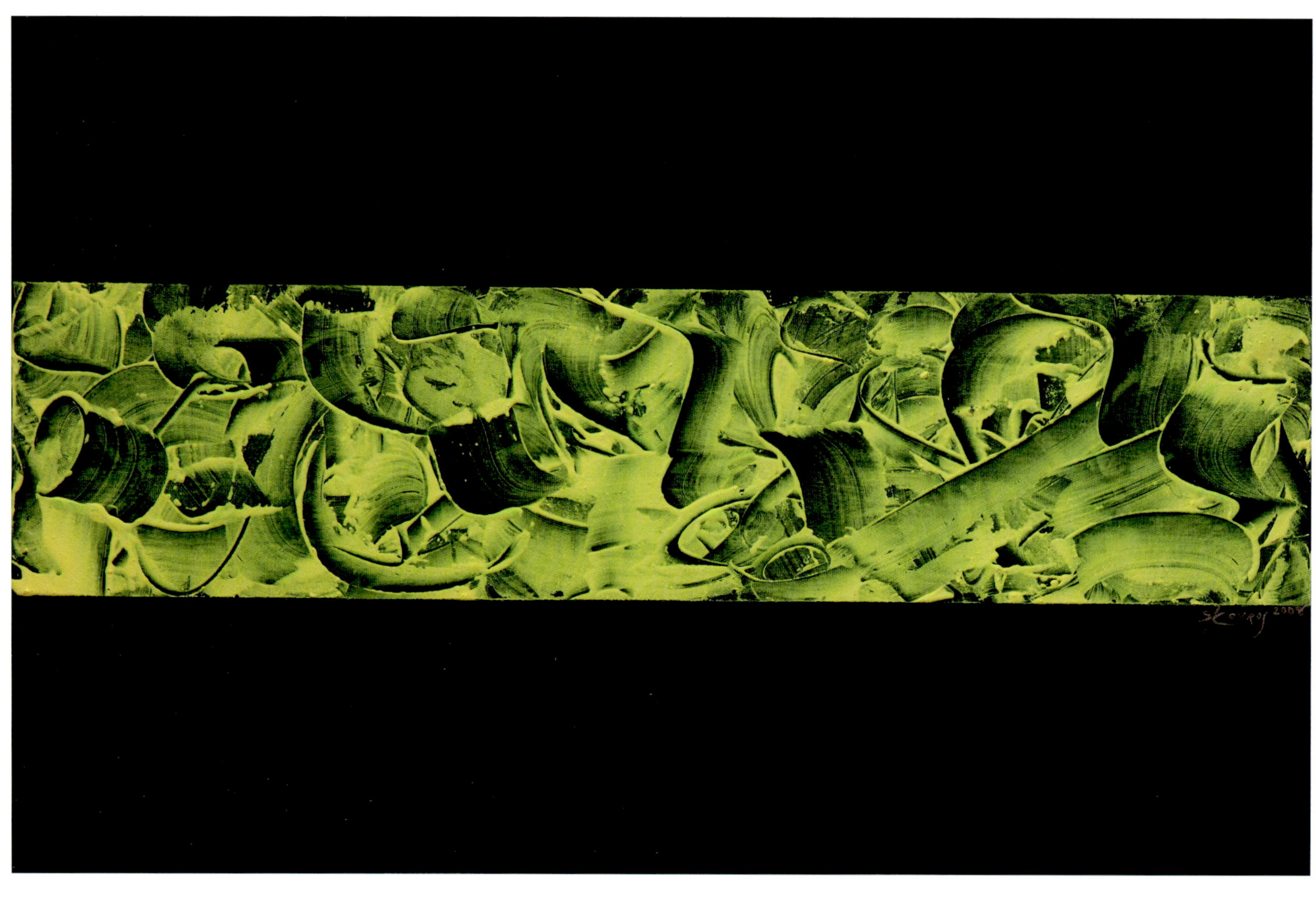

2008, acrylic on canvas,
50 x 70 cm

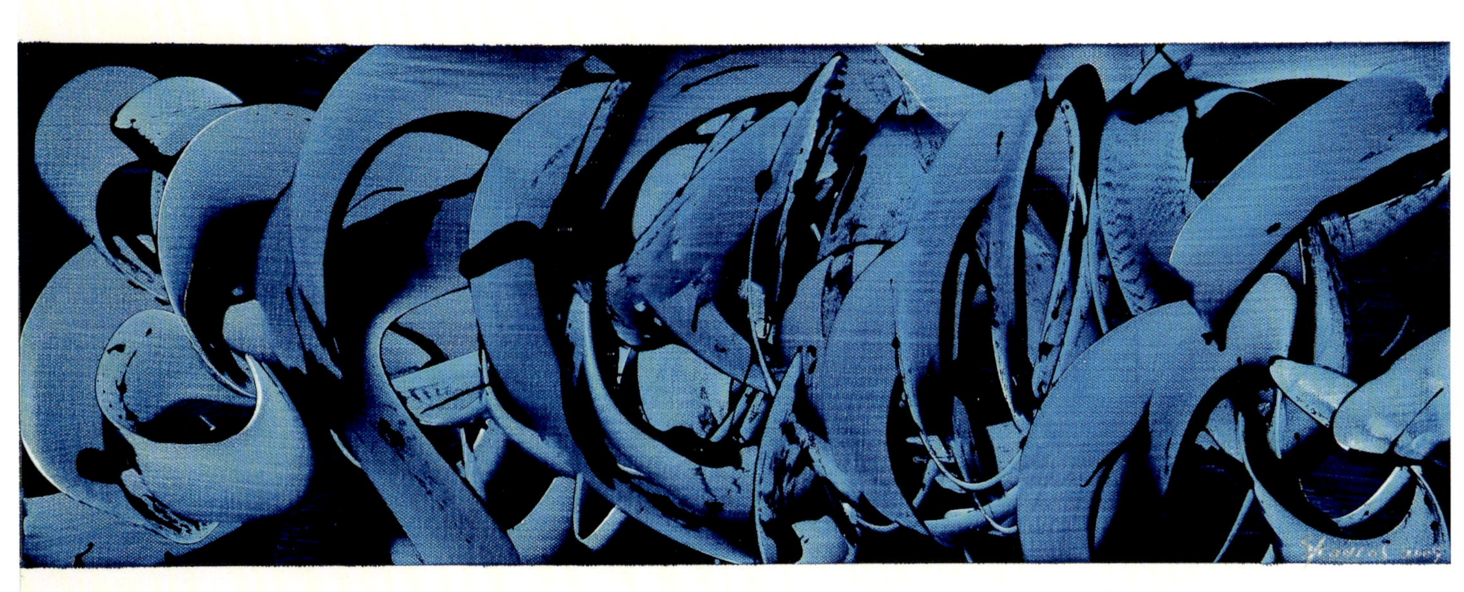

2009, acrylic on canvas,
50 x 70 cm

2009, acrylic on canvas,
100 x 100 cm

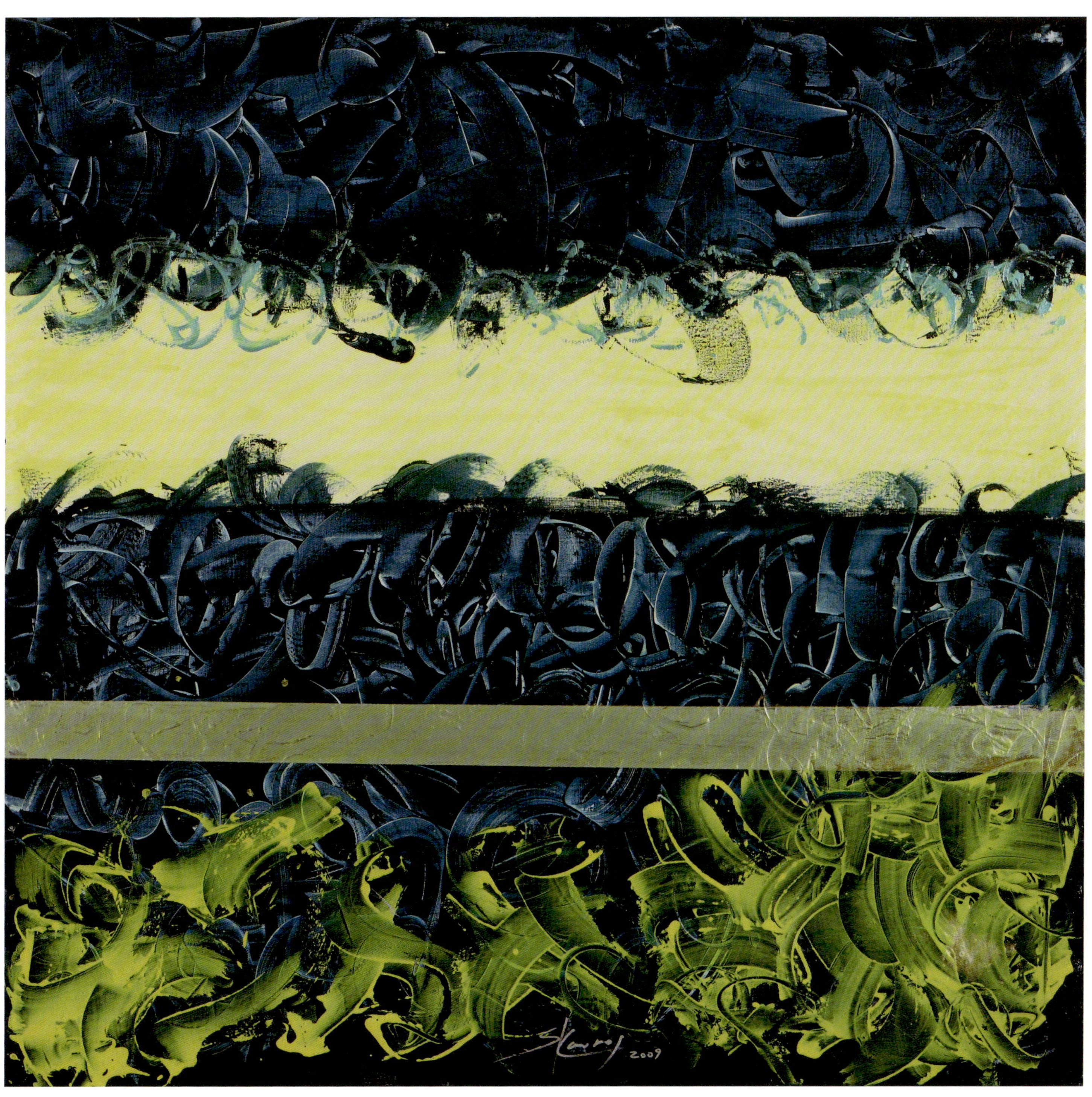

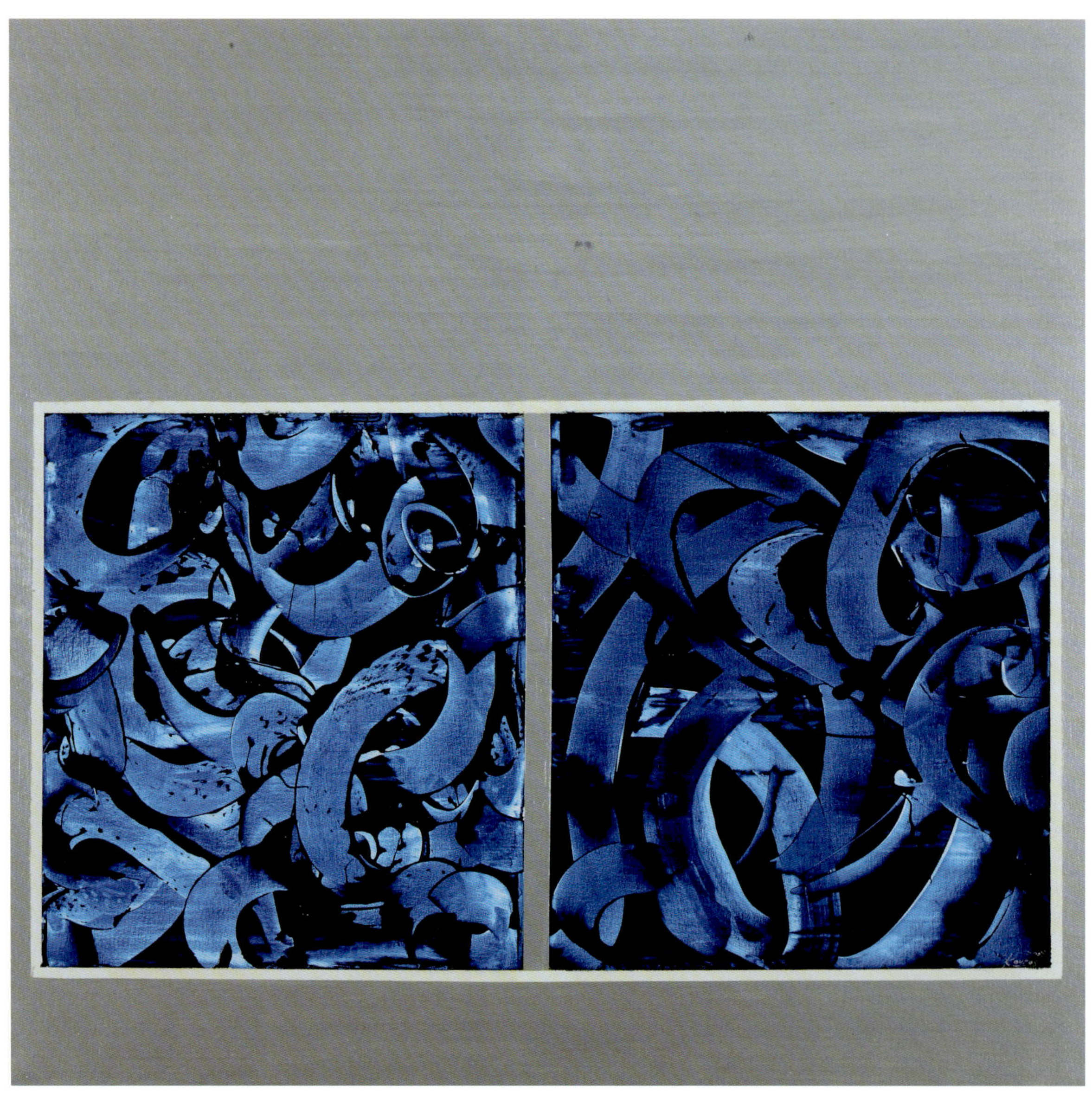

2009, acrylic on canvas,
100 x 100 cm

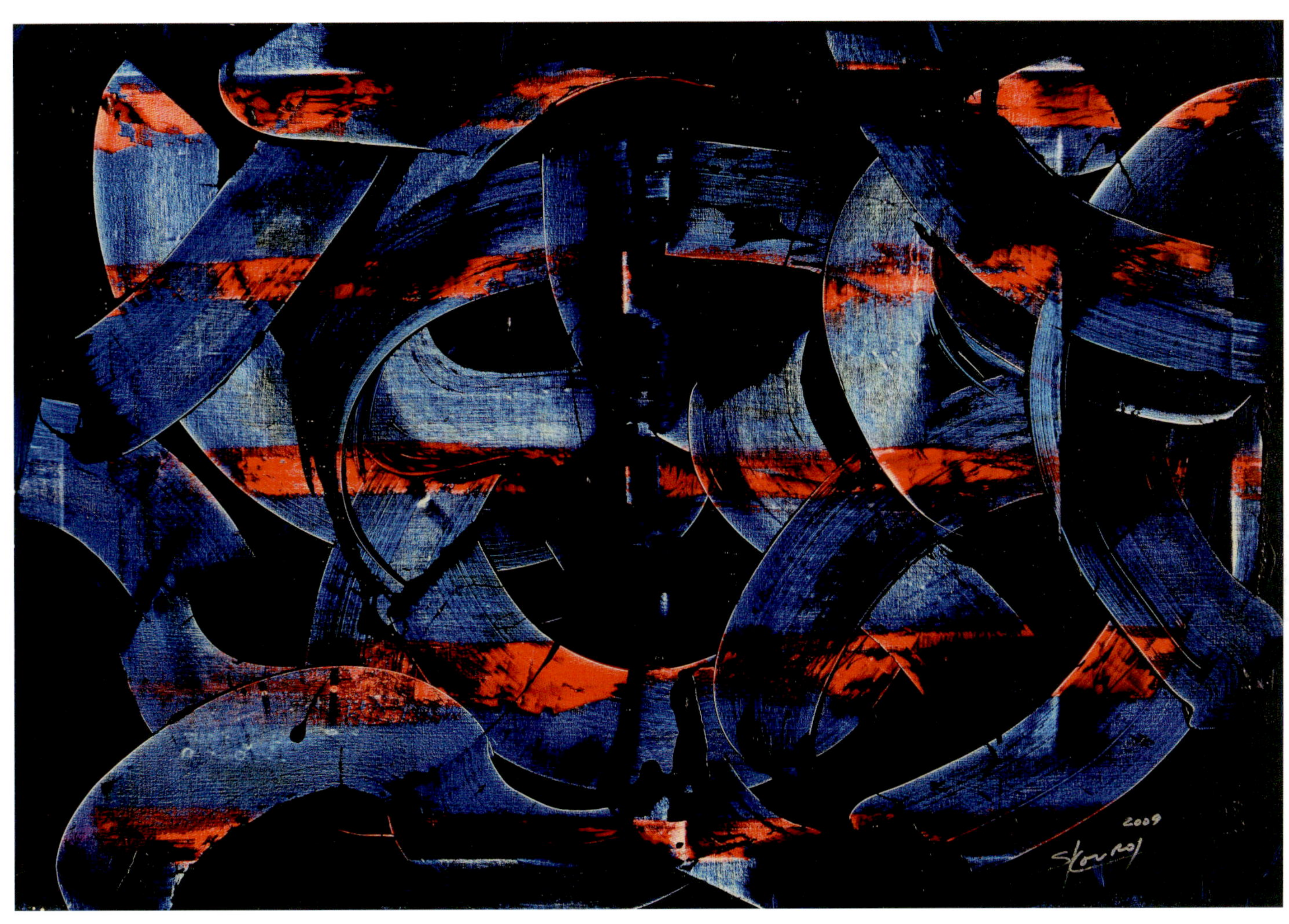

2009, acrylic on canvas,
70 x 100 cm

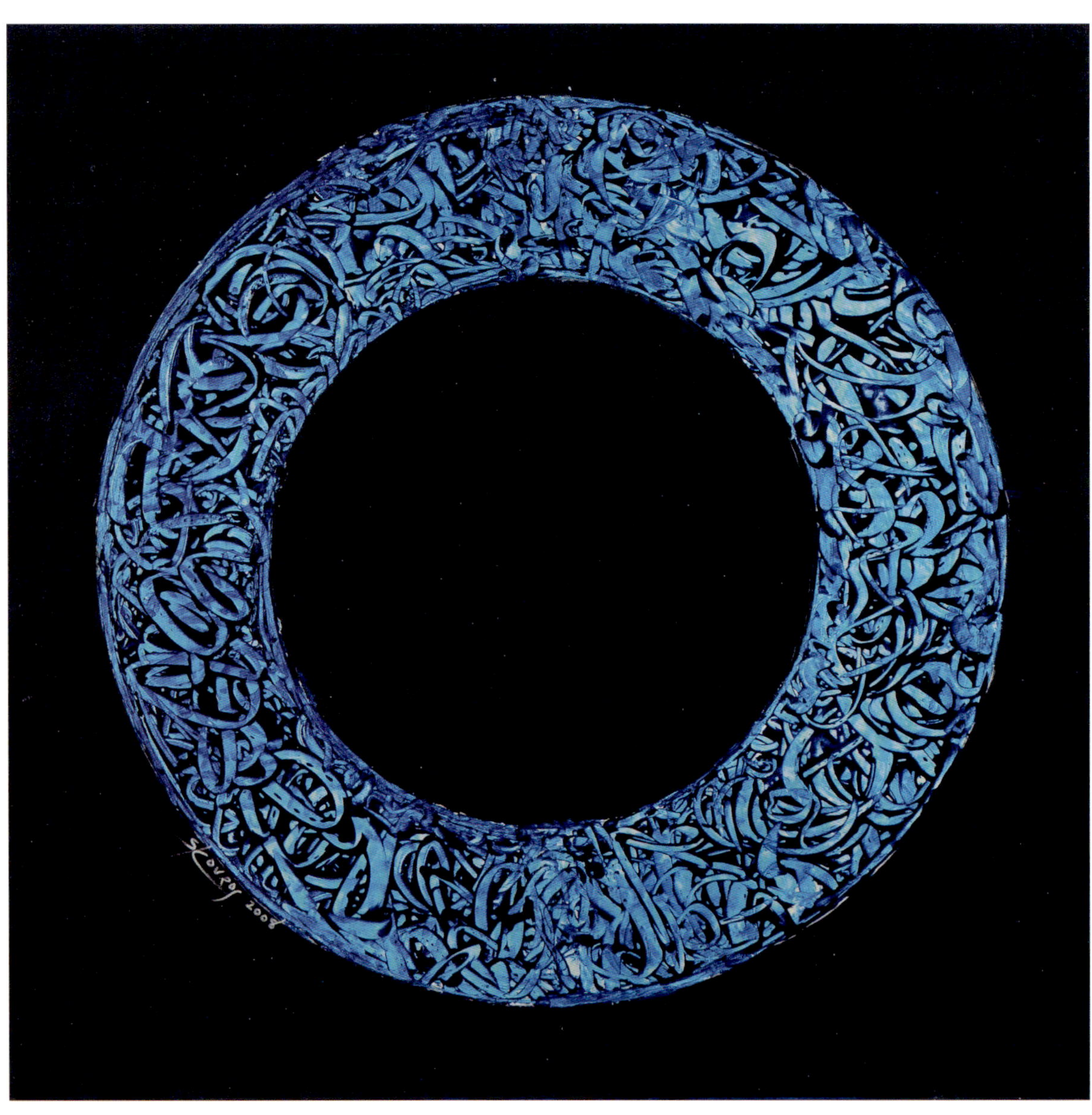

2008, mixed media on canvas,
120 x 120 cm

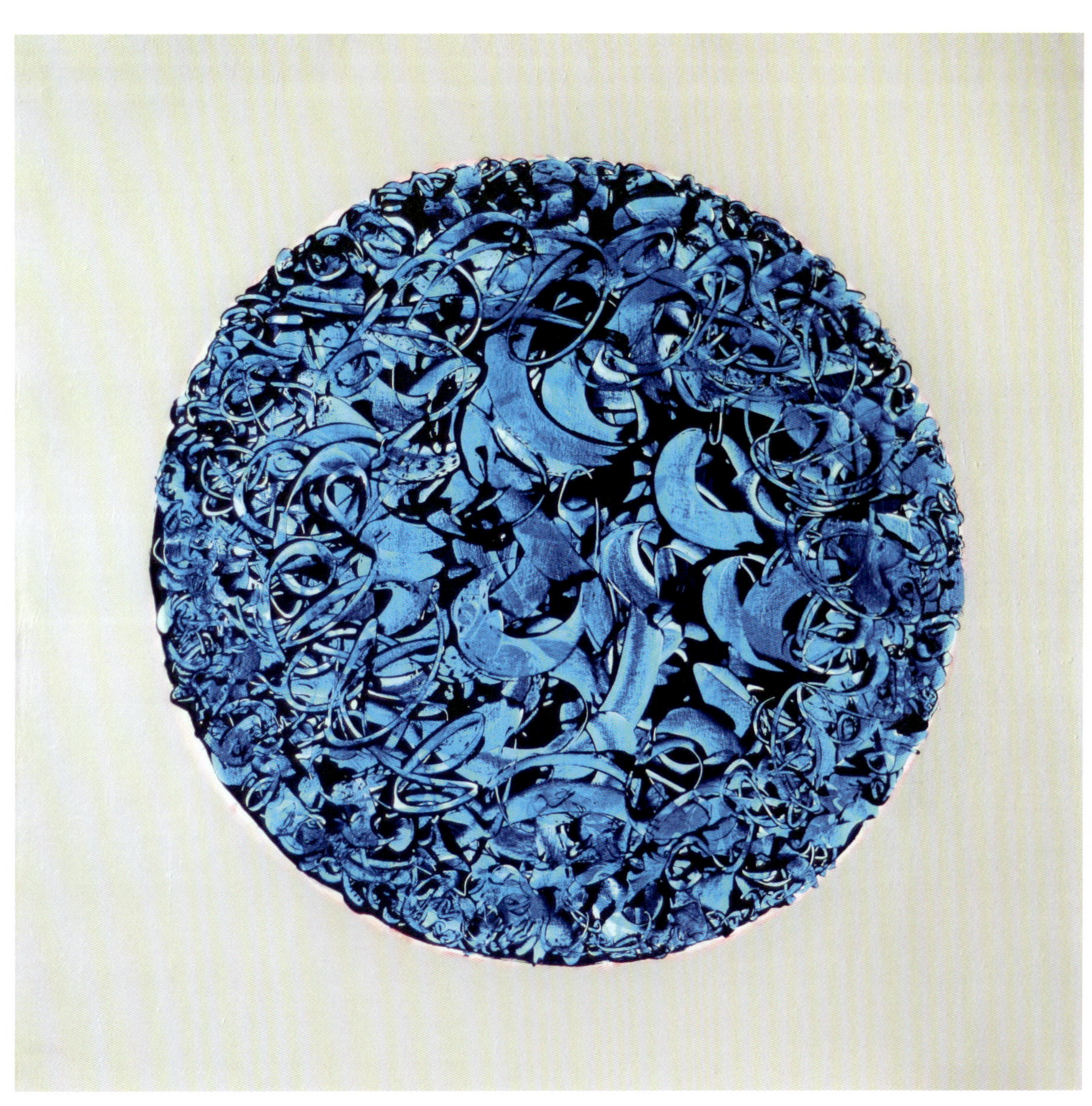

2009, mixed media on canvas,
120 x 120 cm

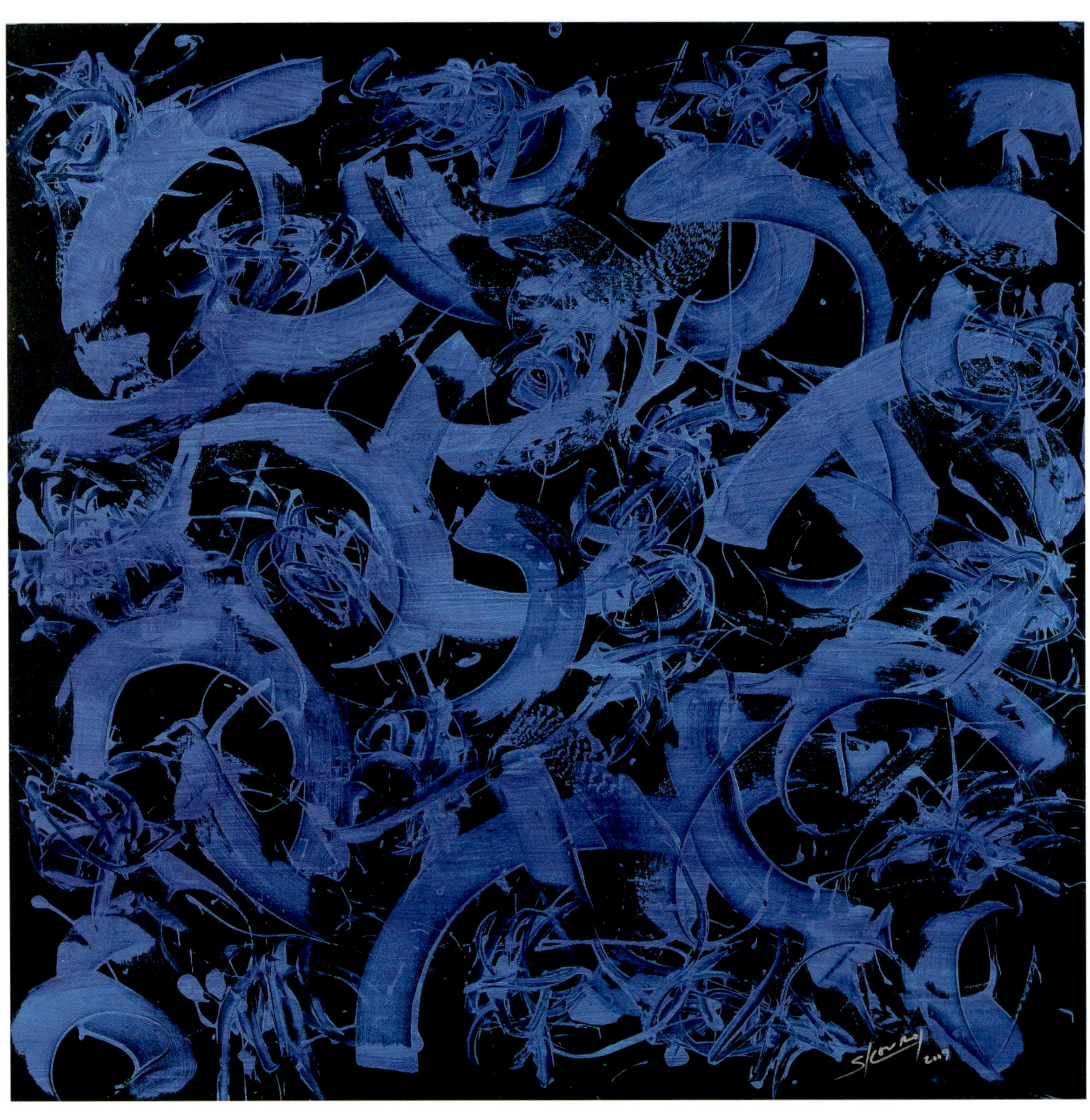

2009, acrylic on canvas,
120 x 120 cm

2009, acrylic on canvas,
70 x 90 cm

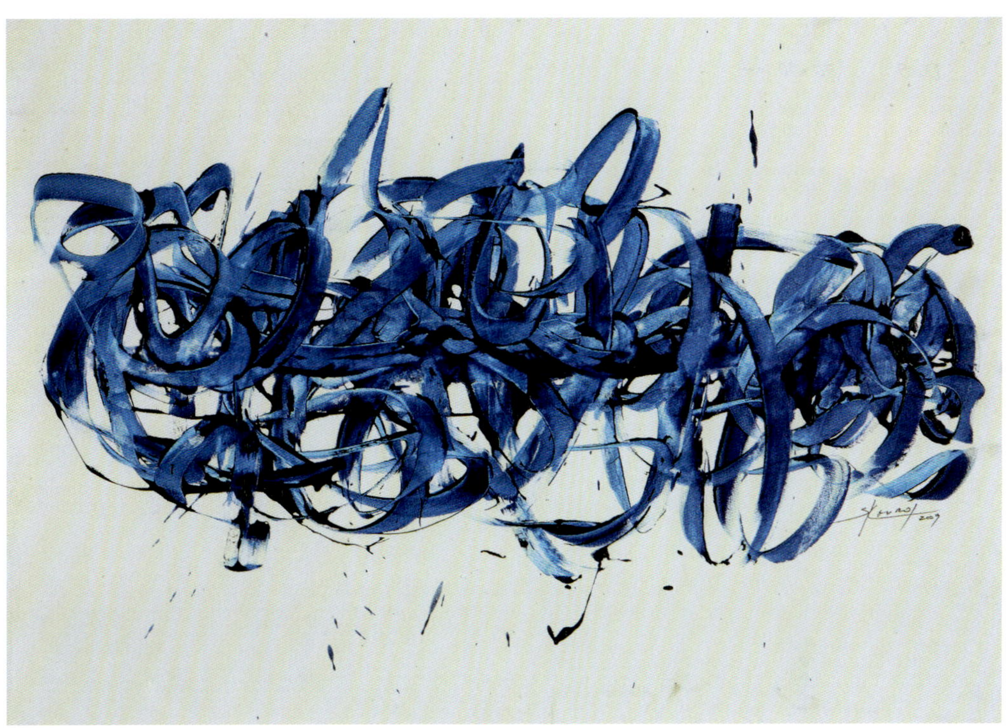

2009, acrylic on canvas,
100 x 70 cm

2009, acrylic on paper,
100 x 70 cm

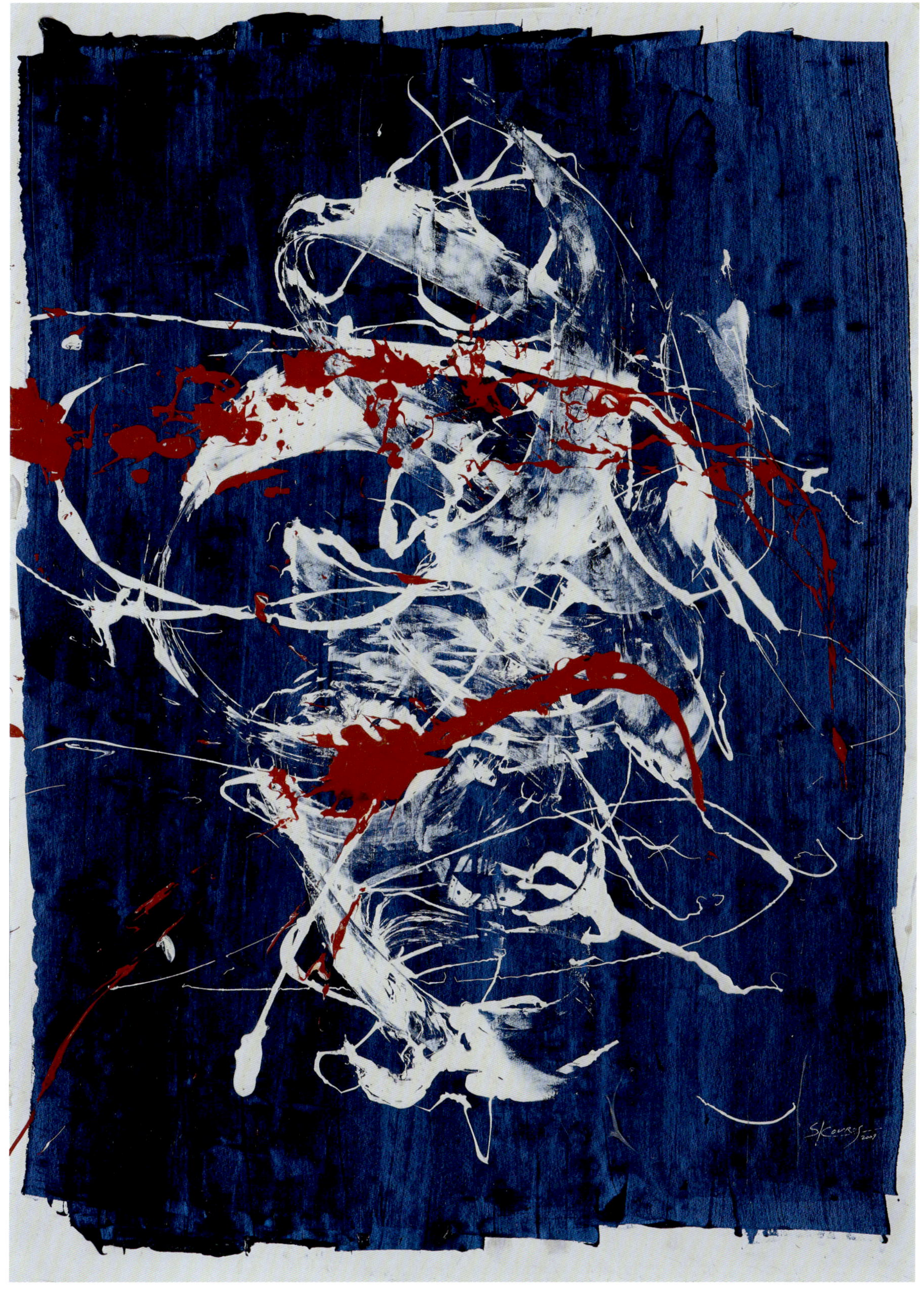

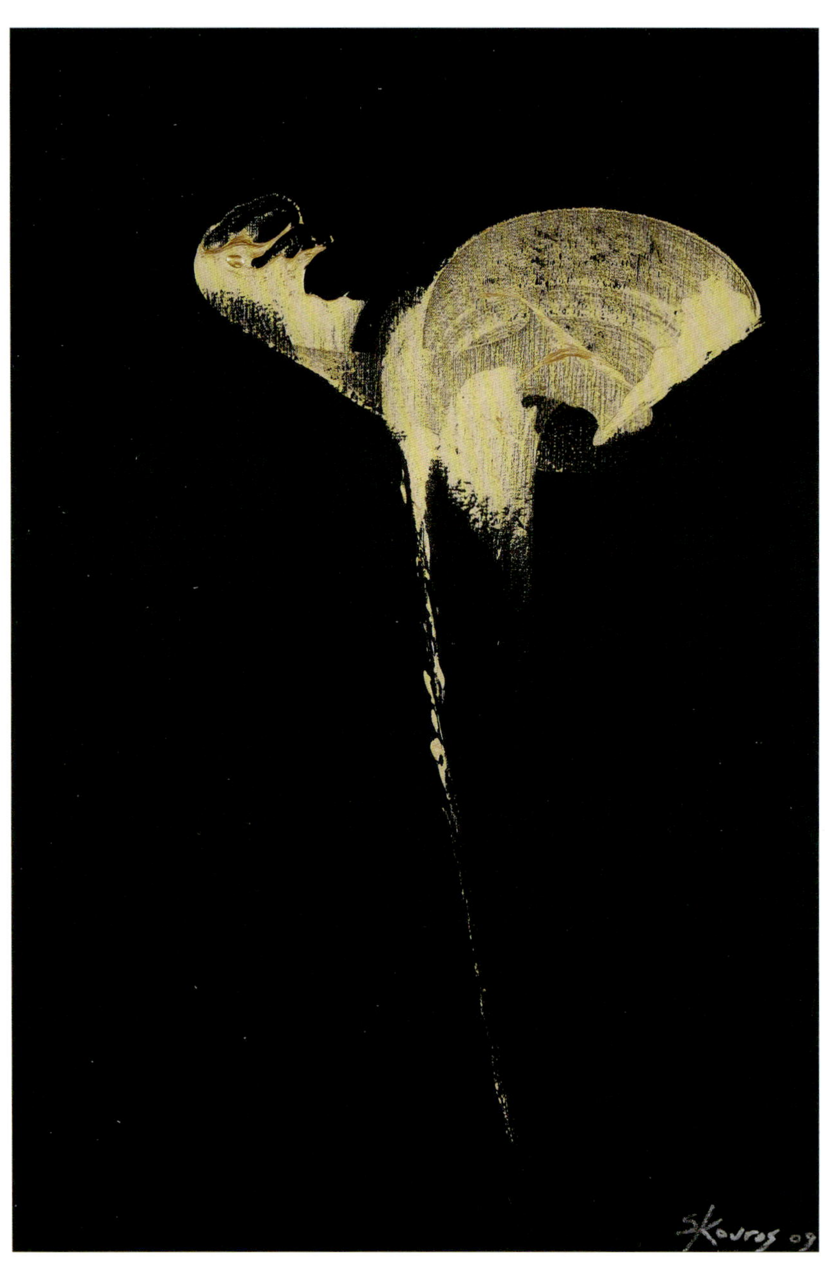

2009, acrylic on canvas,
60 x 30 cm

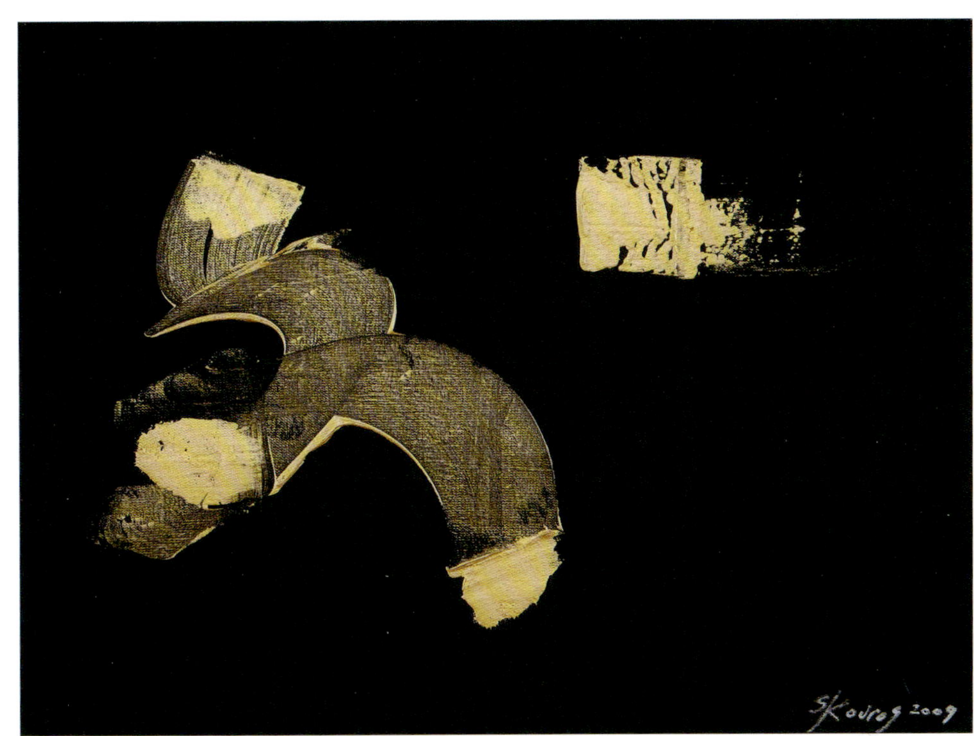

2009, acrylic on canvas,
40 x 60 cm

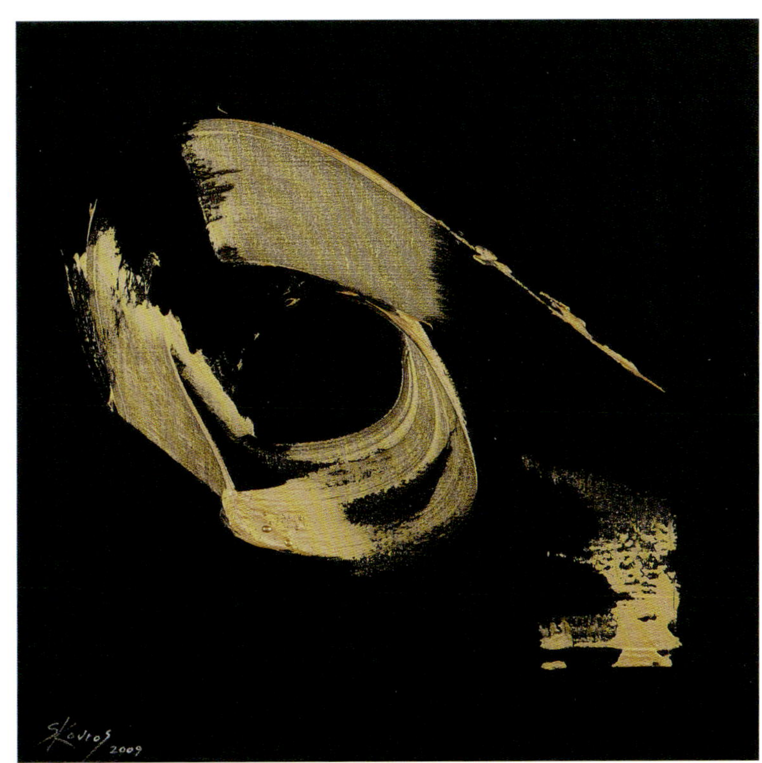

2009, acrylic on canvas,
50 x 50 cm

2010, acrylic on canvas,
100 x 100 cm

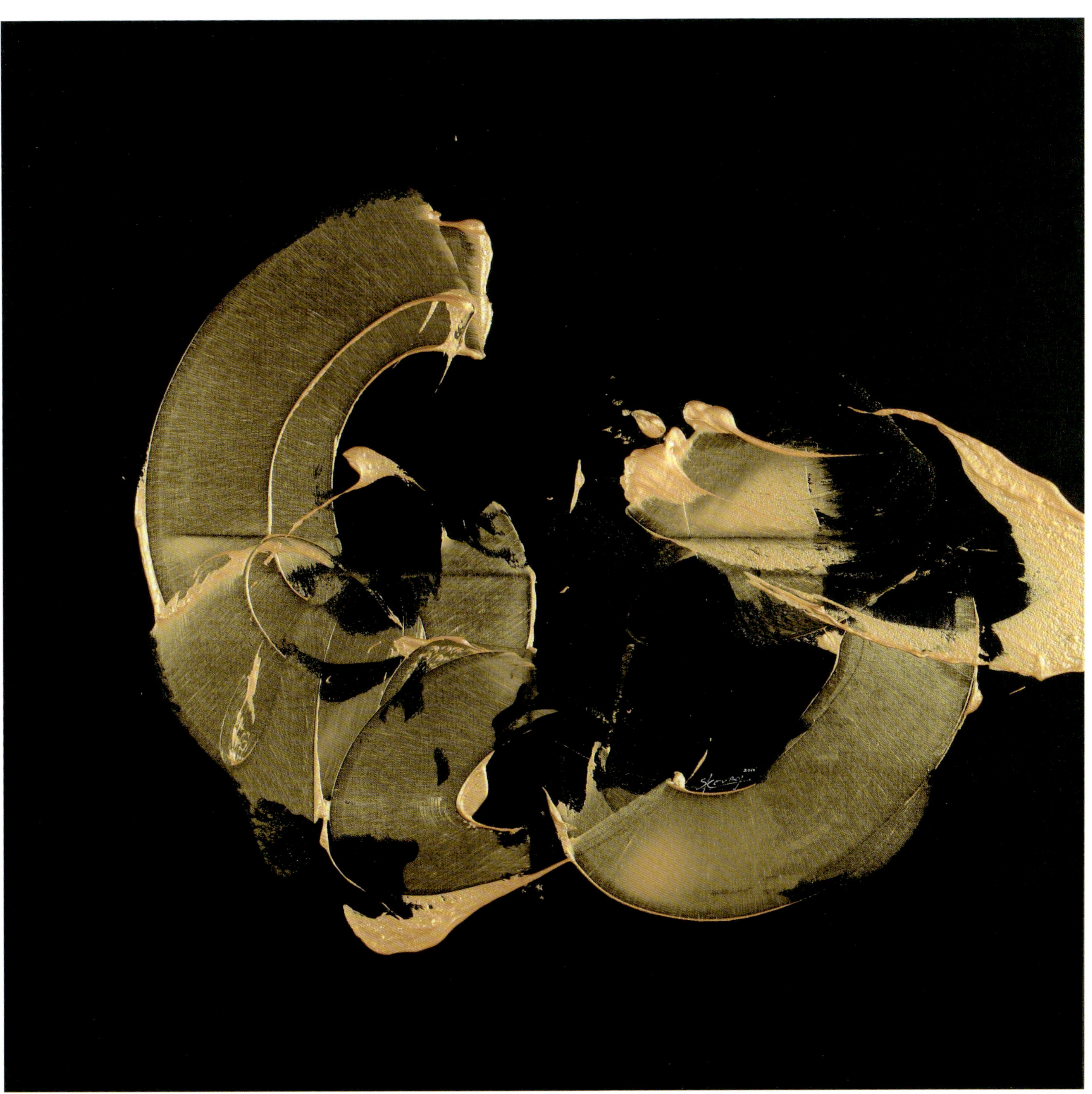

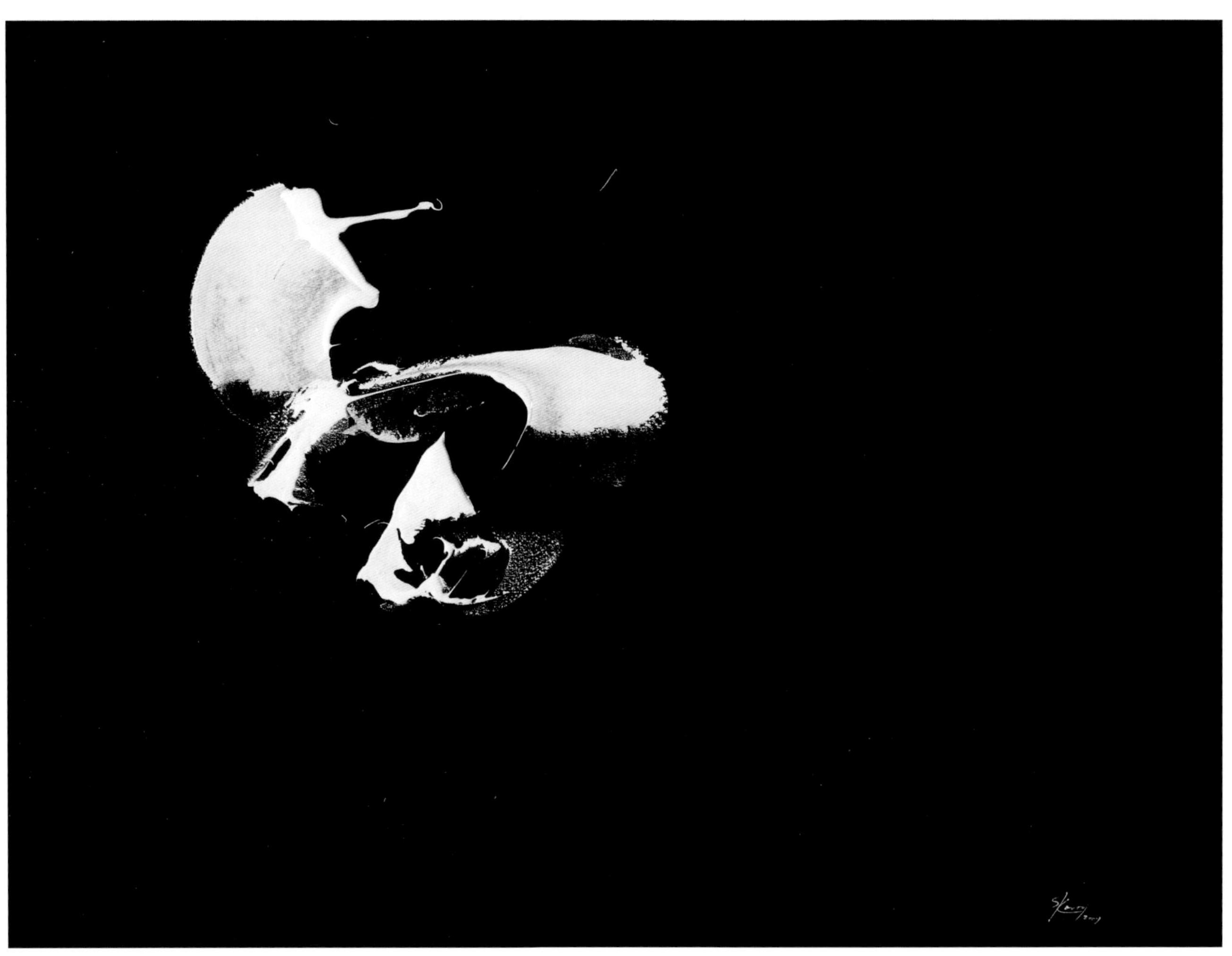

2009, acrylic on cardboard,
50 x 65 cm

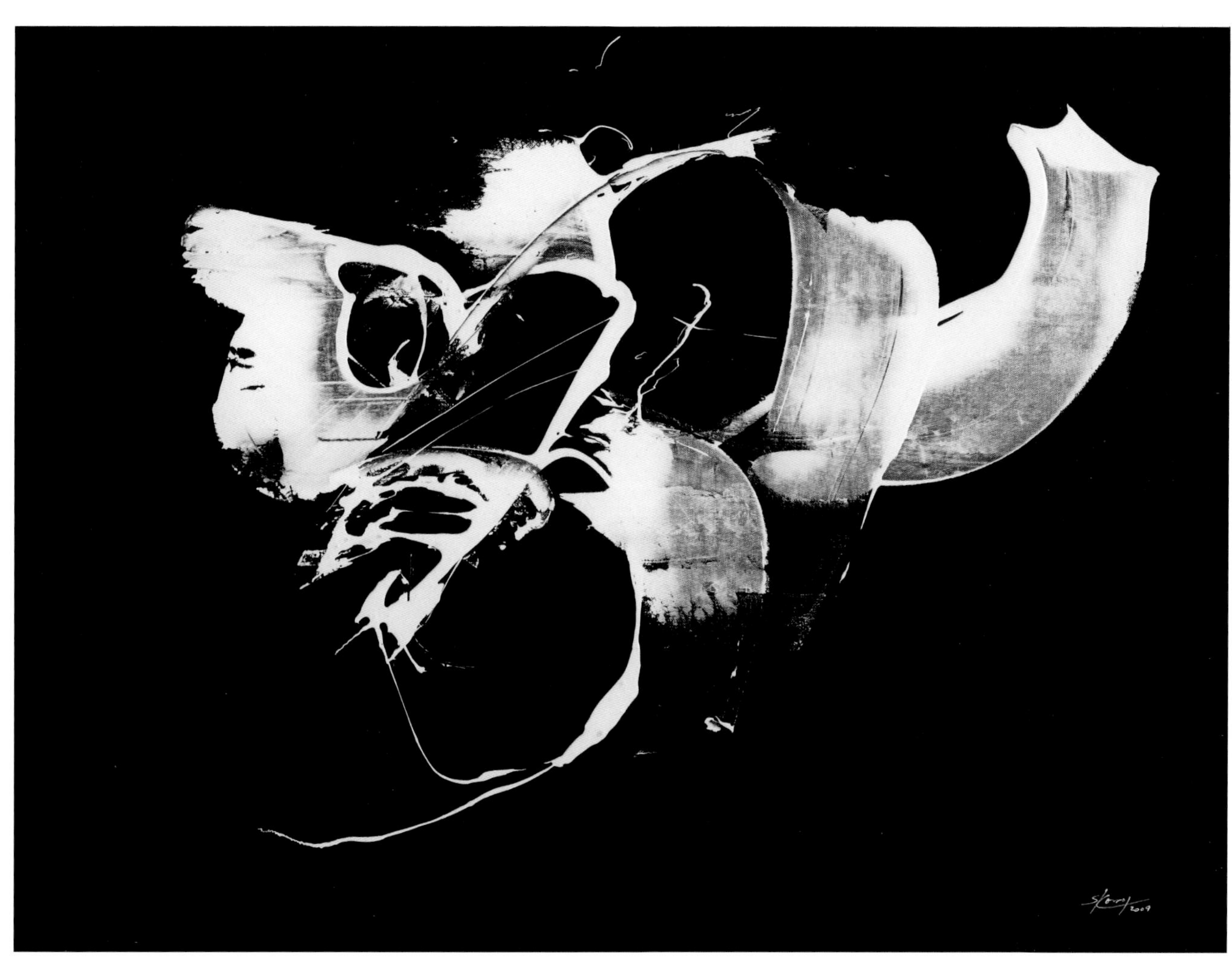

2009, acrylic on cardboard,
50 x 65 cm

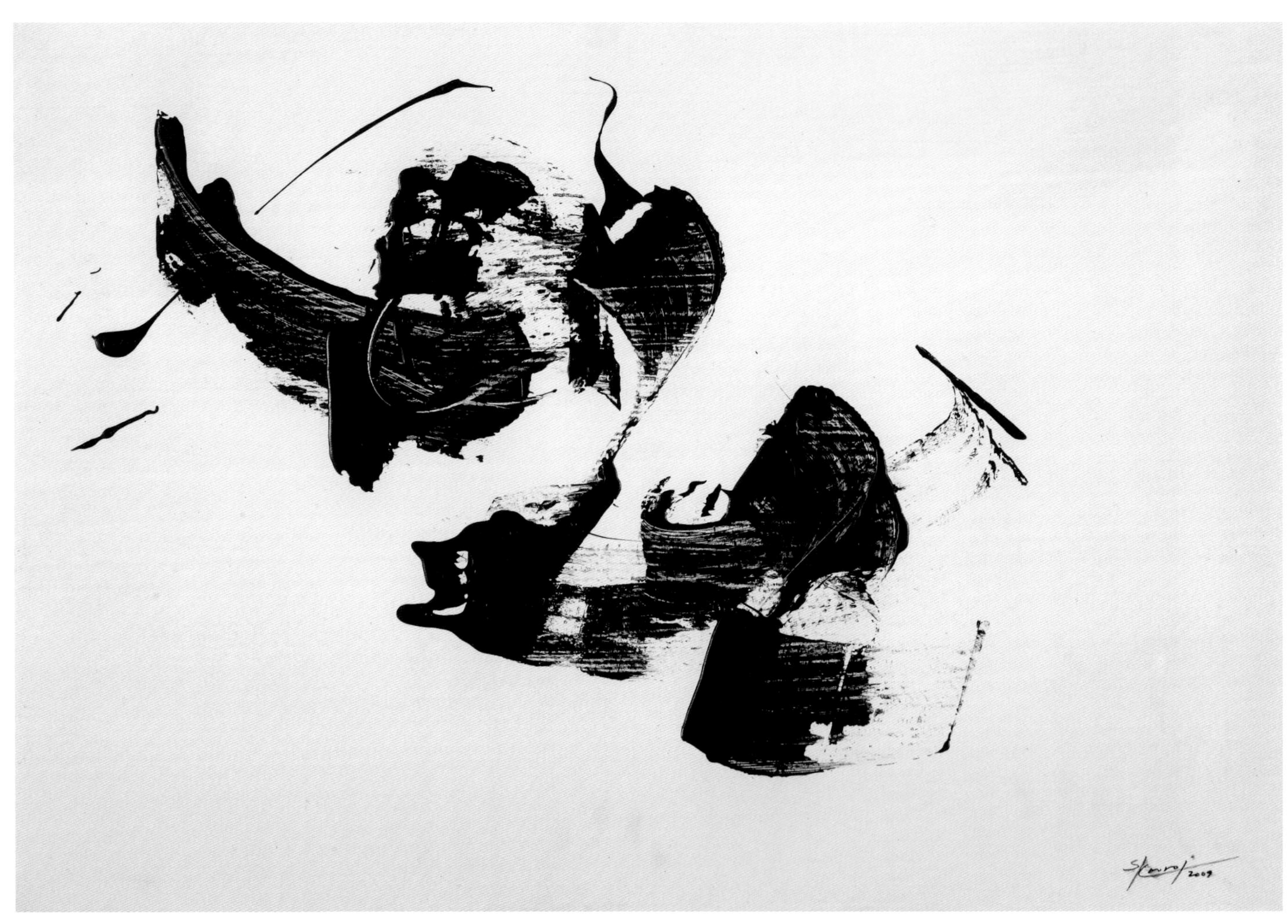

2009, acrylic on cardboard,
50 x 69 cm

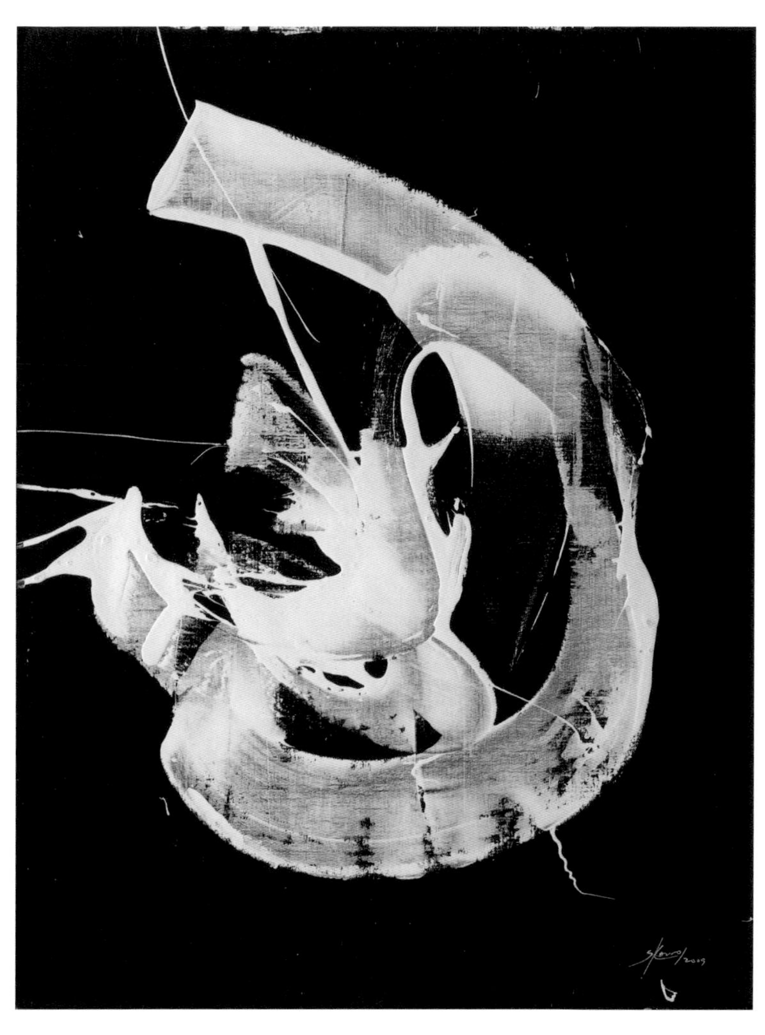

2009, acrylic on cardboard,
65 x 50 cm

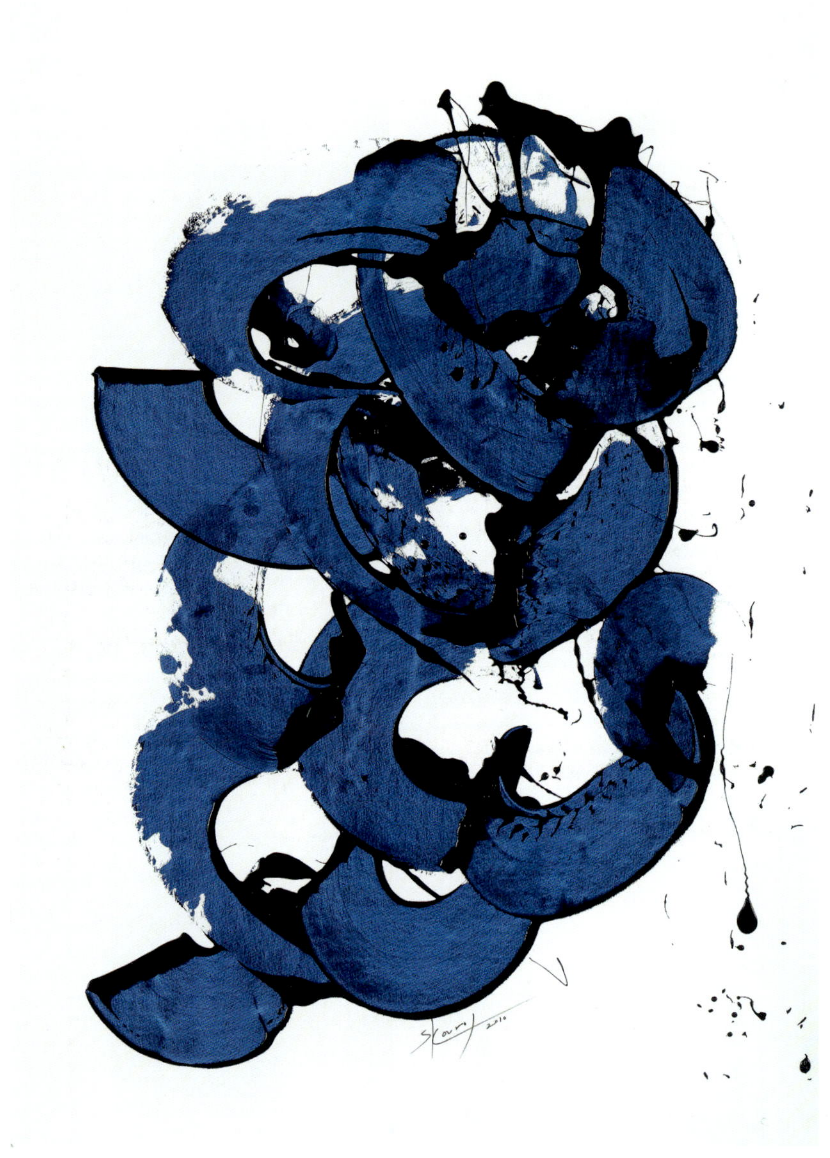

2010, acrylic on cardboard,
100 x 70 cm

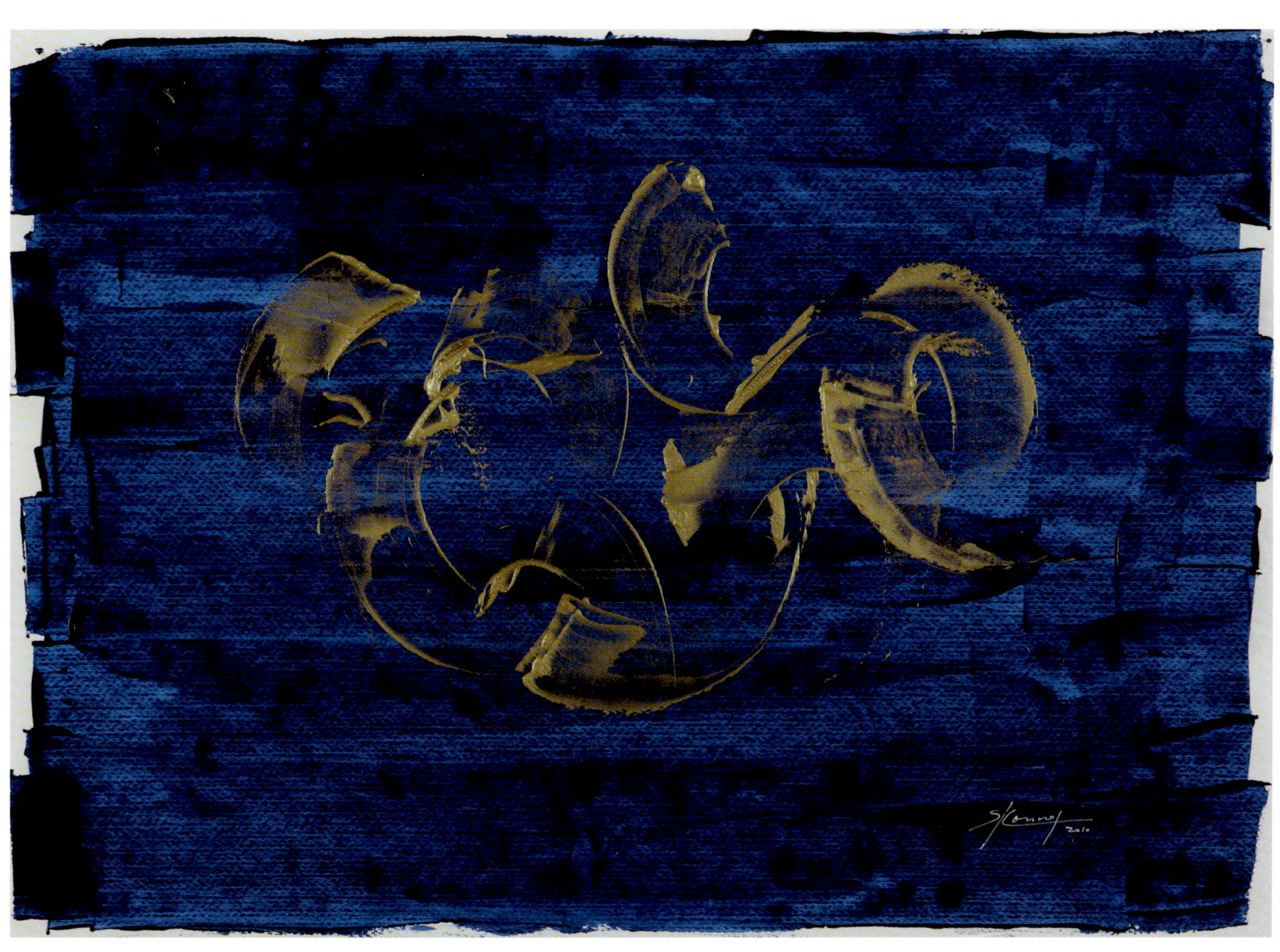

2010, acrylic on cardboard,
50 x 70 cm

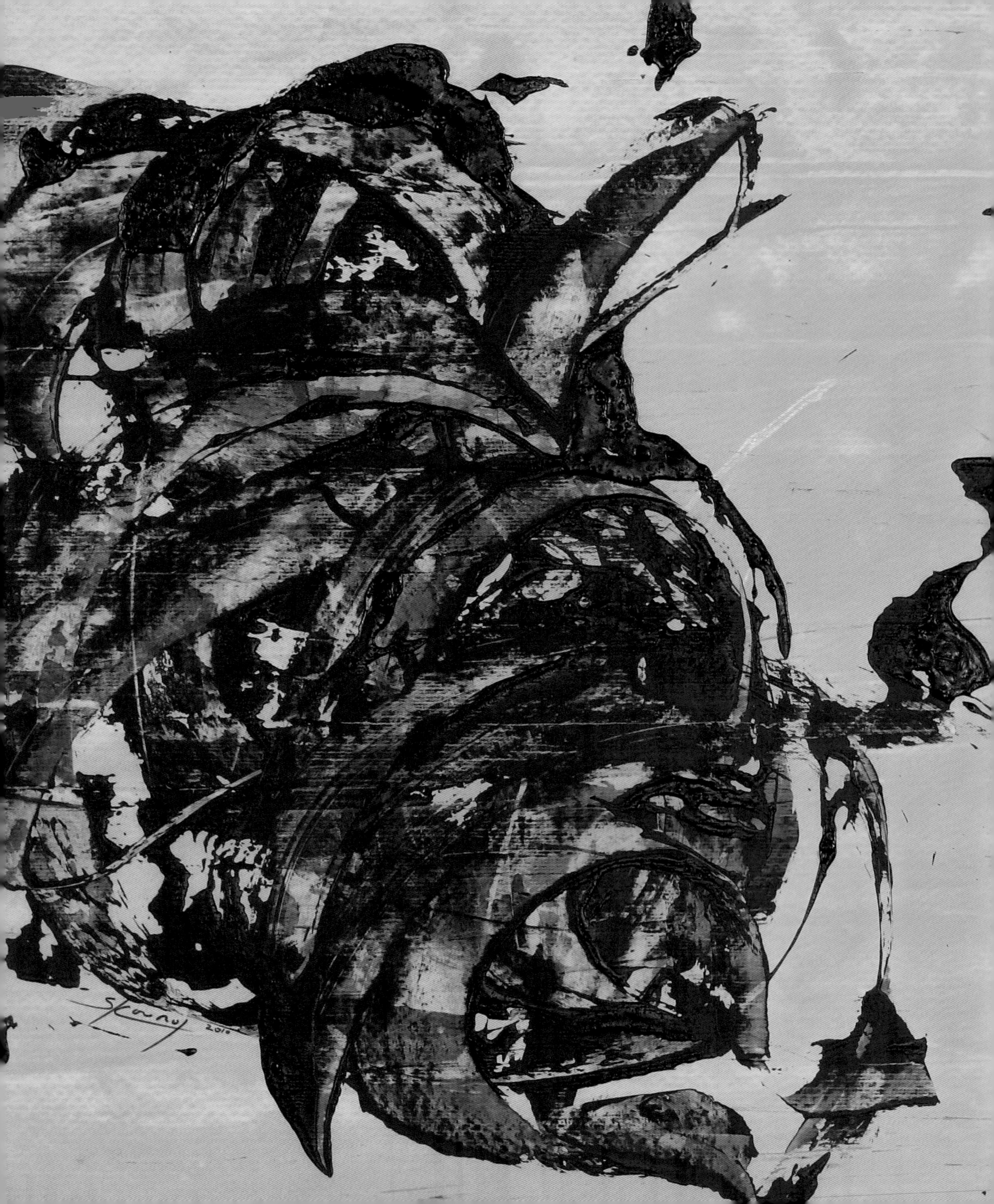

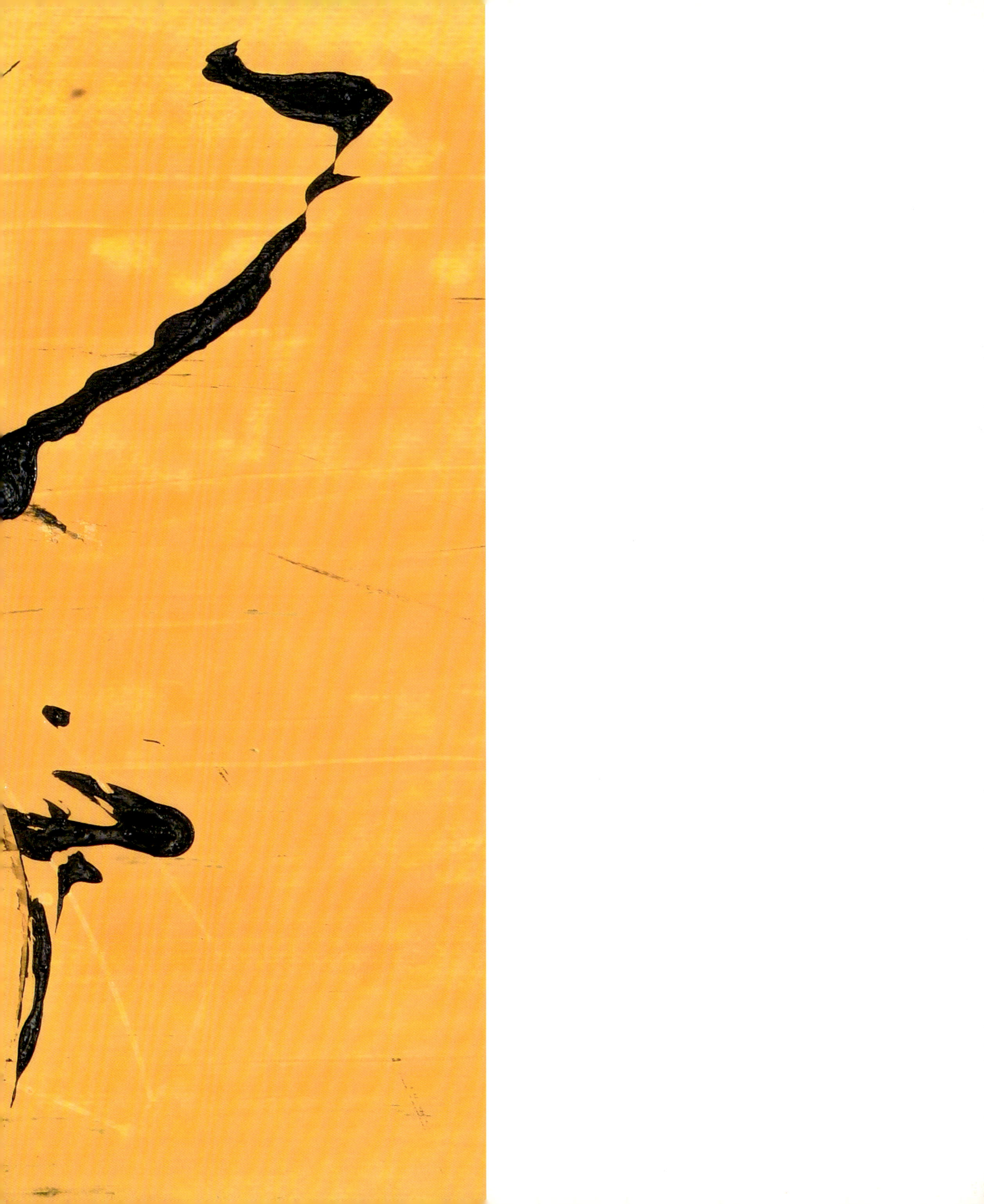

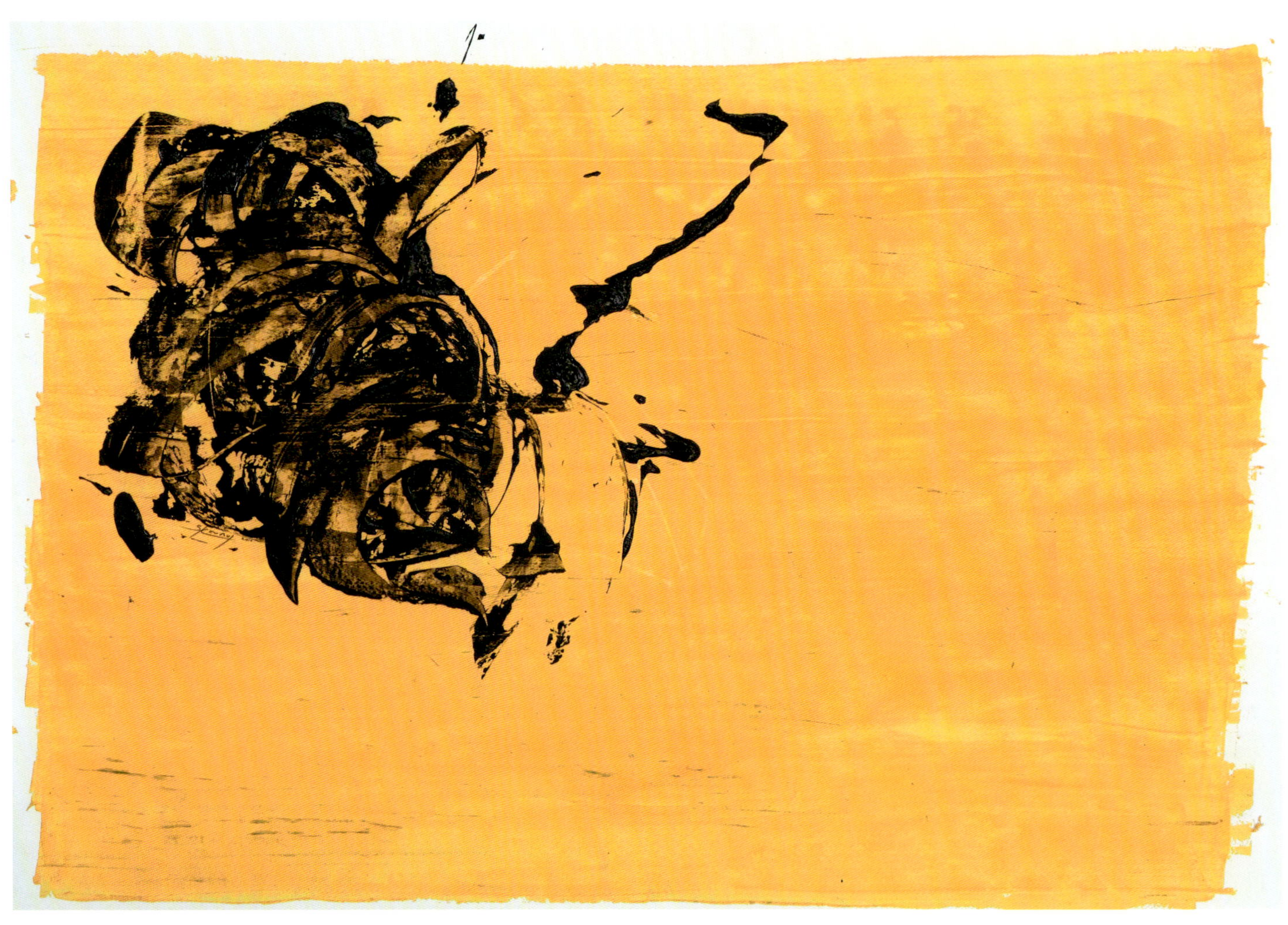

2010, acrylic on cardboard,
70 x 100 cm

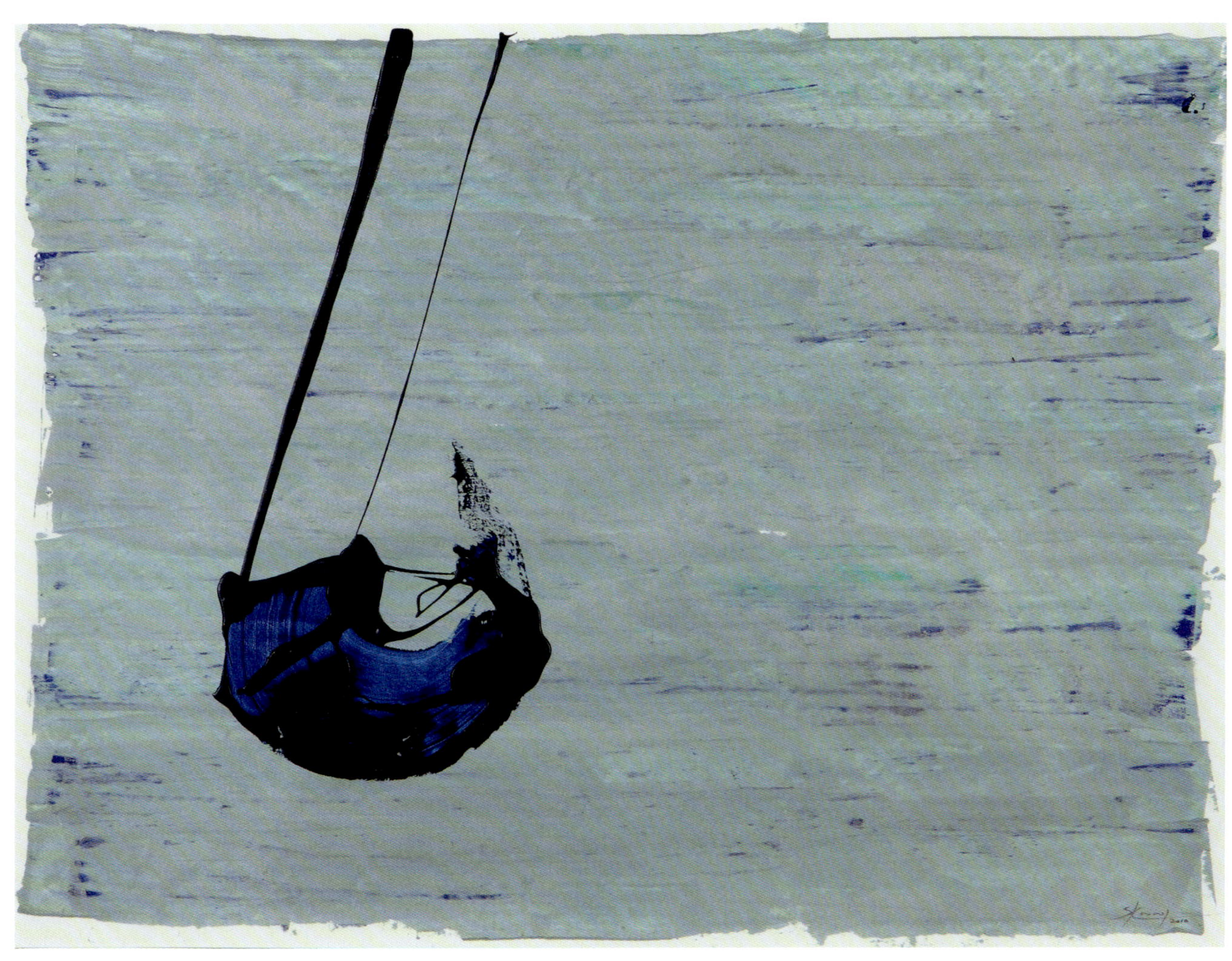

2010, acrylic on cardboard,
50 x 65 cm

2010, acrylic on canvas,
80 x 80 cm

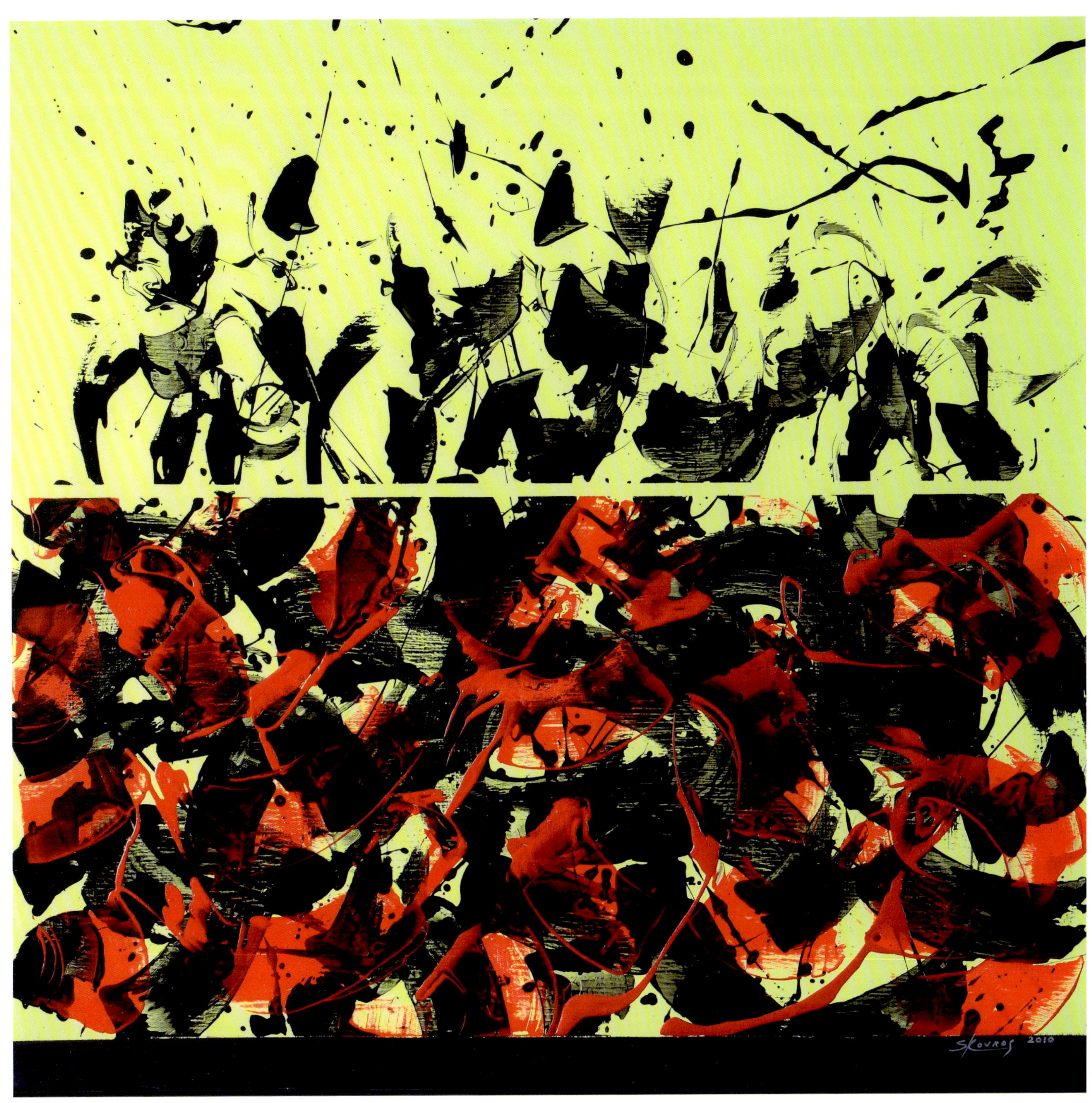
SKouros 2010

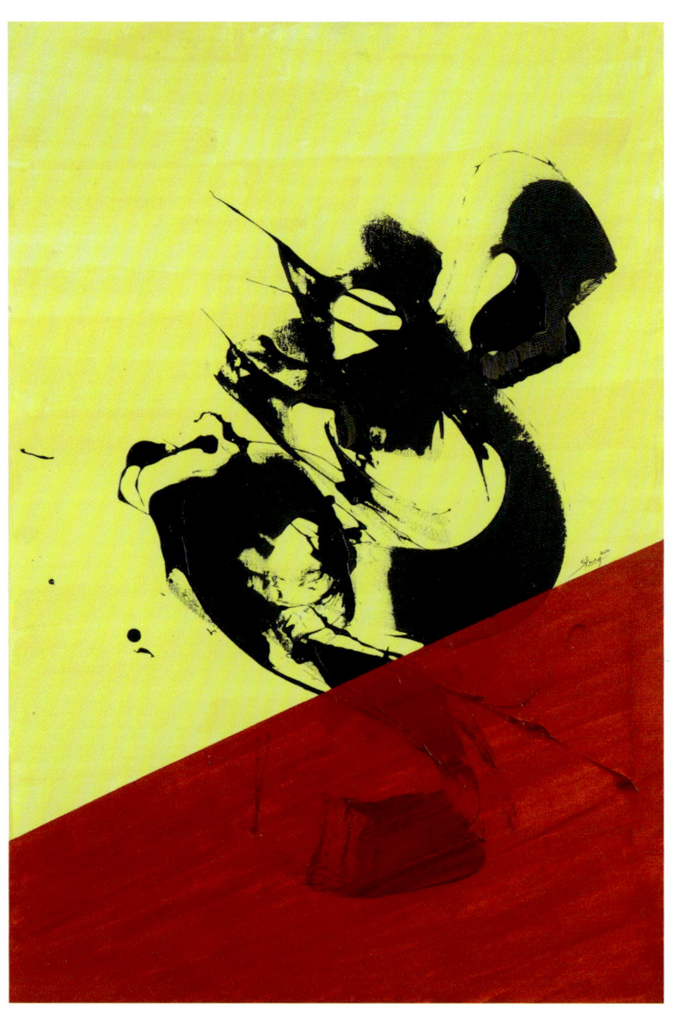

2010, acrylic on canvas,
120 x 80 cm

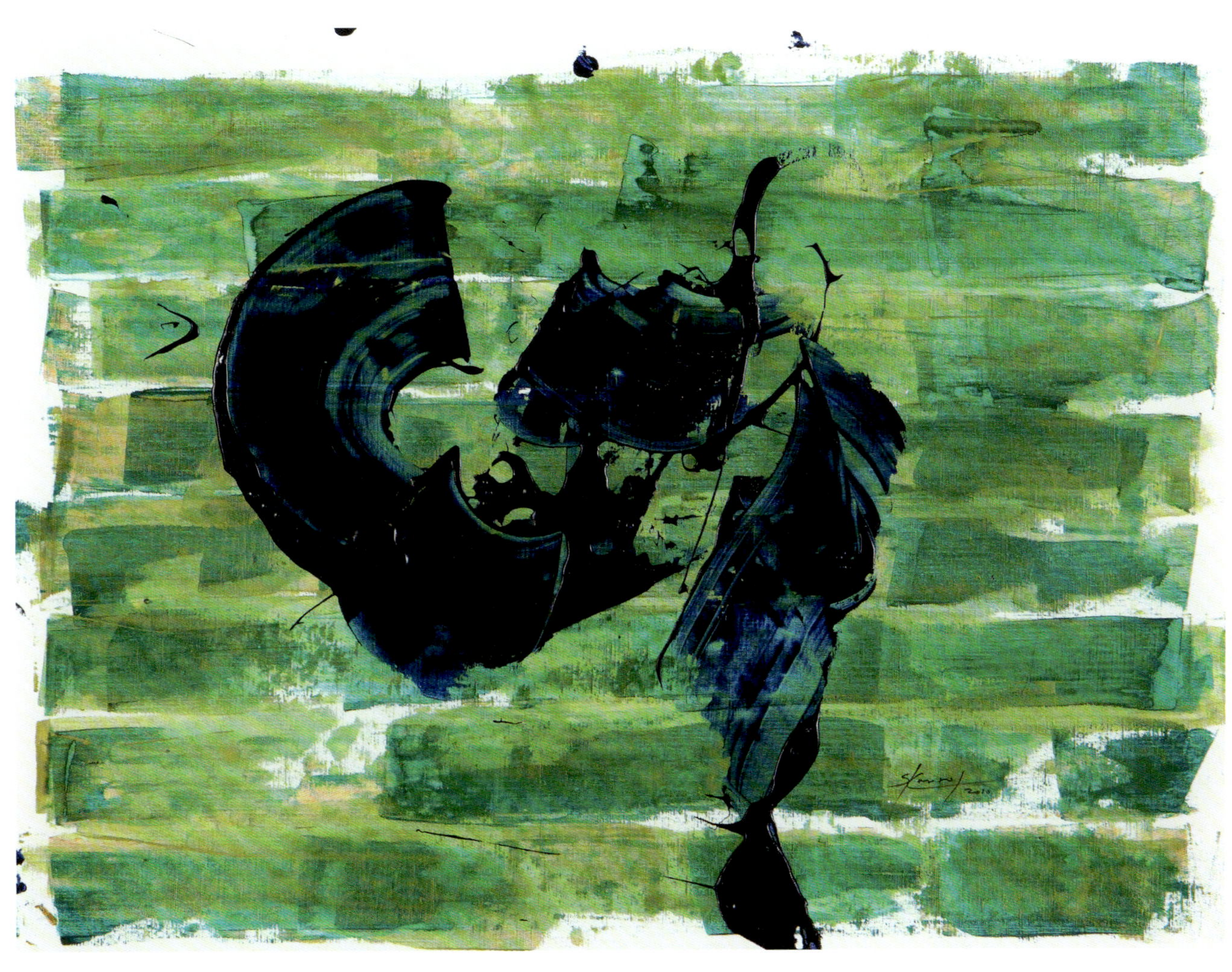

2010, acrylic on canvas,
50 x 70 cm

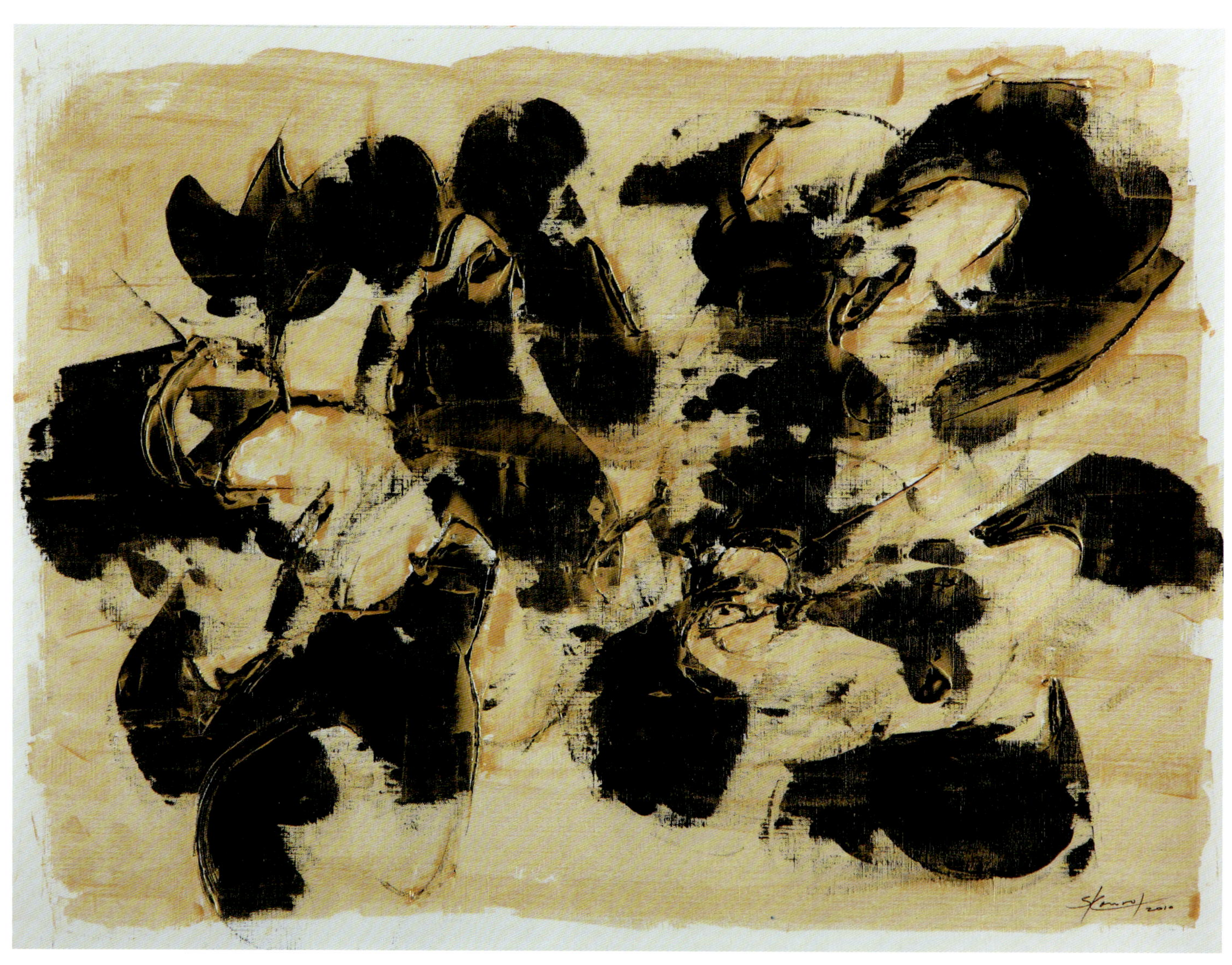

2010, acrylic on canvas,
50x70cm

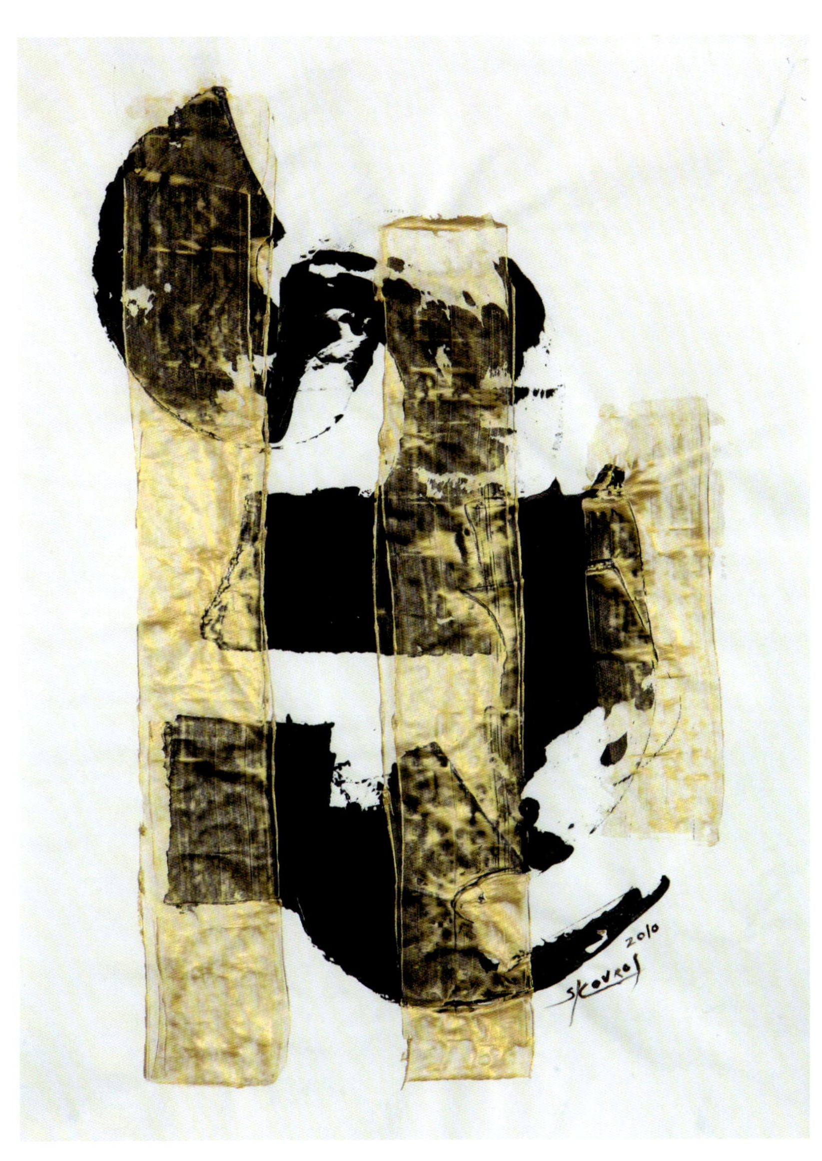

2010, acrylic and crydon on paper,
70 x 50 cm

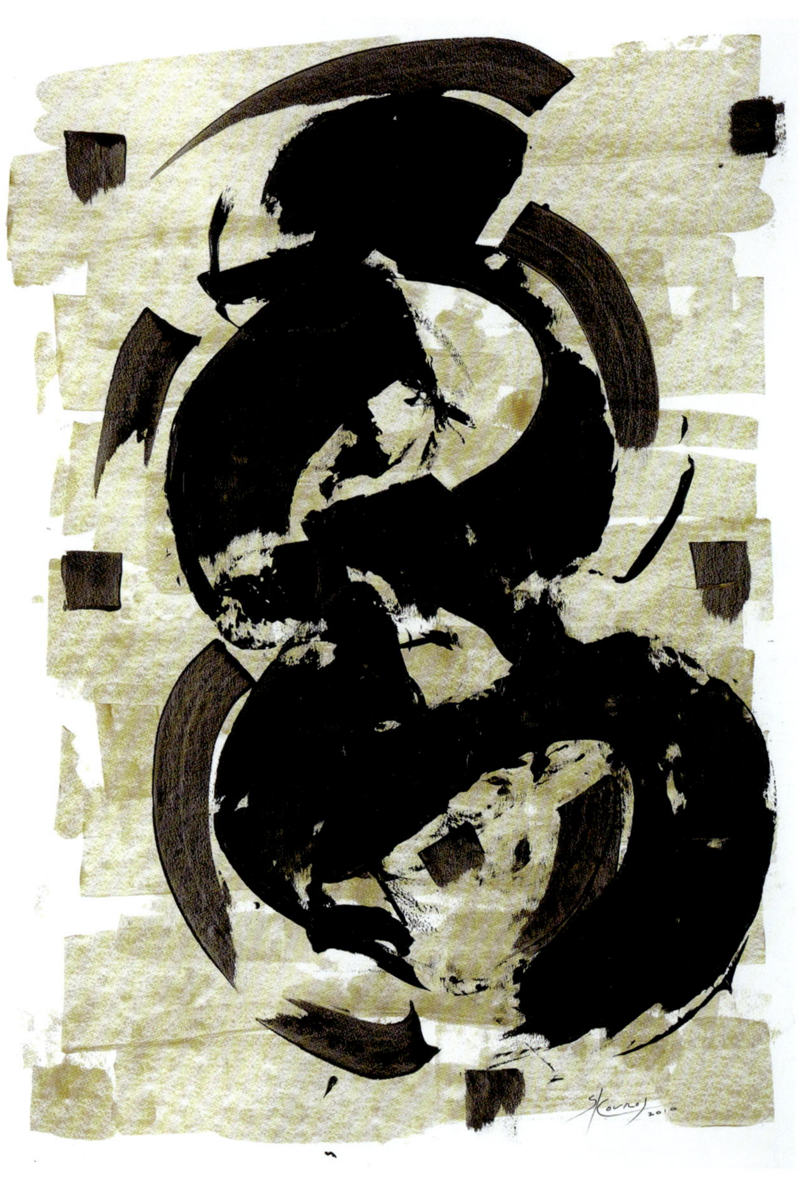

2010, acrylic on cardboard,
100 x 70 cm

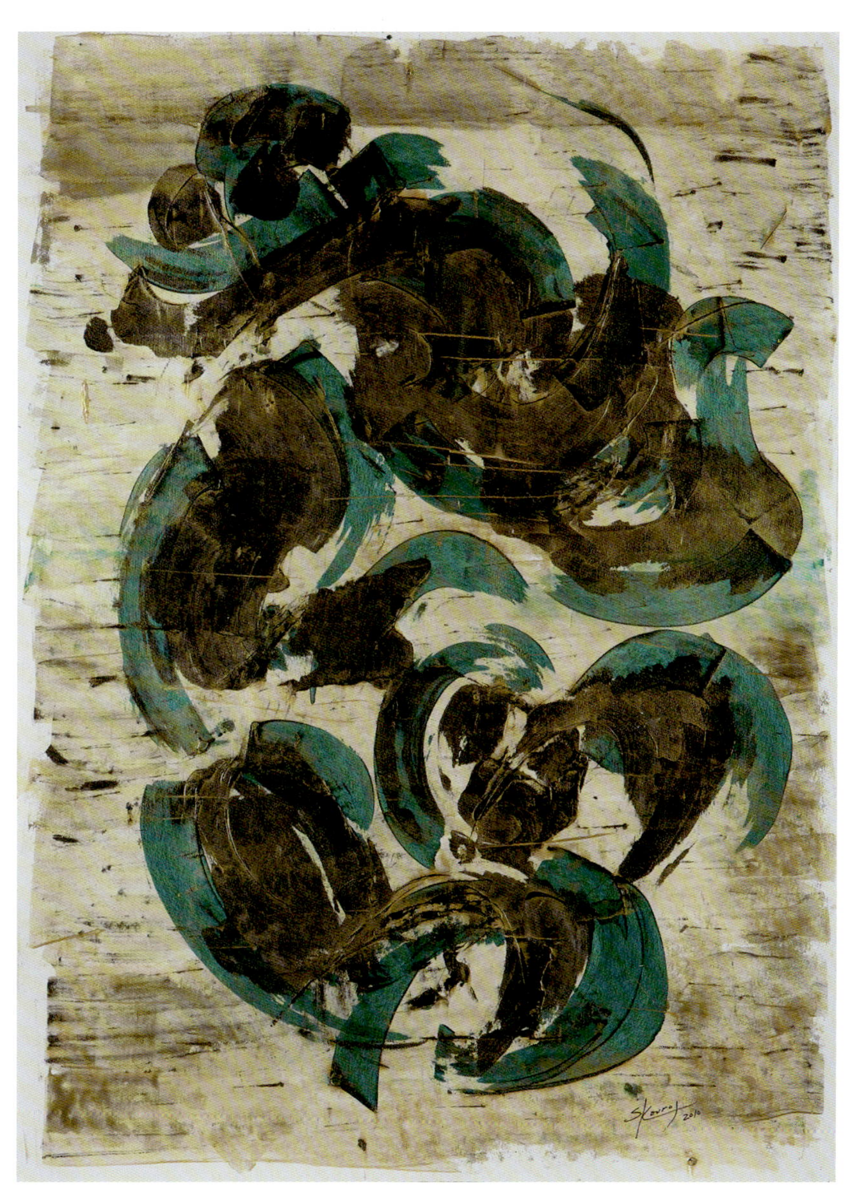

2010, acrylic on paper,
100 x 70 cm

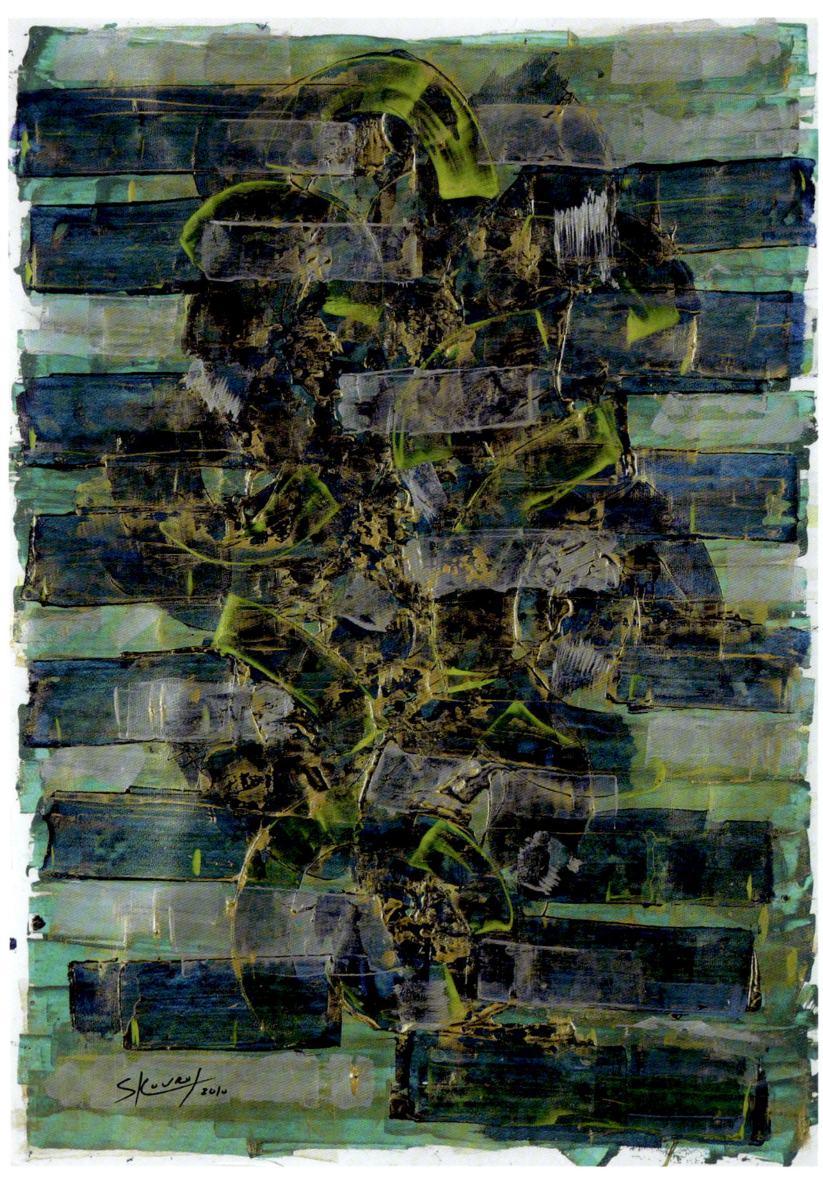

2010, acrylic on cardboard,
100 x 70 cm

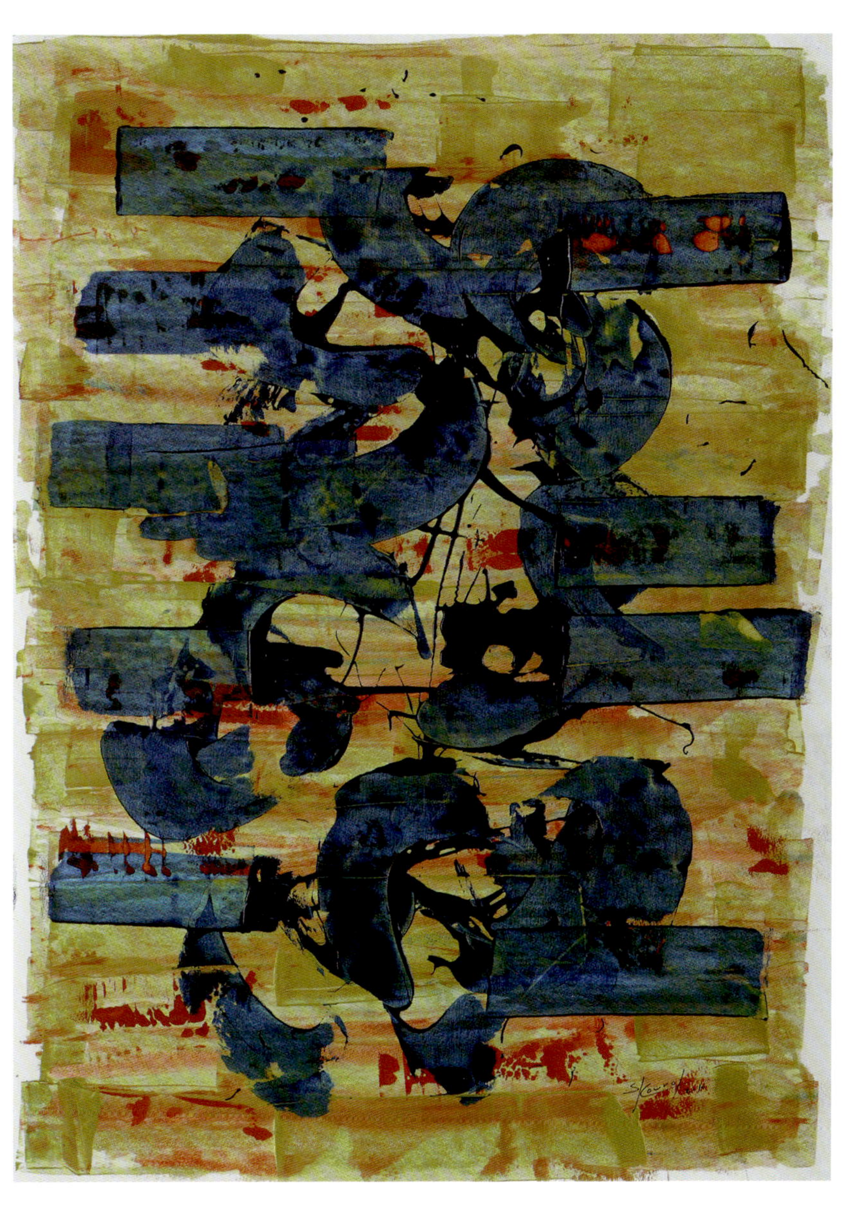

2010, acrylic on cardboard,
100 x 70 cm

2010, acrylic on cardboard,
100 x 70 cm

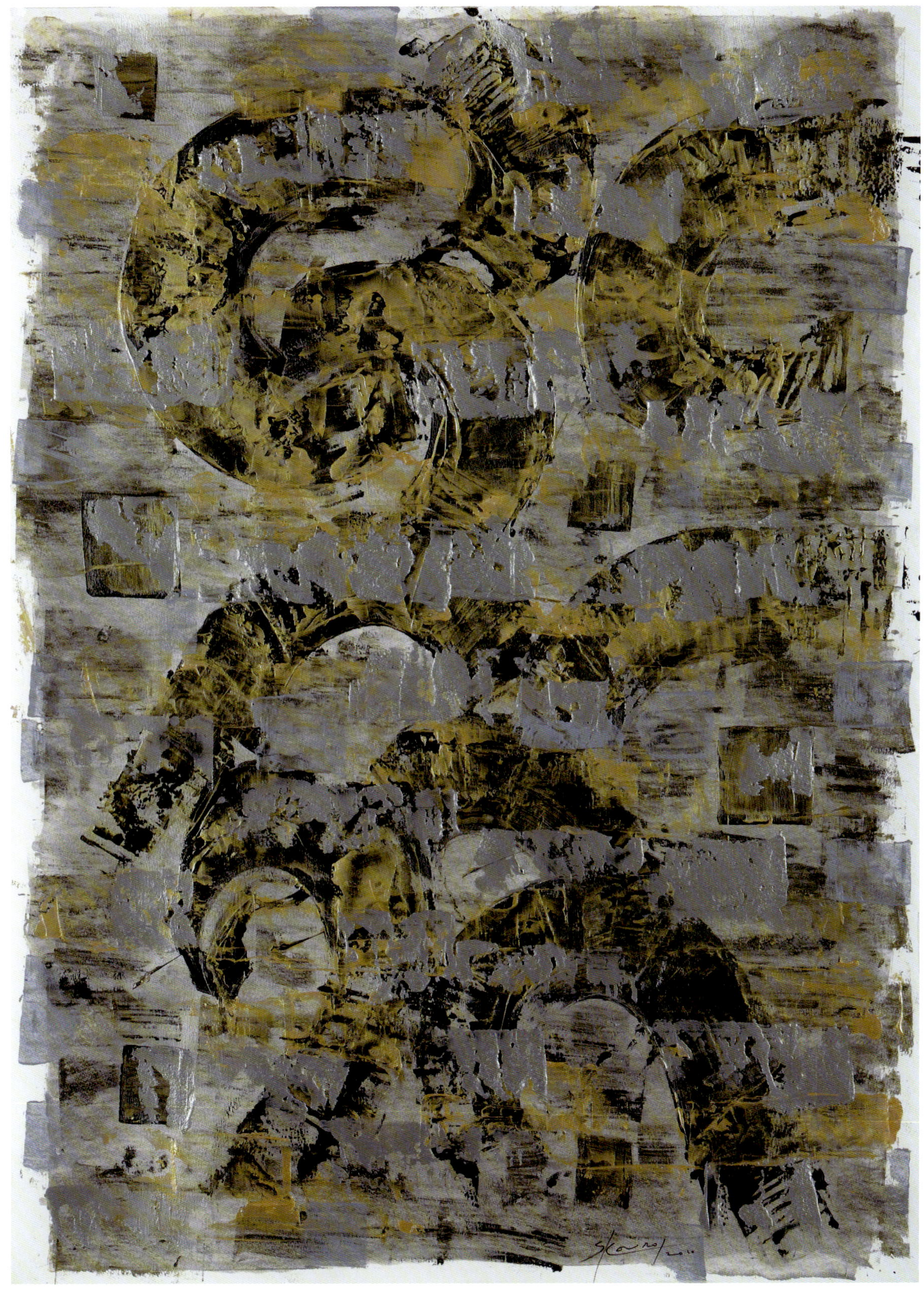

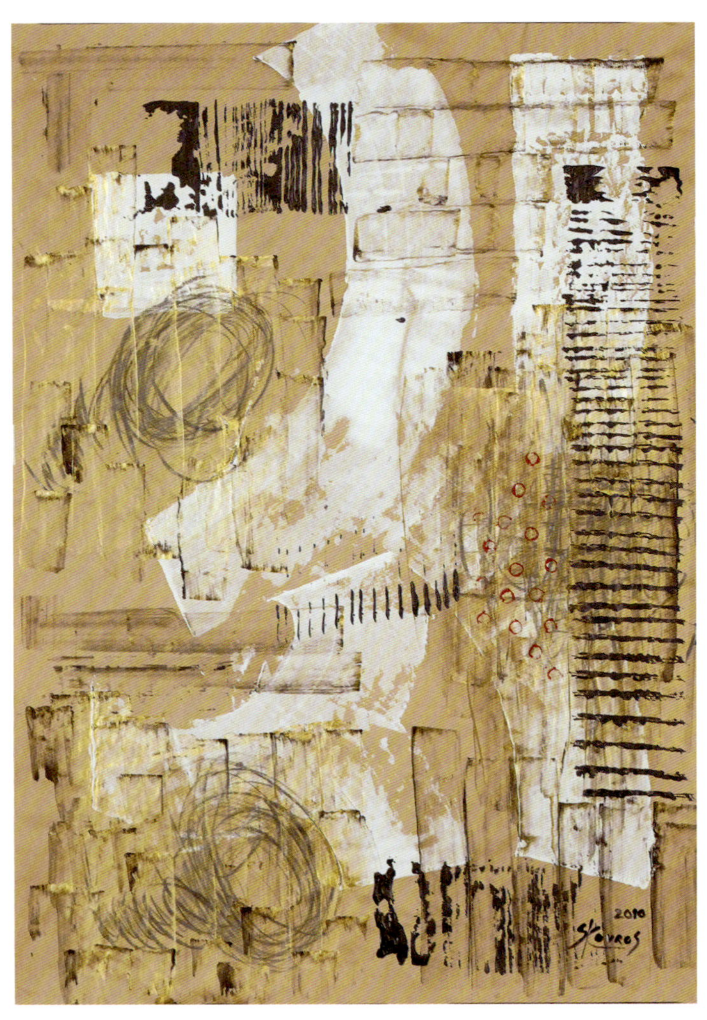

2010, acrylic and crydon on paper,
100 x 70 cm

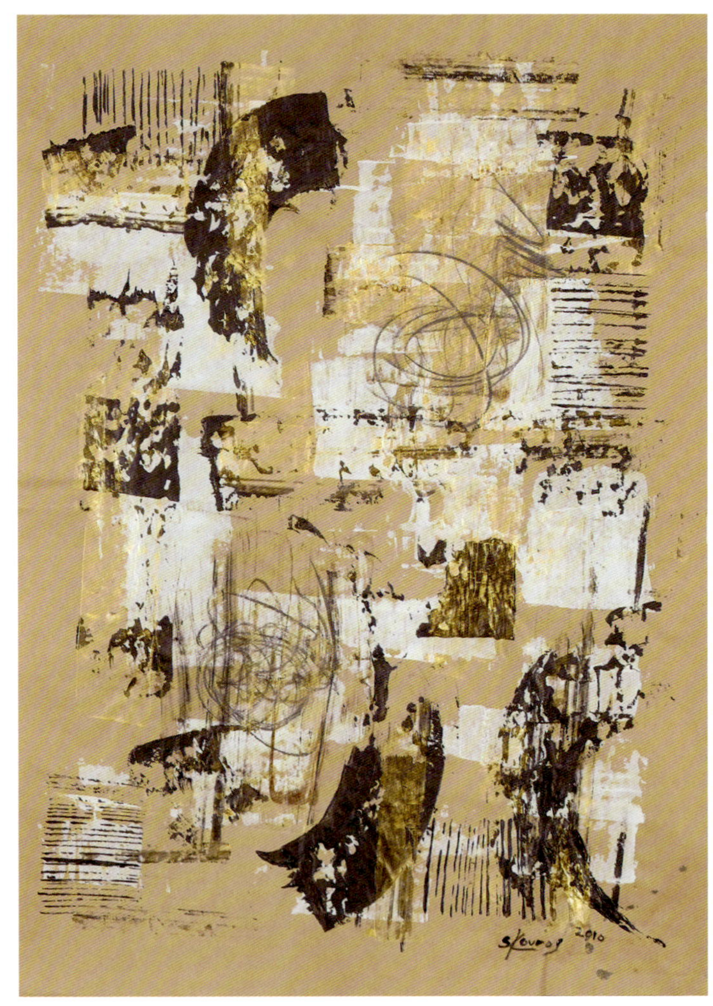

2010, acrylic and crydon on paper,
100 x 70 cm

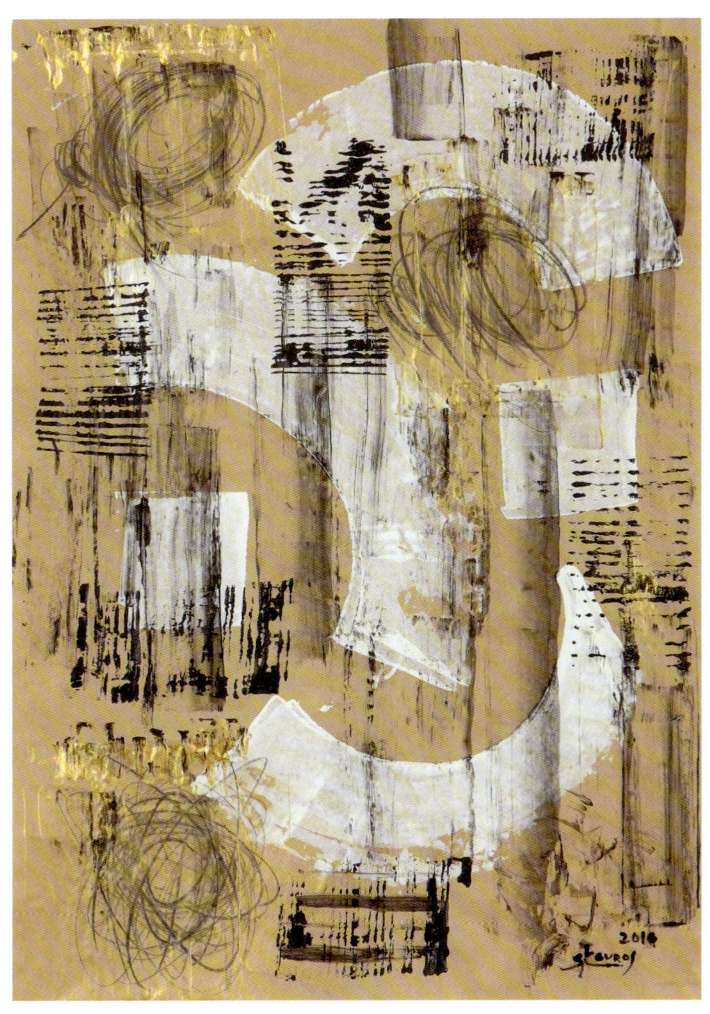

2010, acrylic and crydon on paper,
100 x 70 cm

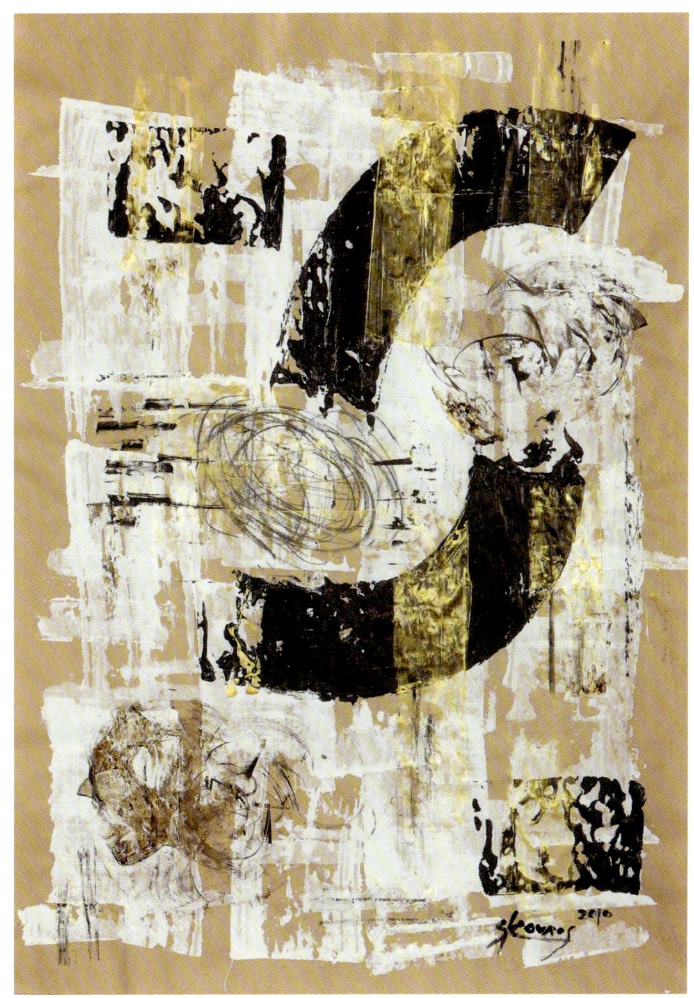

2010, acrylic and crydon on paper,
100 x 70 cm

2011, acrylic on cardboard,
50 x 70 cm

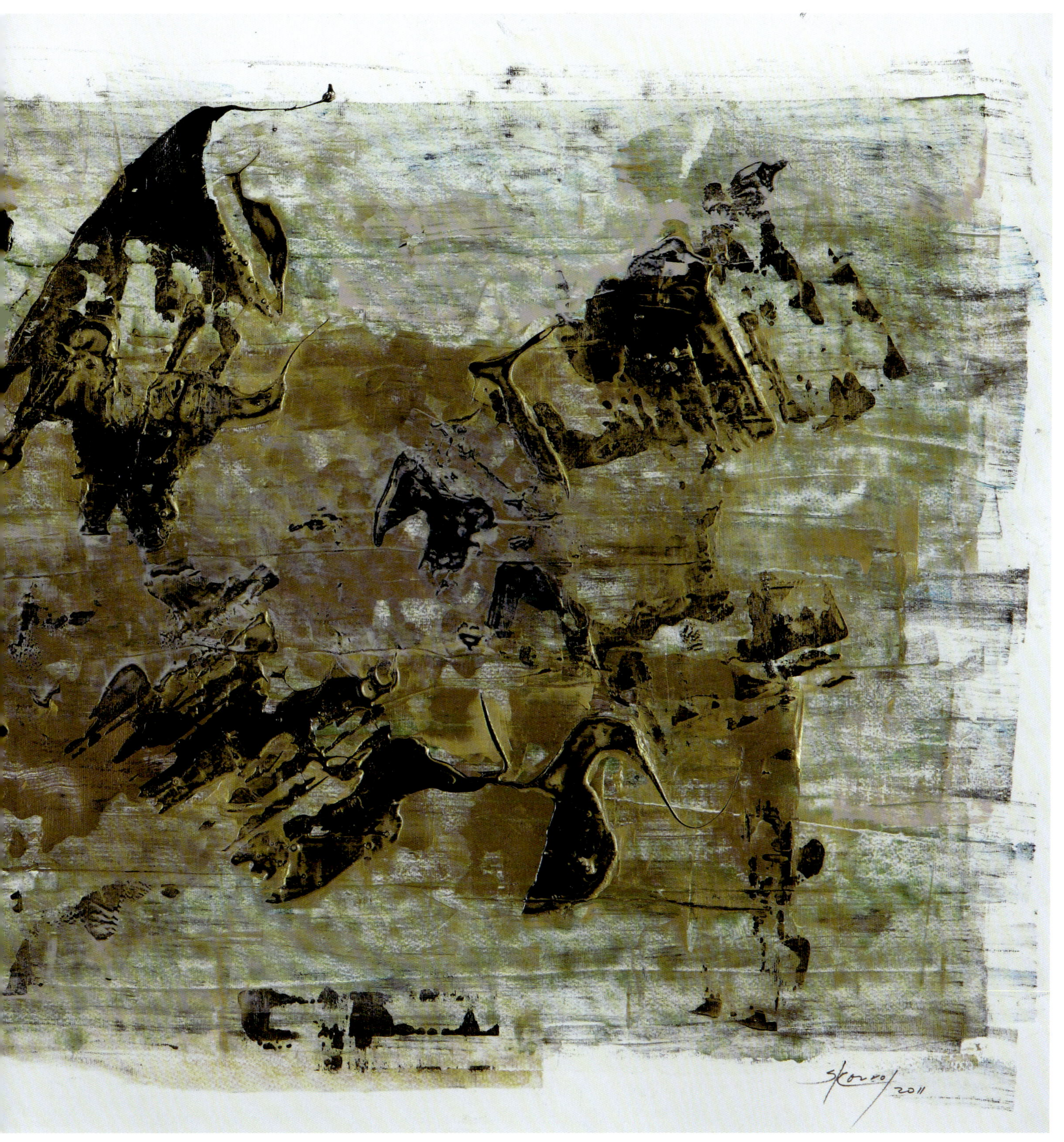

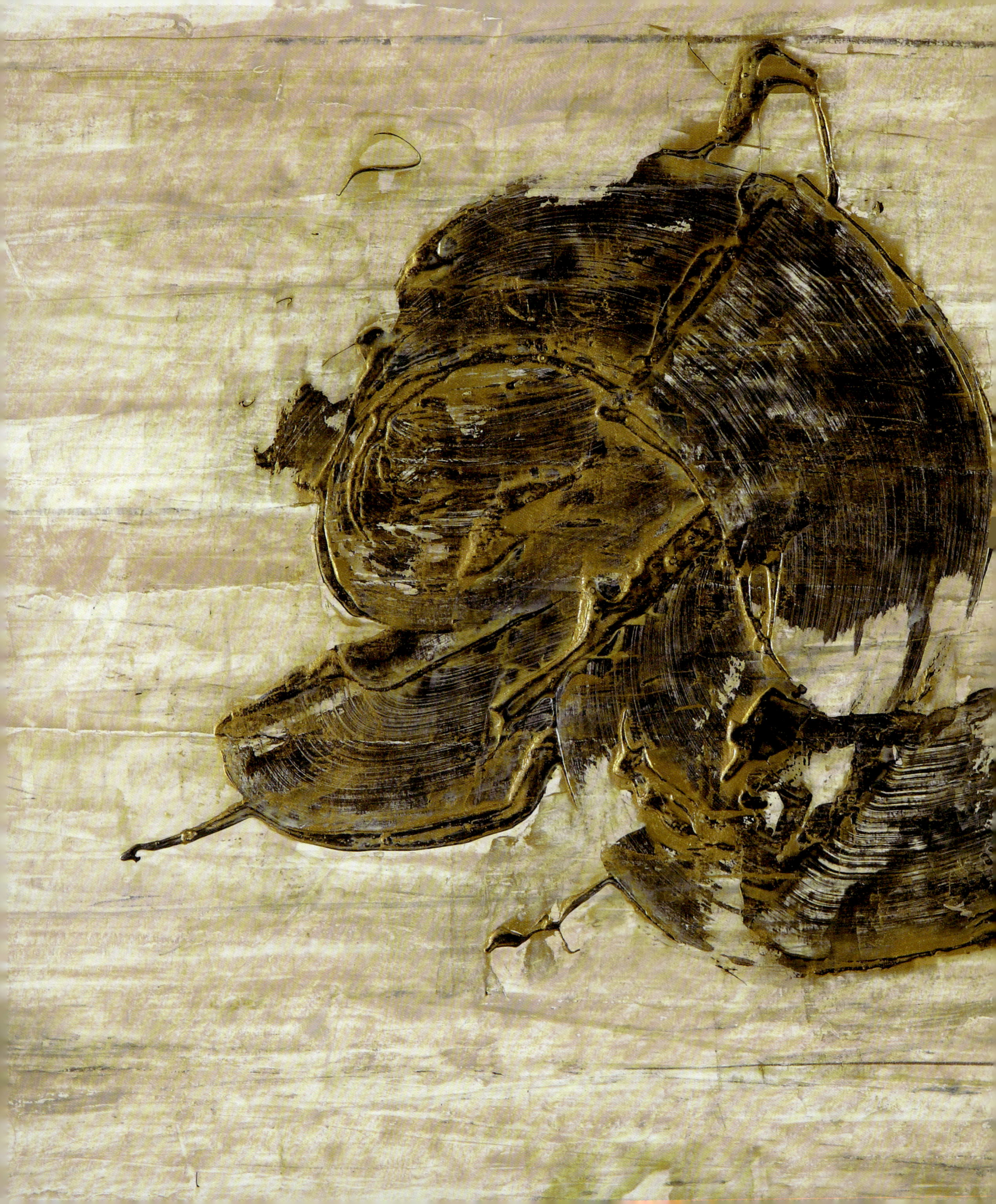

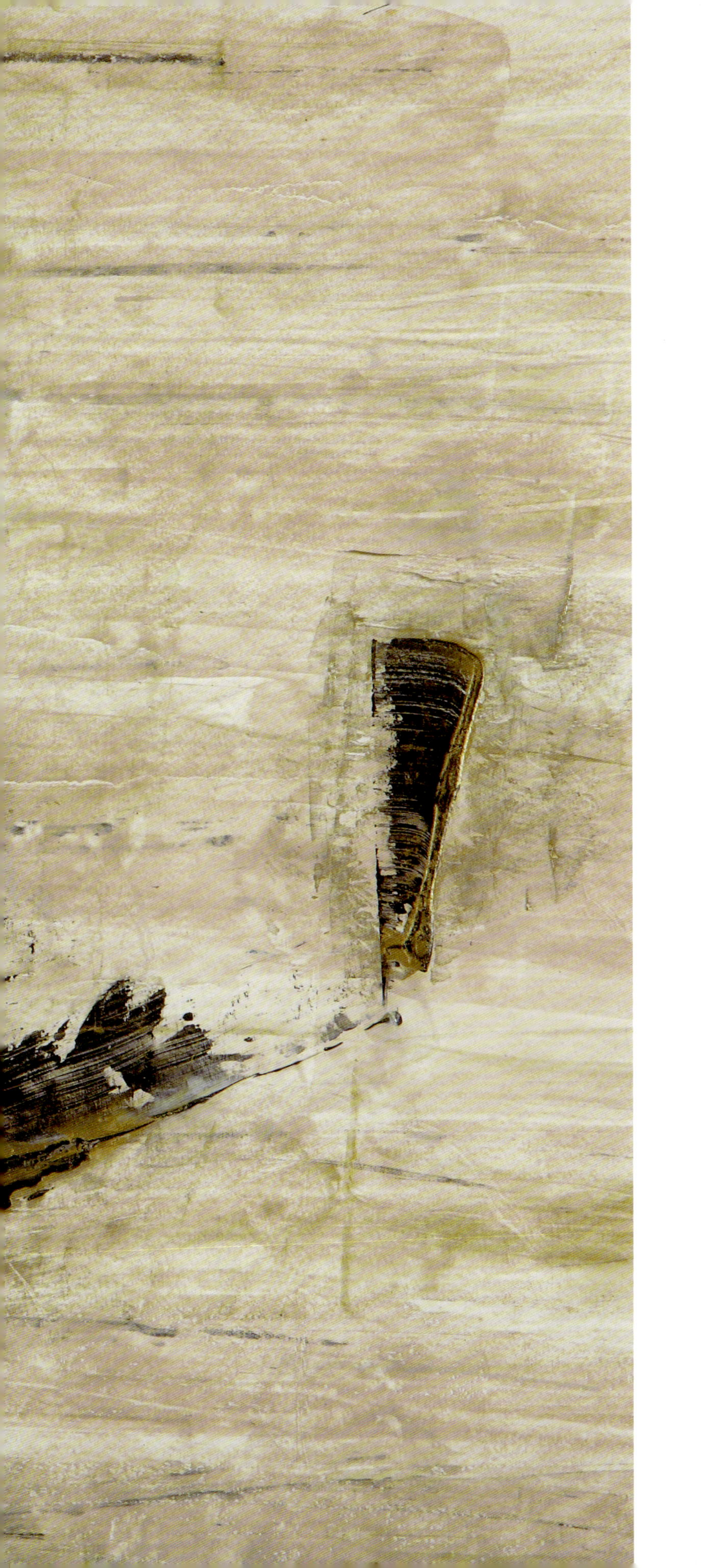

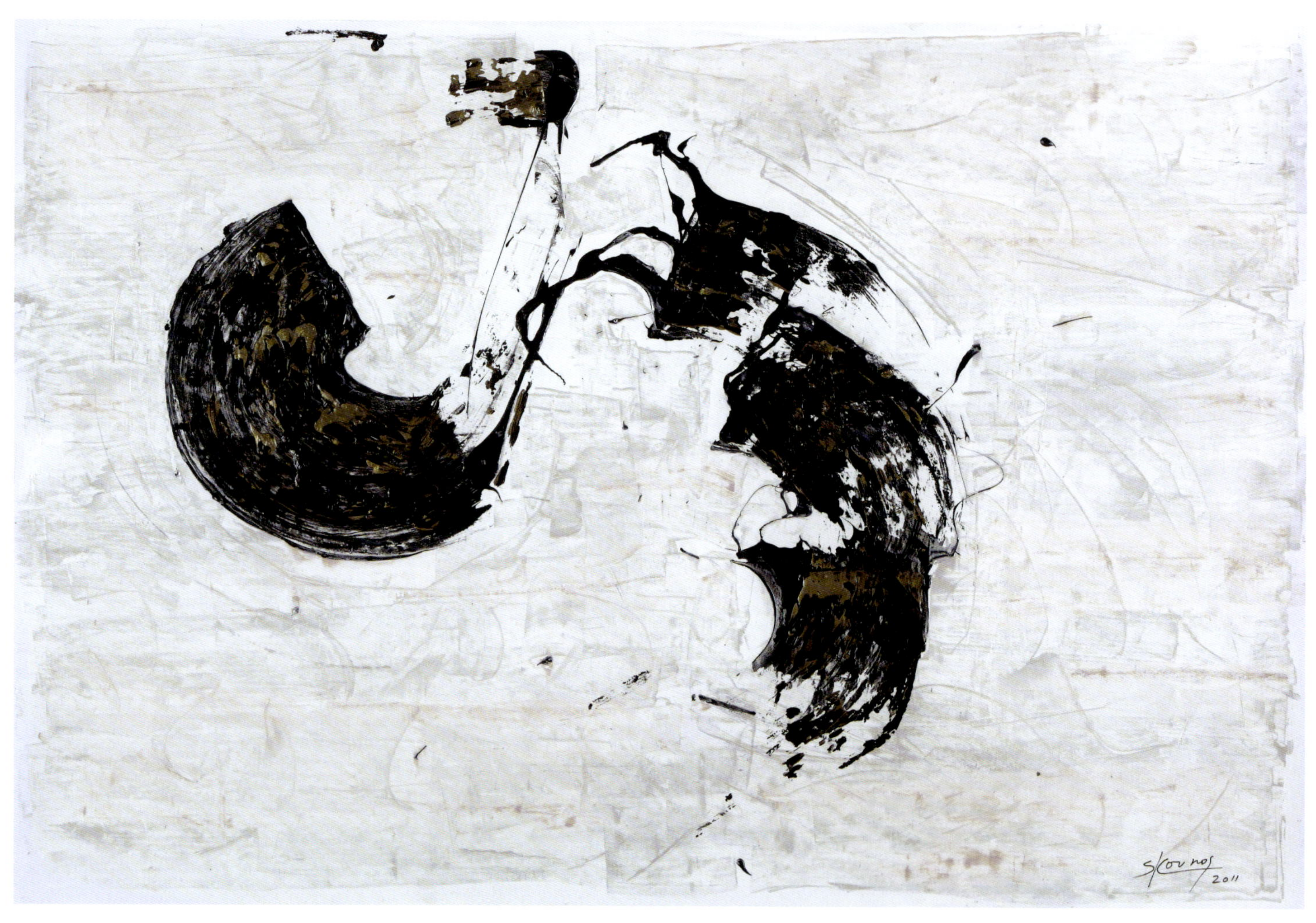

2011, acrylic on cardboard,
70 x 100 cm

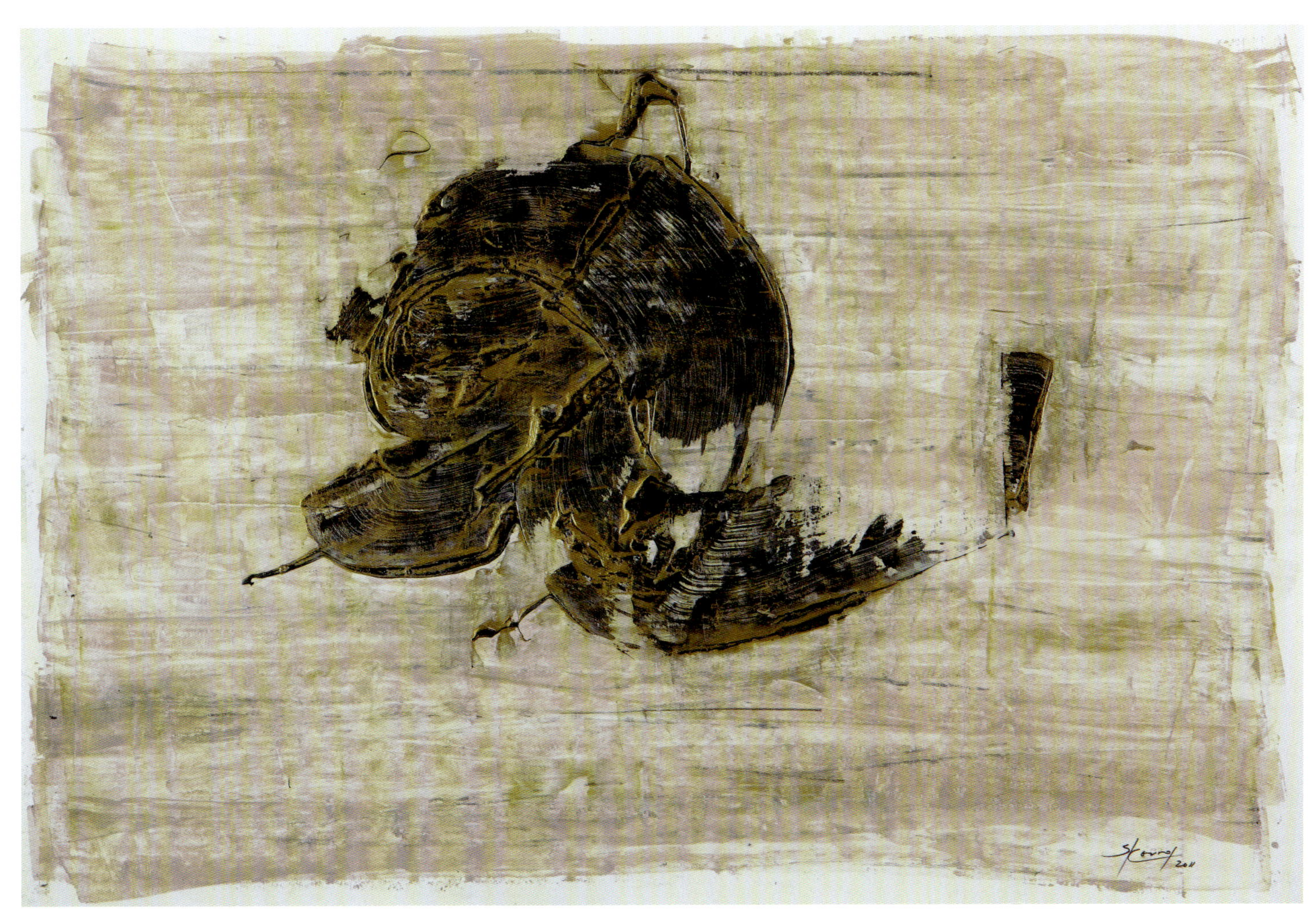

2011, acrylic on cardboard,
50 x 70 cm

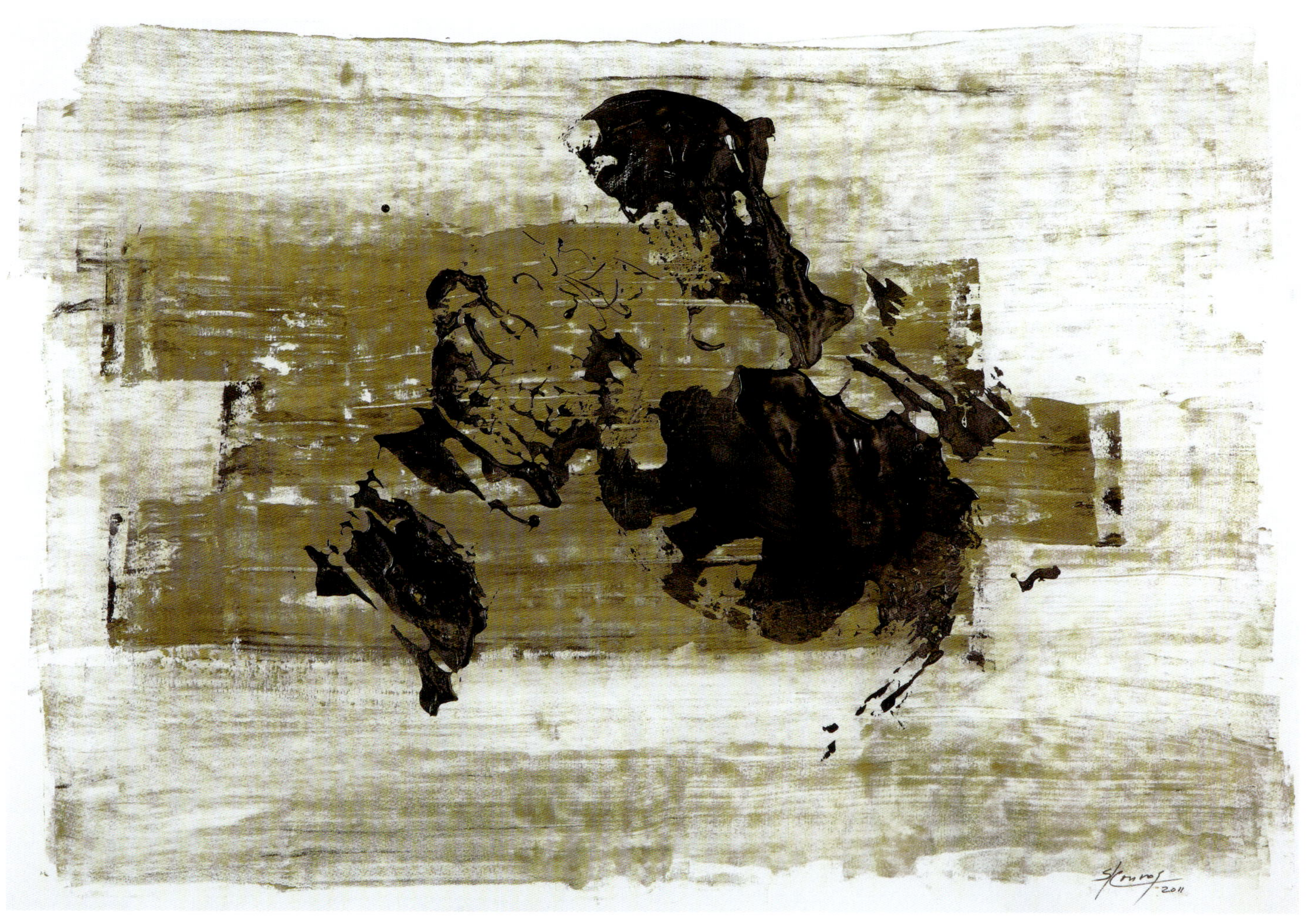

2011, acrylic on cardboard,
50 x 70 cm

2011, acrylic on cardboard,
50 x 70 cm

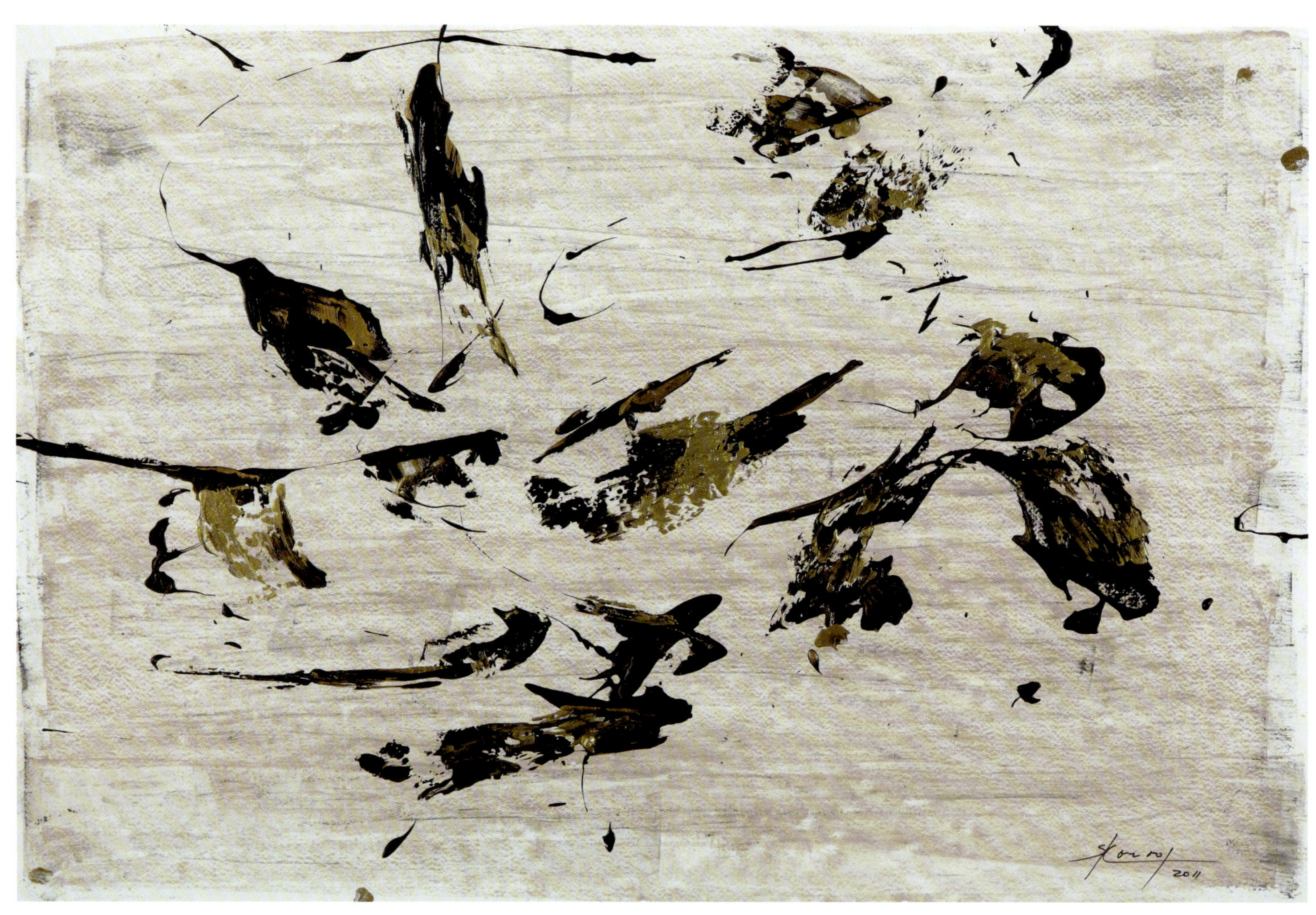

2011, acrylic on cardboard,
50 x 70 cm

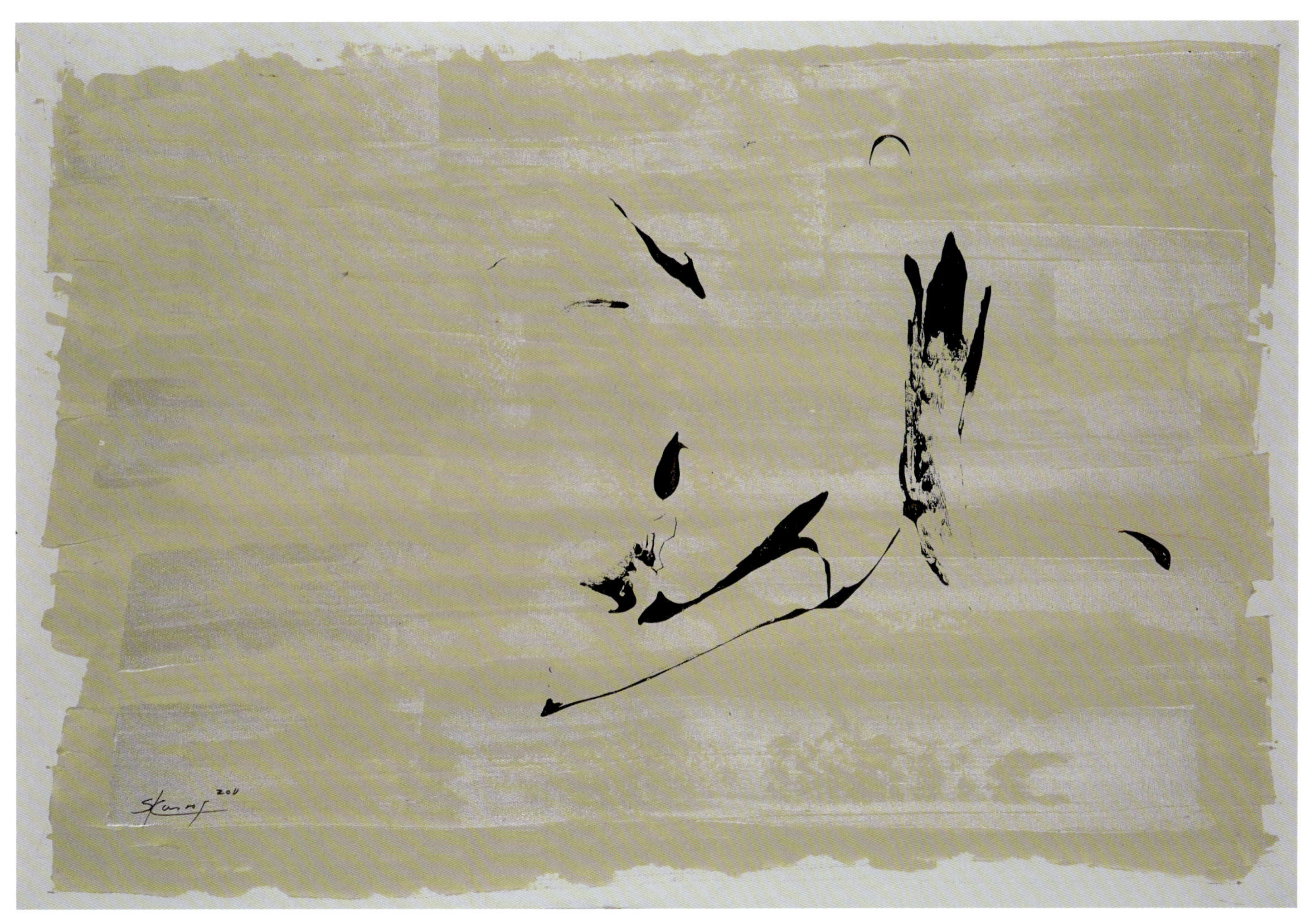

2011, acrylic on canvas,
70 x 100 cm

2011, mixed media on canvas,
120 x 120 cm

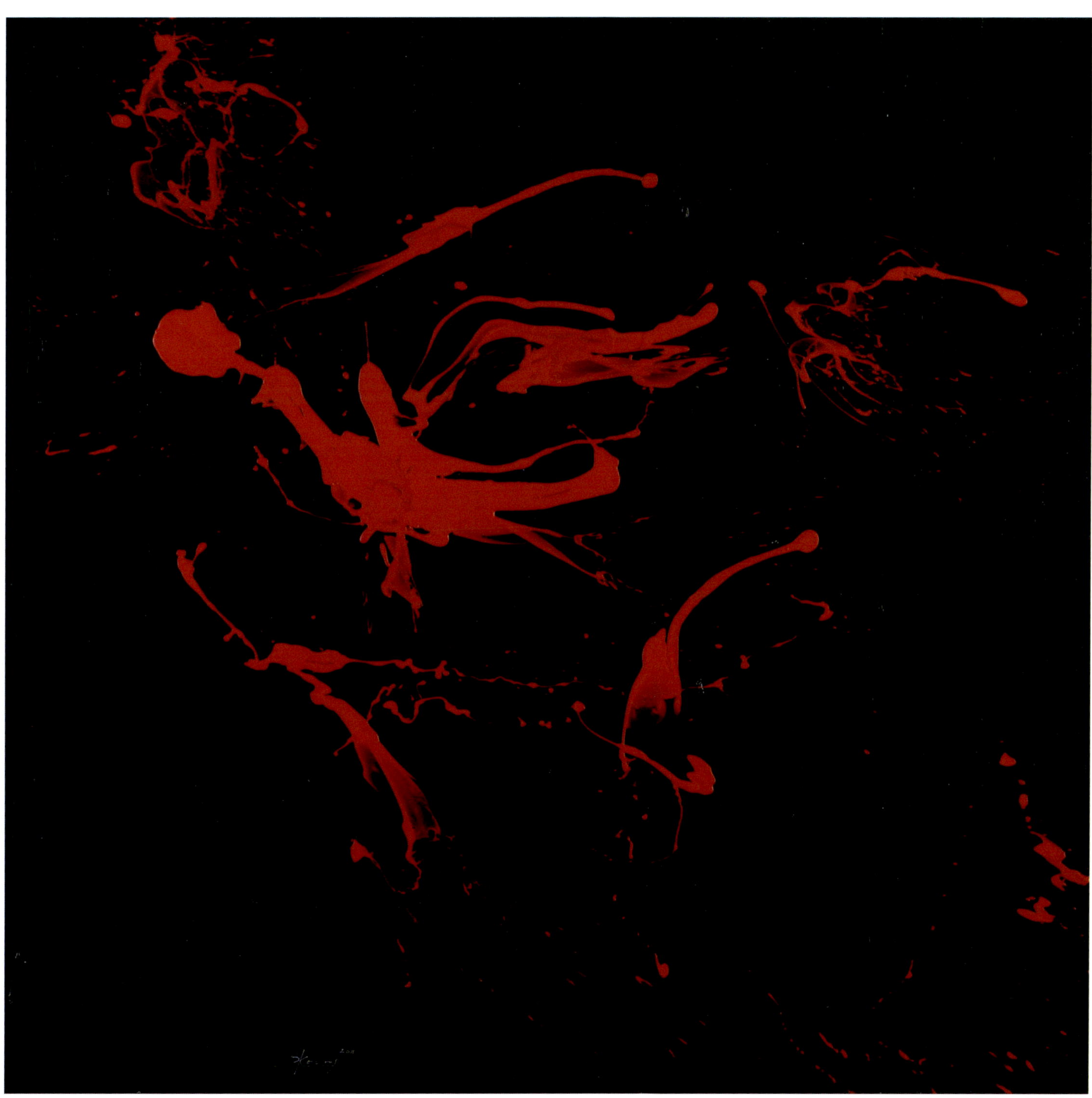

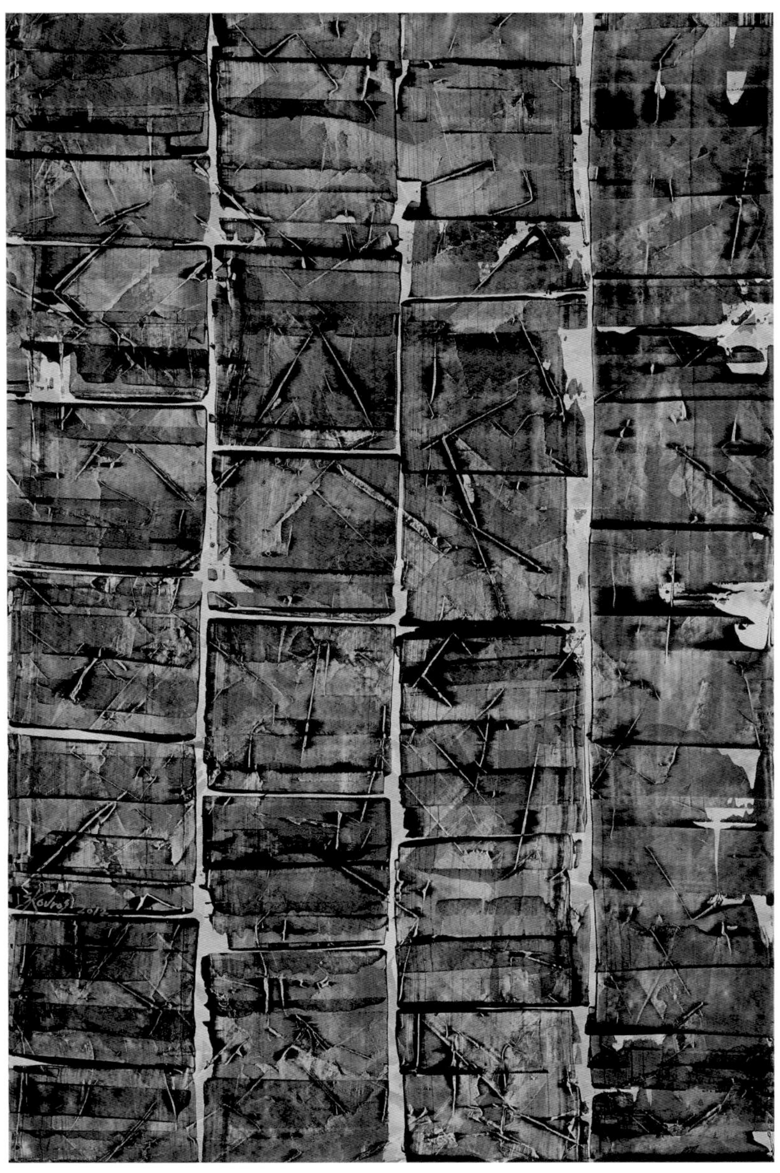

2011, acrylic on cardboard,
120 x 80 cm

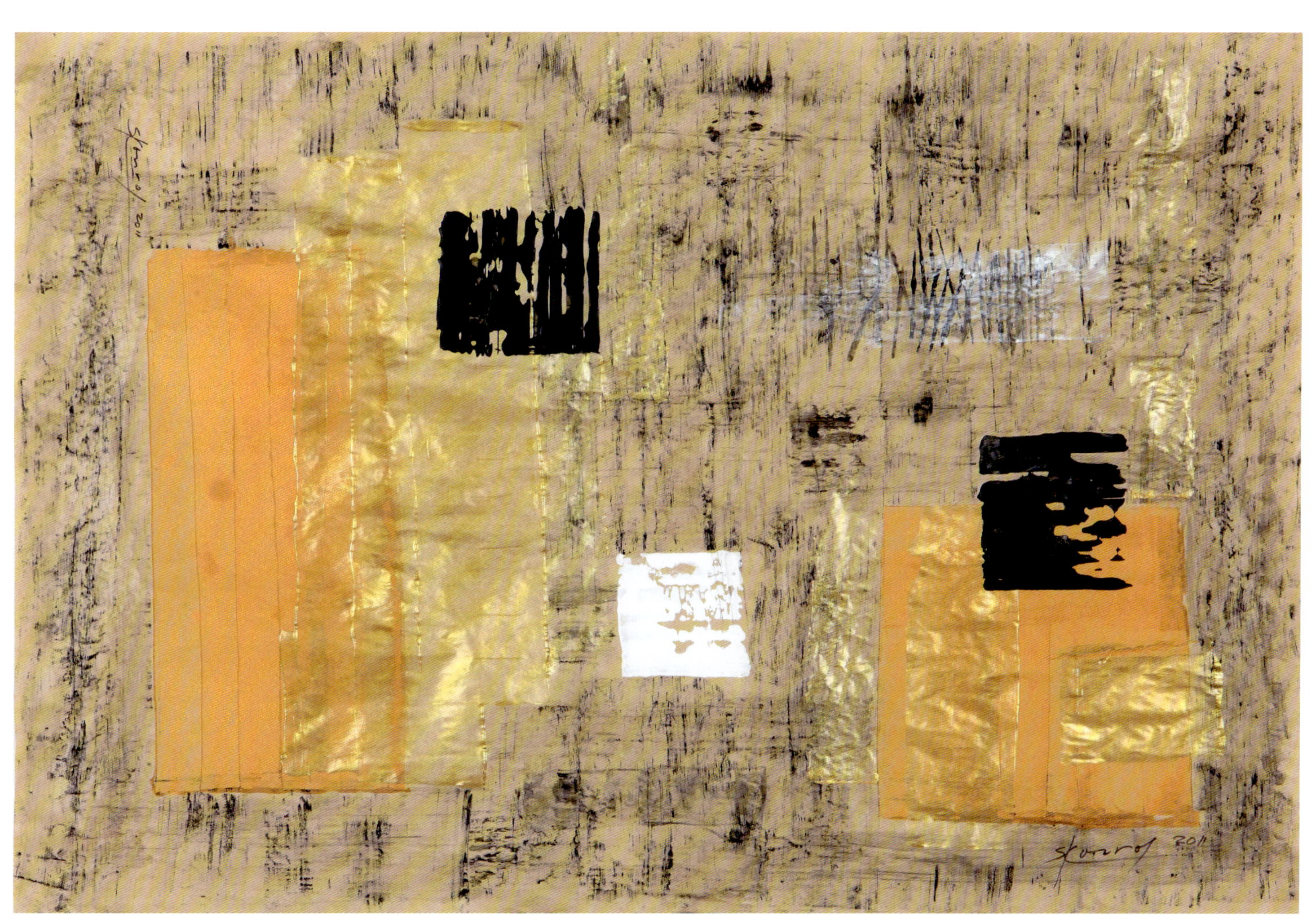

2011, acrylic on paper,
70 x 100 cm

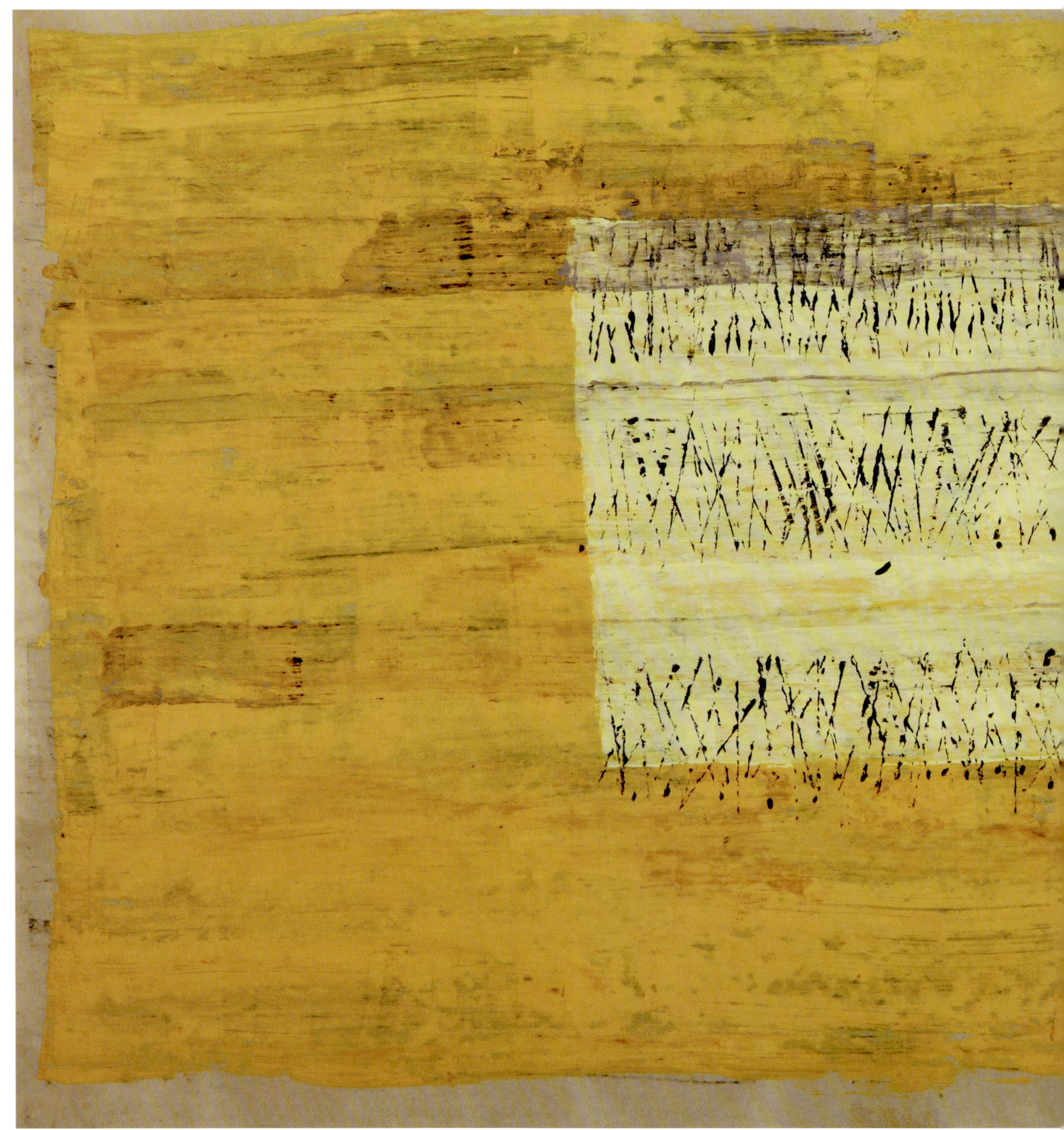

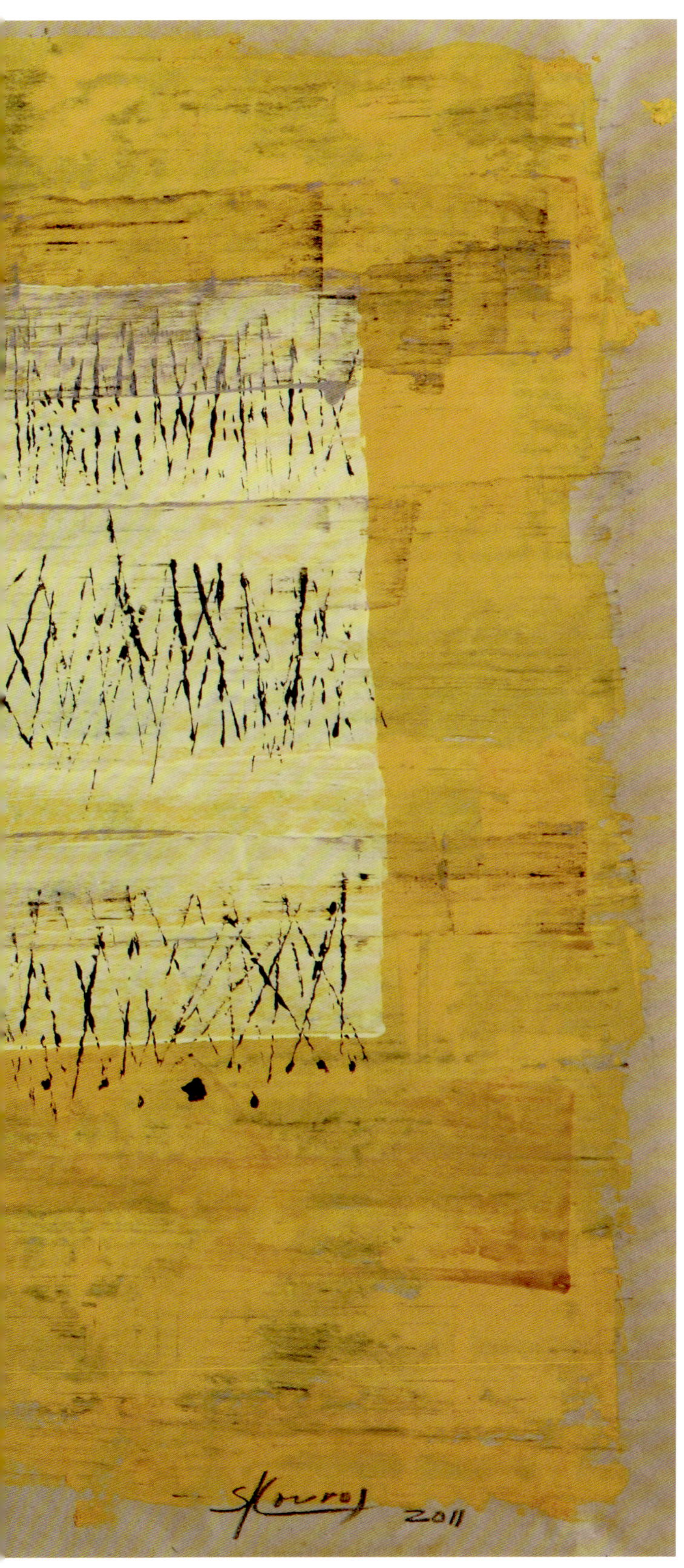

2011, acrylic on paper,
70 x 100 cm

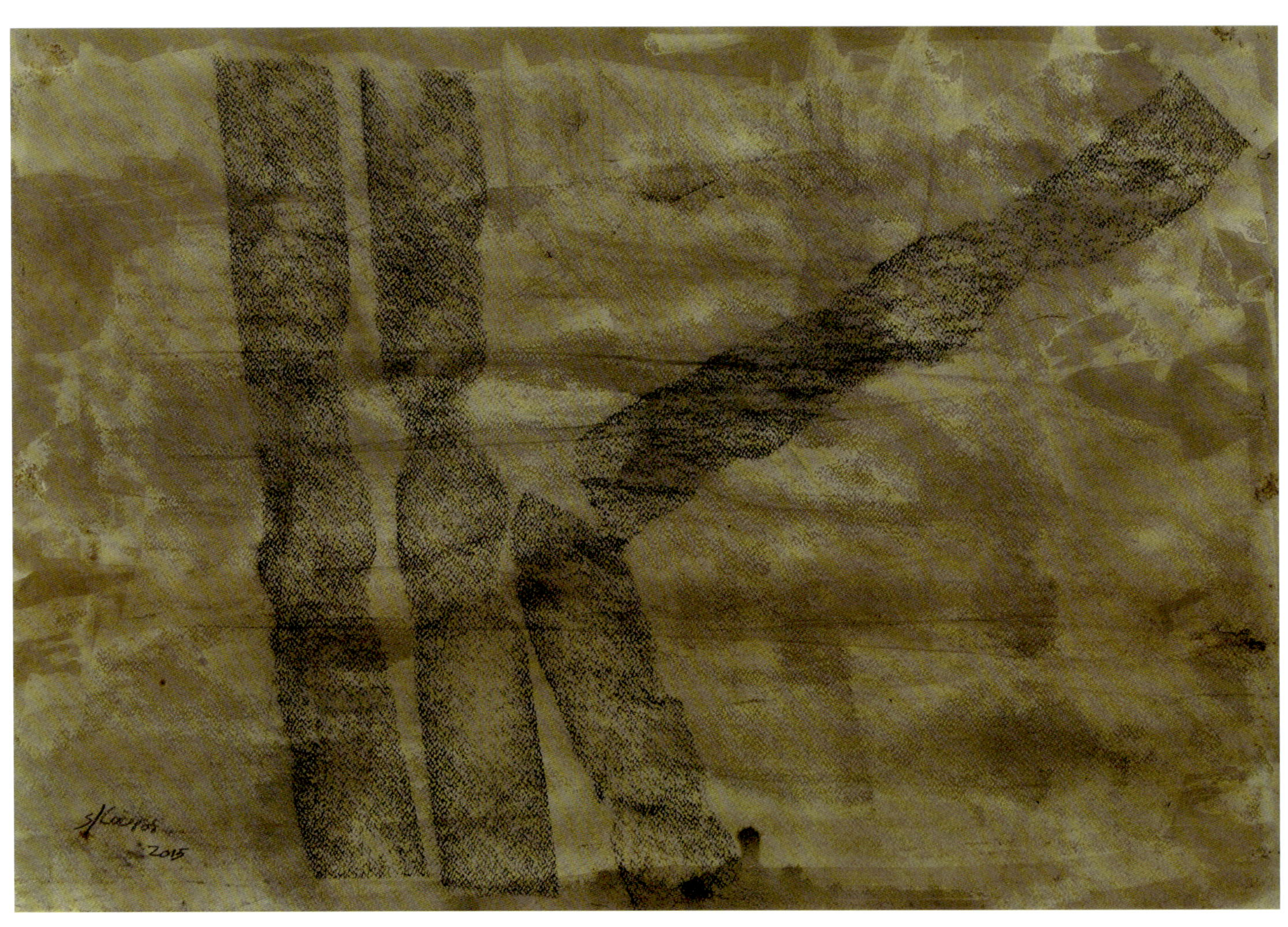

2015, charcoal,
acrylic and graphite on paper,
50 x 70 cm

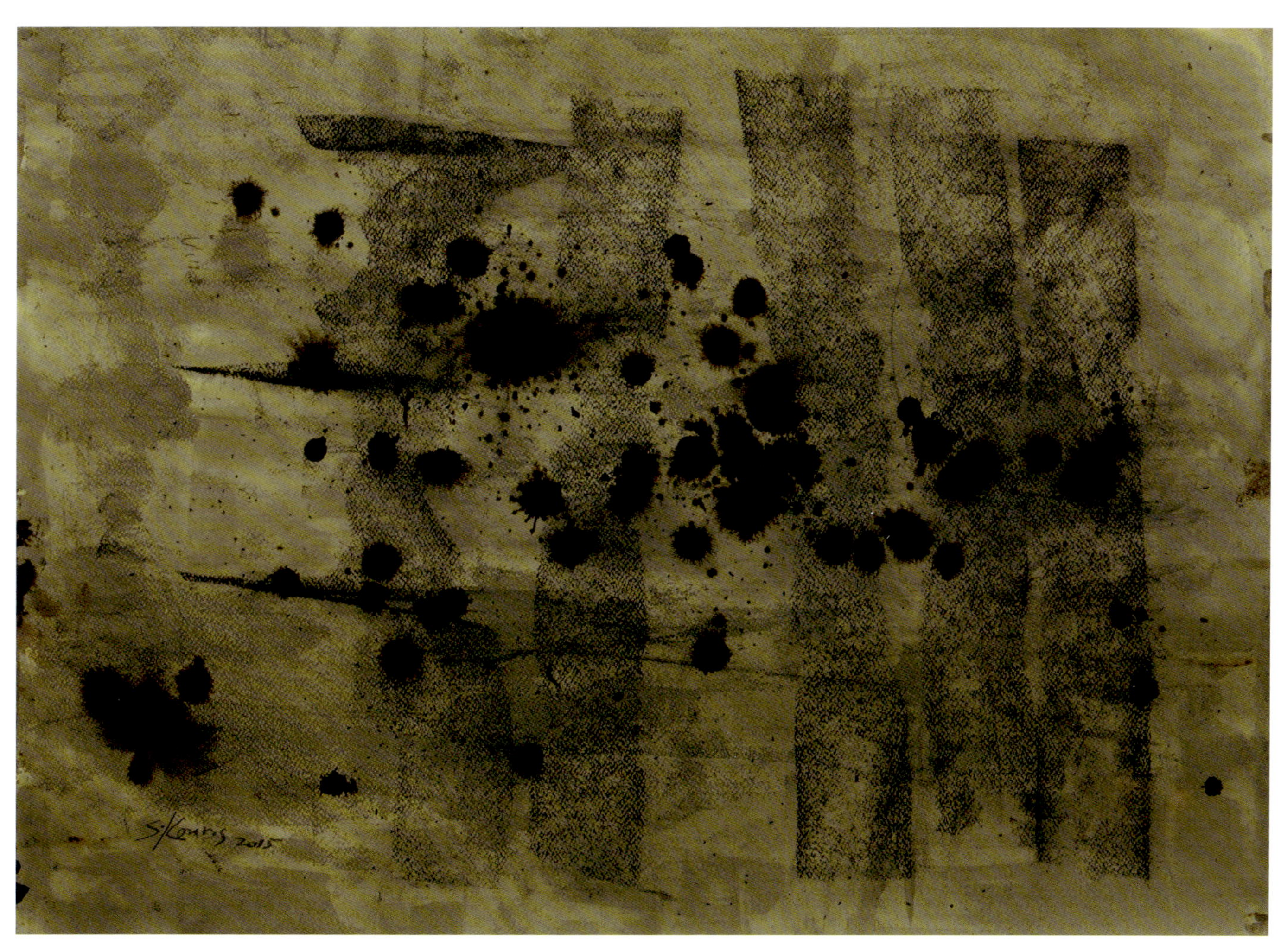

2015, charcoal,
acrylic and graphite on paper,
50 x 70 cm

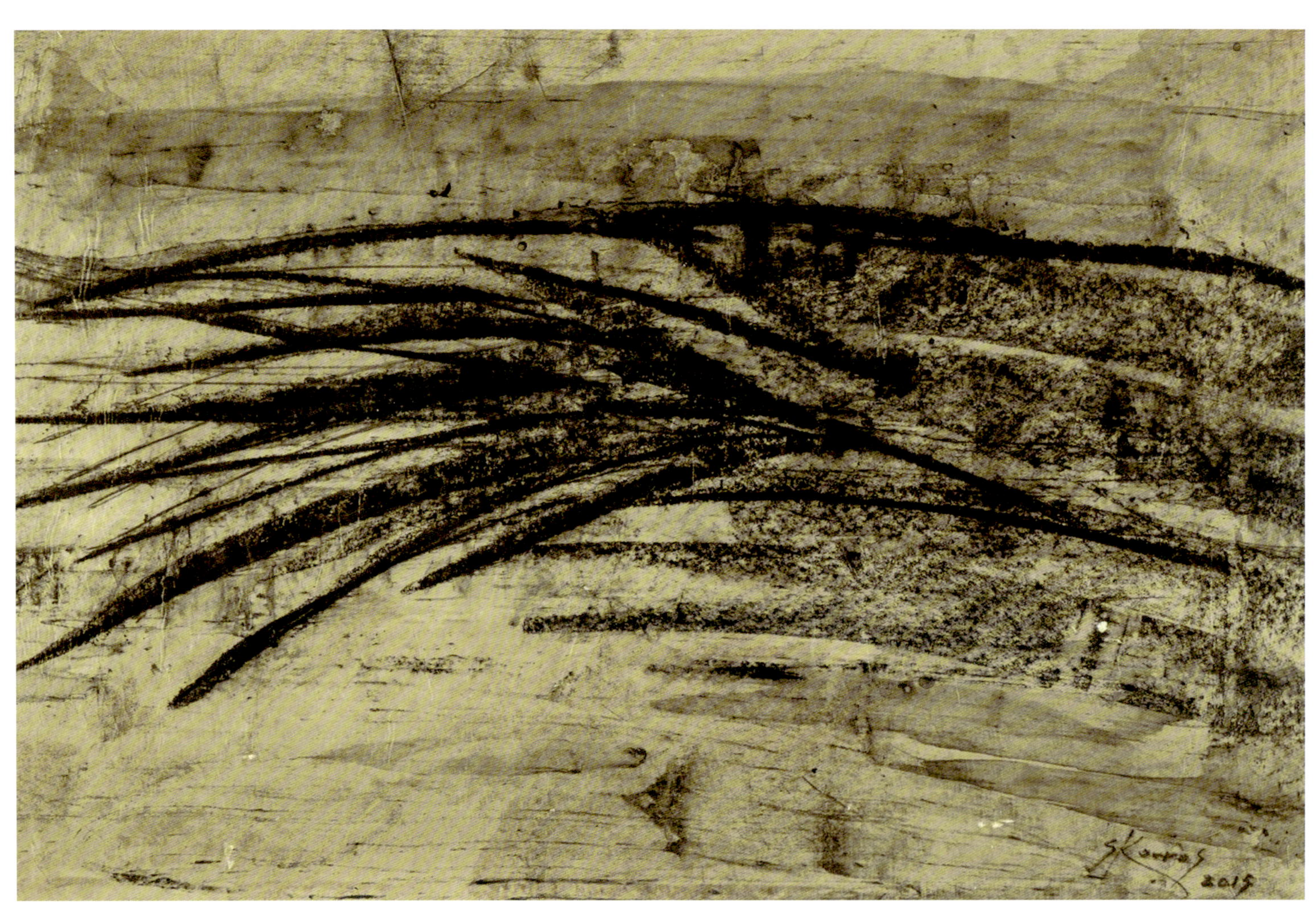

2015, charcoal,
acrylic and graphite on paper,
50 x 70 cm

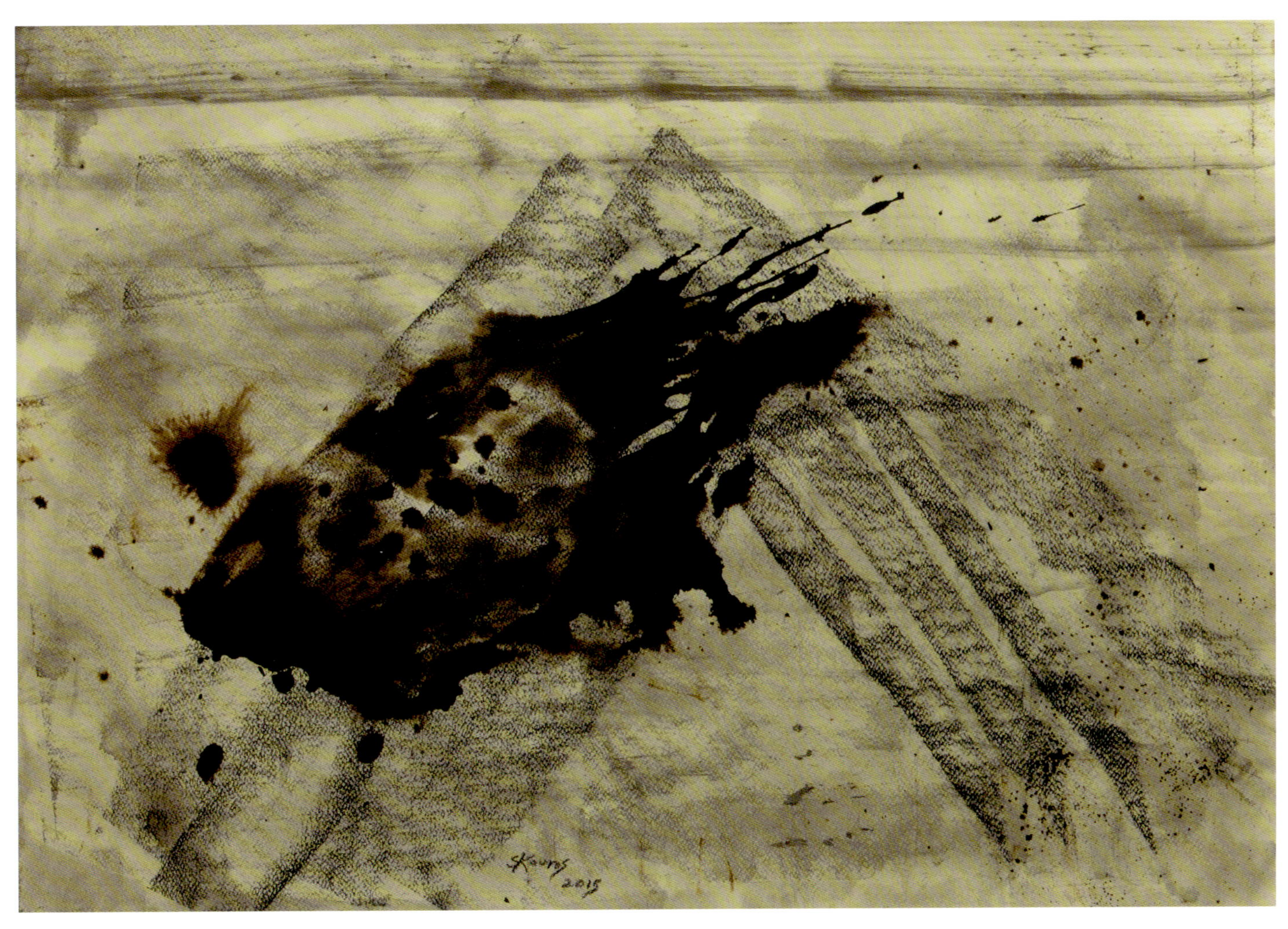

2015, charcoal,
acrylic and graphite on paper,
50 x 70 cm

2015, charcoal,
acrylic and graphite on paper,
50 x 70 cm

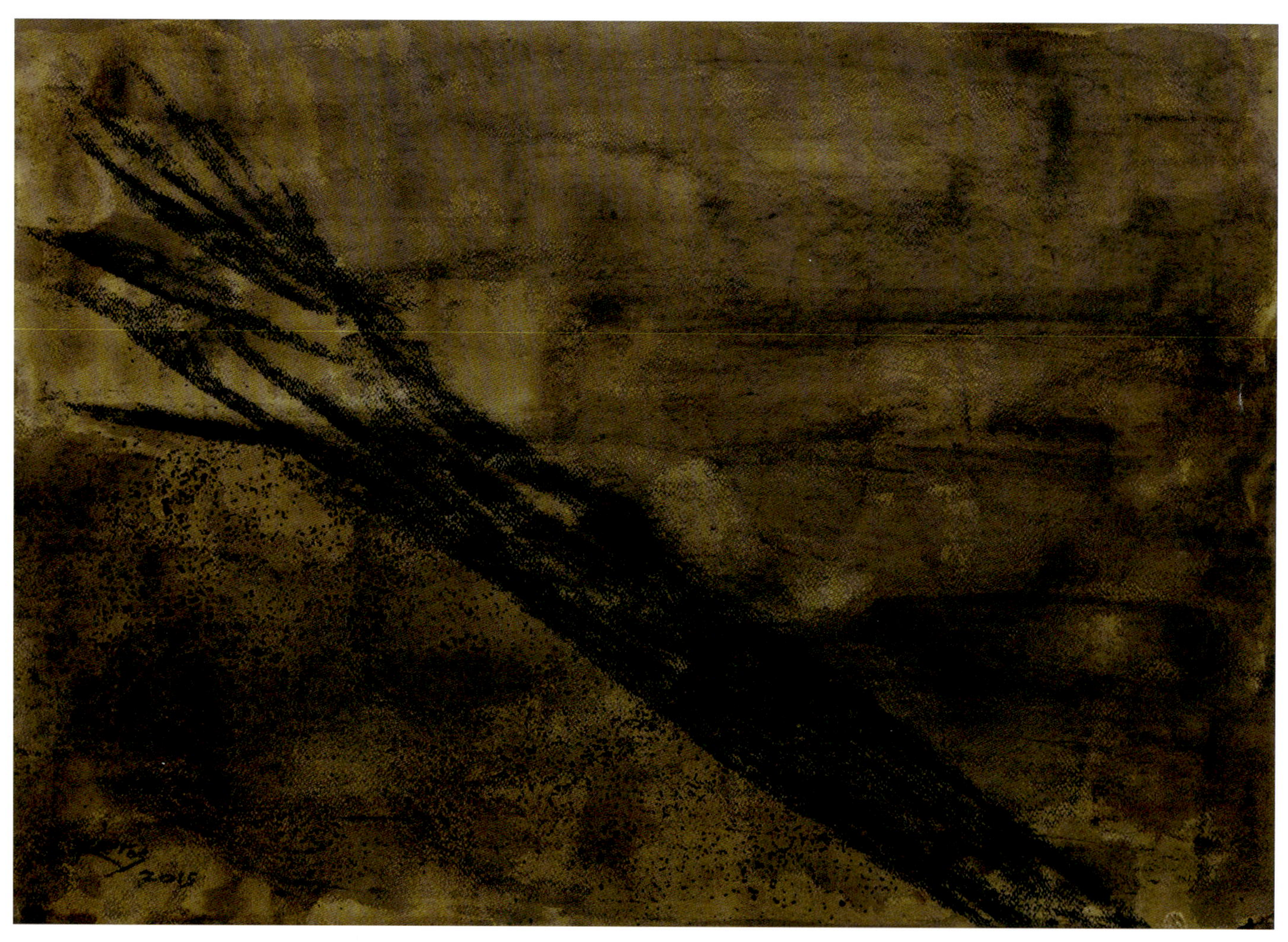

2015, charcoal,
acrylic and graphite on paper,
50 x 70 cm

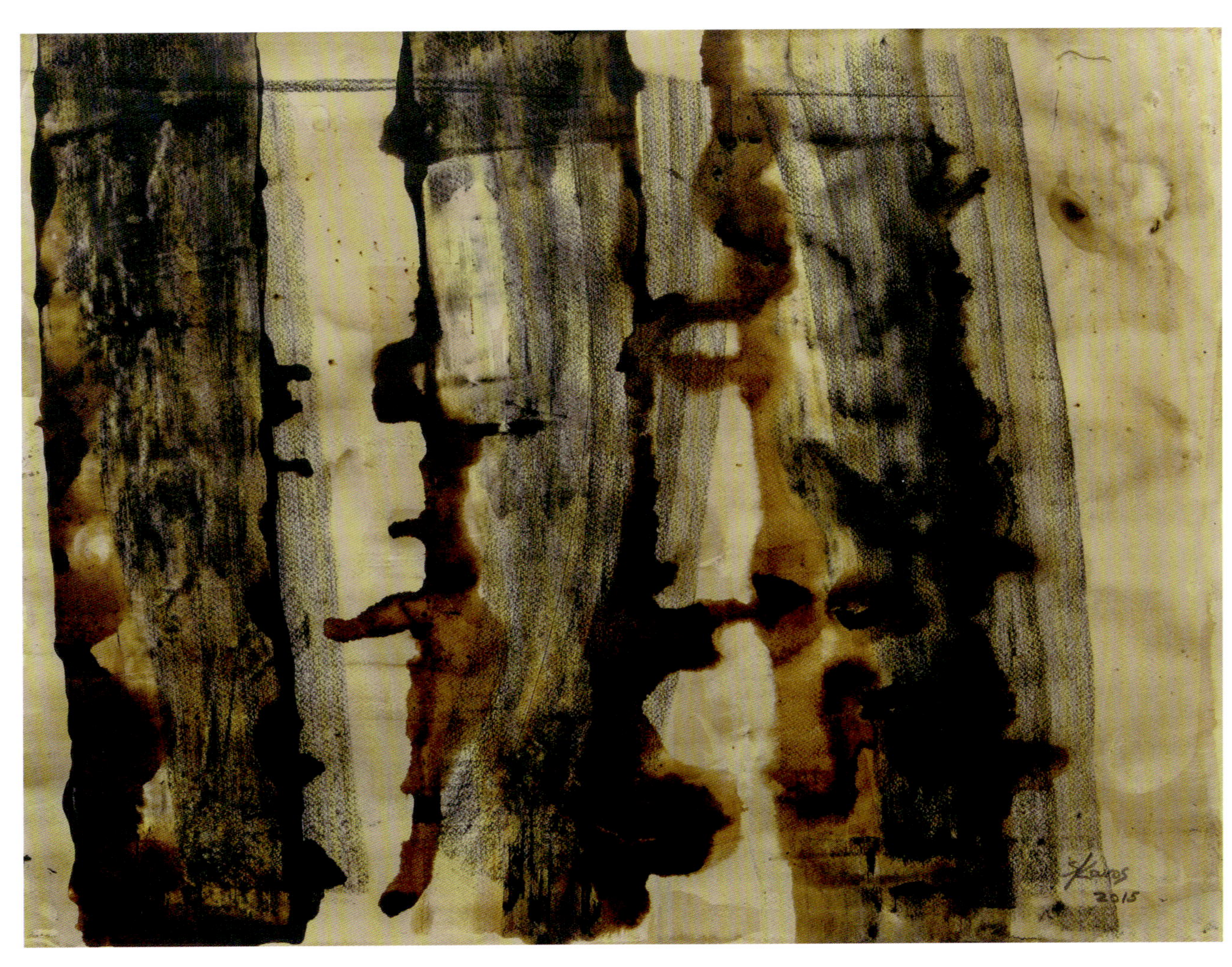

2015, charcoal,
acrylic and graphite on paper,
50 x 70 cm

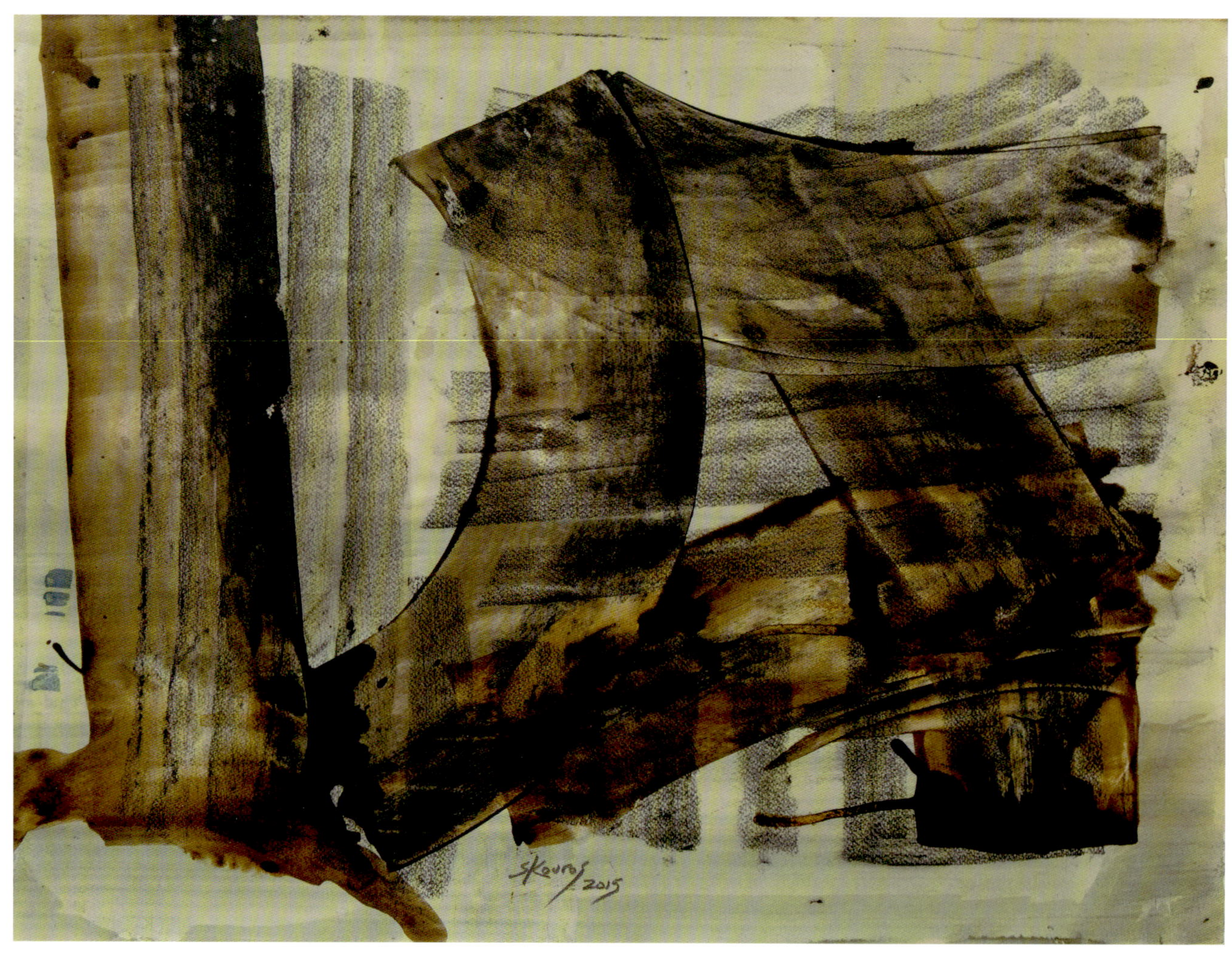

2015, charcoal,
acrylic and graphite on paper,
50 x 70 cm

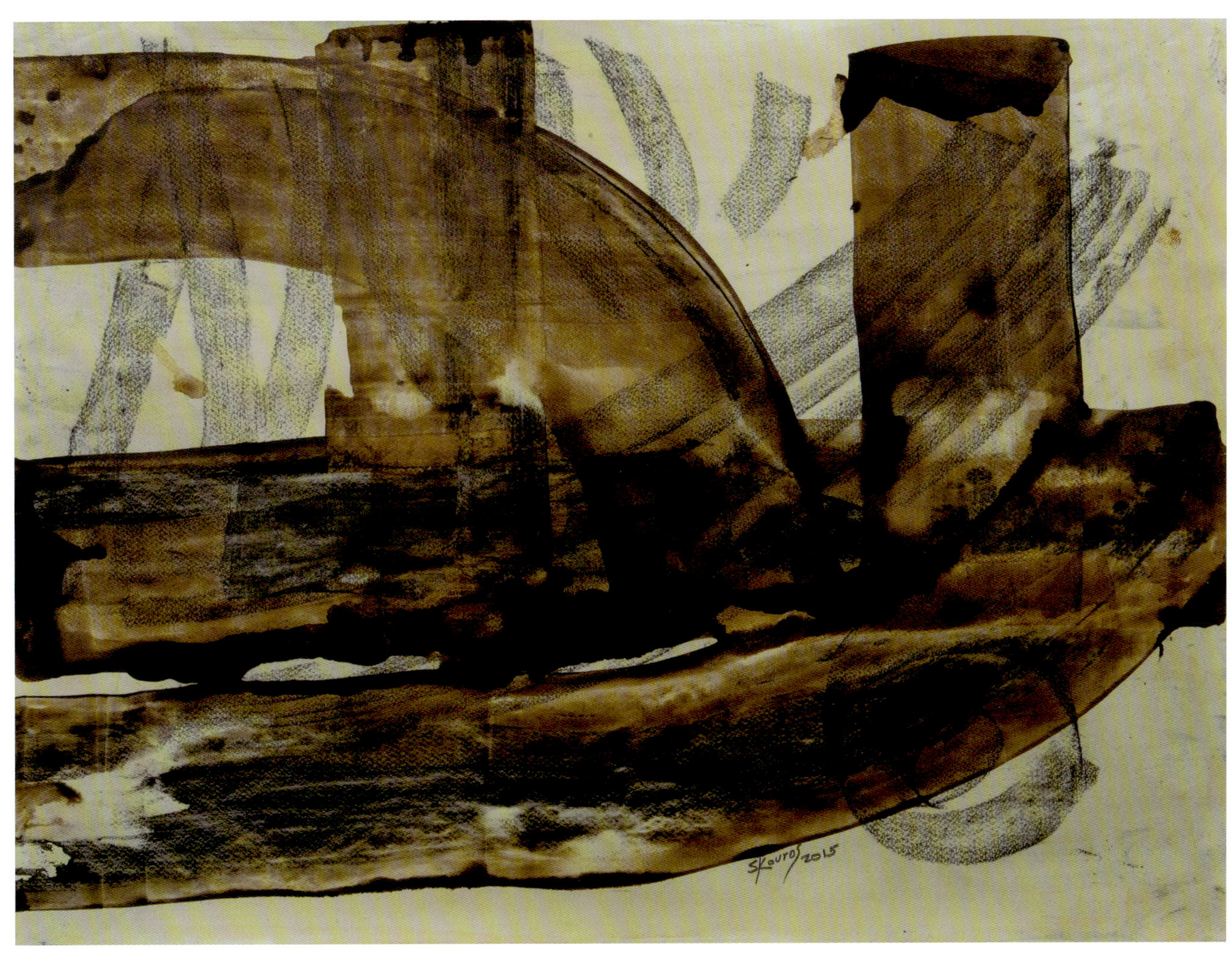

2015, charcoal,
acrylic and graphite on paper,
50 x 70 cm

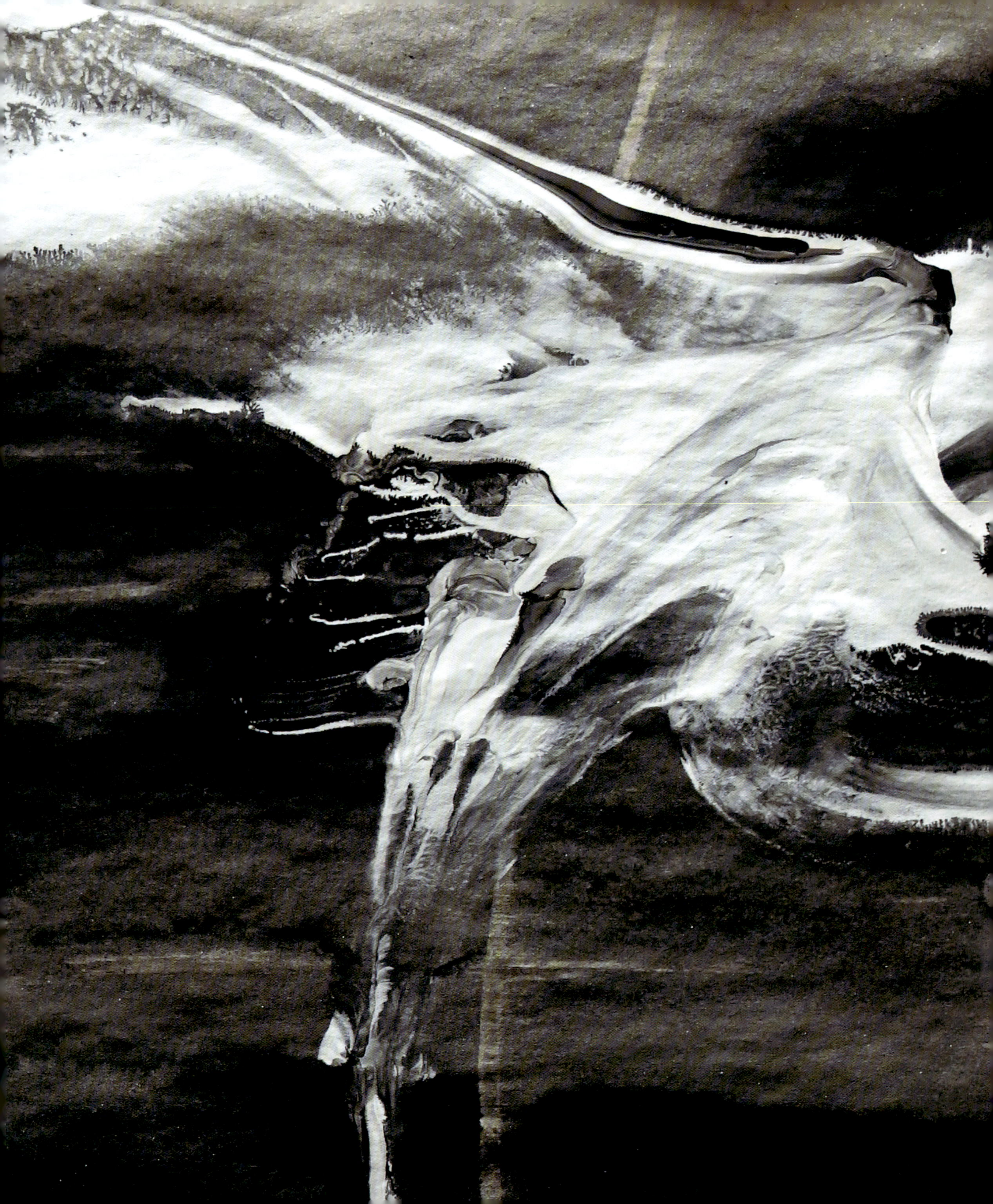

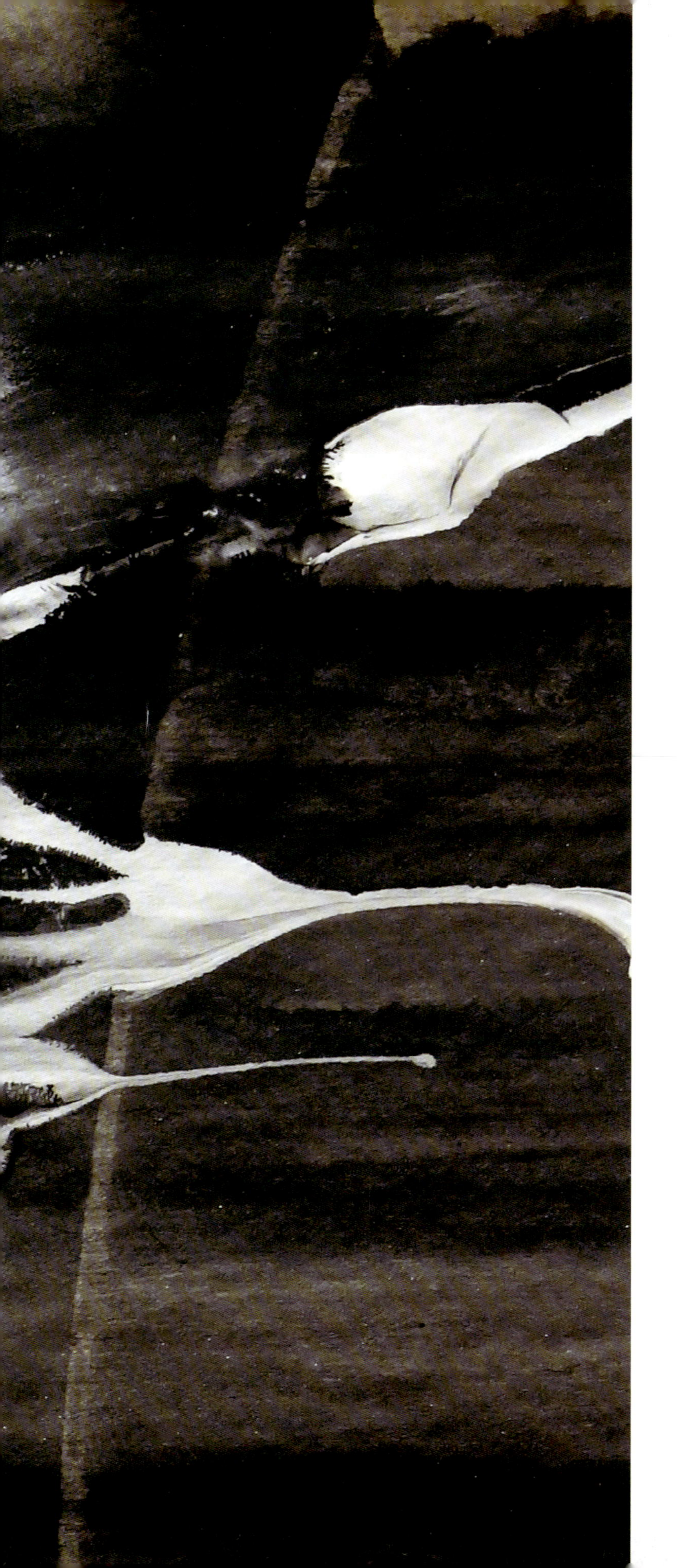

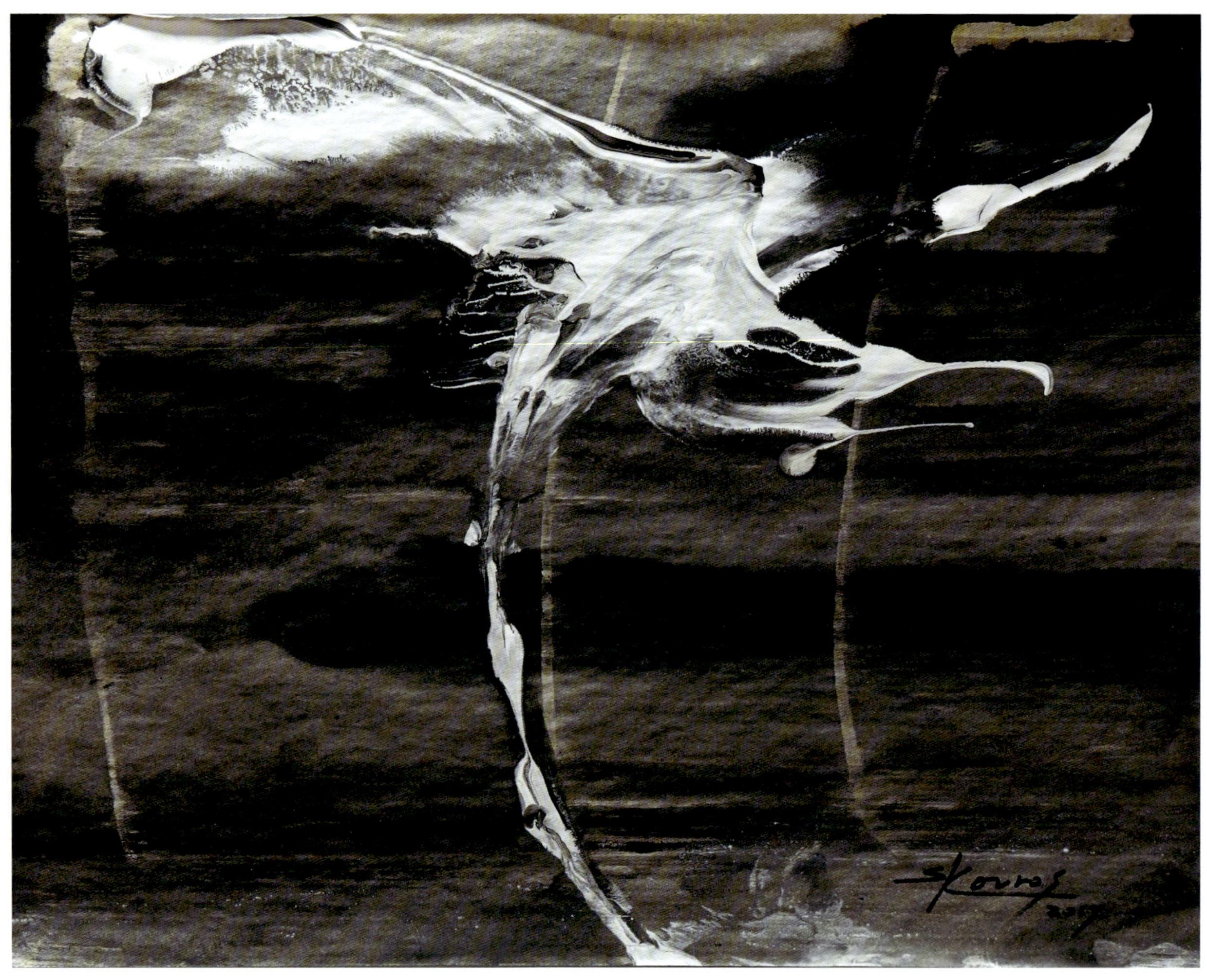

2015, mixed media on paper,
33.5 x 43 cm

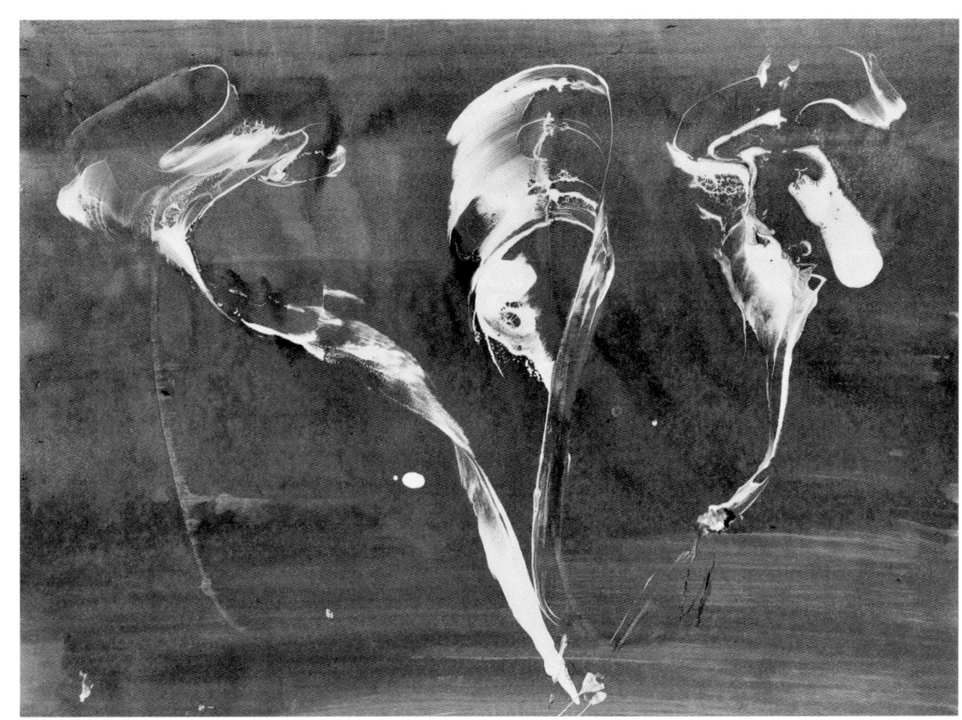

2016, mixed media on paper,
46 x 61cm

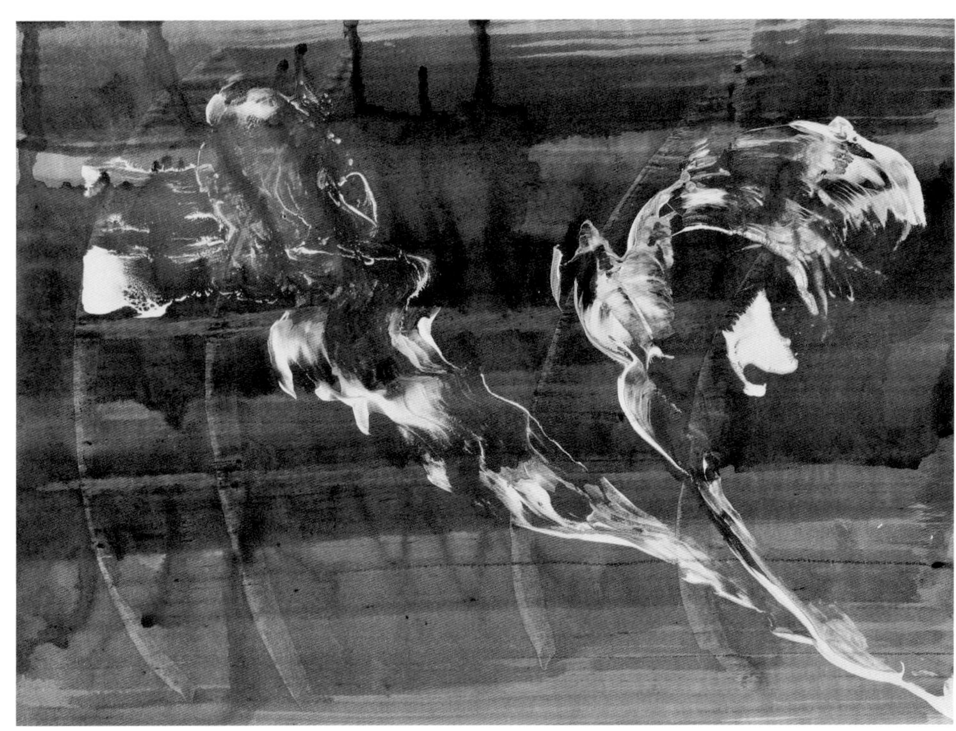

2016, mixed media on paper,
46 x 61cm

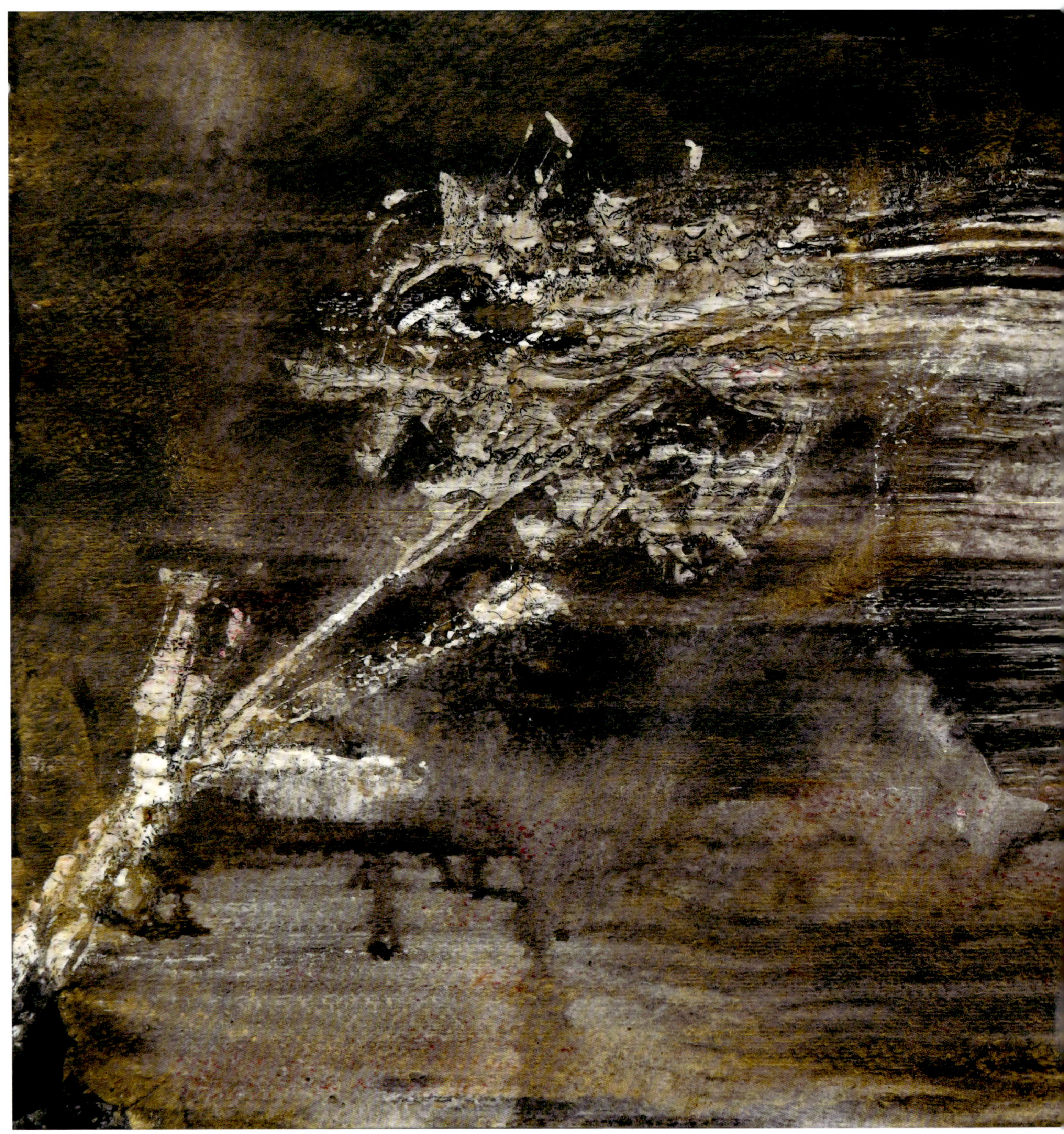

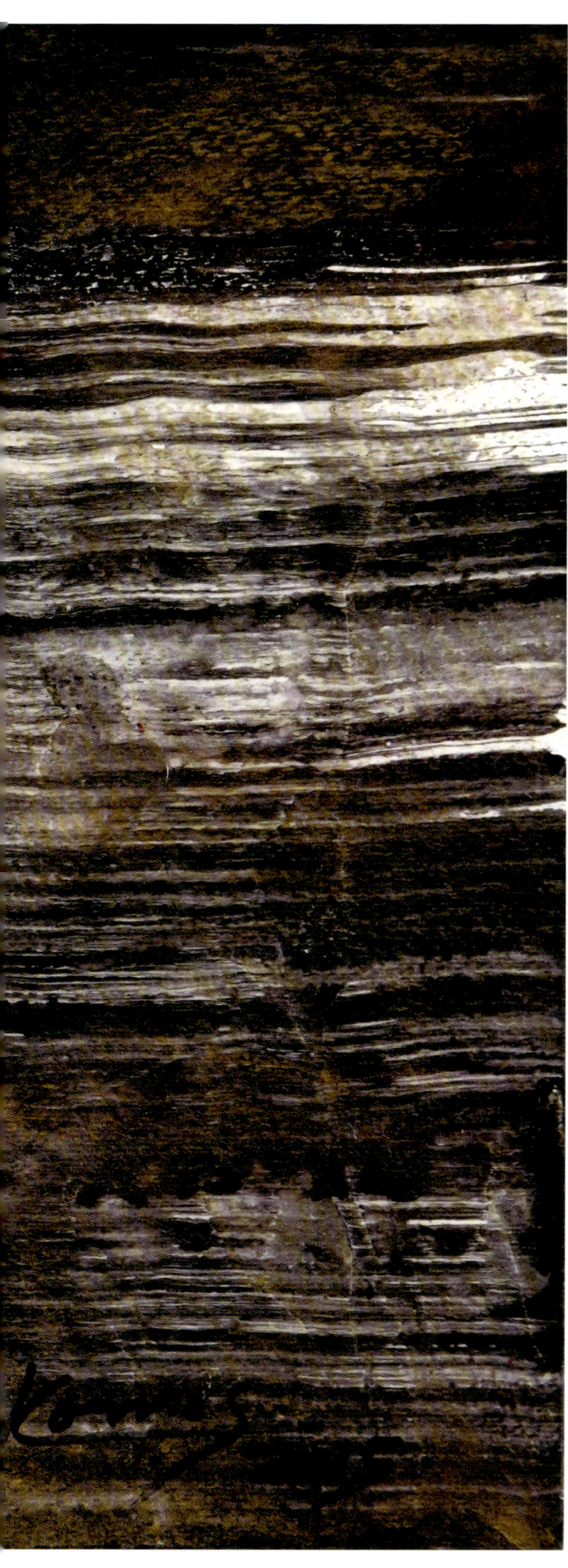

2016, mixed media on paper,
28 x 38 cm

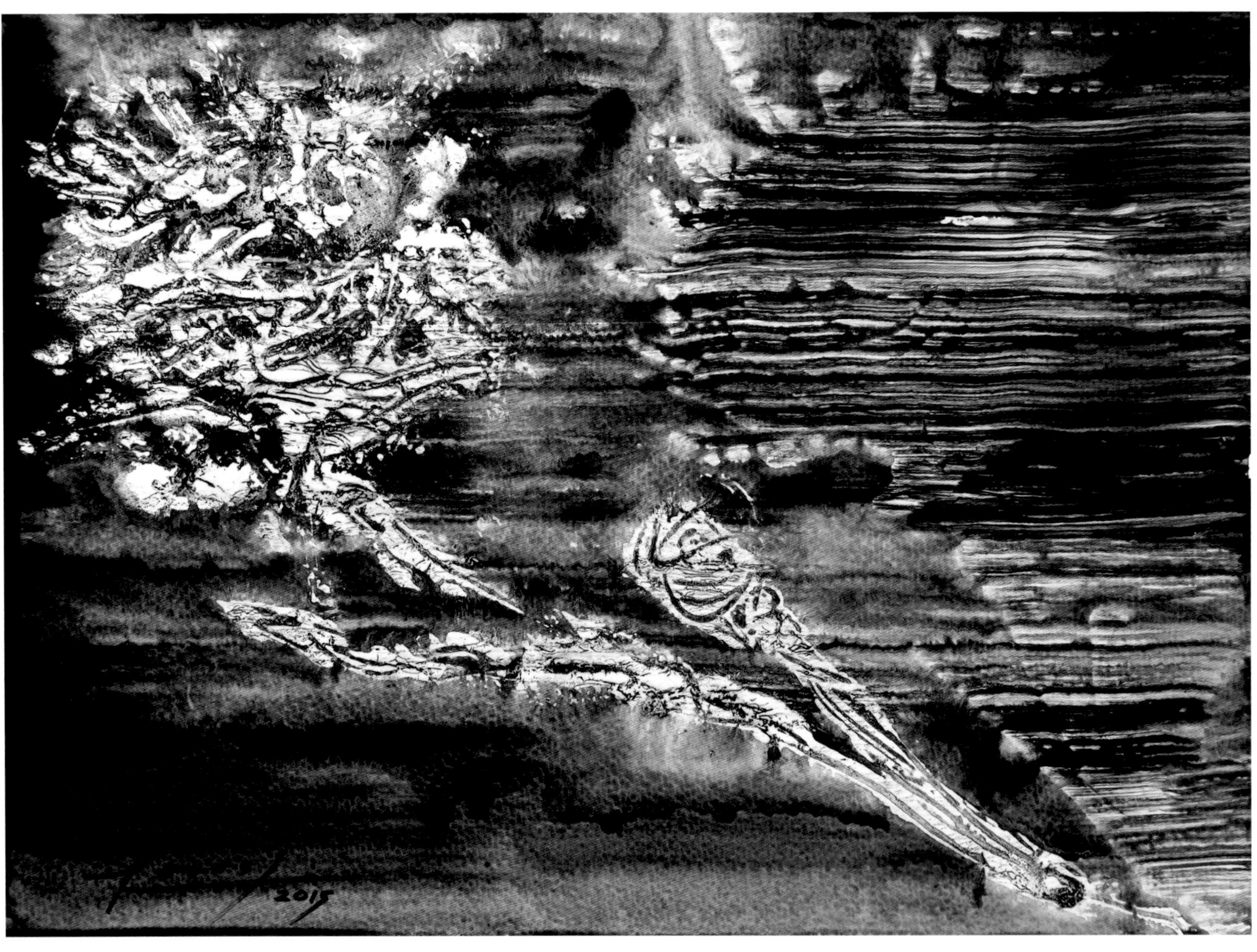

2016, mixed media on paper,
28 x 38 cm

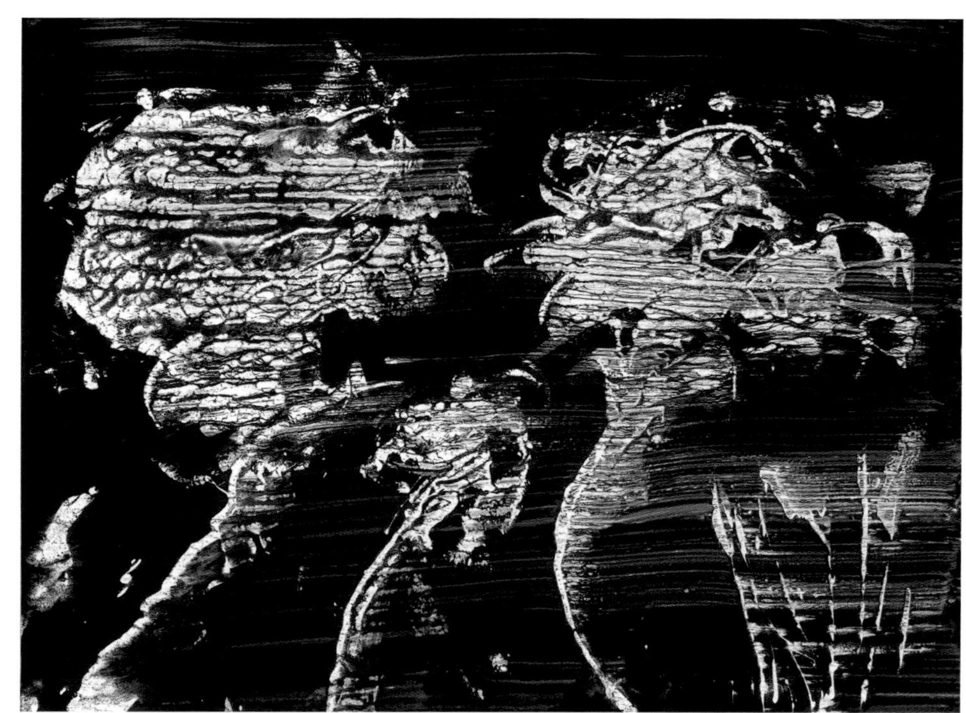

2016, mixed media on paper,
46 x 61cm

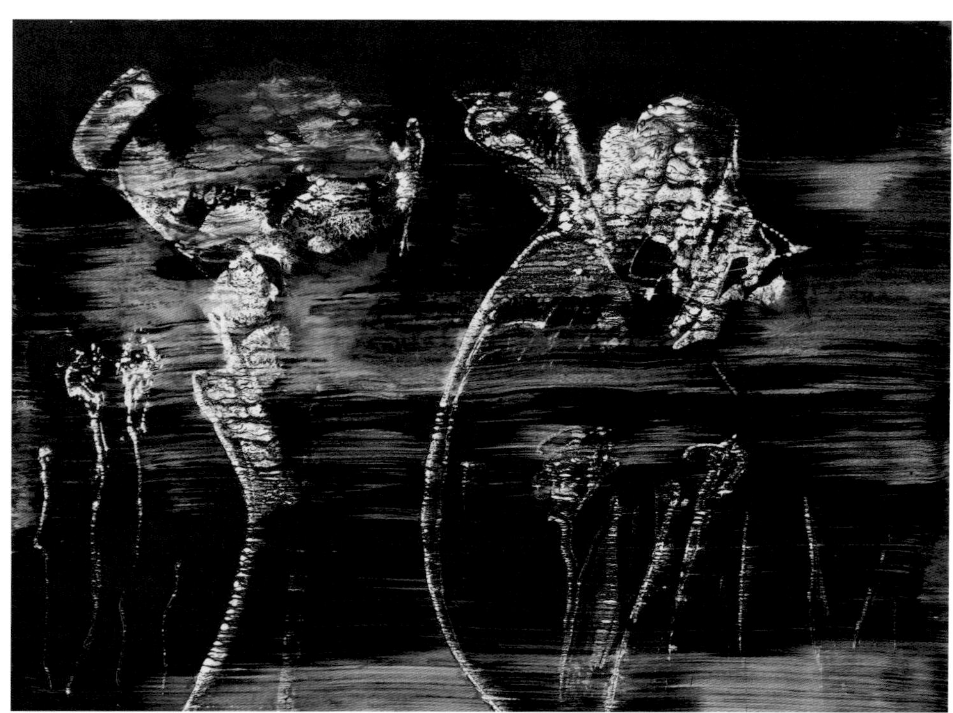

2016, mixed media on paper,
46 x 61cm

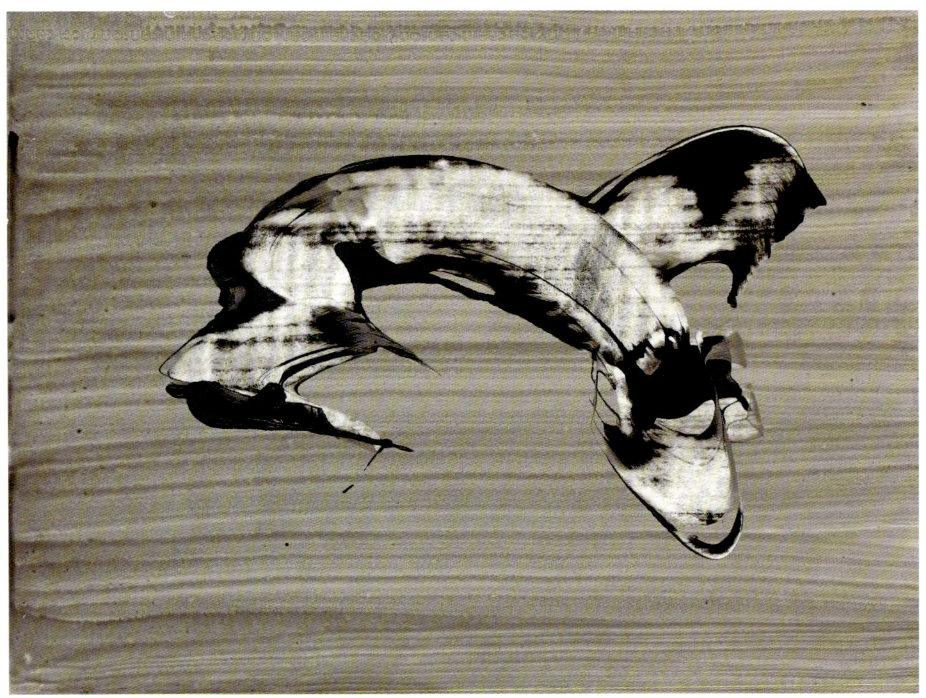

2016, mixed media on paper,
46 x 61cm

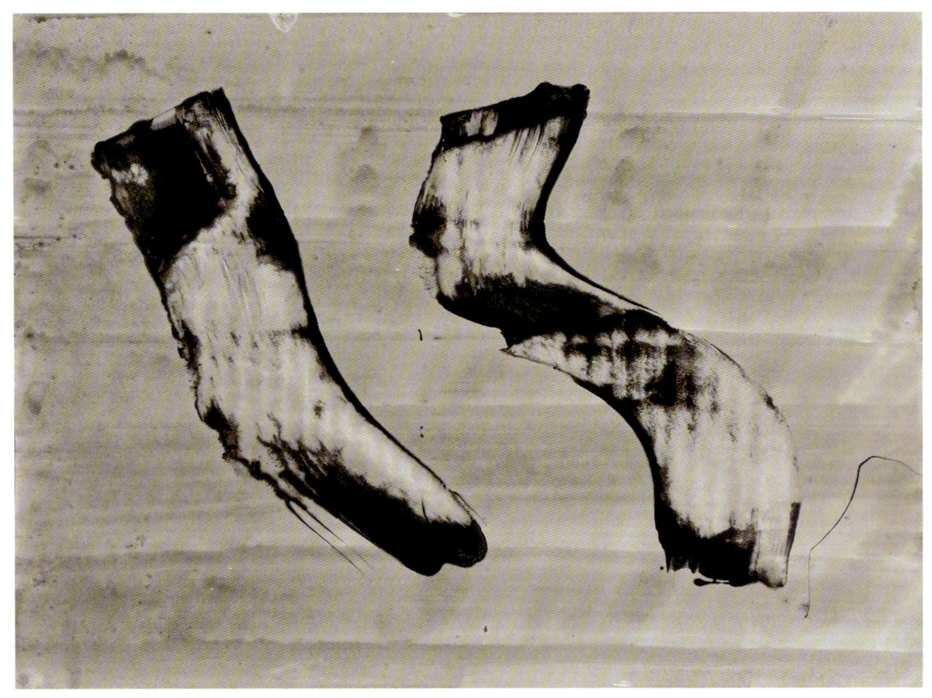

2016, mixed media on paper,
46 x 61cm

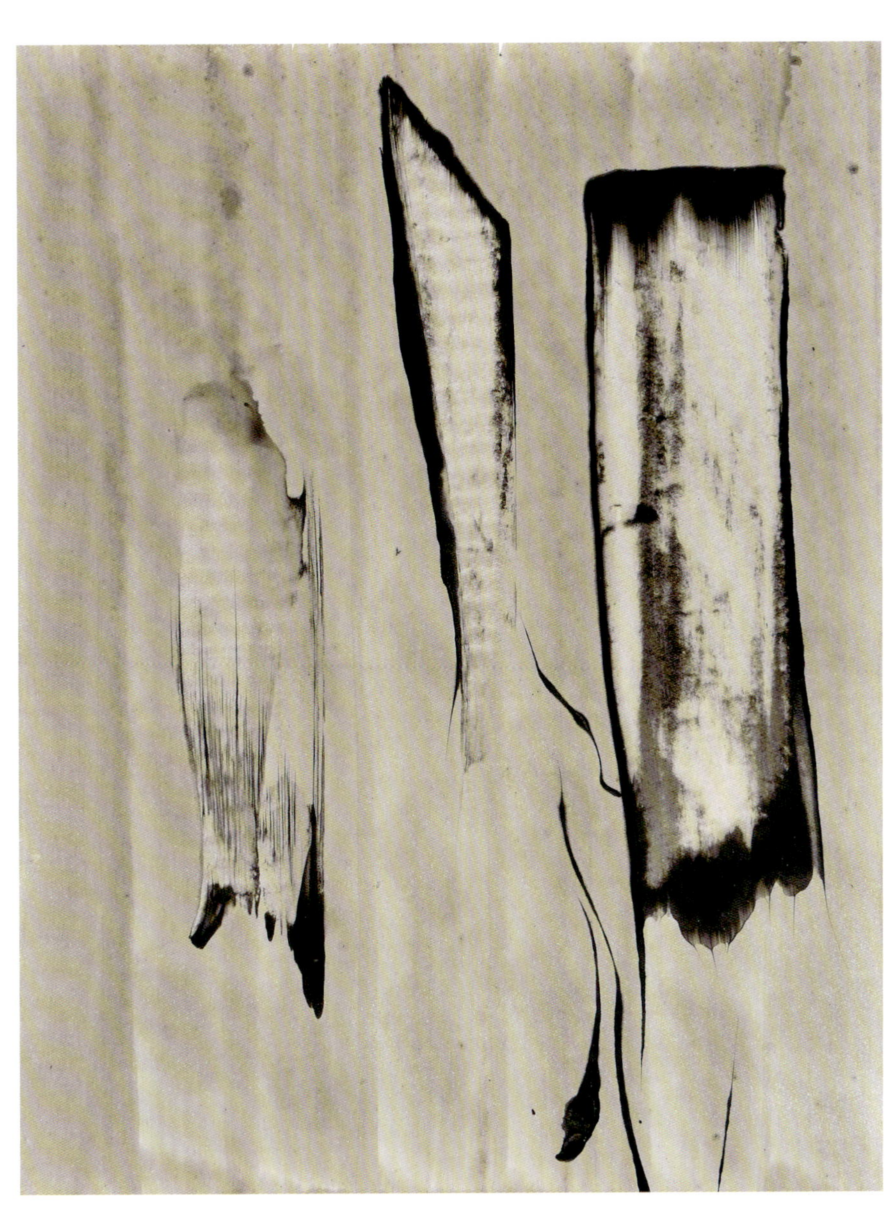

2016, mixed media on paper,
61 x 46 cm

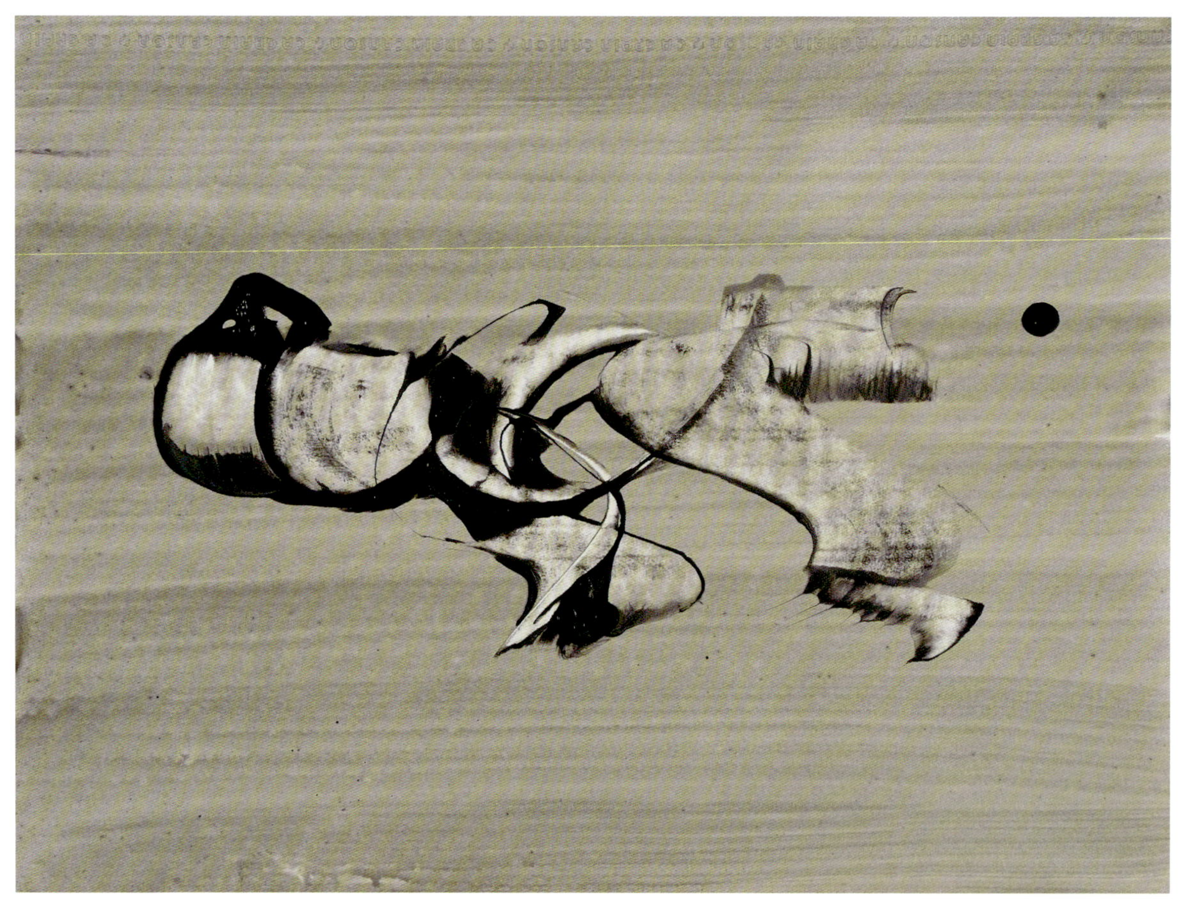

2016, mixed media on paper,
49.5 x 64.5 cm

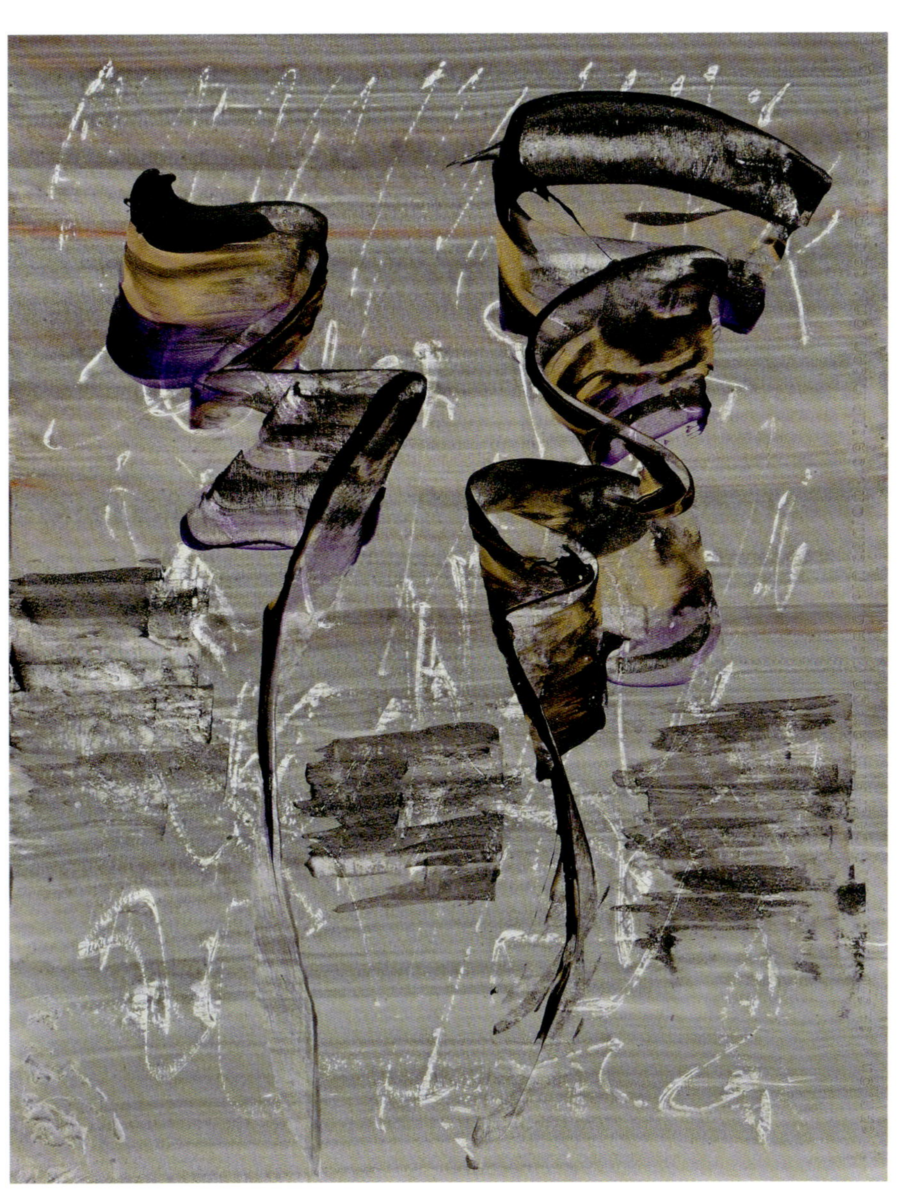

2016, mixed media on paper,
49.5 x 64.5 cm

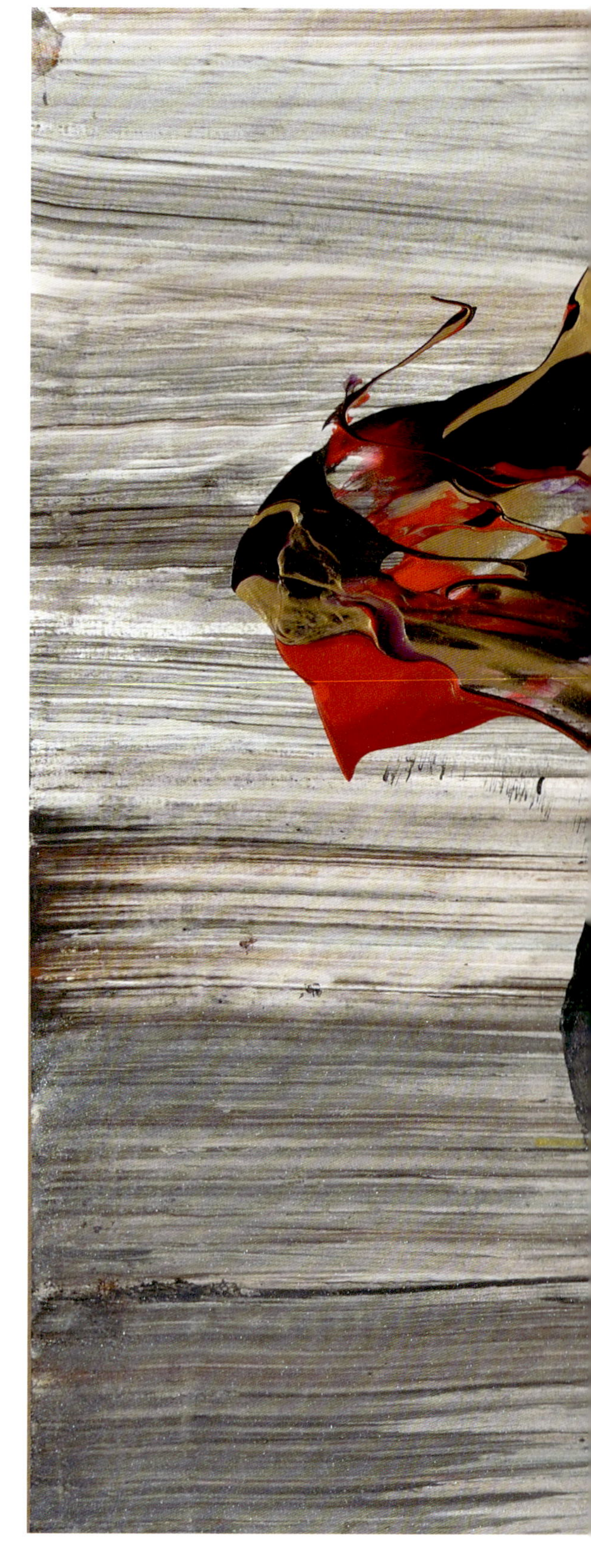

2016, mixed media on paper,
46 x 61cm

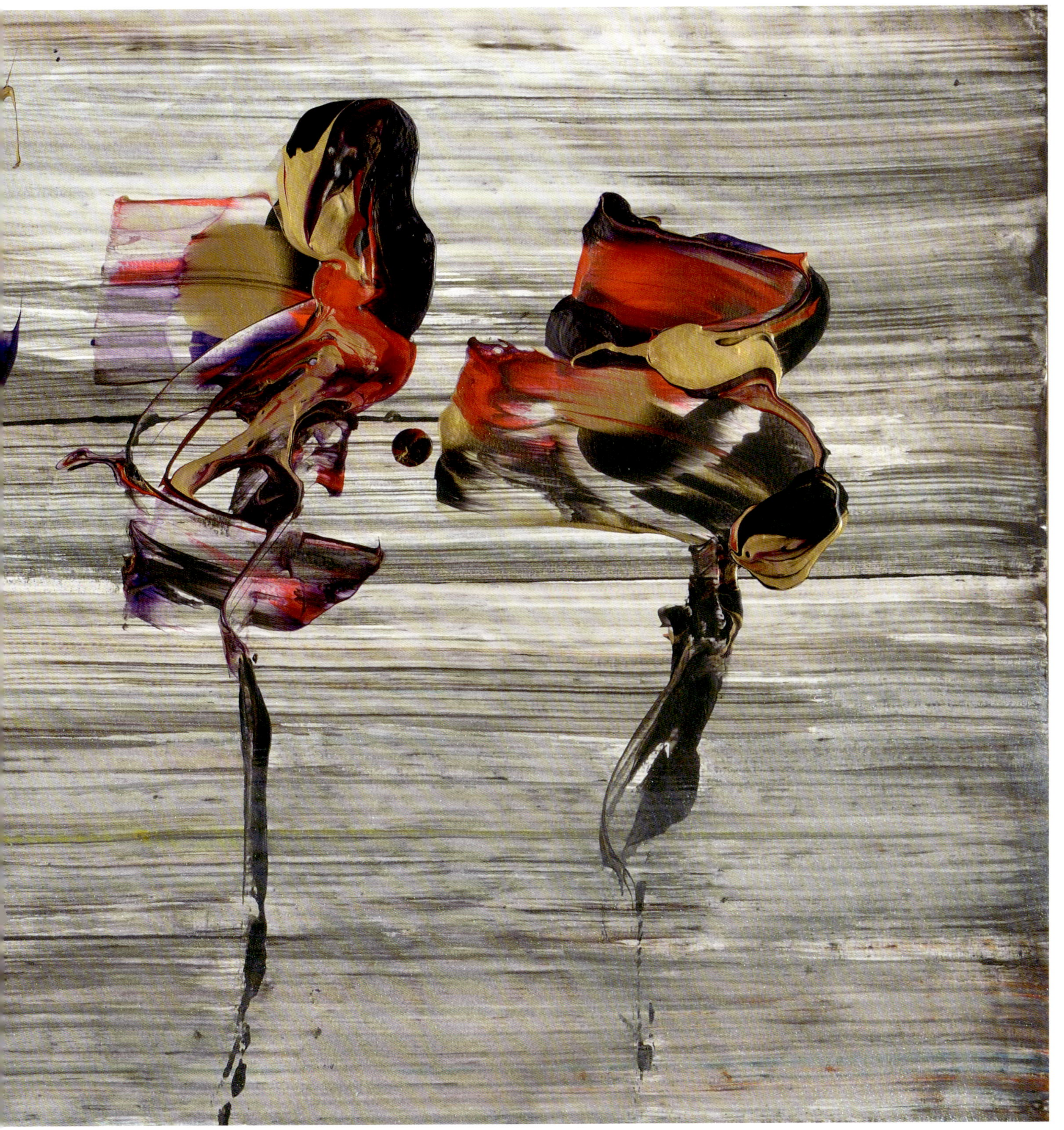

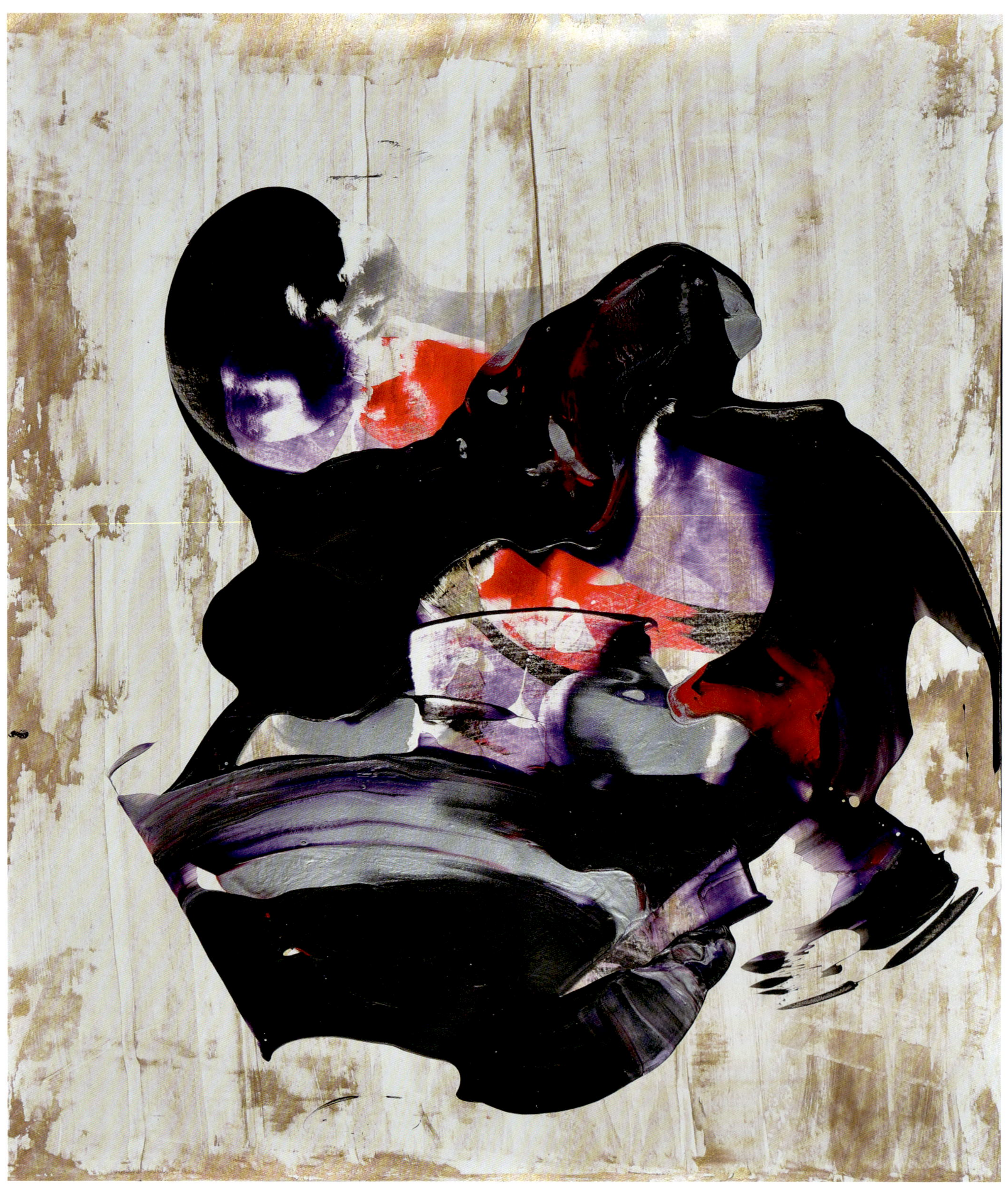

2016, mixed media on paper,
64.5 x 49.5 cm

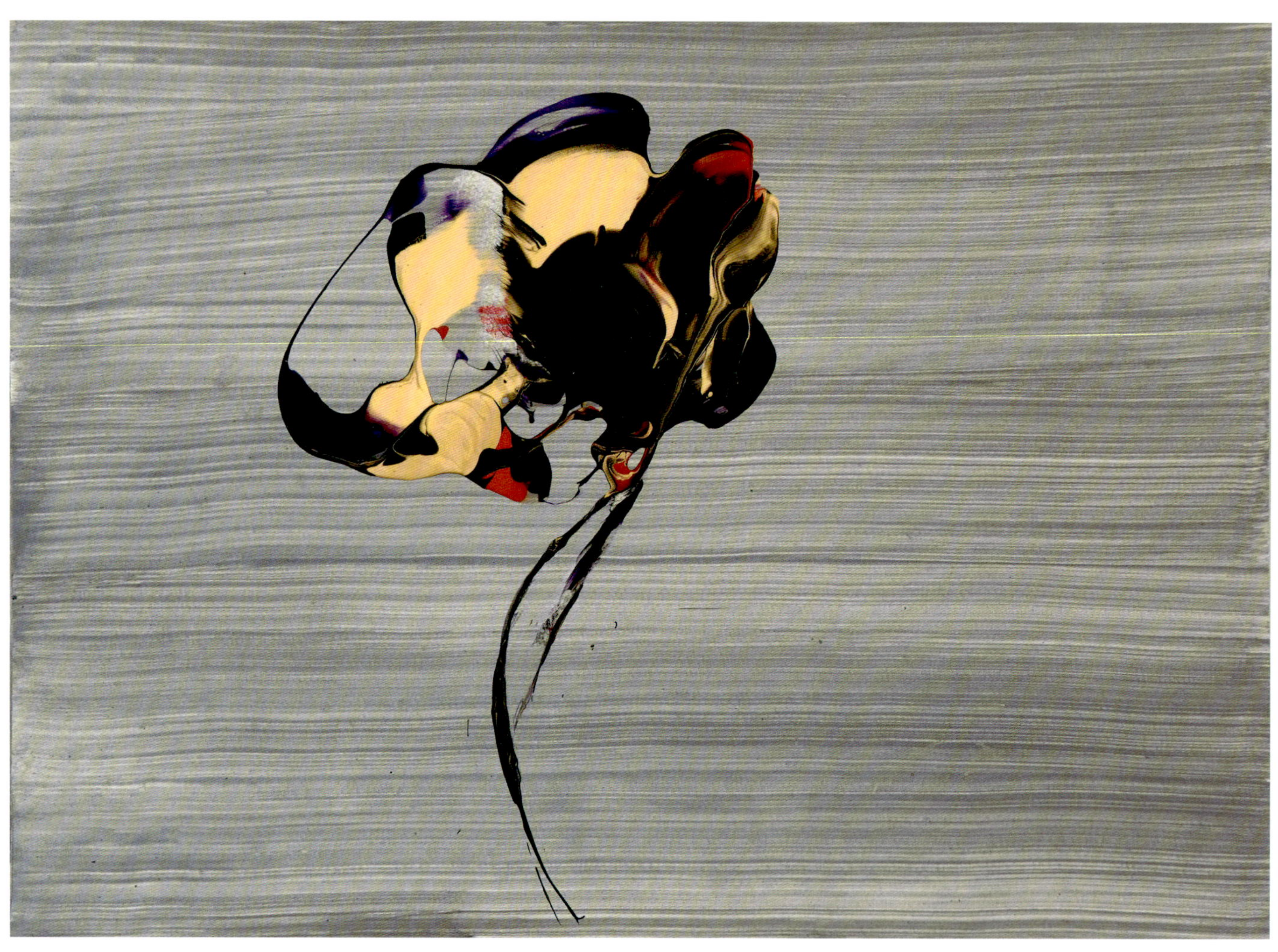

2016, mixed media on paper,
46 x 61 cm

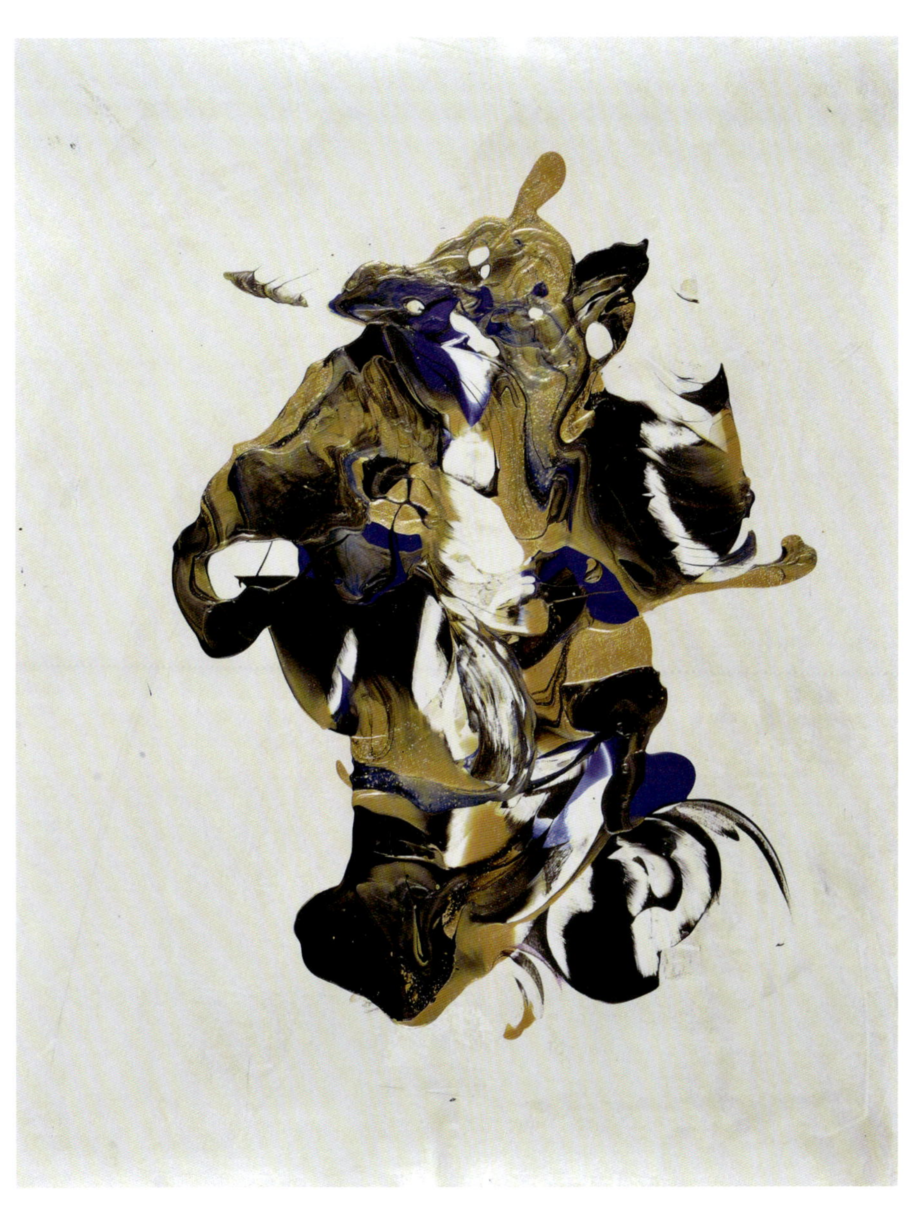

2016, mixed media on paper,
49.5 x 64.5 cm

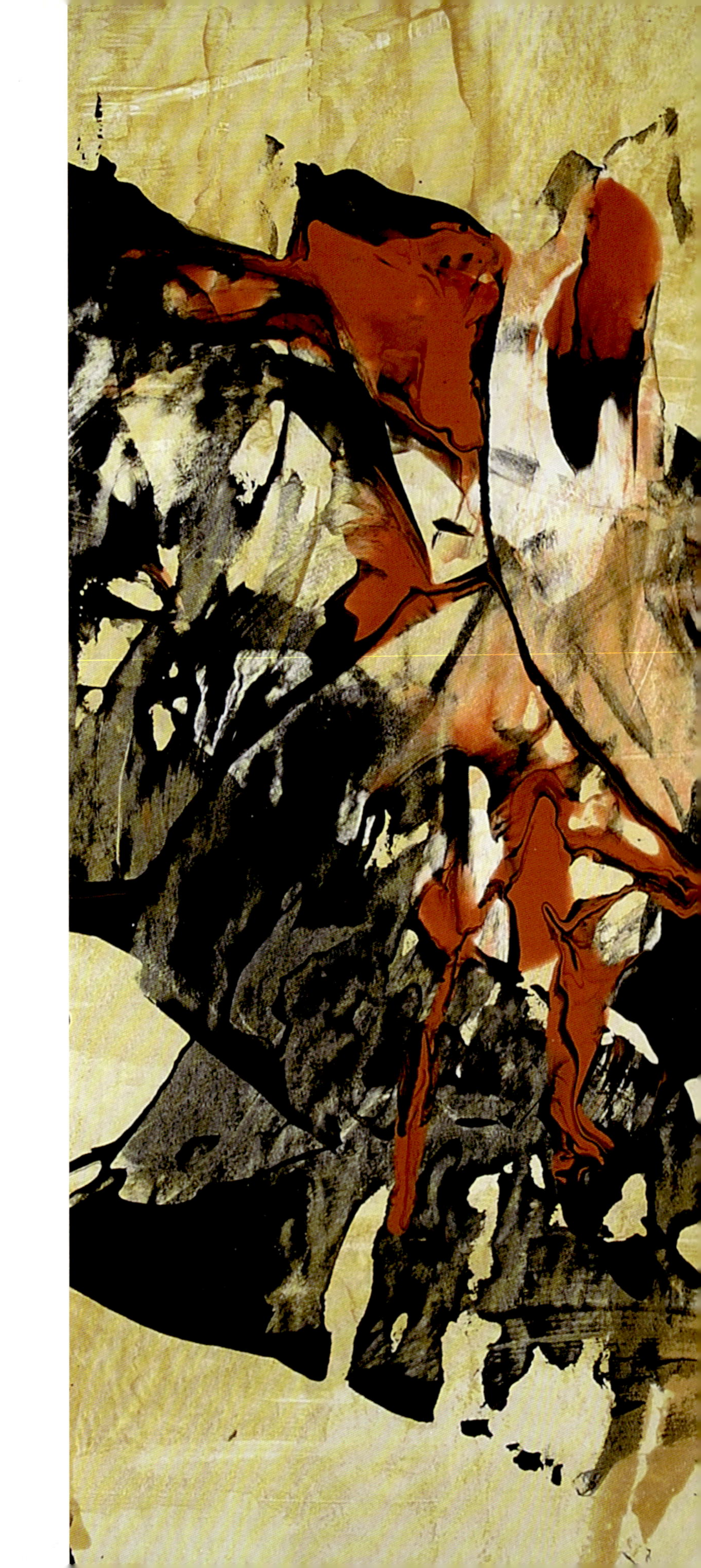

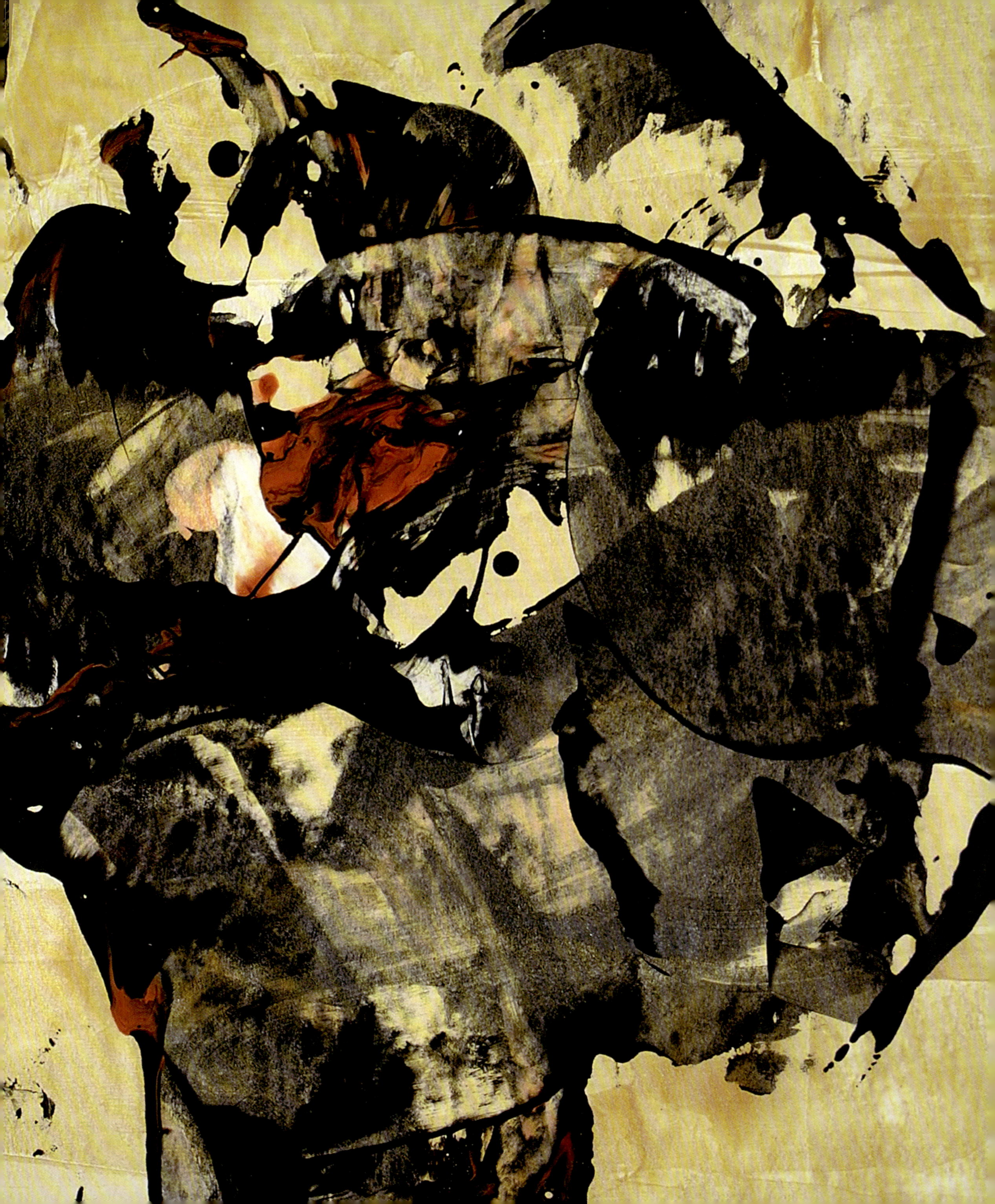

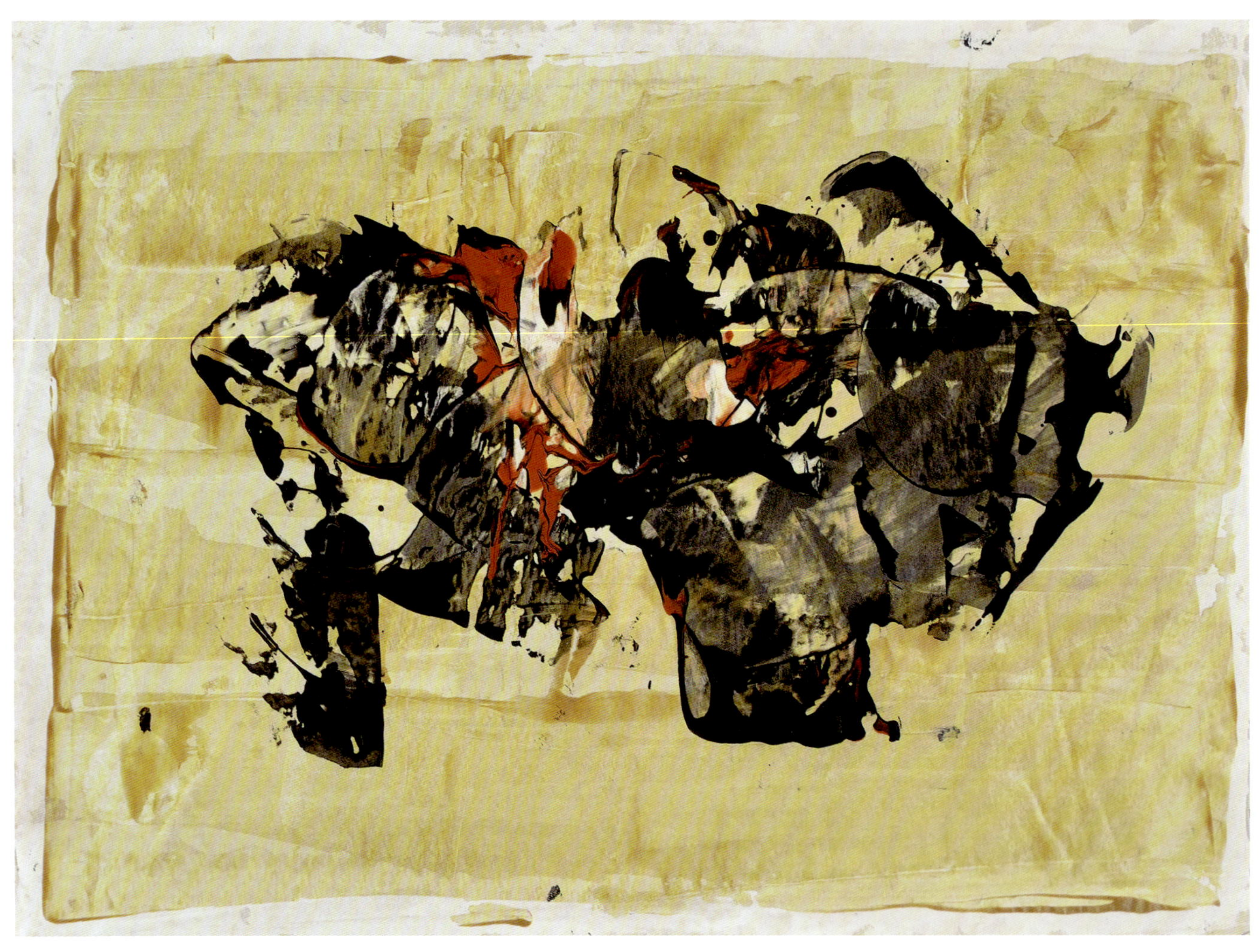

2016, mixed media on paper,
46 x 61cm

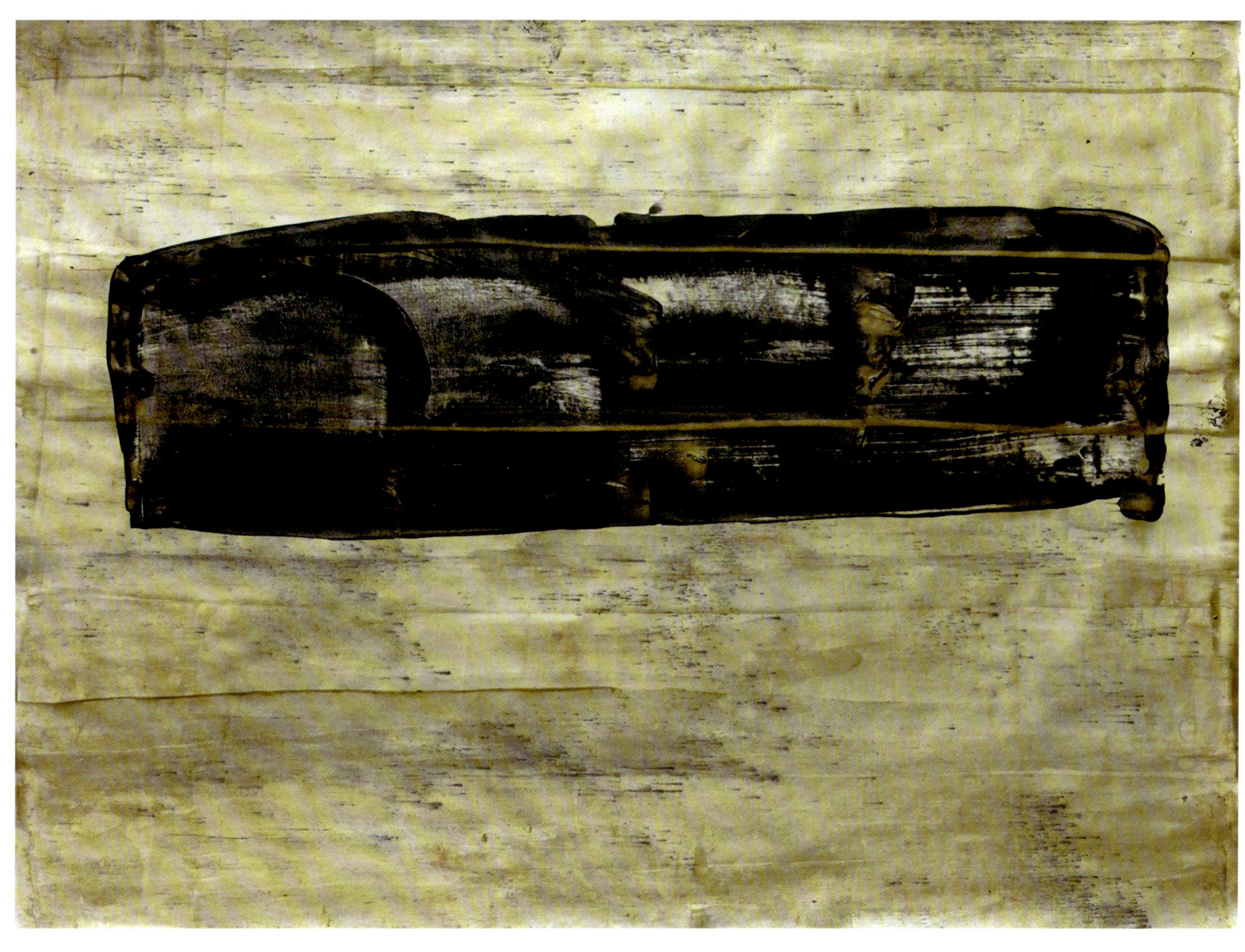

2016, mixed media on paper,
46 x 61cm

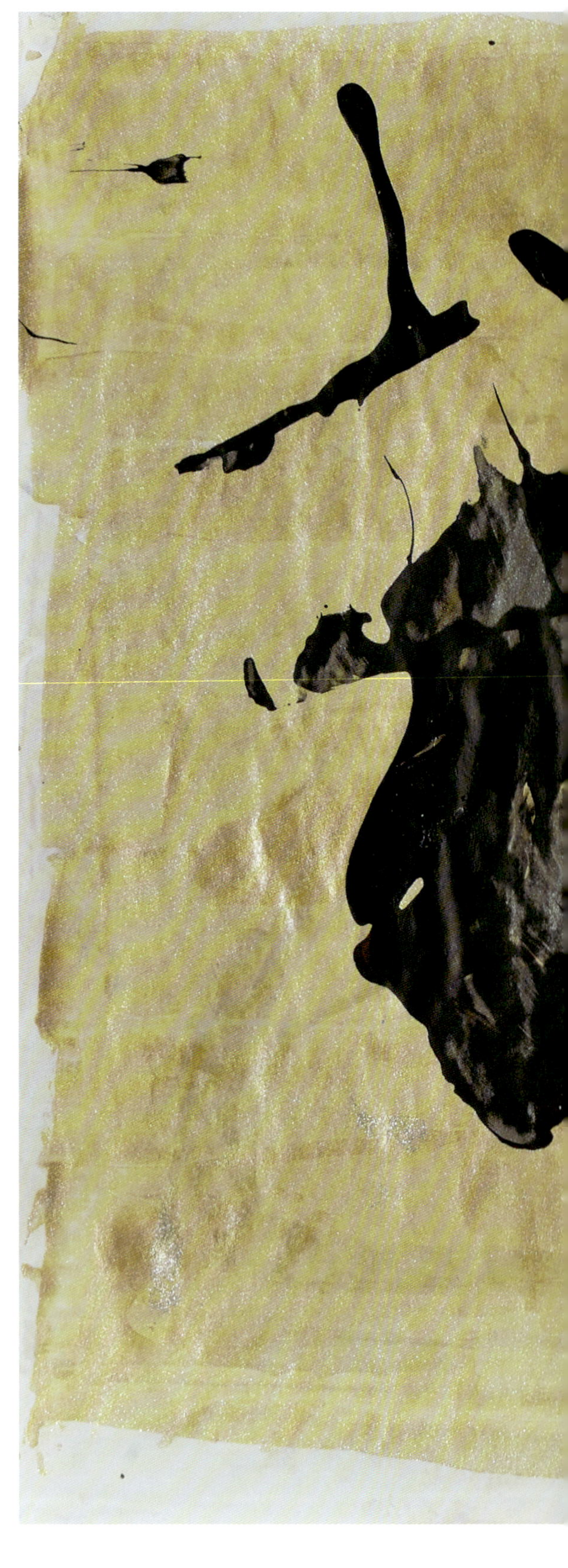

2016, mixed media on paper,
46 x 61cm

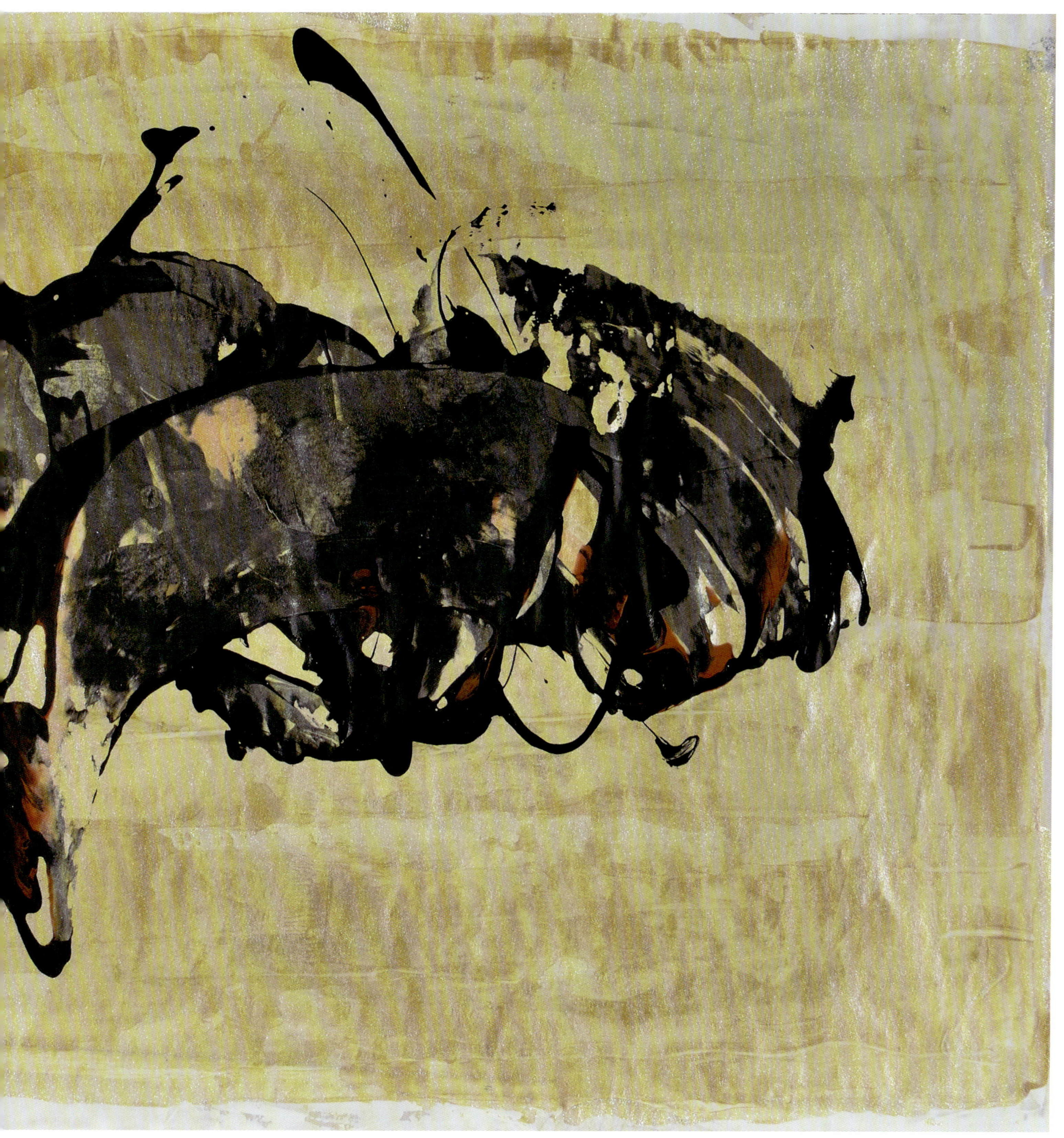

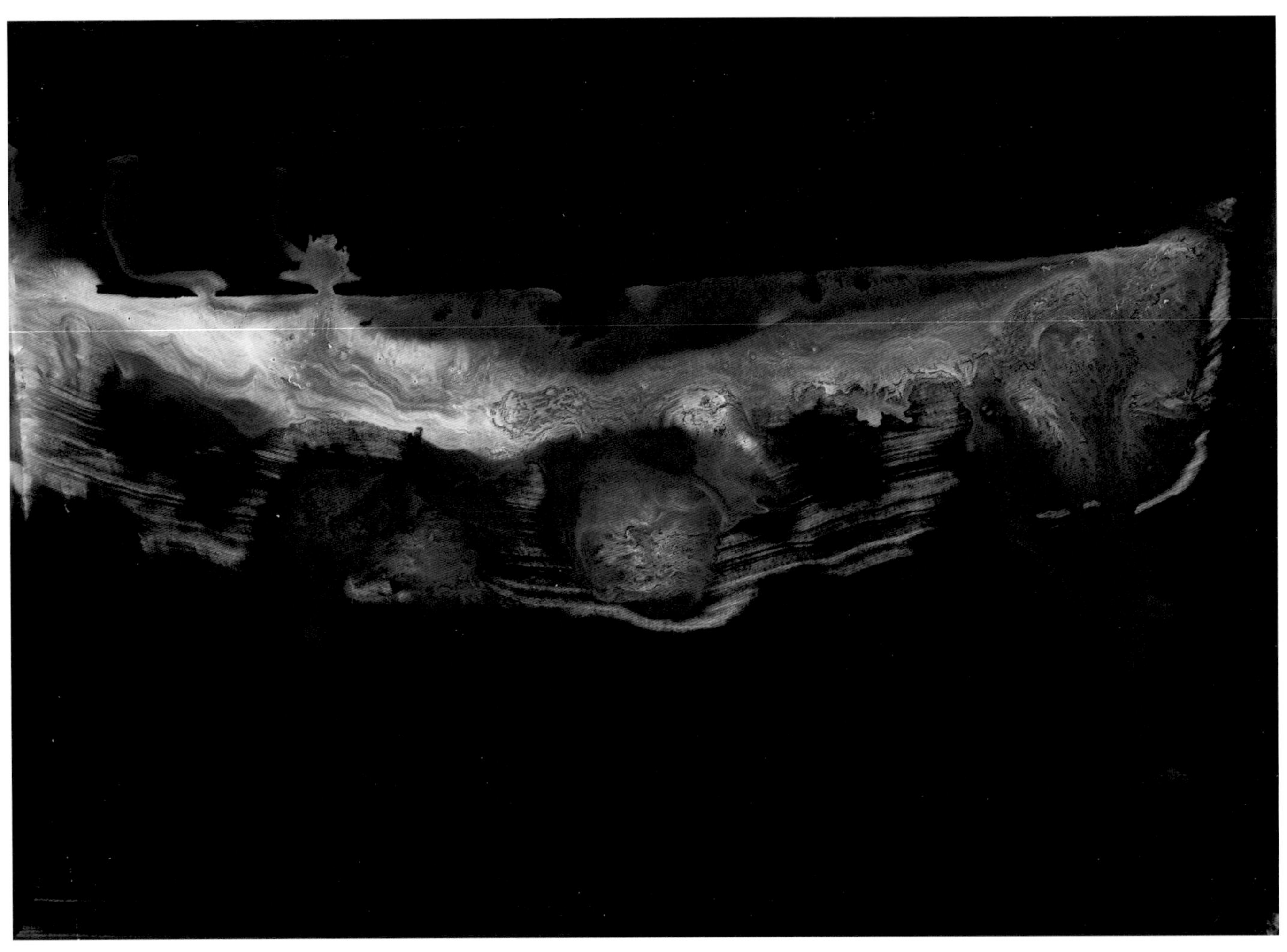

2016, mixed media on paper,
46 x 61 cm

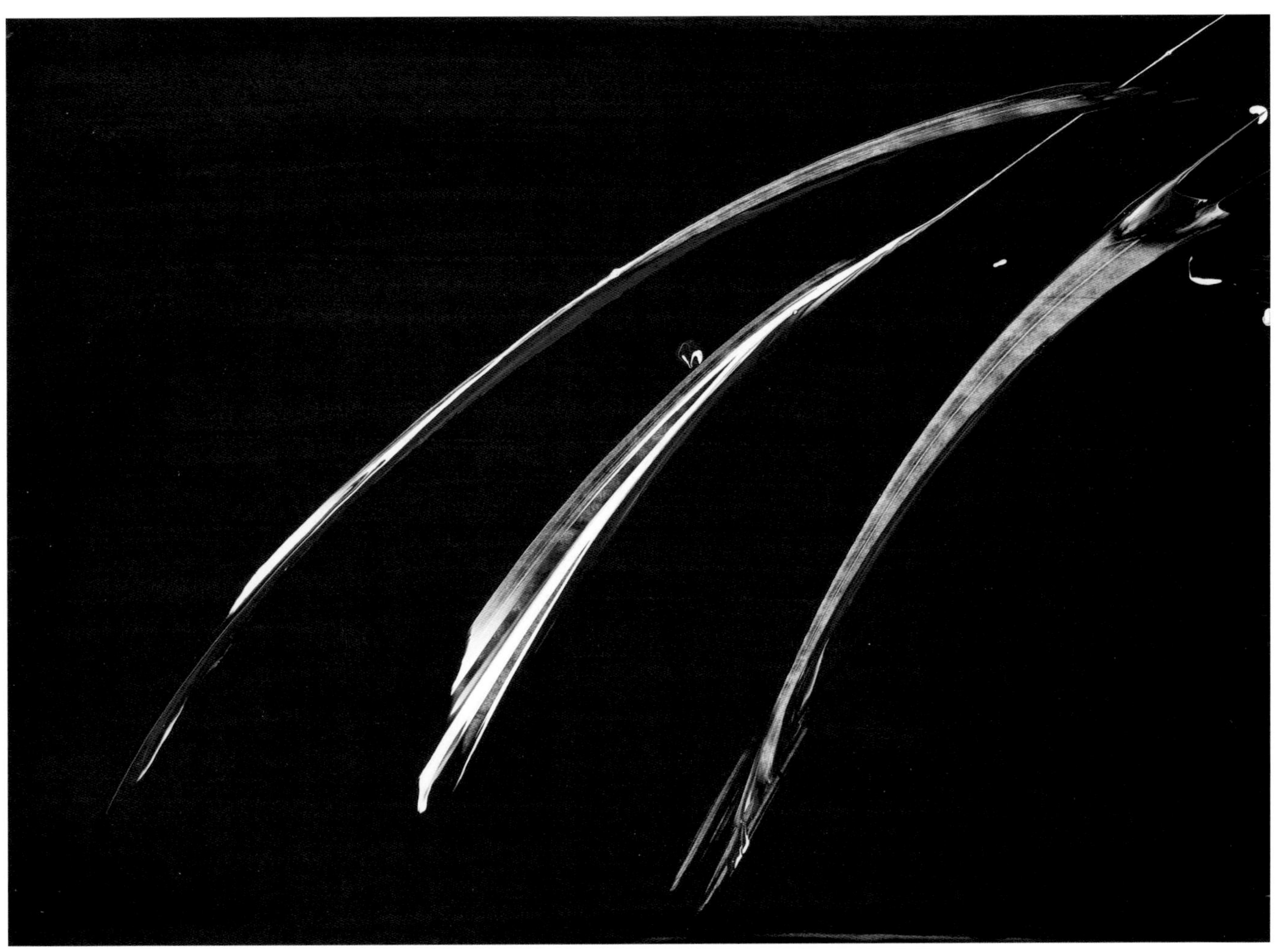

2016, mixed media on paper,
46 x 61 cm

2016, mixed media on paper,
46x61cm

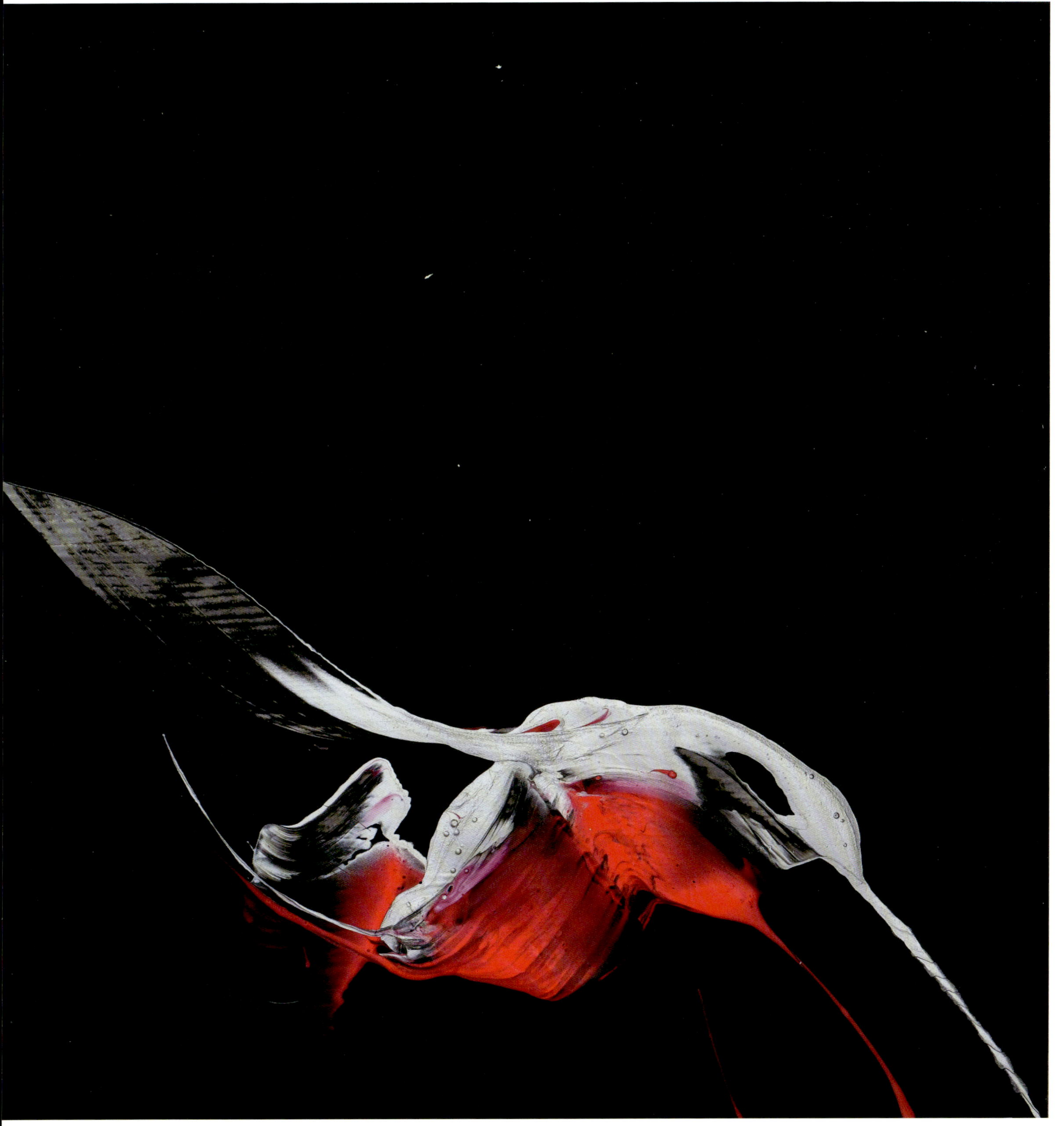

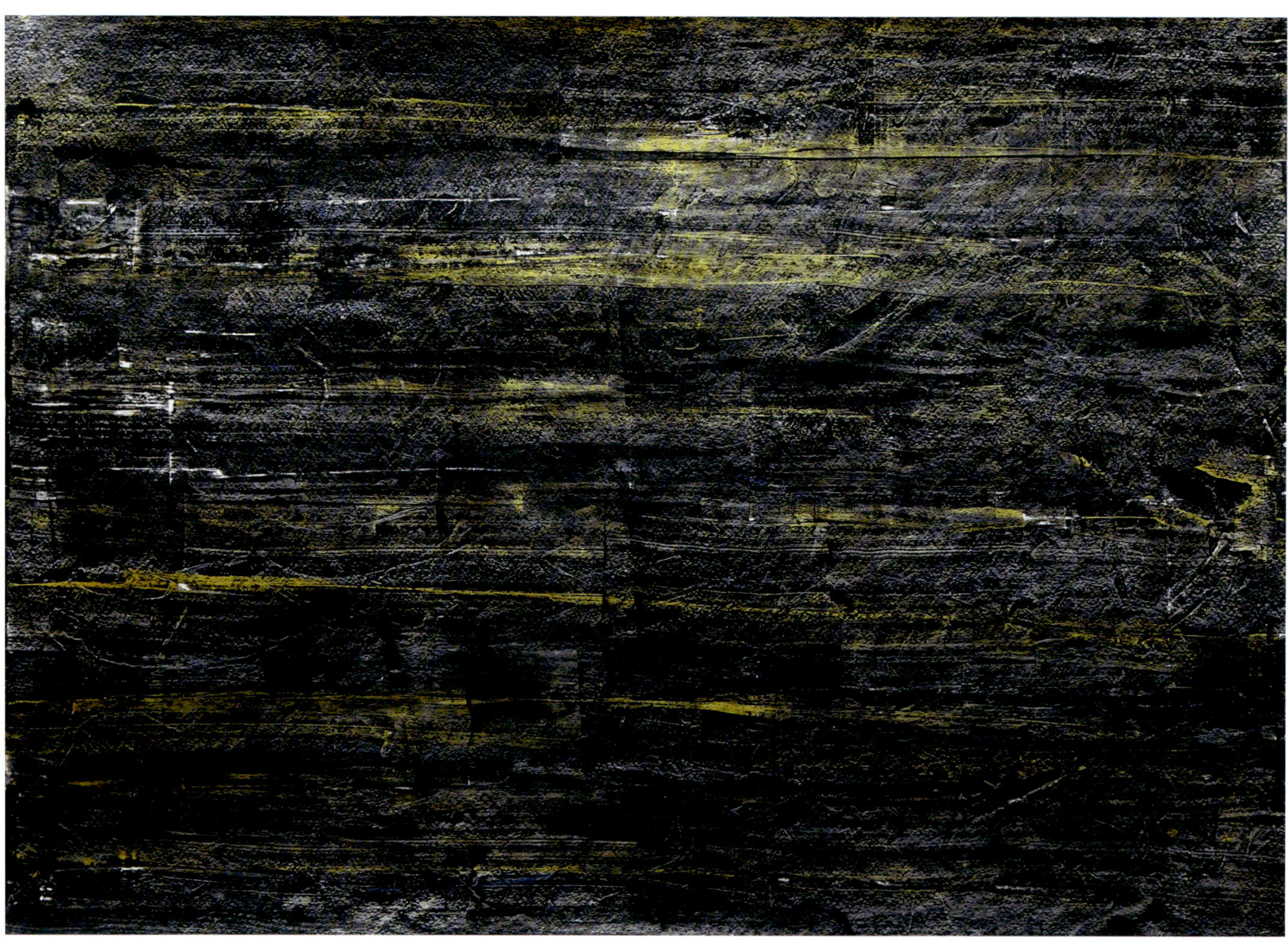

2016, mixed media on paper,
56 x 76 cm

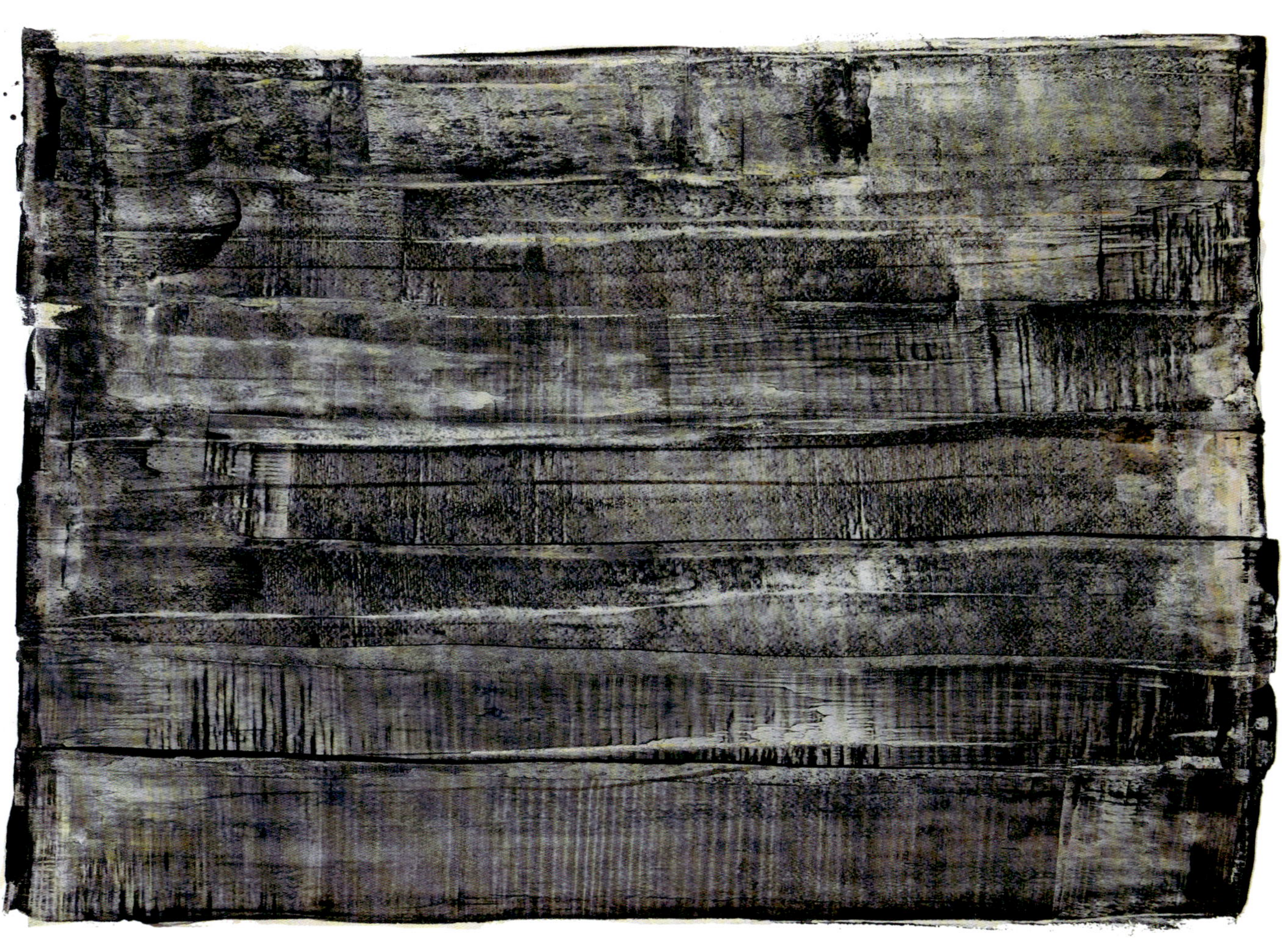

2016, mixed media on paper,
56 x 76 cm

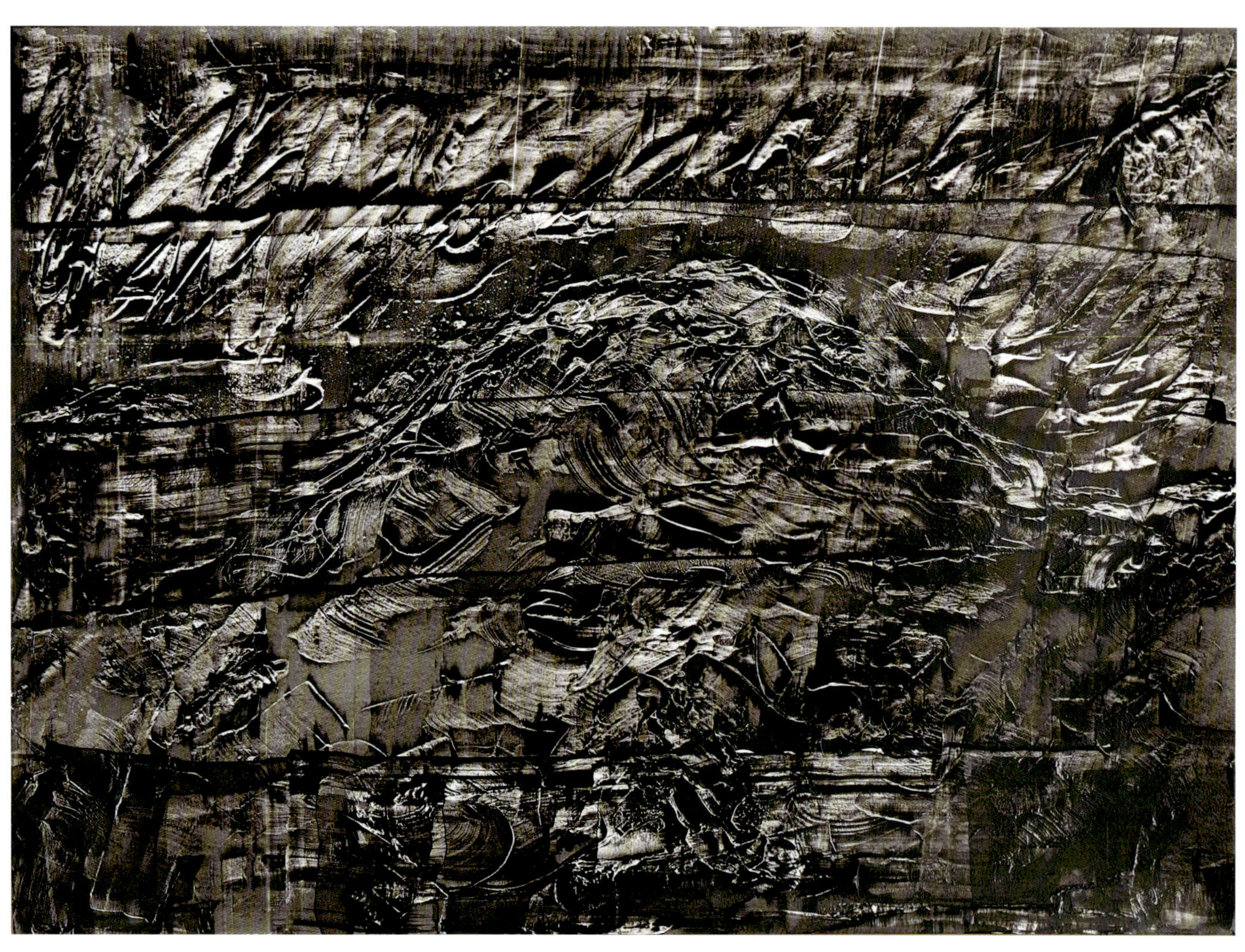

2016, mixed media on paper,
46 x 61cm

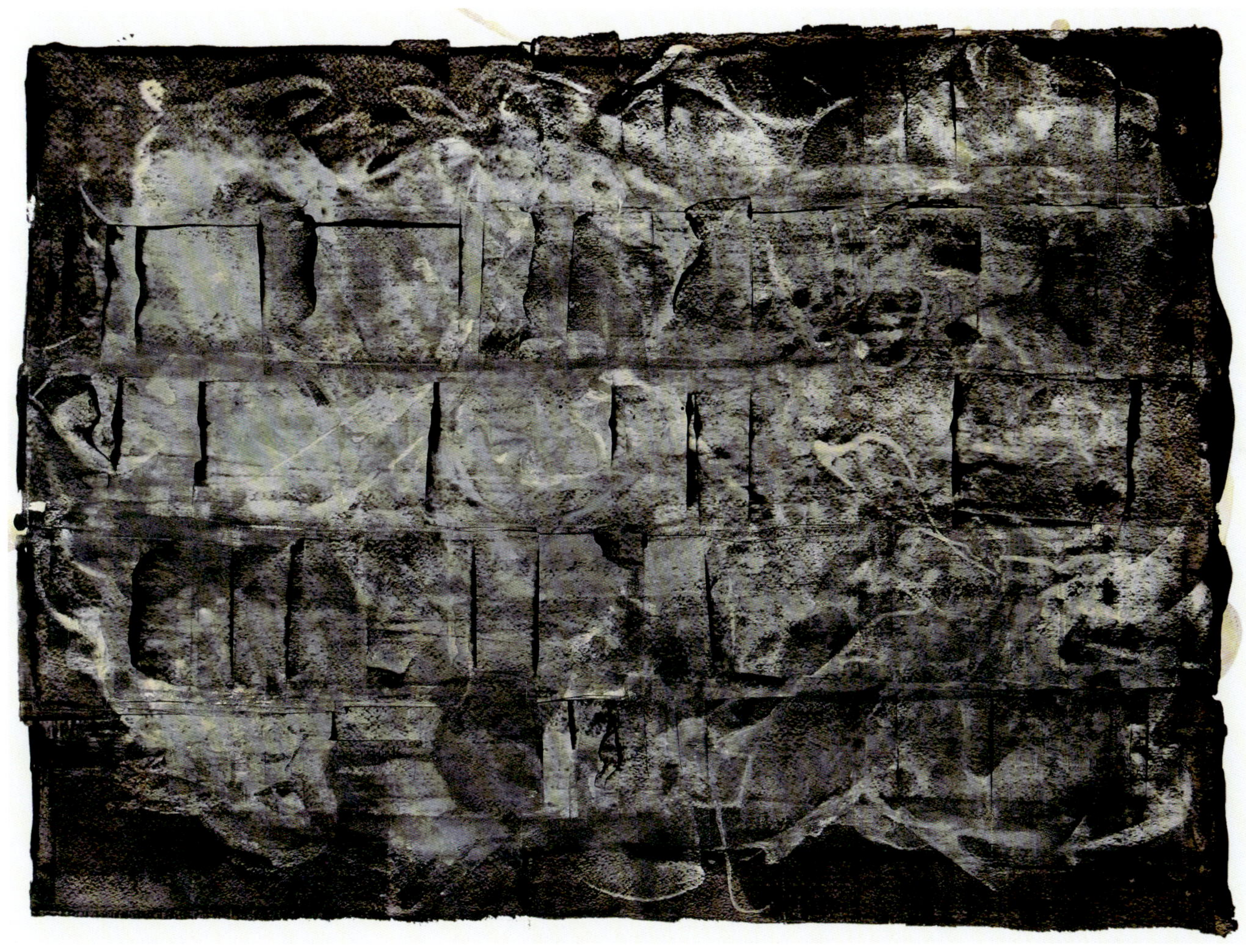

2016, mixed media on paper,
56 x 76 cm

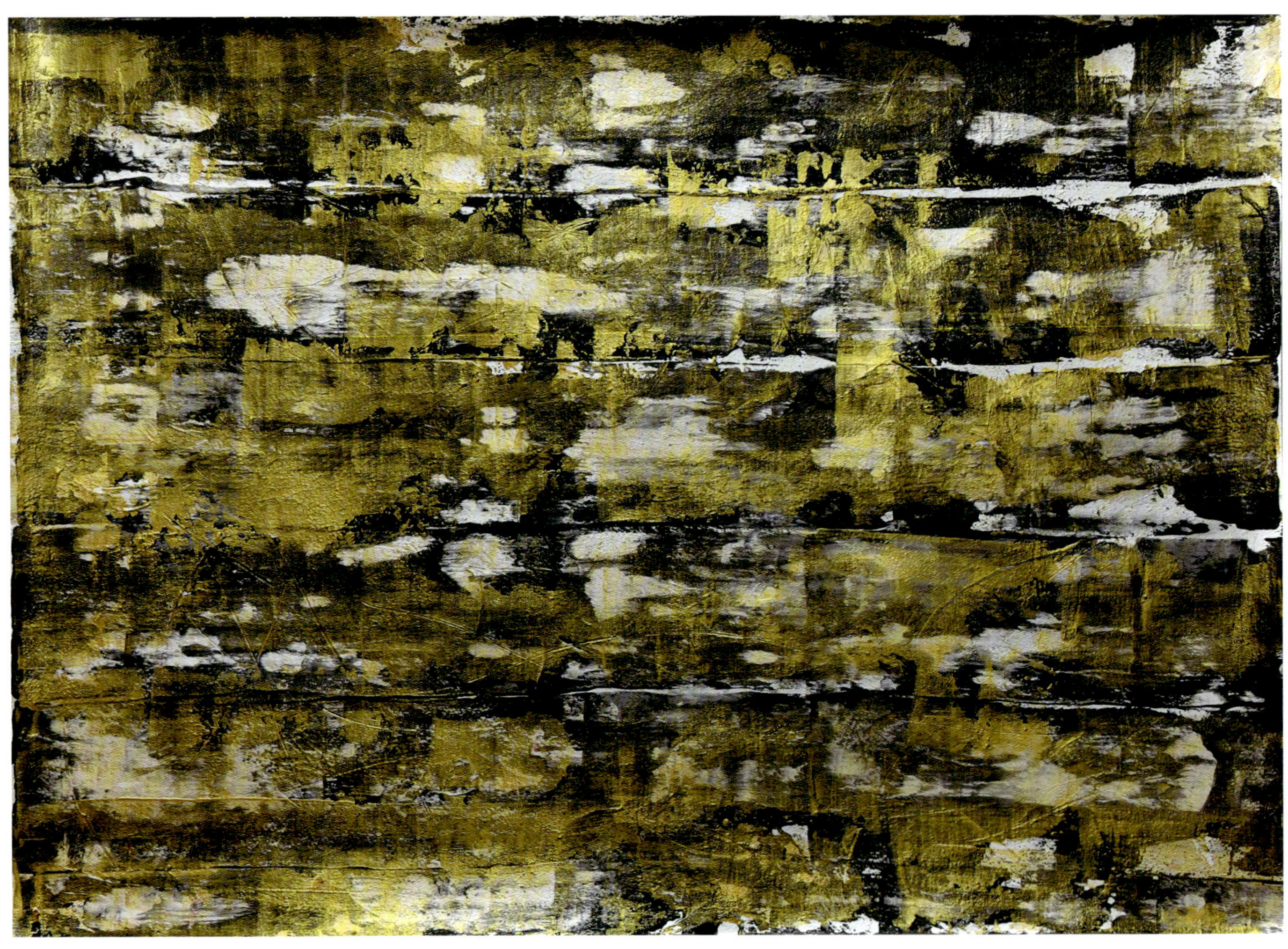

2016, mixed media on paper,
56 x 76 cm

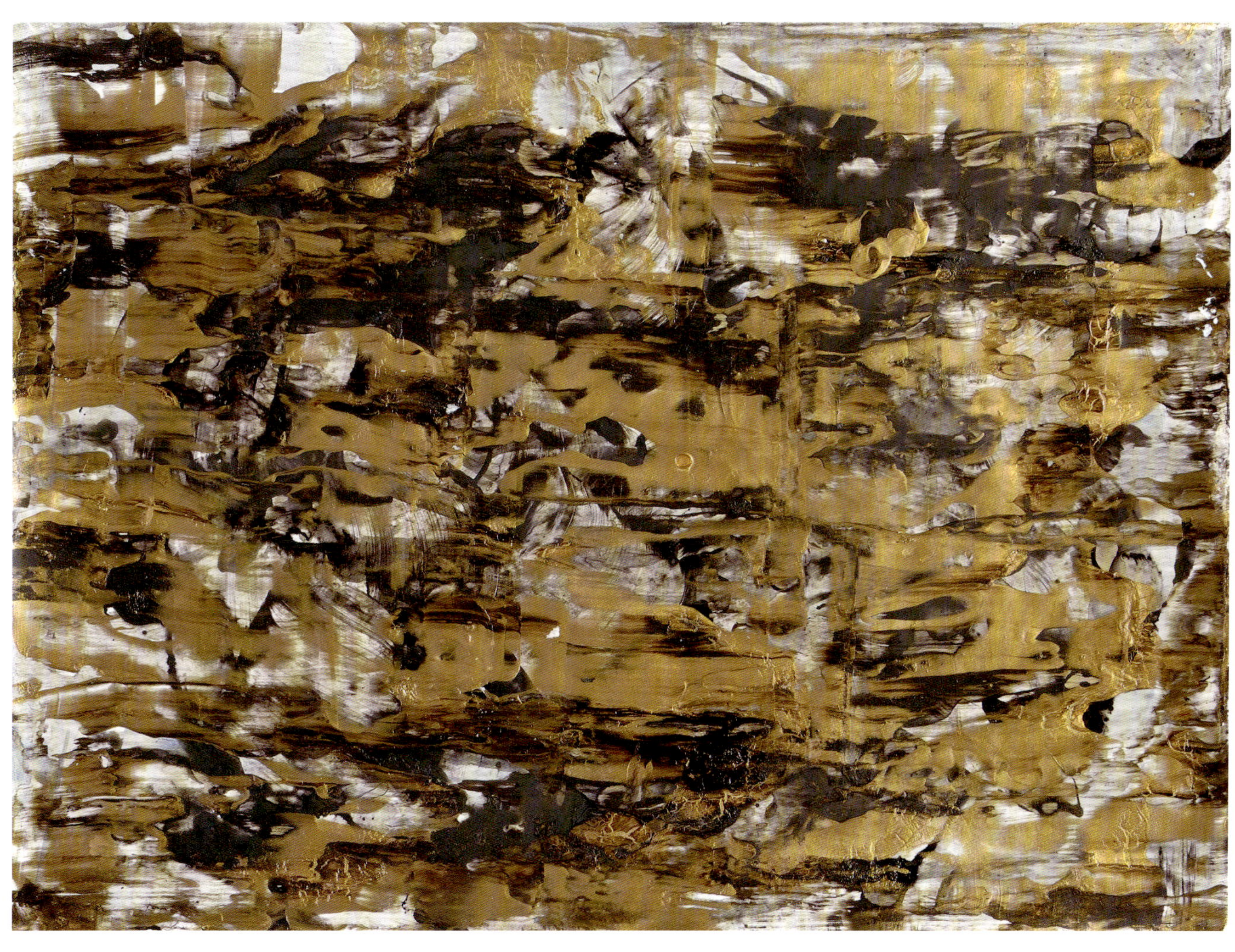

2016, mixed media on paper,
46 x 61cm

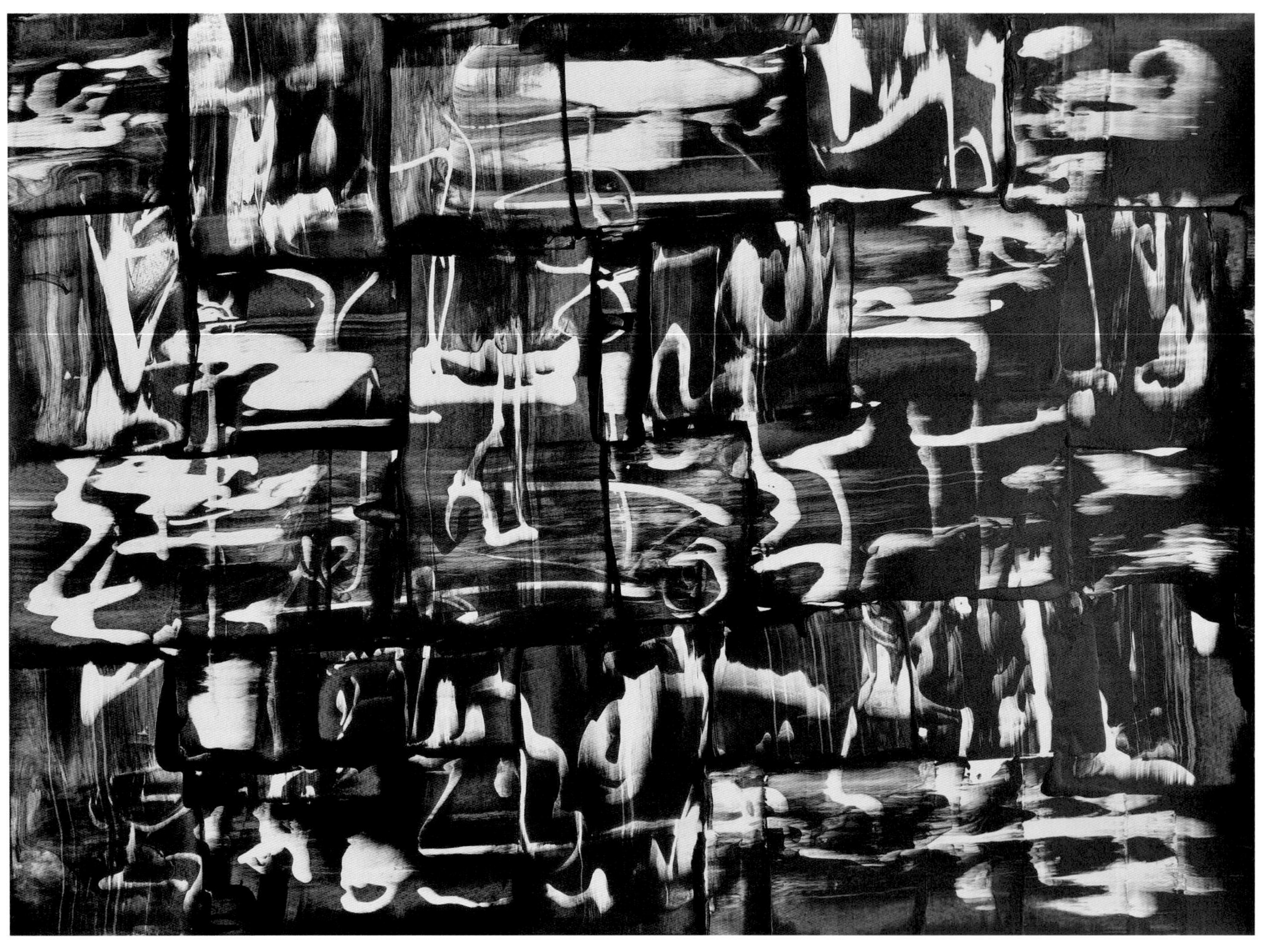

2016, mixed media on paper,
46 x 61cm

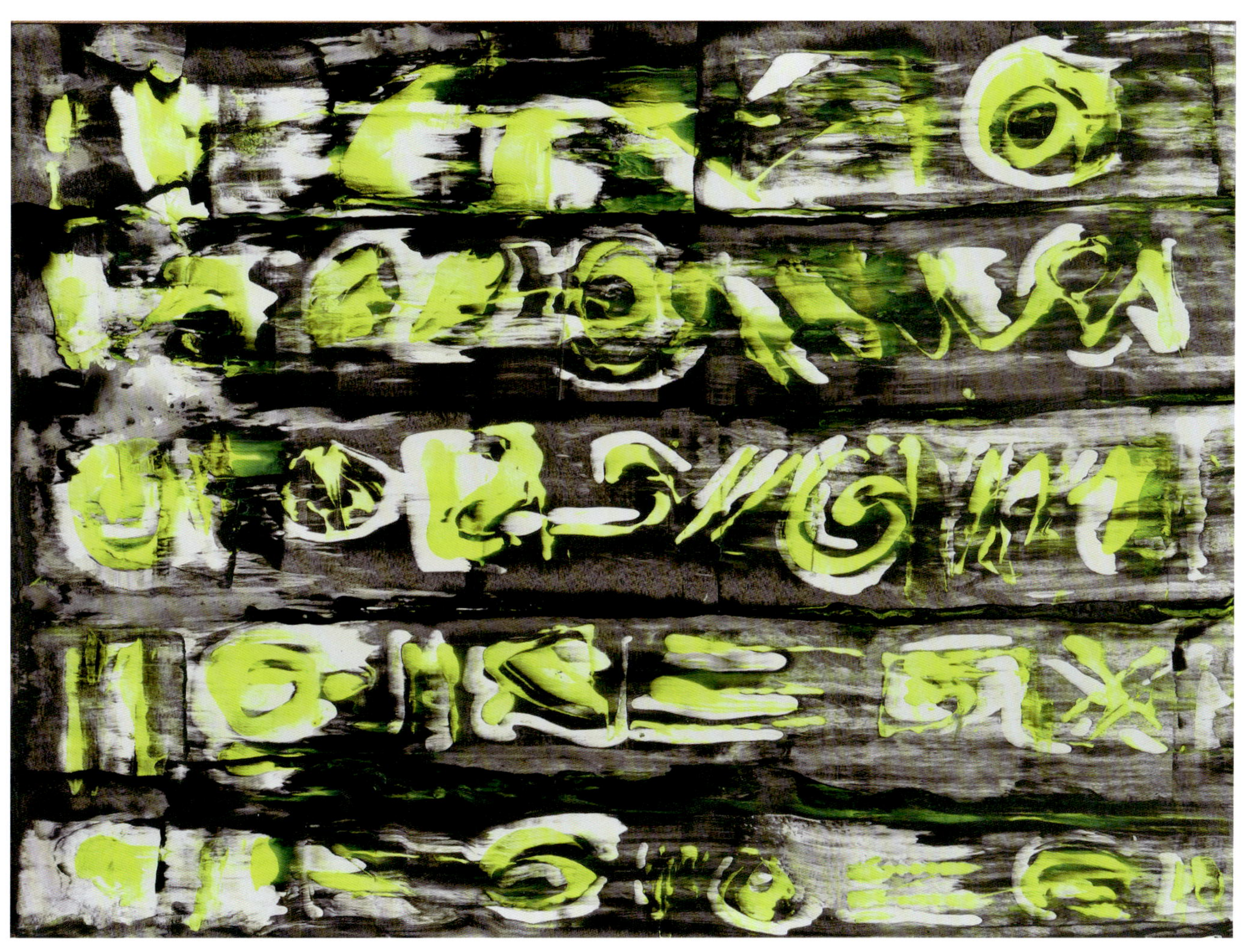

2016, mixed media on paper,
46 x 61 cm

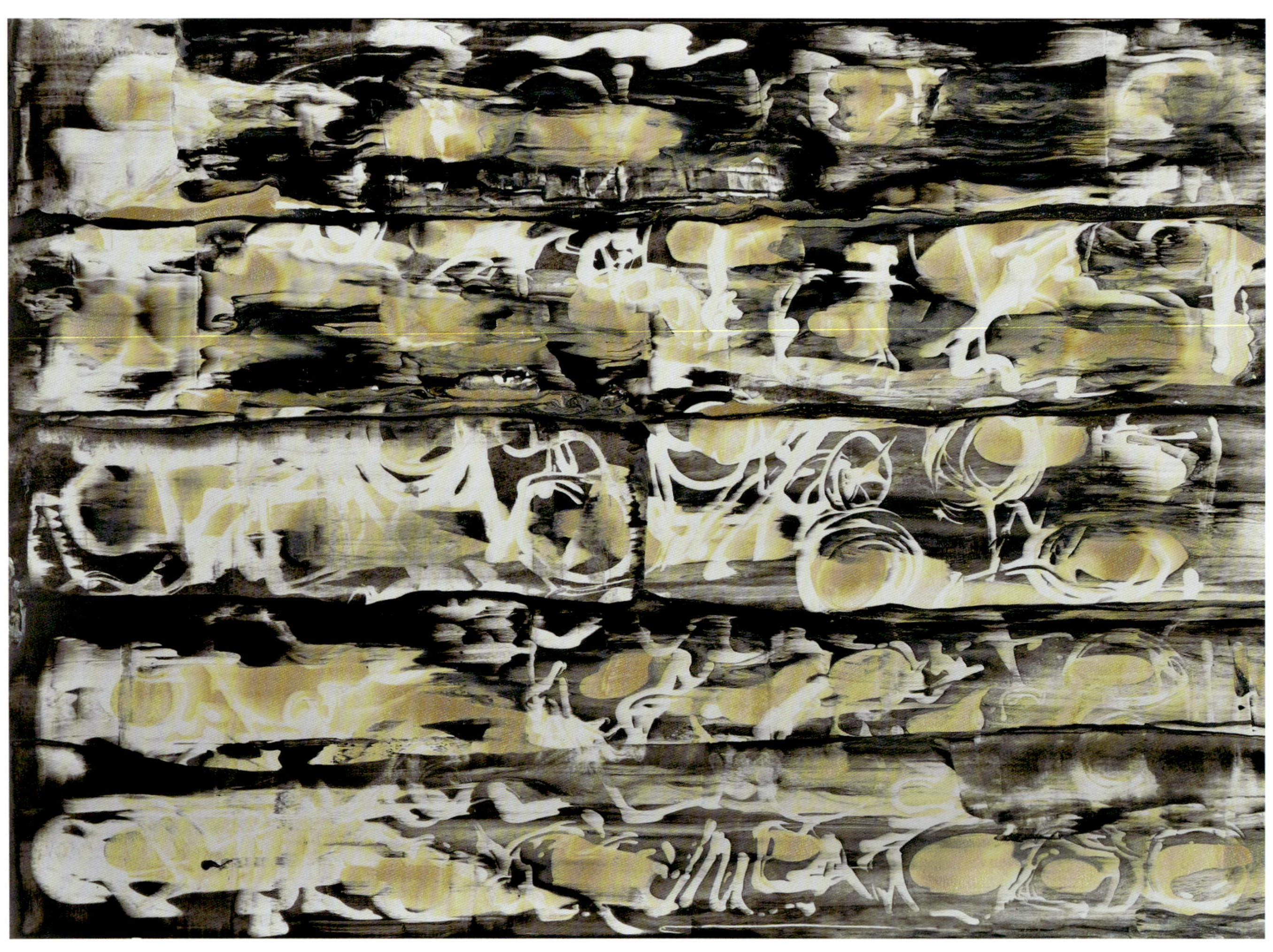

2016, mixed media on paper,
46 x 61cm

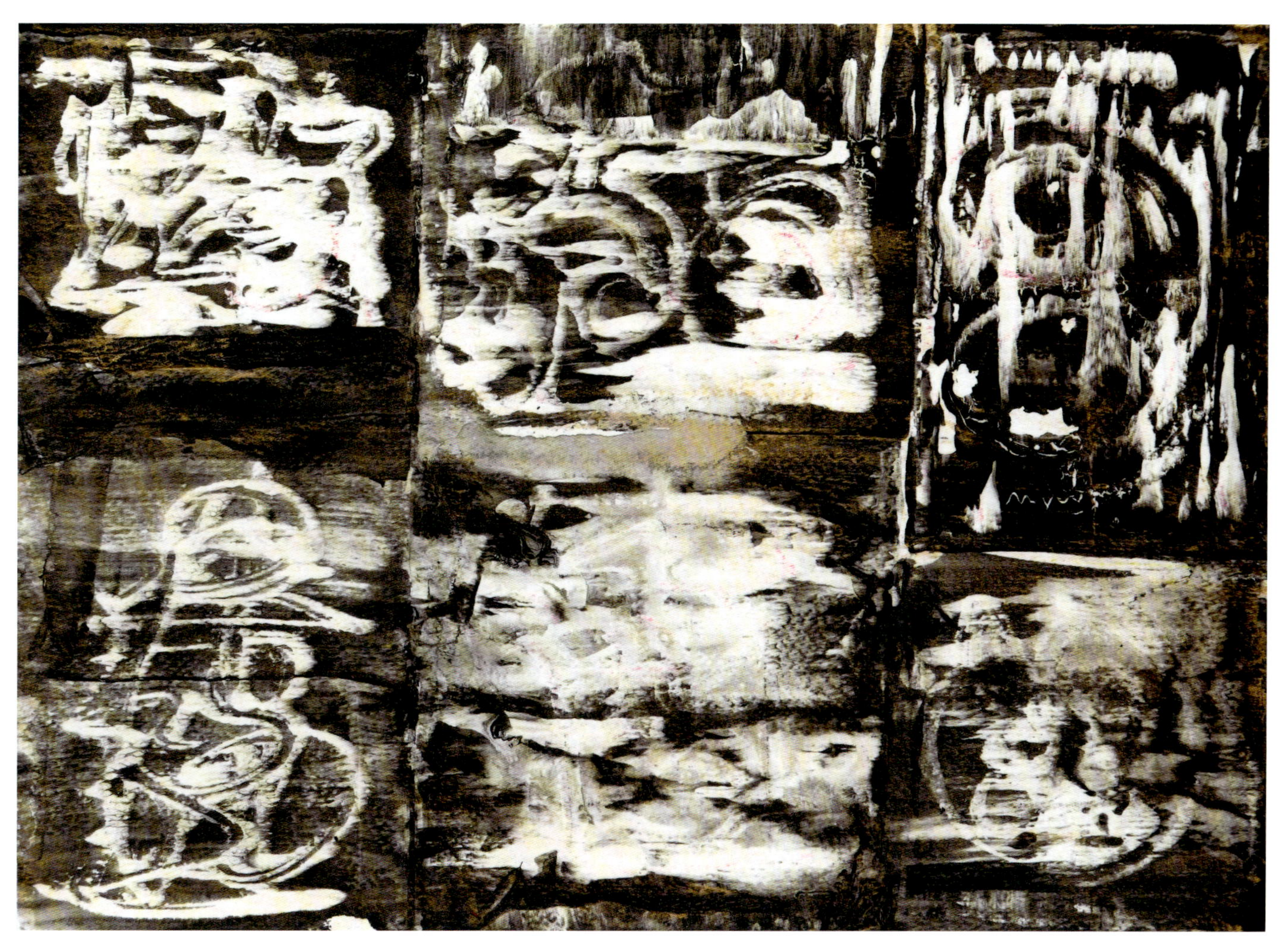

2016, mixed media on paper,
28 x 38 cm

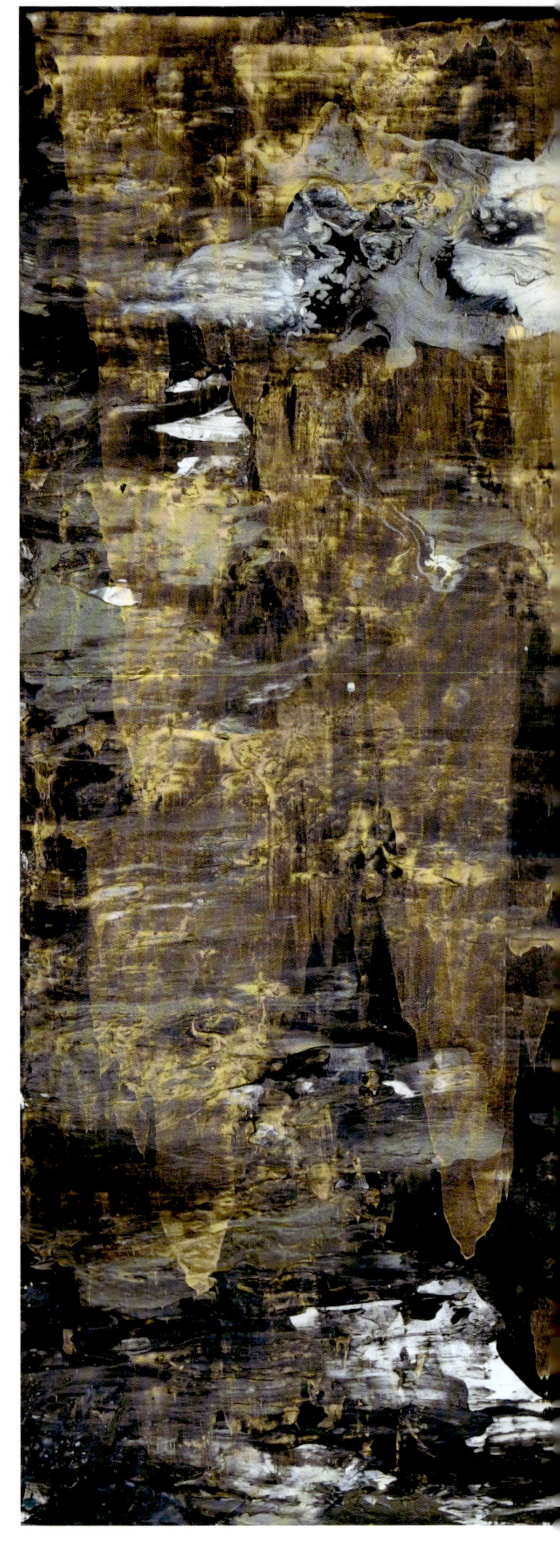

2016, mixed media on paper,
56 x 76 cm

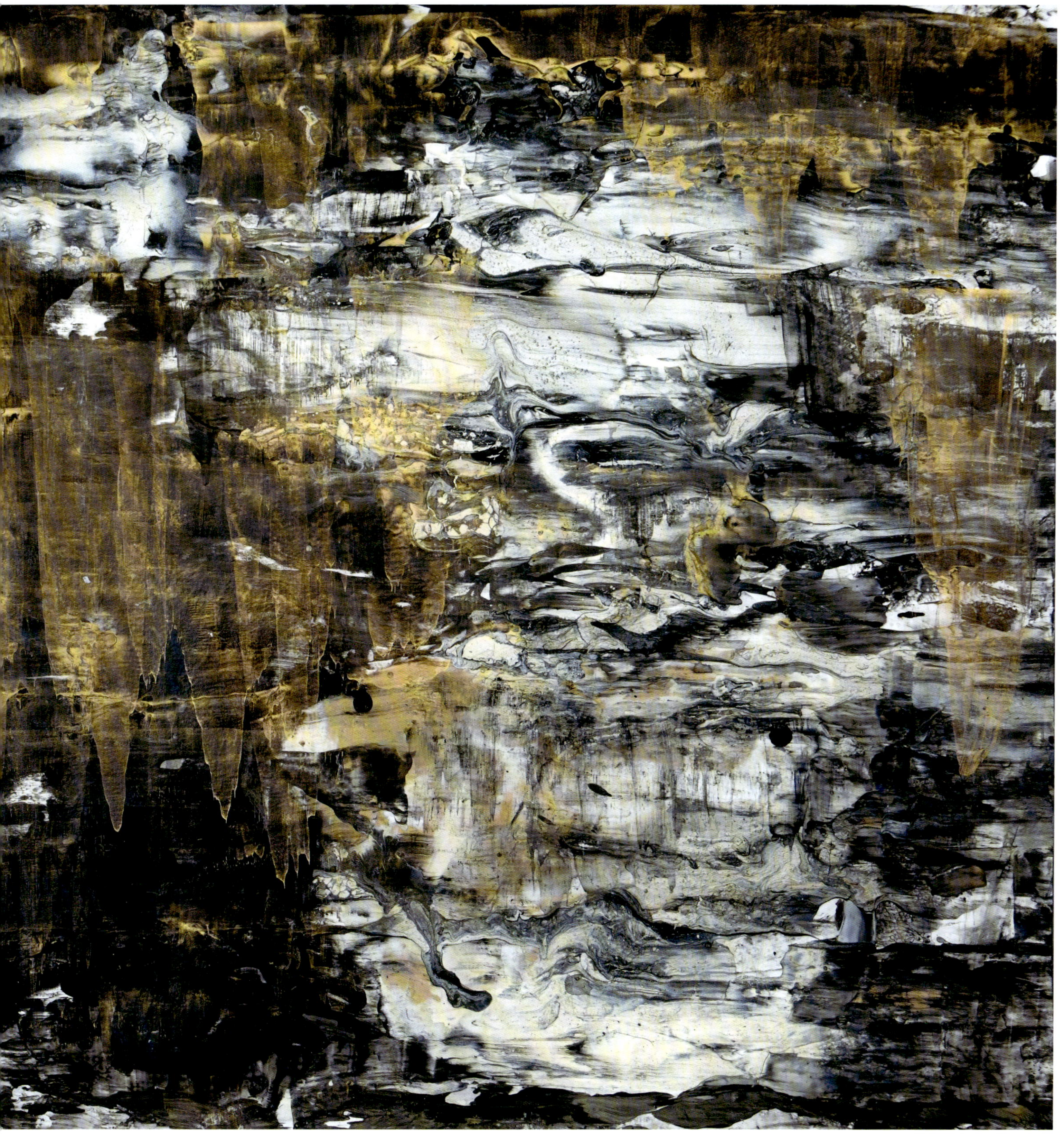

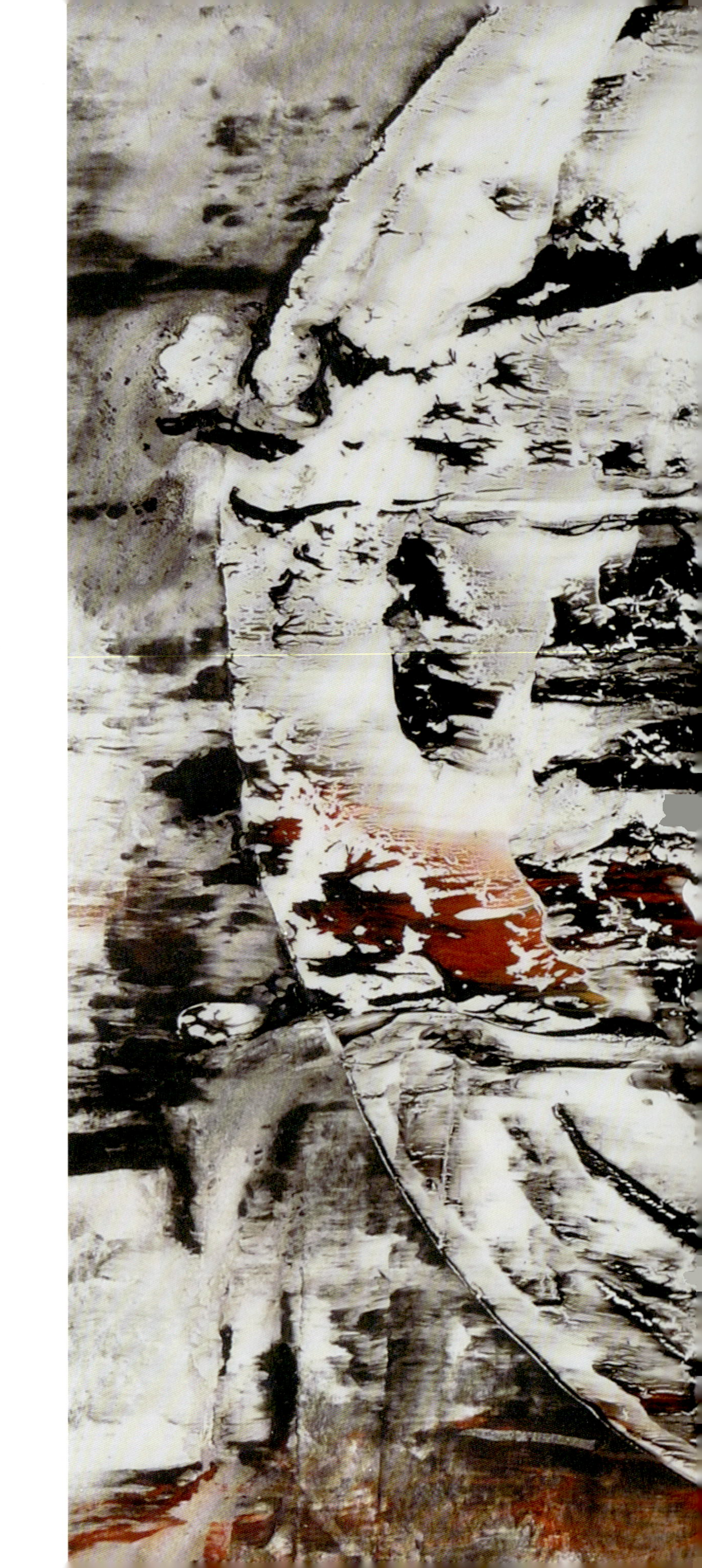

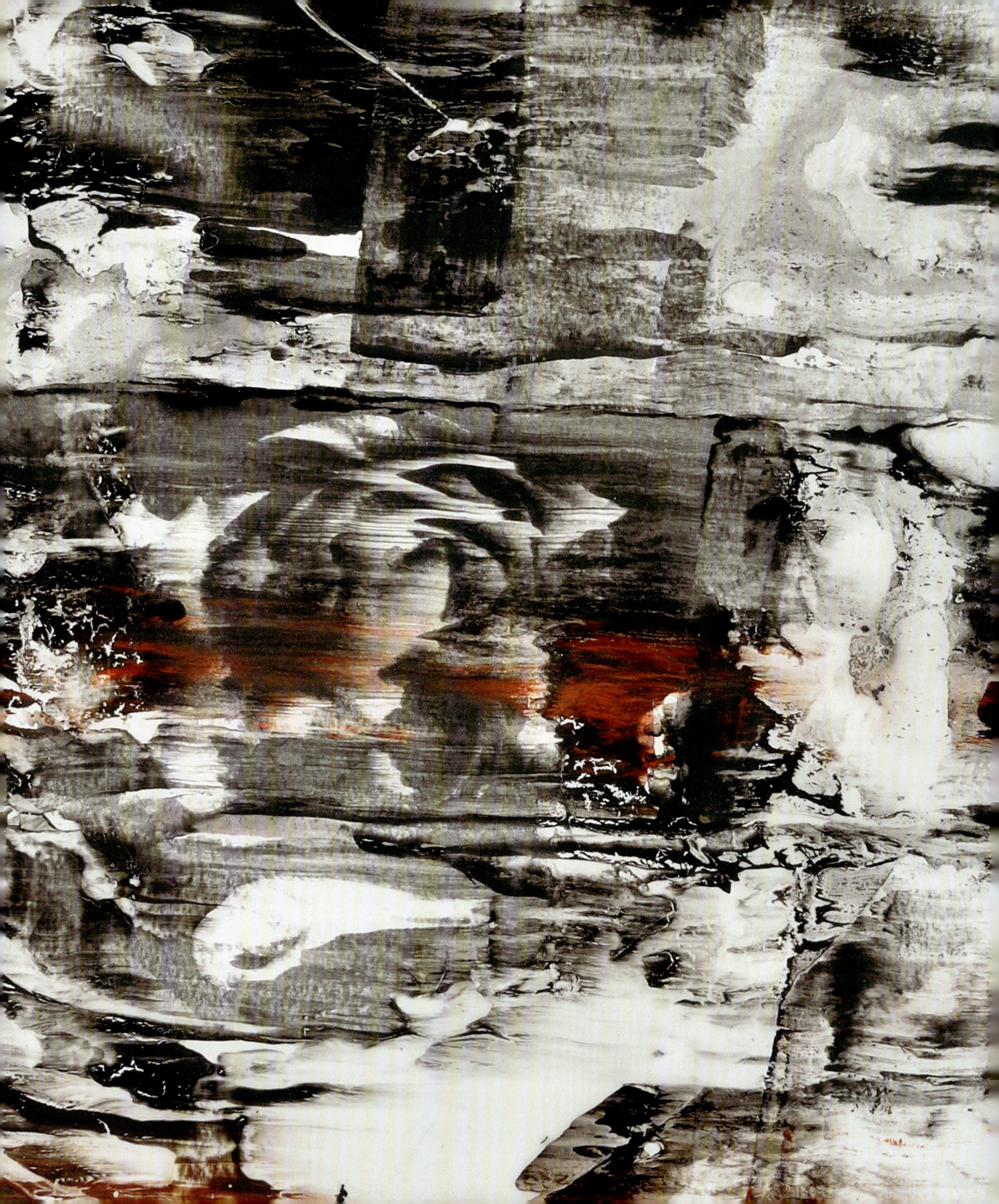

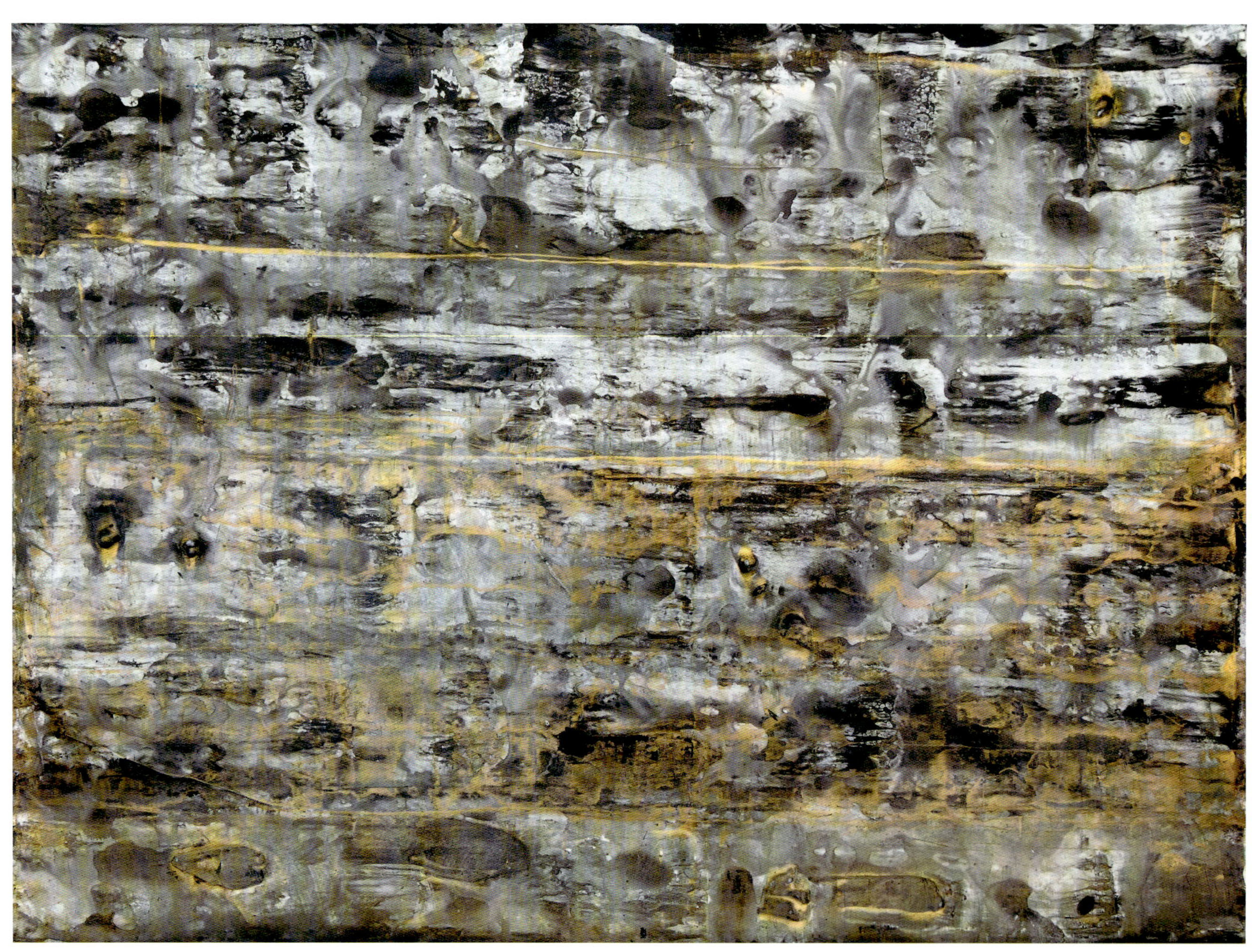

2016, mixed media on paper,
56 x 76 cm

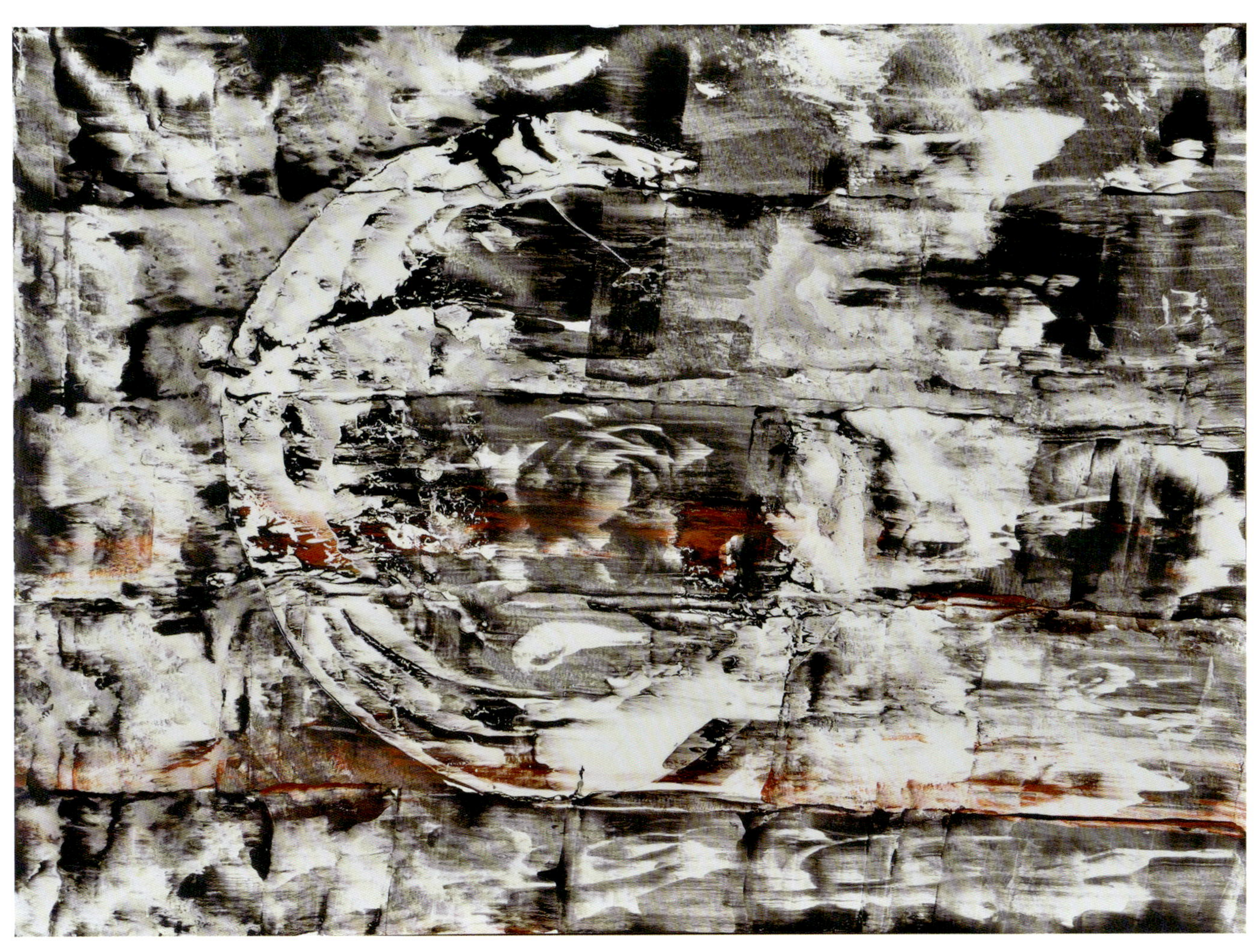

2016, mixed media on paper,
46 x 61 cm

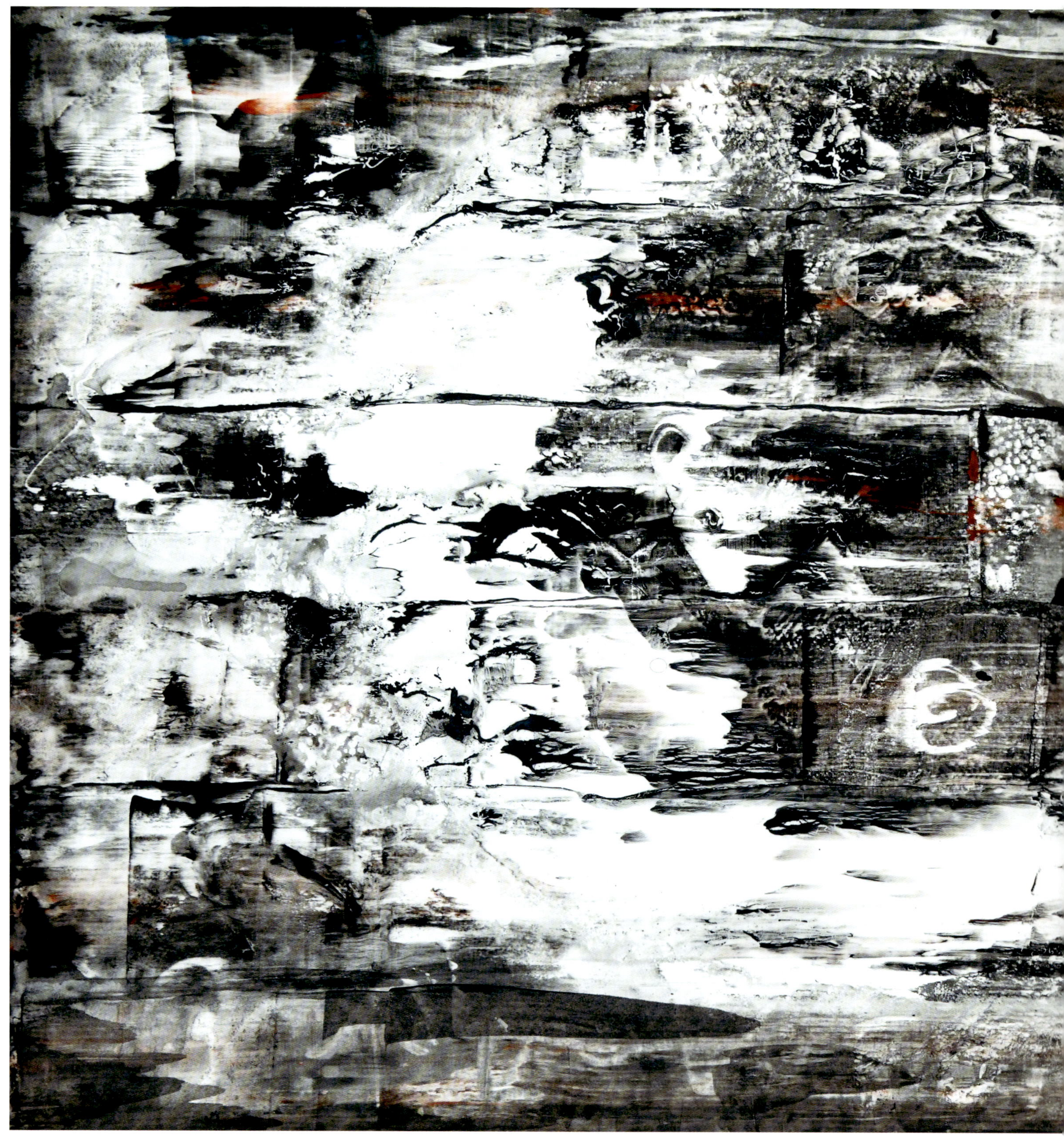

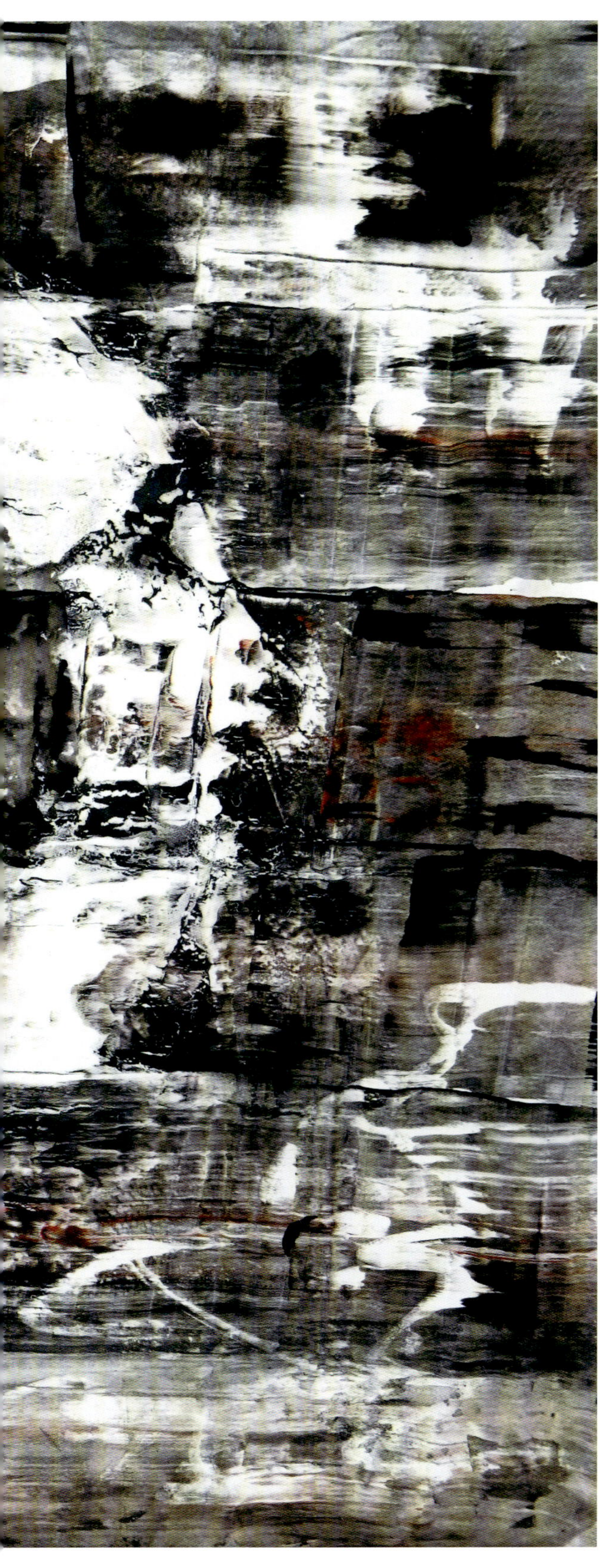

2016, mixed media on paper,
56 x 76 cm

2016, mixed media on paper,
46 x 61cm

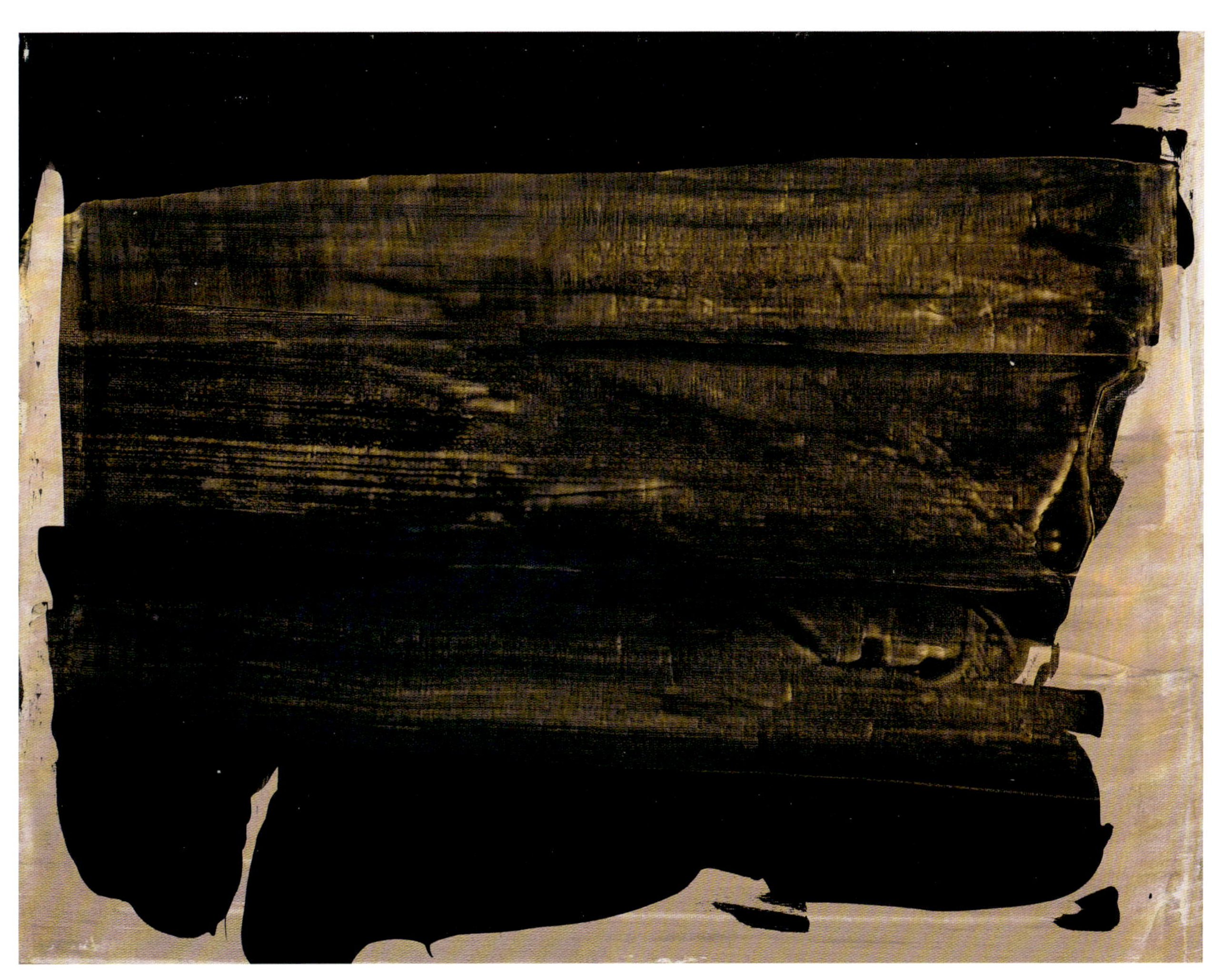

2016, mixed media on canvas,
40.5 x 51cm

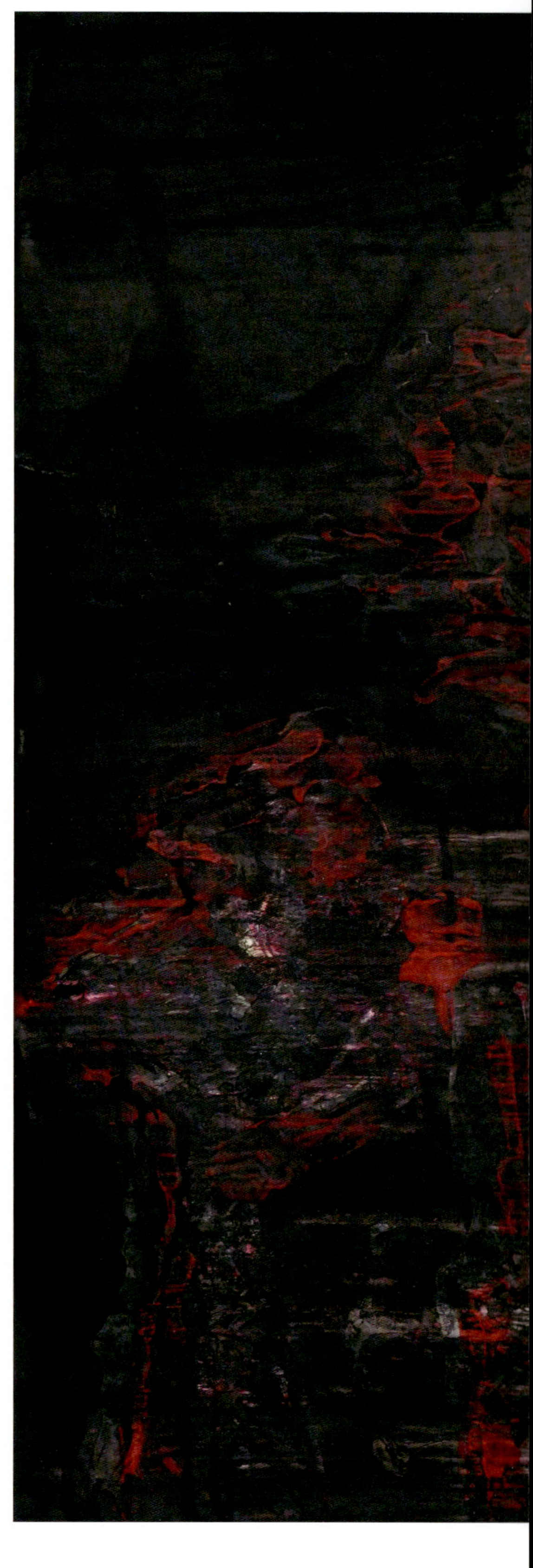

2016, mixed media on paper,
46 x 61cm

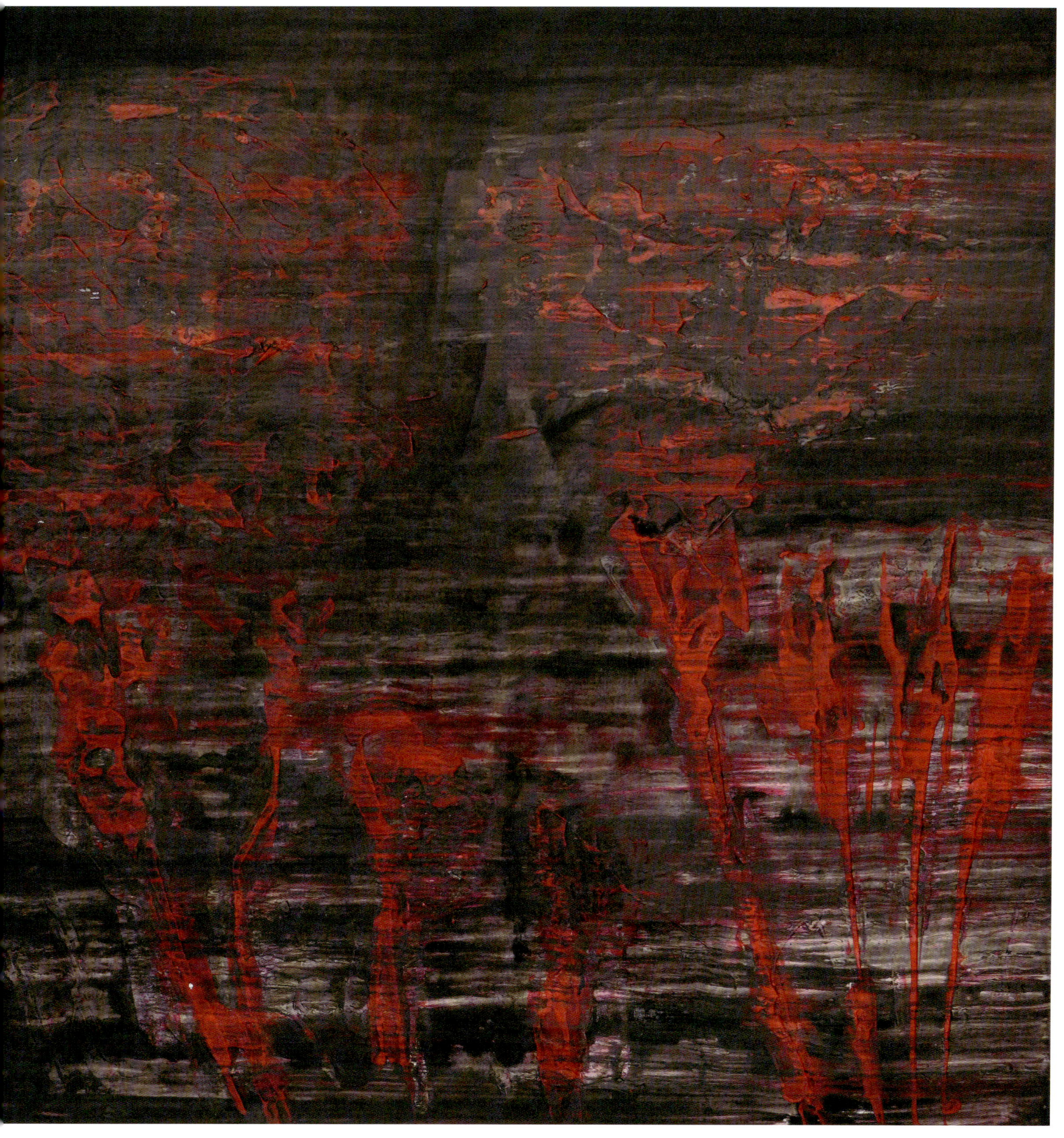

2016, mixed media on canvas,
61 x 76 cm

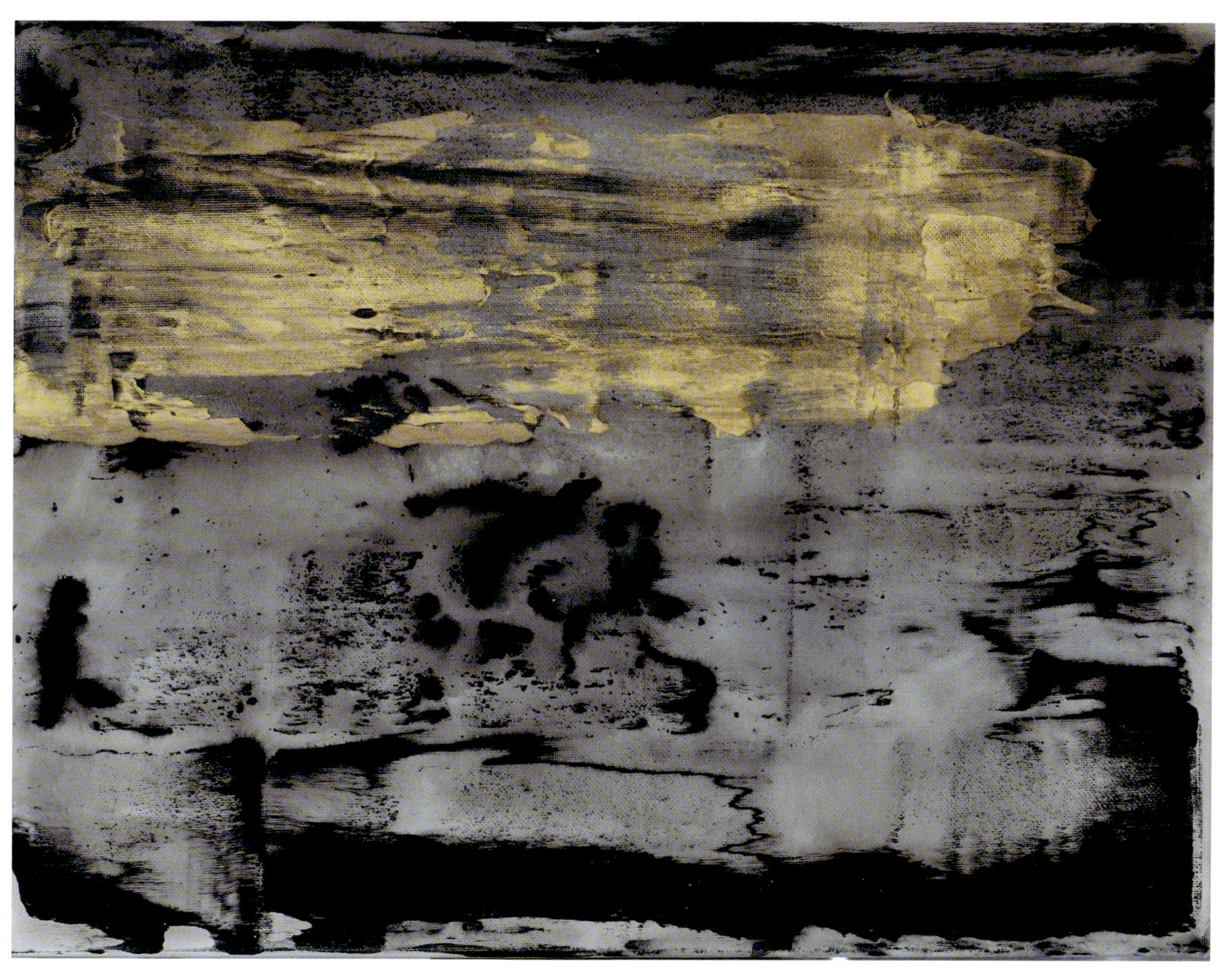

2016, mixed media on canvas,
40.5 x 51cm

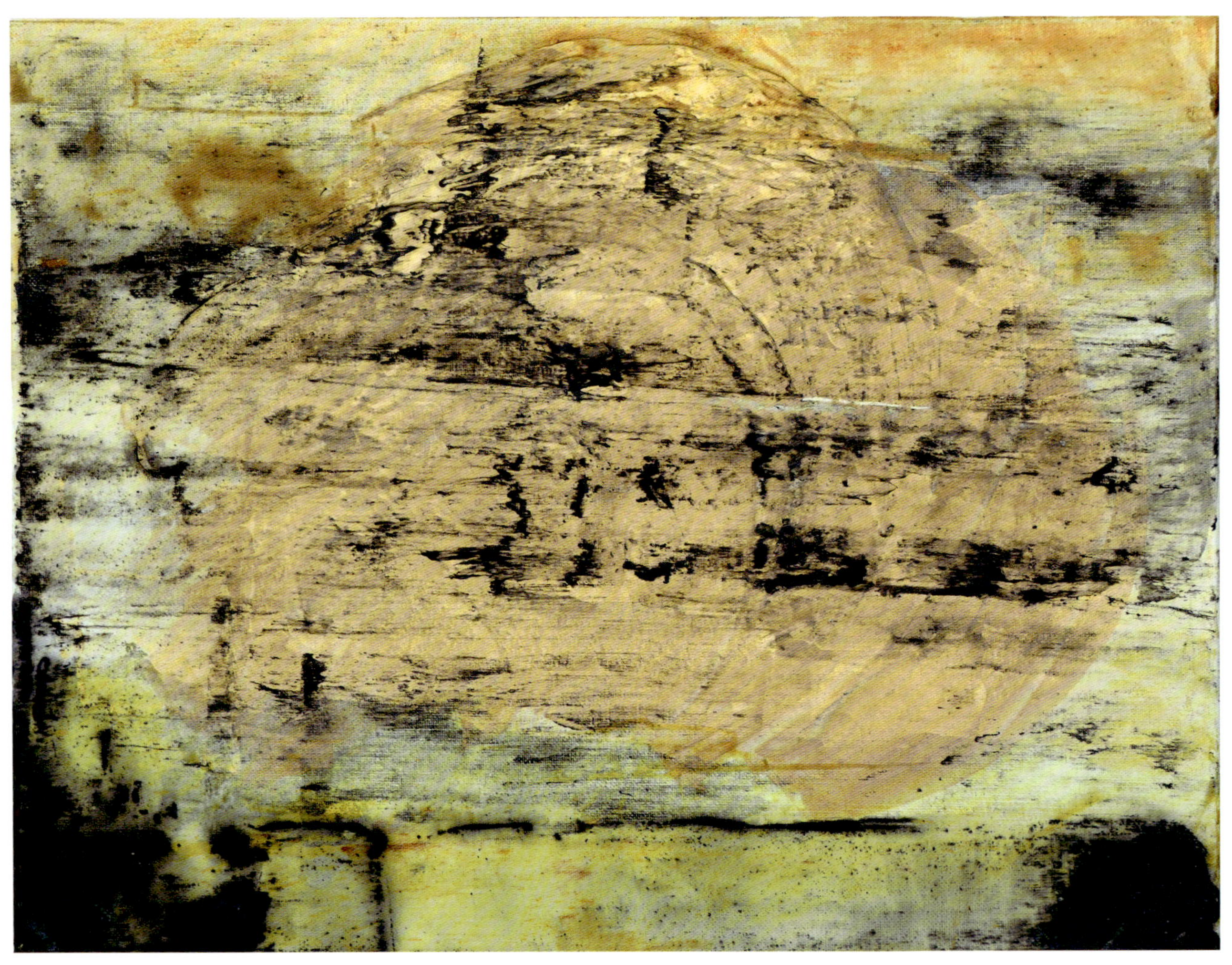

2016, mixed media on canvas,
40.5 x 51cm

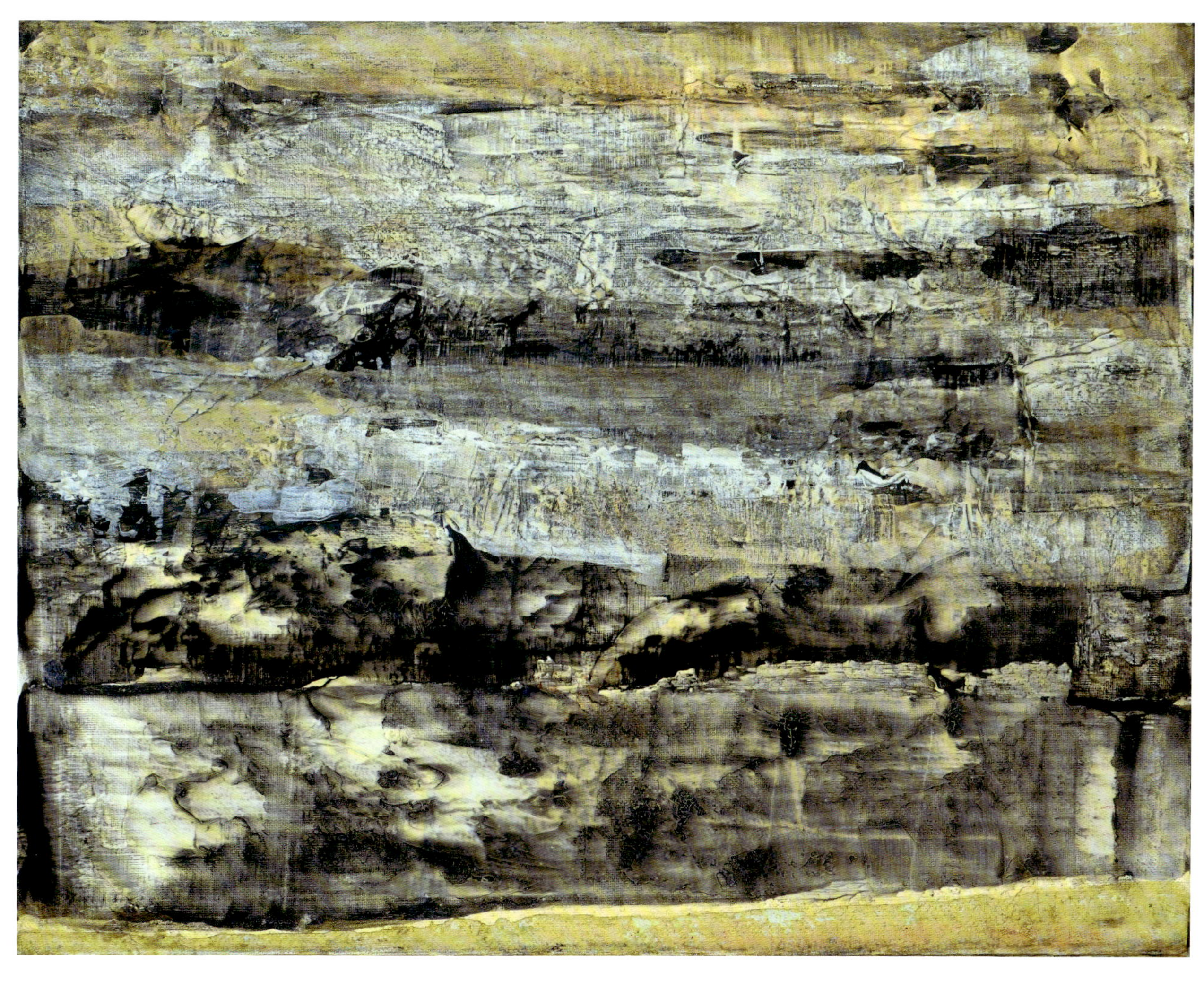

2016, mixed media on canvas,
40.5 x 51cm

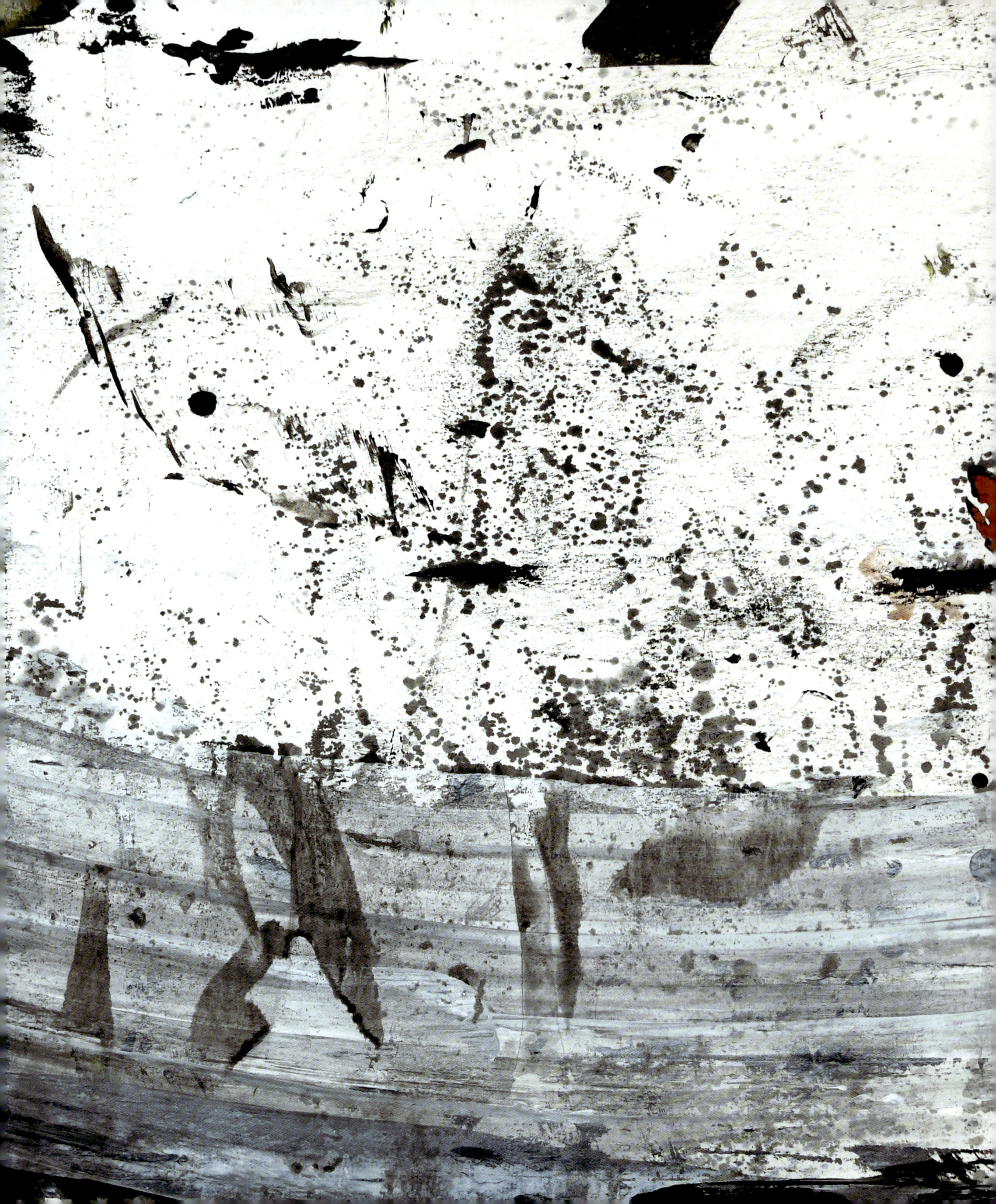

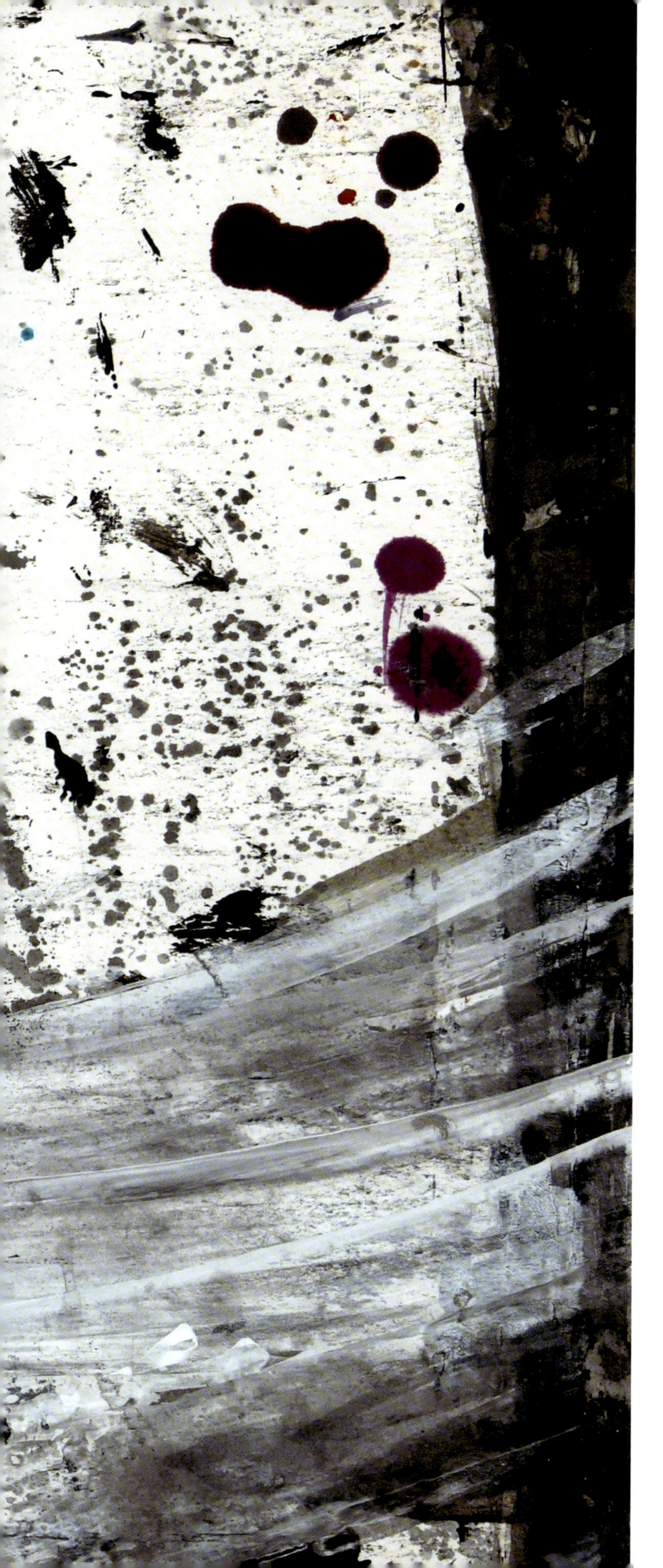

2016, mixed media on paper,
56 x 76 cm

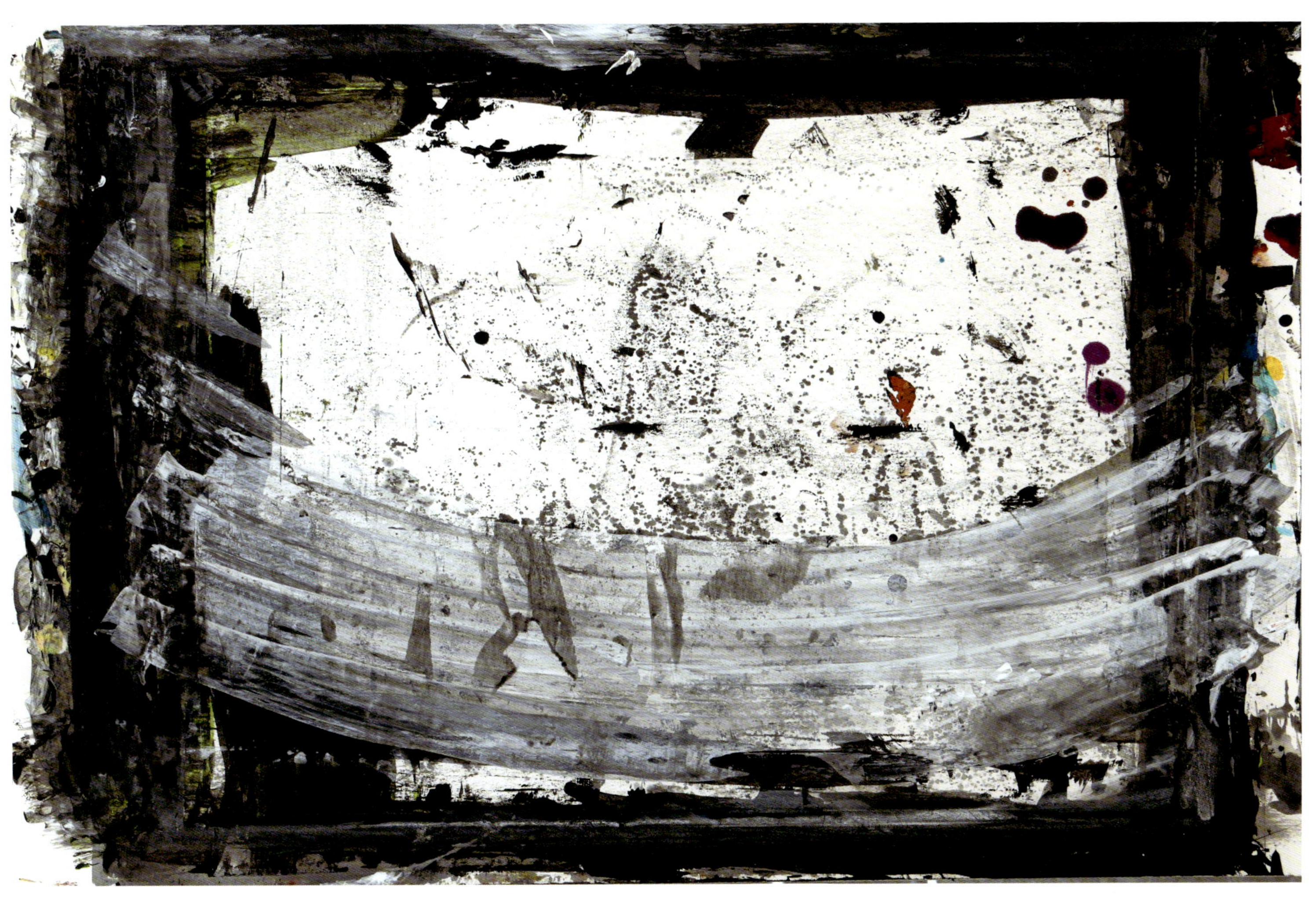

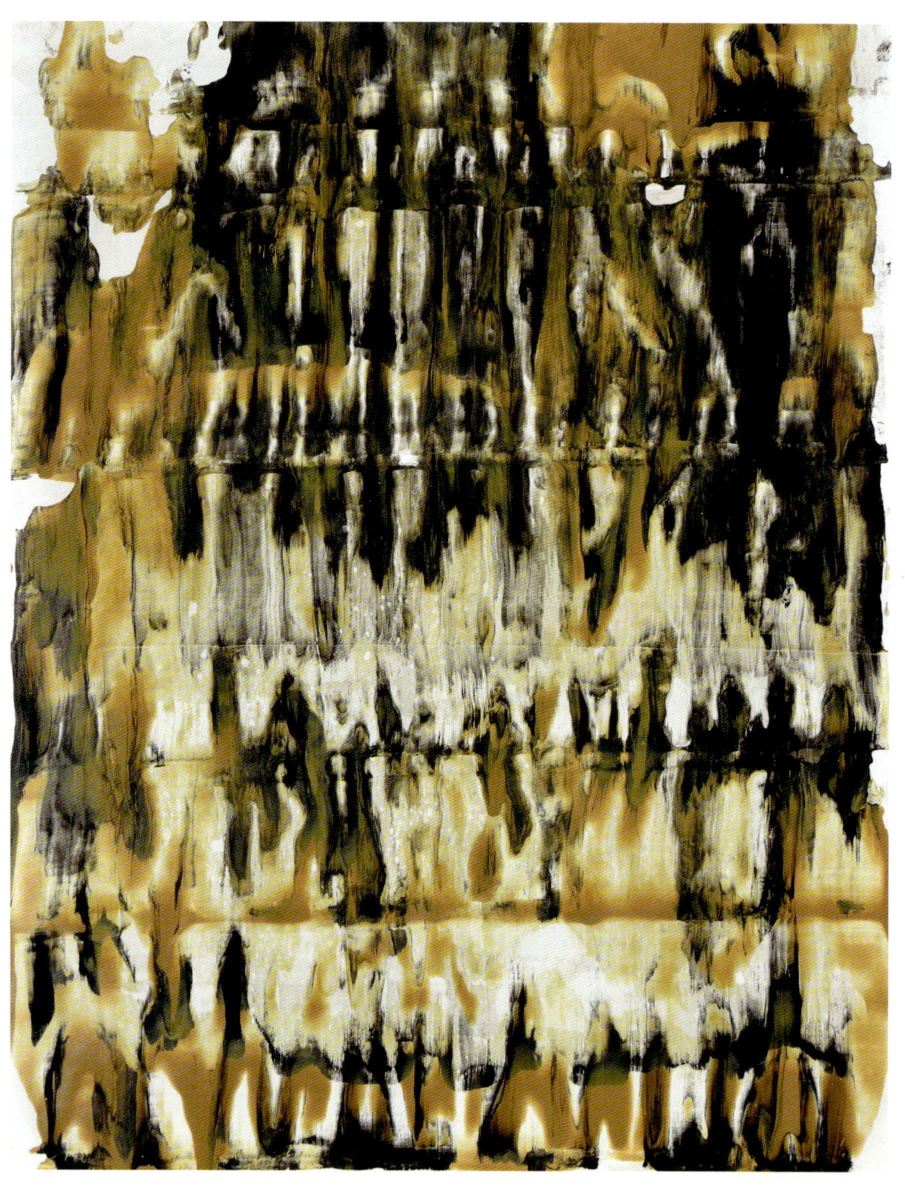

2016, mixed media on paper,
61 x 46 cm

2016, mixed media on paper,
61 x 46 cm

2016, mixed media on paper,
61 x 46 cm

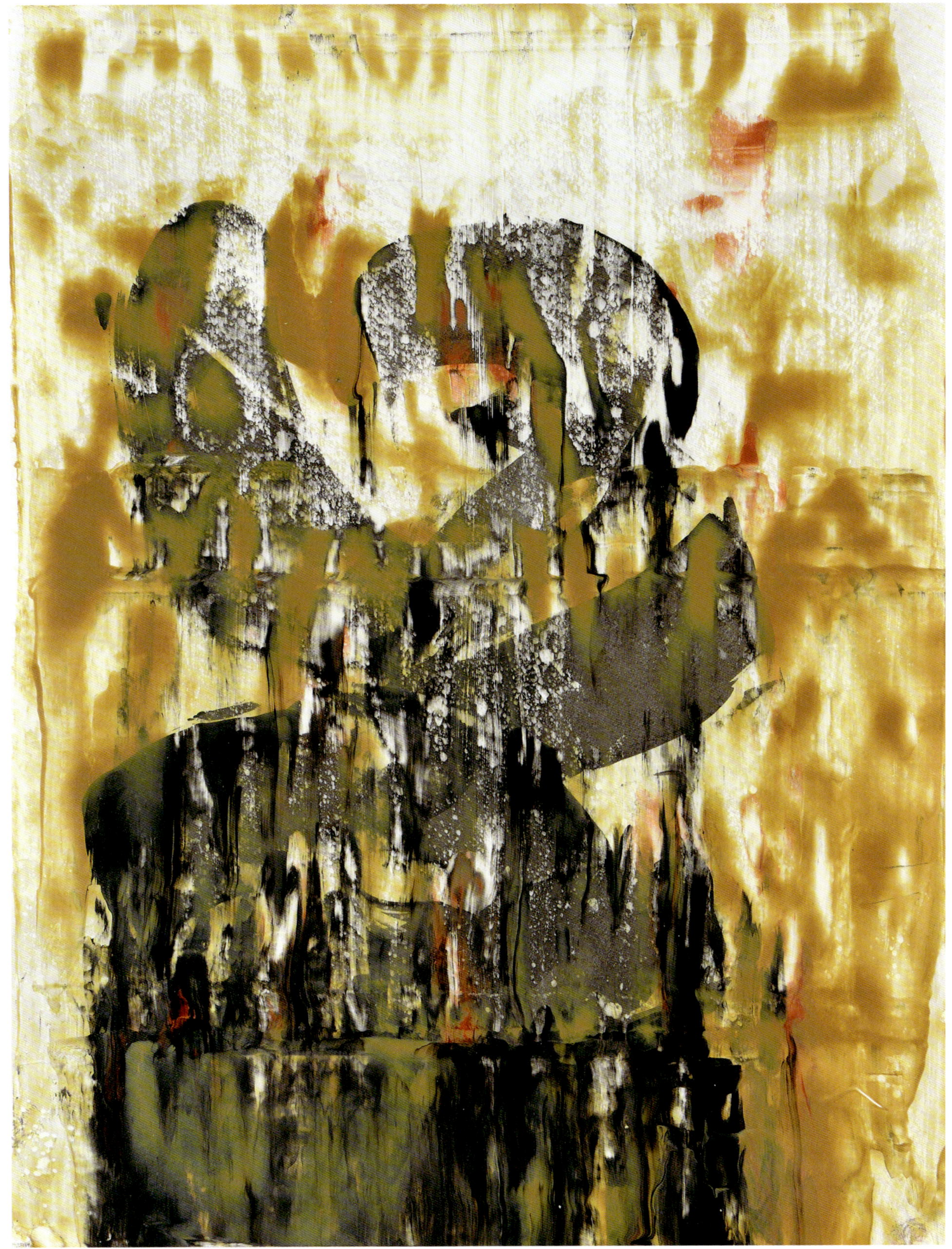

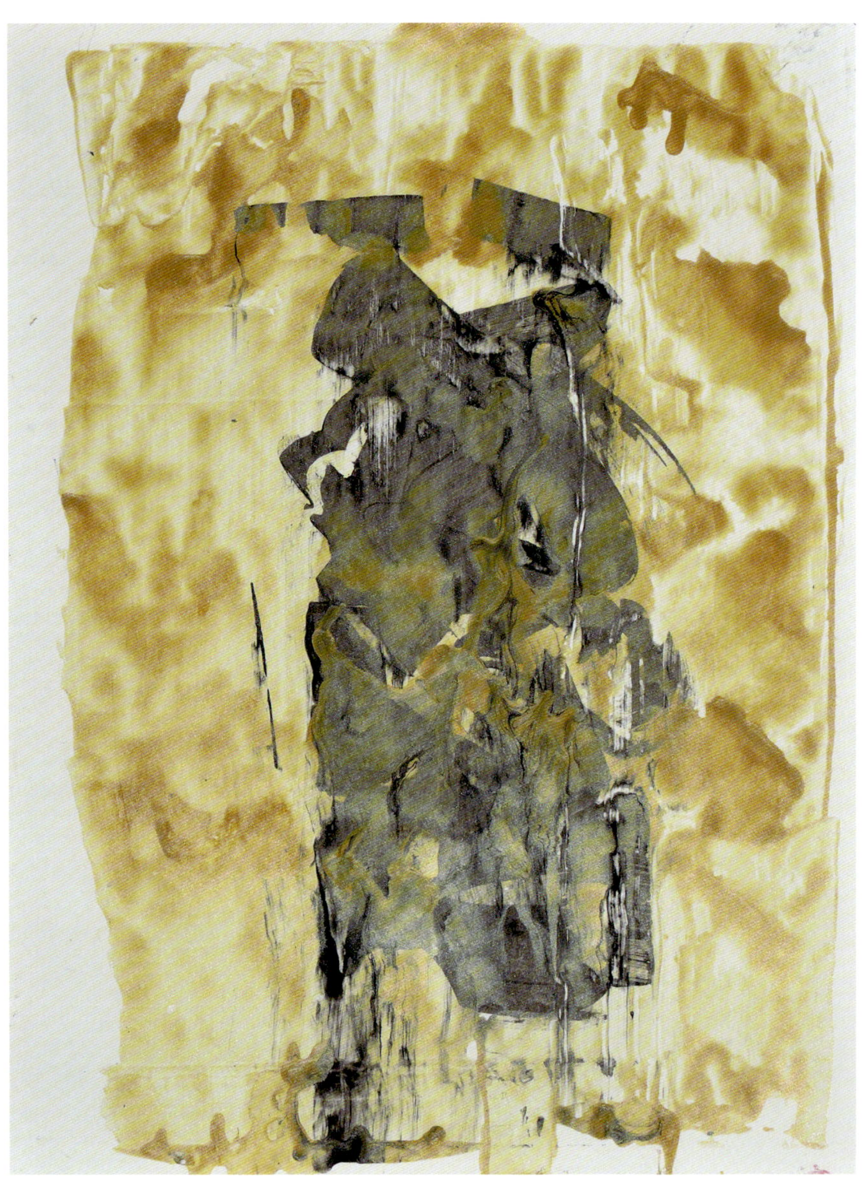

2016, mixed media on paper,
61 x 46 cm

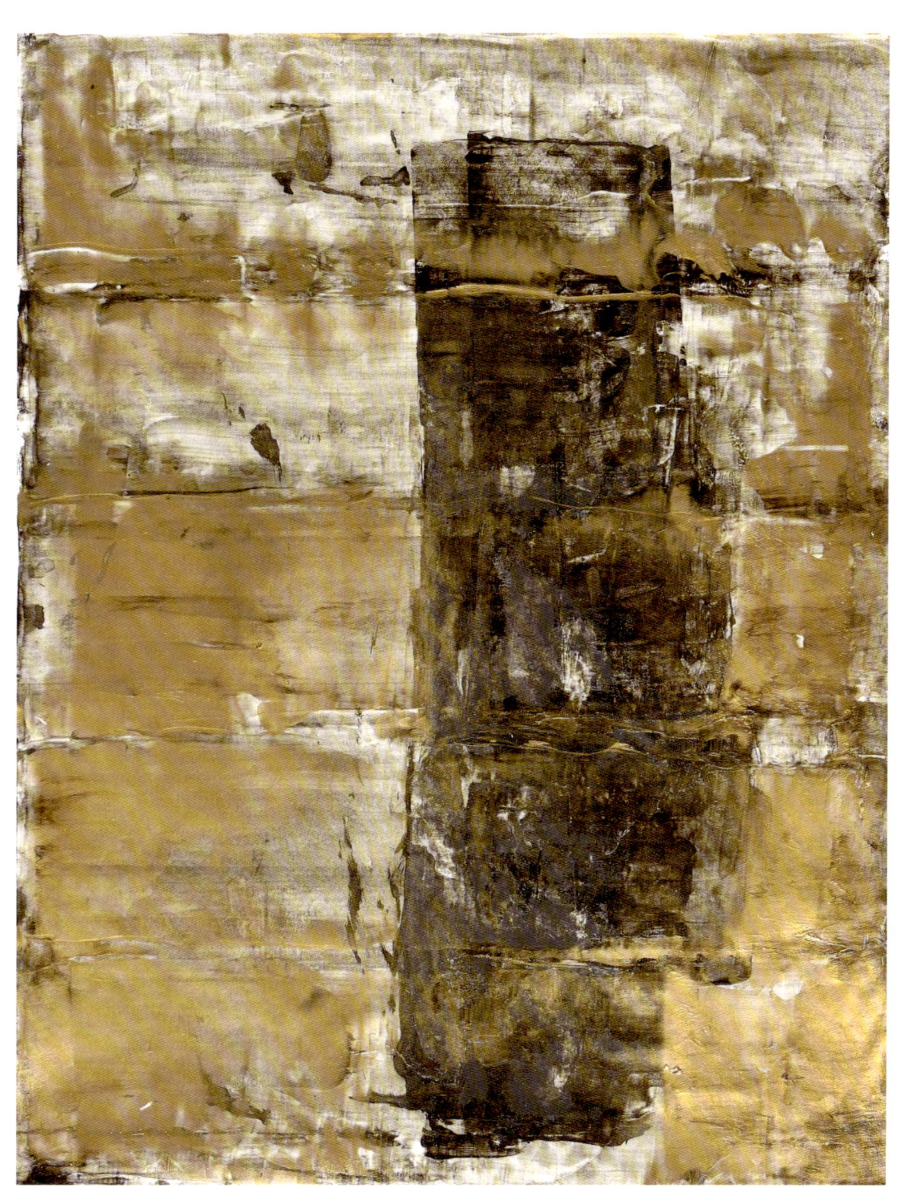

2016, mixed media on paper,
61 x 46 cm

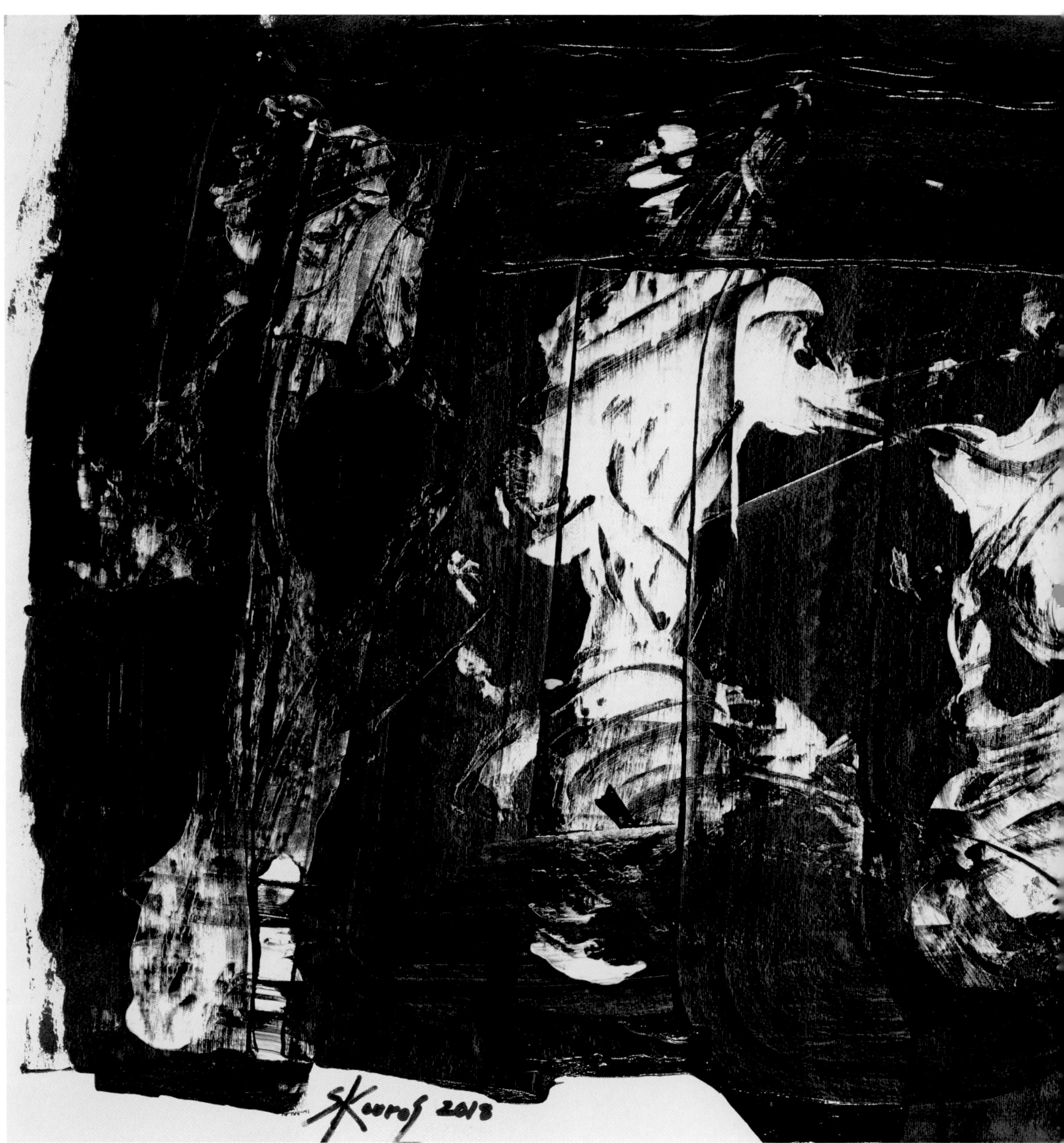
SKouros 2018

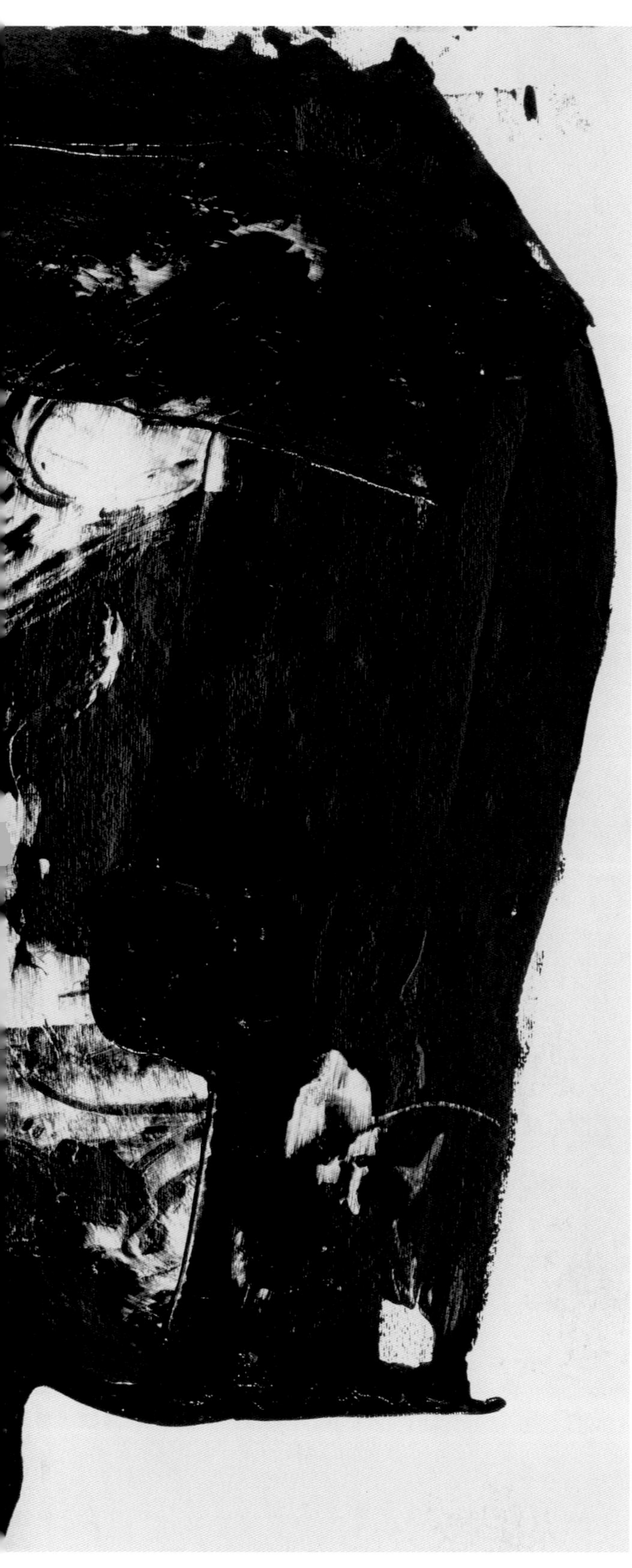

2018, acrylic on paper,
50 x 70 cm

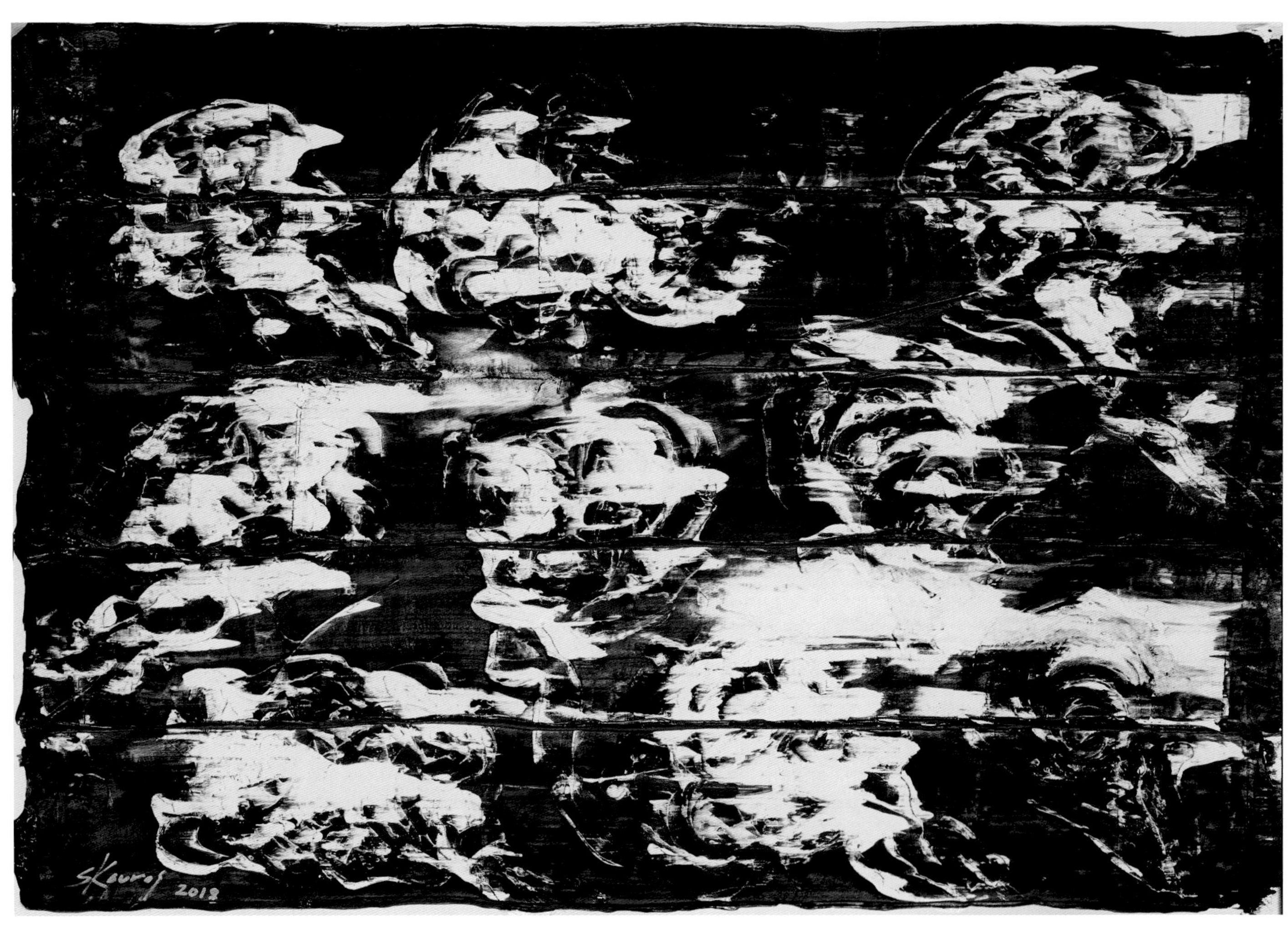

2018, acrylic on paper,
50 x 70 cm

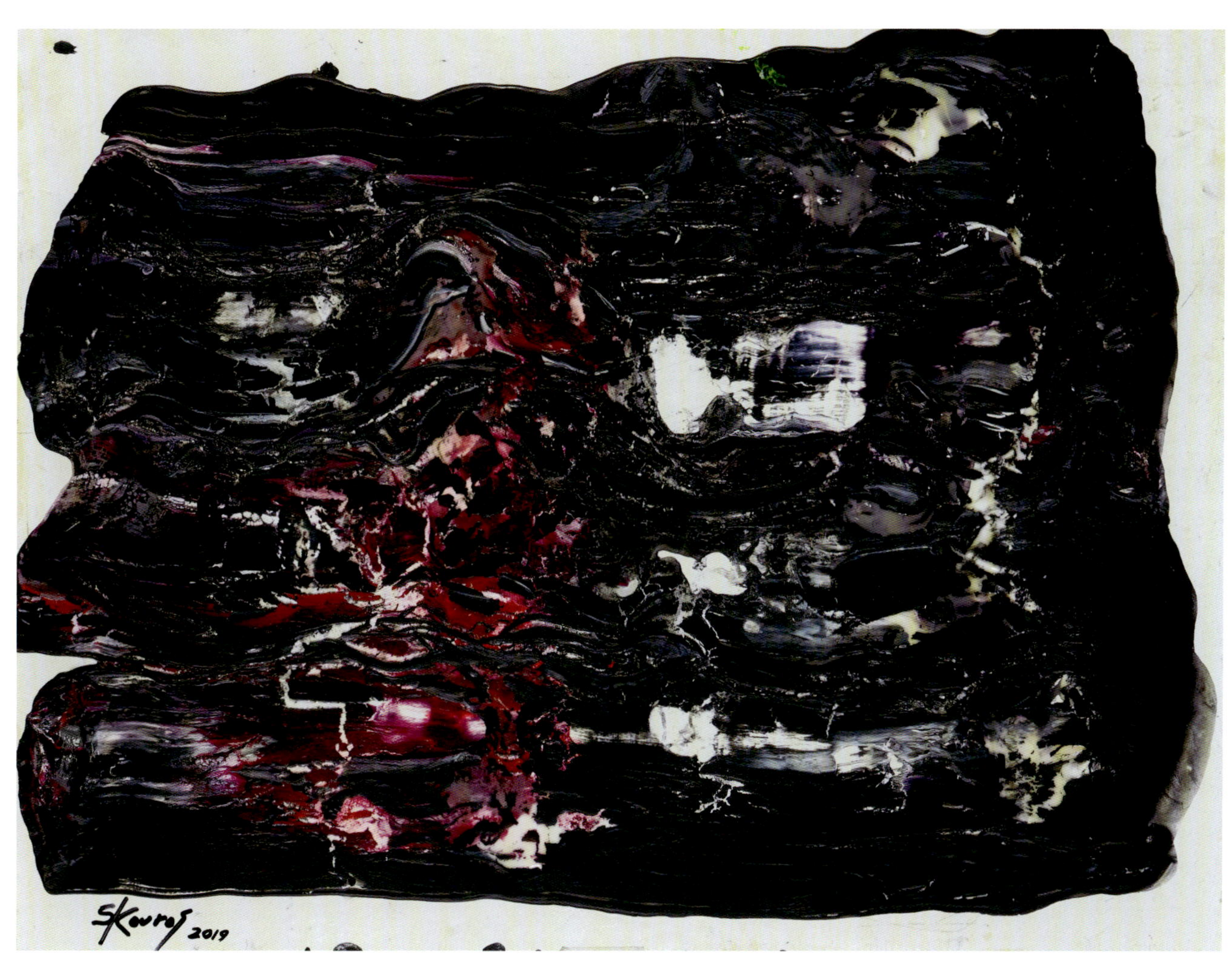

2019, acrylic on paper,
50 x 70 cm

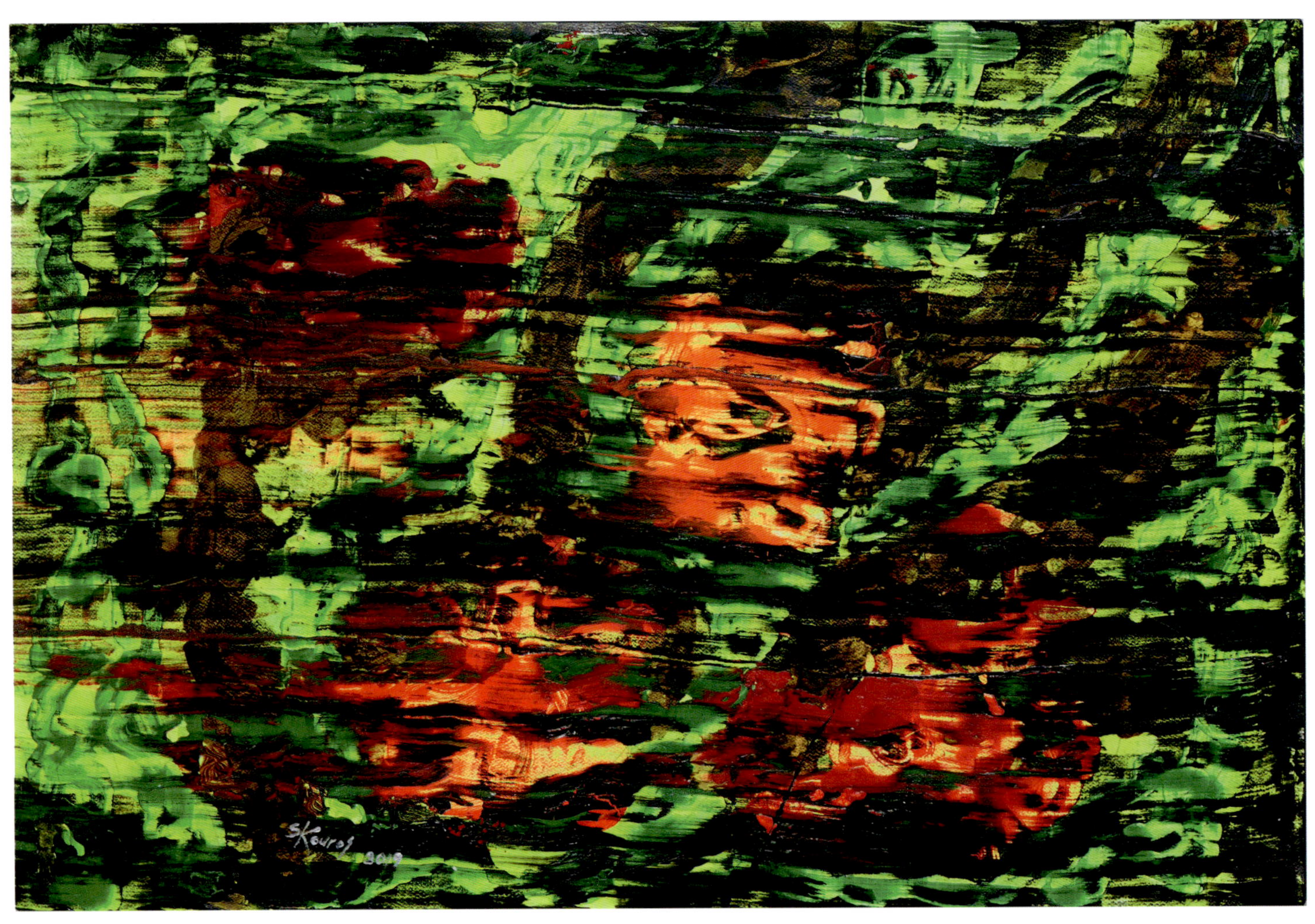

2019, acrylic on paper,
50 x 70 cm

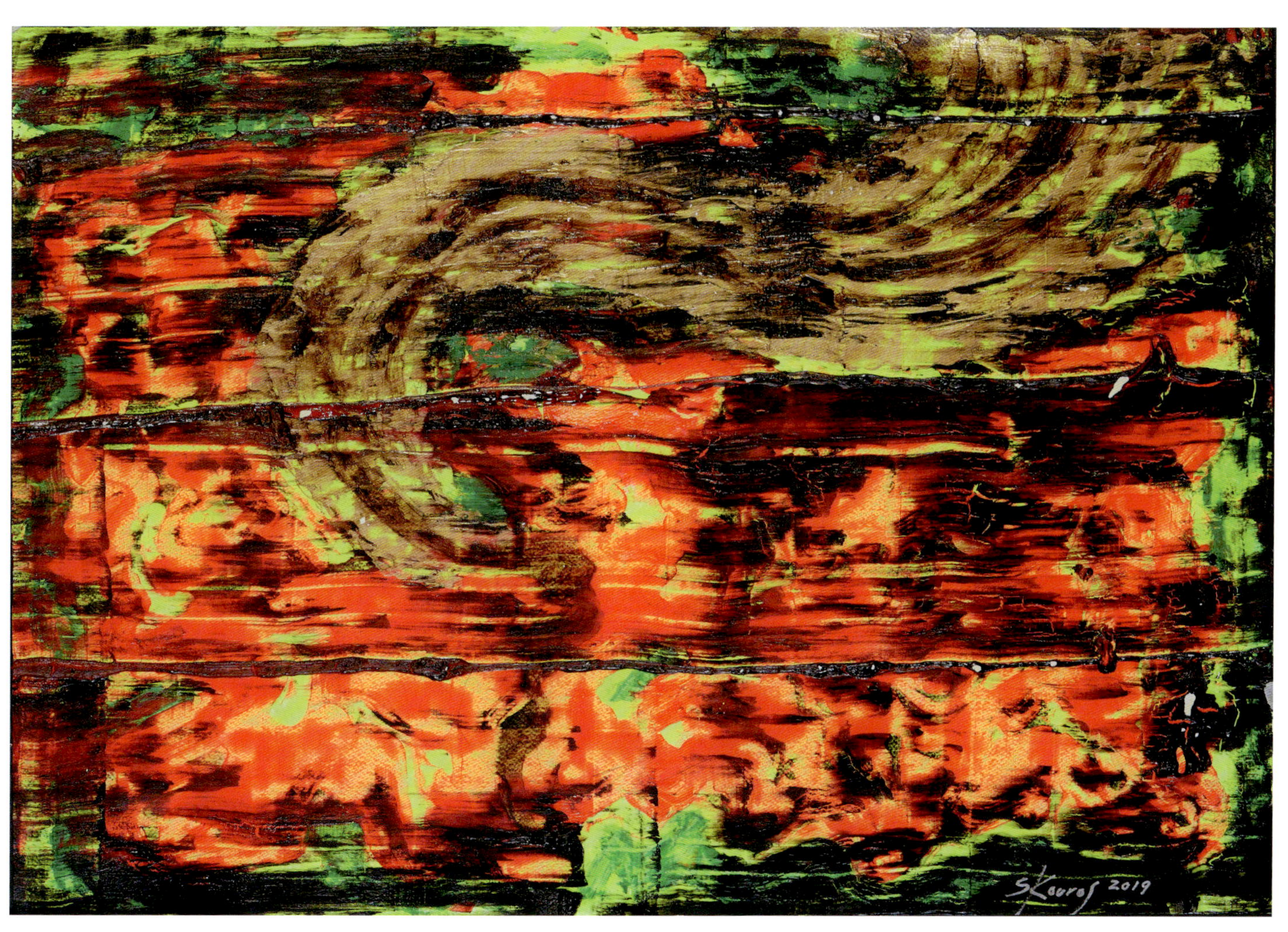

2019, acrylic on paper,
50 x 70 cm

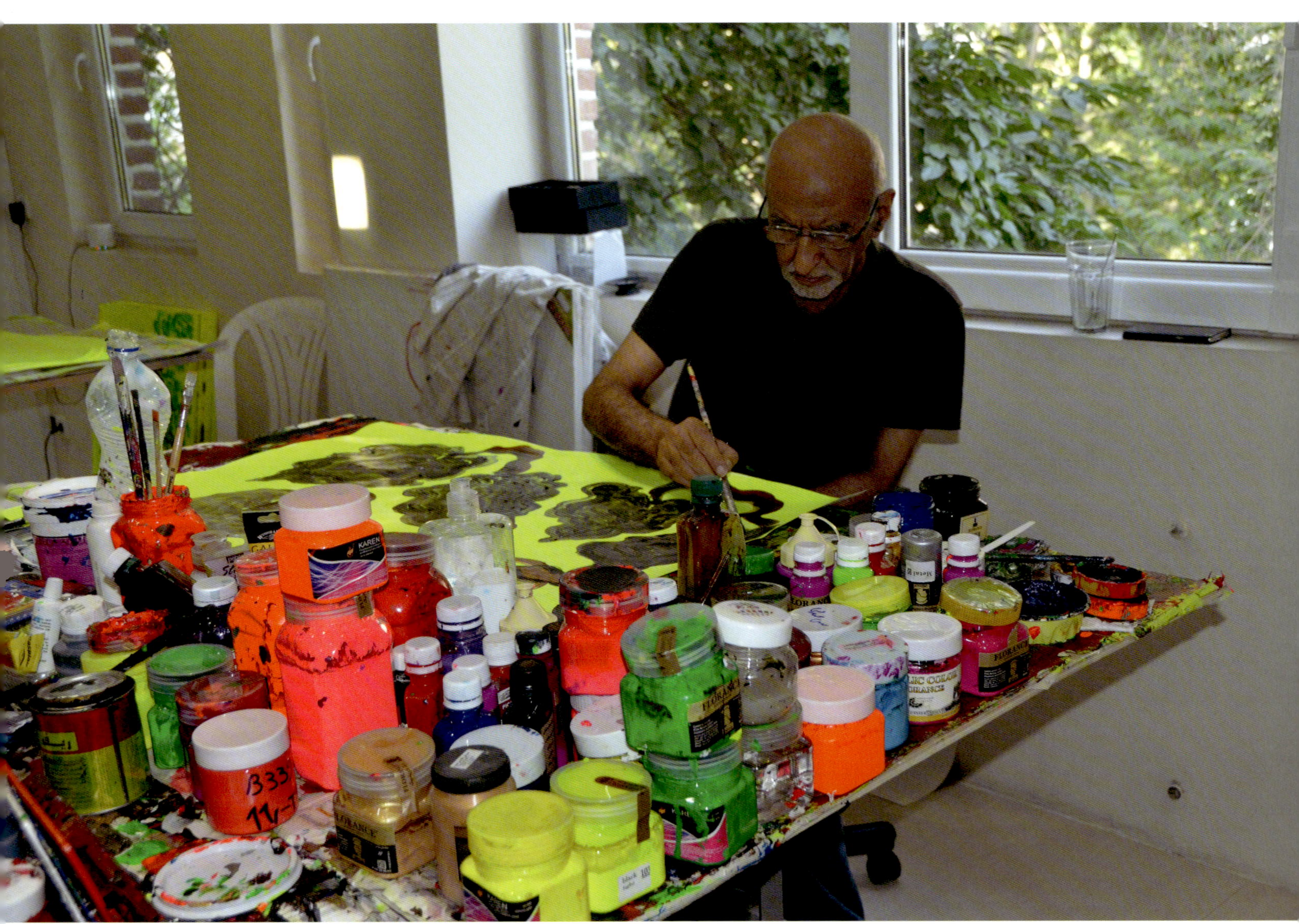
KAREN
FLORANCE

Chronology

1942

Saeed Kouros was born in Tehran.

His mother Ensieh Gheissari (Kouros, 1921-2013) was a painter who had leant painting from Ali Mohammad Heydarian (1896-1990), a distinguished realist painter and one of Kamal al-Mulk's (the famous court artist in the late Qajar period) best-known students. His father, Kazem Kouros (1907-2010), was an influential industrialist and pioneer of printed cotton and chintz factory in Iran, among others *Chit-sazi-e Rey* factory, an MP, senator and collector of Islamic art and objects.

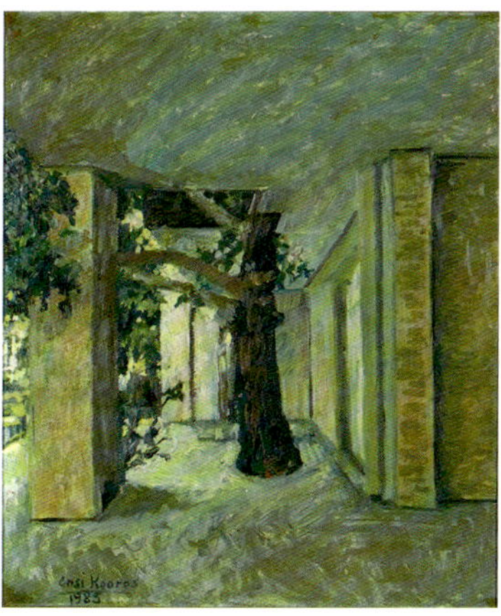

Ensieh Gheissari (Kouros), *The Garden*, 1985, oil on canvas, 60 x 50cm

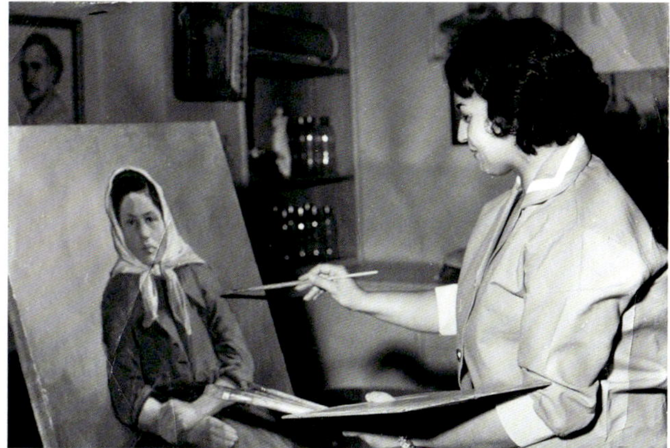

Ensieh Gheissari (Kouros), Saeed's mother working on a painting in Ali Mohammad Heydarian's studio, circa 1938-9

1946

He was four years old having to accompany his father on a mission to Egypt, Palestine and Lebanon when he was diagnosed with tuberculosis infection. He was taken to Marseille, France, from Beirut and then to Leysin, Switzerland. It was just a few years after the World War II and he started treatment for TB infection in a hospital in Leysin what took about three years.

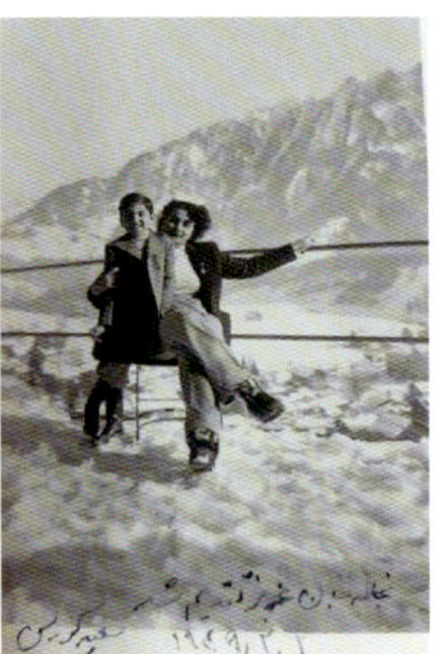

Saeed Kouros and his mother in the Alps,
Leysin, Switzerland, 1949

1949

He was enrolled in a boarding school in Lausanne. His younger brother Hamid (b. 1944) joined him after a few years.

1954

Kouros was allowed by the doctors to leave Switzerland and travel back to his home country, Iran, when he was twelve. He met his younger brother Vahid (b. 1949) for the first time!

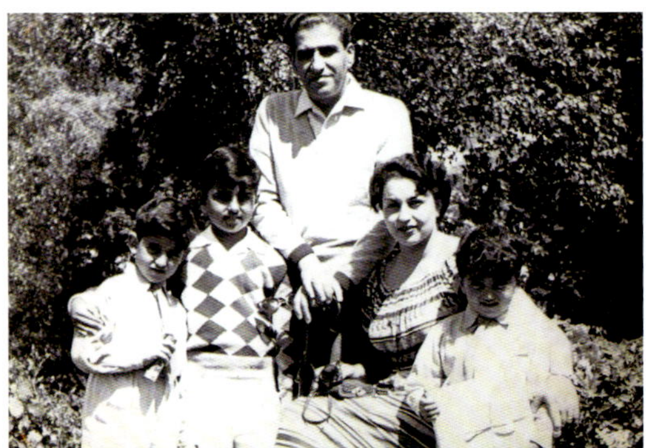

Kouros's family (Kazem, Ensieh, Saeed,
Hamid and Vahid) in Germany

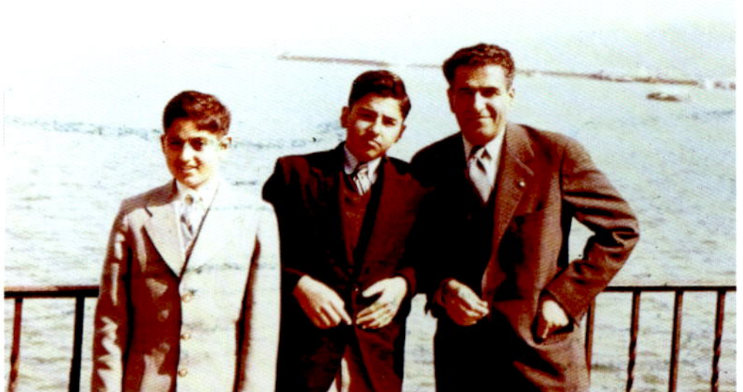

Kouros together with his father and brother,
Hamid in Switzerland

1962 He went to Canada from Switzerland to study business. He enrolled for an MBA in economics at the Montreal University but left it unfinished.

1964 In Montreal at the age of twenty-one, he started working on his early artworks. As a self-taught artist, he experimented with materials such as sand and plaster on huge canvases and installation made up of hundreds of coloured black and white geometrical forms of triangle and circle. He exhibited his works in a solo and a group exhibition.

1965 This fruitful period of art practice ended as a result of his emotional breakdown and he left Canada and returned to Iran and became involved in his family business in industry, production and finance.

1978 He married Avid Moazami Goodarzi and their children Ali, Roxana and Mandana were born in 1979, 1985 and 1991 respectively.

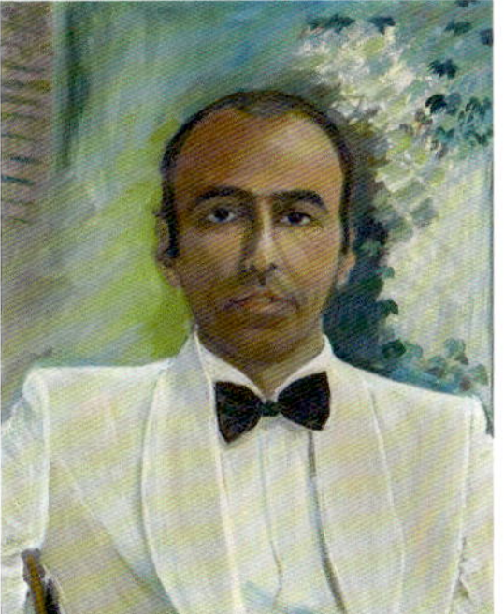

Ensi Kouros, Saeed Kouros's Portrait, 1985,
oil on canvas, 50 x 40cm

2000 He was suddenly diagnosed with liver, stomach and pancreas failure. He had to go through a long and painful period of treatment and medication in the US. He was then introduced to a Chinese lady who offered him and "alternative medication" to cure the severe inflammation caused by the disease. Although the treatment was useful, it was a very long process and Kouros did not get cured fully.

2003

Curing process continued through a psychoanalyst in North London as after a long period of discomfort and medication, Korous felt deeply depressed. After the process of diagnosing he was prescribed to start painting again to help him transfer the pains to his art. He started painting with simple art materials such as pencil, colour pencil, paper and ink. His early works in Greece, mainly in abstract forms, show experimentation with those materials. All the works of this period were mainly based on spontaneity and improvisation.

2005-6

He started to establish a formal structure on a canvas and then develop it to several canvases trying to experiment with different colour and texture. This approach continued in his later periods too. Most of the works created in this period were experimental abstraction paintings and had a close affinity with Abstract Expressionism, both in terms of the act of painting and formal characteristics.

2007-8

He painted a series of geometrical-shaped paintings. In these works the elements and textures were positioned on theses basis. Economical use of colour and attention to the texture and pattern and composition were the main features in these canvases. He gradually moved again toward a kind of more spontaneous paintings now with the use of calligraphic-like elements executed in a variety of formats and colour-scheme. One of the most important characteristics of these works were the intensity of colours and textures.

2008

He had his second solo show at the Gallery 10., Tehran. It consisted of the collection of his works created during 2007 and 2008. The art critic Behzad Hatam writes in the introduction to the catalogue of the exhibition:

"[There are] different periods in this exhibition. In each one a single colour prevails and black, the colour that he claims to be his character is always present. It isn't only the colour that changes with every period, the shapes and compositions ... also change completely. The size of the brush or what he uses to place the paint on the canvas, the sizes of the shapes and their density in each period is different and you think it is closely entangled with his mood on the night that was created."

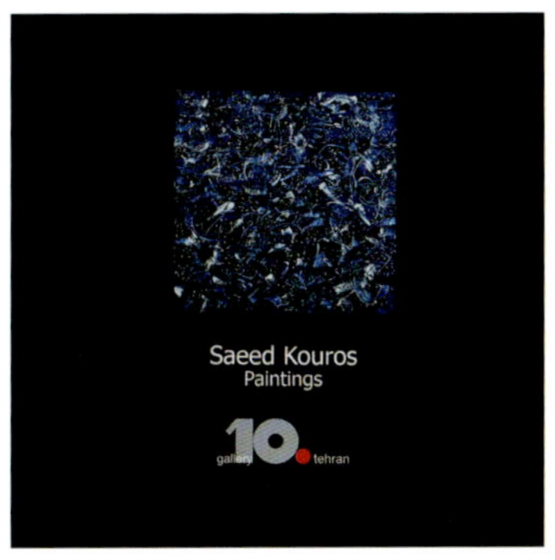

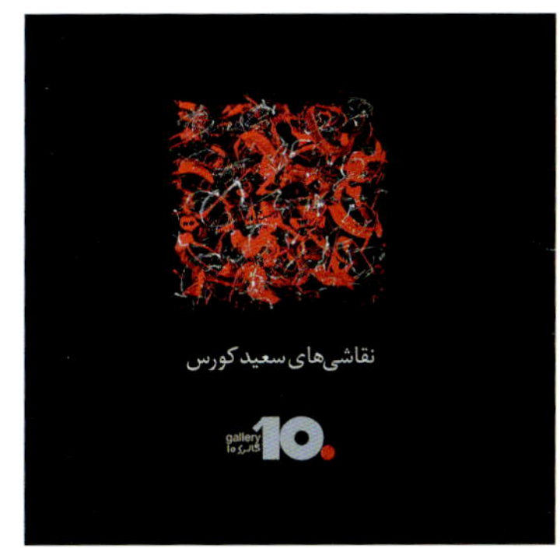

2013

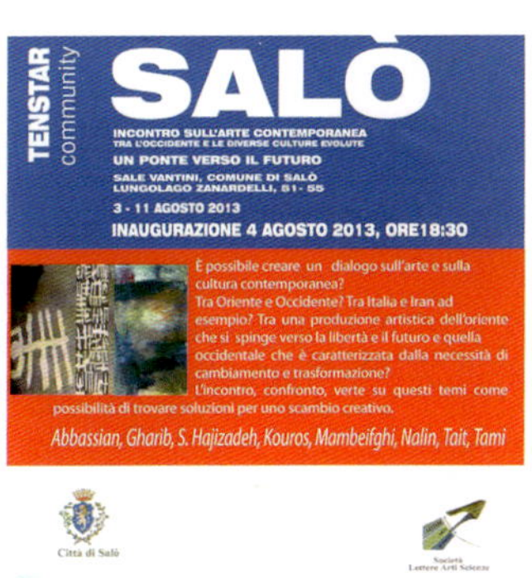

His works were exhibited in a group show in Salò, Italy, curated by Abbas Gharib, architect, artist and founder of Tenstar Community. The exhibition included works of both Iranian and Italian artists: Pooya Abbasian, Abbas Gharib, Ghasem Hajizadeh, Saeed Kouros, Fereydoun Mambeygi, Nalin, Tait and Tomi.

2014

His third solo exhibition of his works from the collections created from 2008 to 2011 was held in Verona, Italy in October 2014. The show was curated by Abbas Gharib. During the exhibition a panel entitled: "From Suprematism to Post-contemporary" was held to discuss Kouros's works. The panellists included Abbas Gharib, Luigi Menghelli, the Italian art critic and Elisabetta Mezzani.

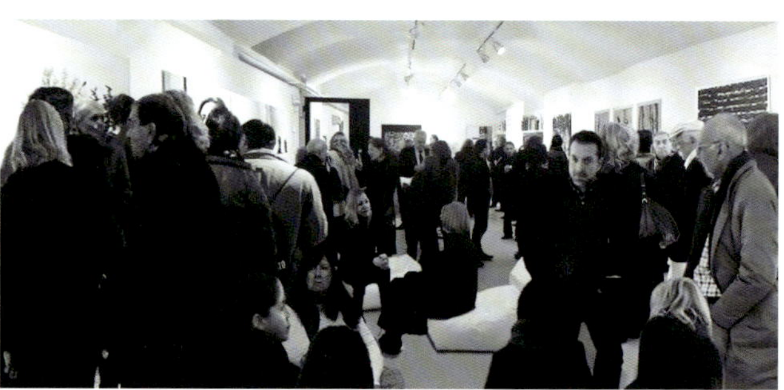

A scene from the opening of the exhibition, Verona, Italy

2015

His fourth solo show was held at the Etemad Gallery, Tehran. The title of this exhibition was "The Ravage of Time, Desperate Aesthetics". He exhibited a series of charcoal and ink on paper works all executed in 2015.

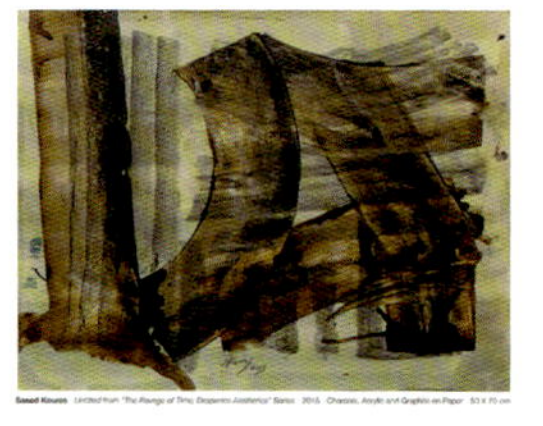

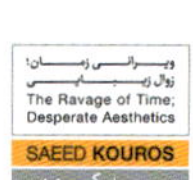

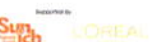

Invitation card of Saeed Kouros's exhibition at the Etemad Gallery, Tehran

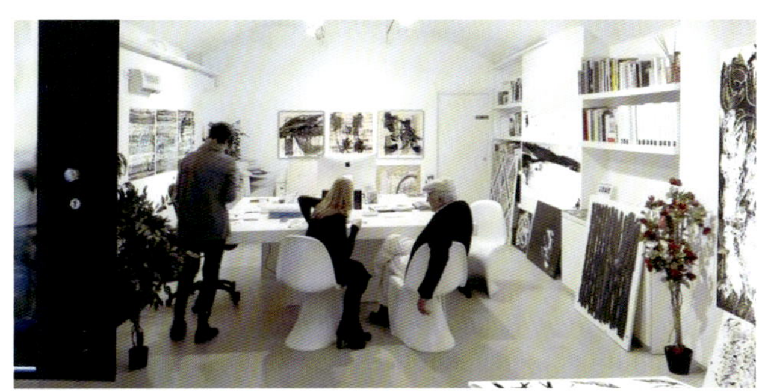

A scene from the exhibition, Milan, Italy

2016

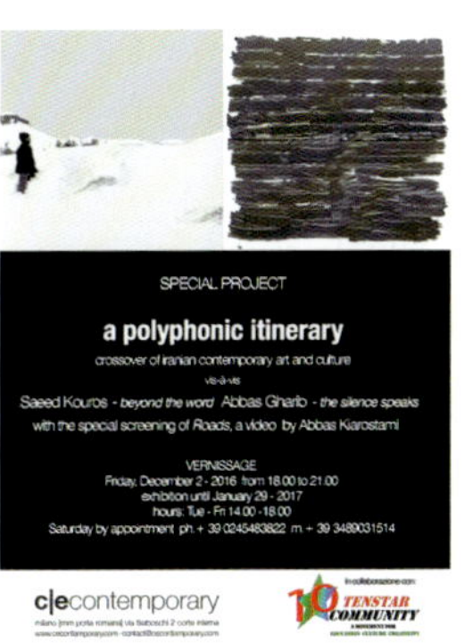

He participated in the group exhibition, entitled "A polyphonic Itinerary, Crossover of Iranian Art and Culture": Abbas Kiarostami, Saeed Kouros and Abbas Gharib, in Milan, Italy, held from December 2016 to January 2017. The exhibition was curated by Abbas Gharib and the Italian art critic Viana Conti.

Acknowledgments

I should, first of all, thank the Kouros's (Kooros) family for their generous support with enthusiasm without which the materialisation of this book project would not have been possible. In particular, I would like to acknowledge Vahid and Hamid Kooros's time and help with collecting the visual materials and documents and also Avid Kouros for providing the required information about the artist's life. Special thank should moreover go to Maryam Motemdi for her extremely useful assistance with gathering information and documents, mainly visual and working with the Studio Lorca, Tehran for obtaining the high-quality pictures of a number of works printed in this book. I am likewise grateful to Abbas Kowsari who shared his brilliant photos taken from Saeed Kouros's exhibition held at the Gallery 10., Tehran, in 2008 to be used in this book. Furthermore, I should thank Abbas Gharib, Amir Hossein Etemad (Etemad Gallery) and Behzad Hatam (Gallery 10.) for their generous time and help with providing information, documents and photos.

I am equally thankful to Pegah Keshmirshekan for her brilliant job in designing this book with excellent care and competence. Last but not least, I should acknowledge Massimiliano Pagani's, the Project Manager at Skira, help, enthusiasm, energy and professional advice throughout this project.

Design:

Pegah Keshmirshekan

Copy-editing:

Mauro Ogliari

First published in Italy in 2019
by Skira editore S.p.A.
Palazzo Casati Stampa
via Torino 61
20123 Milano
Italy
www.skira.net

Printed and bound in Italy. First edition

ISBN: 978-88-572-4118-0

Distributed in USA, Canada, Central & South America by

ARTBOOK | D.A.P. 75 Broad Street Suite 630, New York, NY 10004, USA.

Distributed elsewhere in the world by Thames and Hudson Ltd., 181A High Holborn, London WC1V 7QX, United Kingdom.

Image Credits

Photography:

Abbas Kowsari; pp. 18, 20, 21, 22, 23, 24, 25, 26, 27, 28, 29, 30, 33, 34, 35, 36, 37, 39, 40, 43, 44, 45, 46, 47, 49, 50, 53, 56, 57, 58, 60, 61, 62, 64, 68, 71, 73, 74, 75, 76, 77, 78, 80.

Tehran Studio Lorca; pp. 12, 13, 14, 15, 41, 54, 63, 82, 86, 87, 88, 90, 91, 92, 93, 96, 98, 99, 100, 102, 103, 104, 105, 106, 107, 111, 112, 114, 115, 116, 117, 118, 119, 120, 121, 122, 124, 125, 126, 128, 131, 132, 133, 134, 135, 136, 138, 139, 140, 141, 217, 219, 220, 221, 222, 224, 226.

Maryam Motamedi; pp. 6 and 223.

References:

Pictures selected from books made by Hamid Kooros; pp. 63, 85, 87, 87, 92, 102, 103, 106, 107, 111, 114, 117, 118, 121, 122, 124, 126, 127, 128, 131, 132, 133, 134, 135, 136, 155, 156, 157, 159, 160, 161, 162, 163, 164, 166, 167, 169, 170, 172, 174, 176, 177, 178, 180, 181, 182, 183, 184, 185, 186, 187, 188, 189, 190, 192, 193, 195, 196, 197, 199, 200, 202, 203, 104, 205, 206, 210, 211, 212, 214, 215, 216.

Collections:

Vahid Kooros; pp. 29, 30, 35, 39, 47, 49, 57, 71, 144, 146.

Reza Azhideh; pp. 76, 81, 94, 138.